From TINSELTOWN to BORDERTOWN

Contemporary Approaches to Film and Media Series

A complete listing of the books in this series can be found online at wsupress.wayne.edu.

Celestino Deleyto

From TINSELTOWN to BORDERTOWN

LOS ANGELES ON FILM

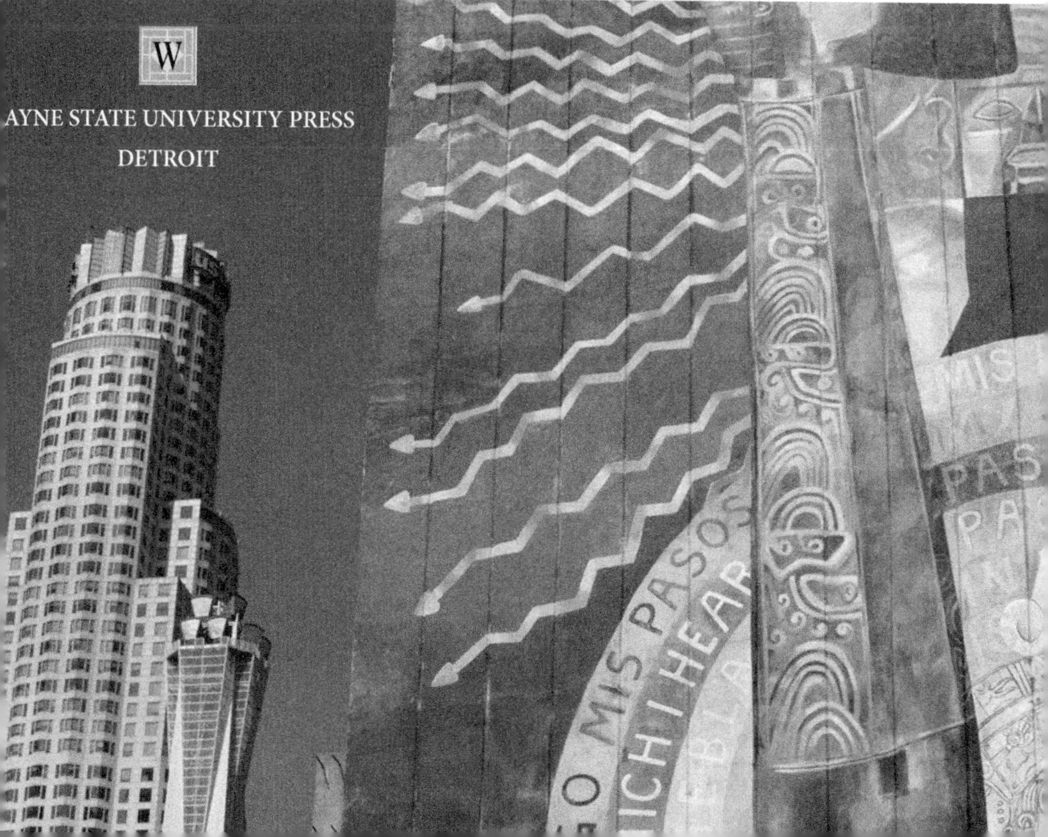

Library of Cataloging Control Number: 2016959426
ISBN 978-0-8143-3985-5 (paperback) | ISBN 978-0-8143-3986-2 (ebook)

Wayne State University Press
Leonard N. Simons Building
4809 Woodward Avenue
Detroit, Michigan 48201–1309

Visit us online at wsupress.wayne.edu

For Alfonso López-Baissón (1951–2016),
Who should have died hereafter

Contents

Acknowledgments

Research toward this book was financed by the Spanish Ministerio de Economía y Competitividad (research projects HUM2007-61183/FILO and FFI2010-15312) and by the Diputación General de Aragón (Ref. H12). The University of Zaragoza partially funded two research stays at UCLA, where I was a visiting scholar in 2010 and 2012. During my two stays at UCLA, the Chicano Studies Research Center was my home. I would like to thank the CSRC's director, Professor Chon Noriega, for welcoming me to the Center and for his advice and encouragement. I am also indebted to Javier Iribarren, Michael Stone, Connie Heskett, and Darling Sianez for their help with practical matters and invaluable advice. Without the infrastructure, the resources, and the warmth of the CSRC, this book would not have seen the light of day.

My research was also carried out at the Charles E. Young Library at UCLA and at the Margaret Herrick Library in Beverly Hills. Susan Anderson, María García, Arlete Pichardo, and José Luis Valenzuela were my guides through various aspects of LA history, culture, and society. Much of what I have learned from them has found its way into this book. Susan also compiled an extremely useful reading list for me, which became the basis of my research on the city of Los Angeles, and she read and gave me most welcome advice on one of my chapters. I would also like to thank José Luis for giving me access to the *Luminarias* production papers and for his candid discussion of his work and Mexican life in the city.

Stephen Gyllenhaal and Kathleen Mann Gyllenhaal were kind enough to share their views on contemporary Hollywood with me. I am grateful to Rosa Urtiaga for letting me use her unpublished interview with *Real Women Have Curves* scriptwriter Josefina López and to Ms. López for allowing me to reproduce her views on the film. My very special thanks go to Kevin and Ascensión, the visible part of the iceberg of my many conversations with Angeleno citizens. Ignacio Deleyto helped me with the music in *The Soloist*, Hilaria Loyo gave me a useful bibliography on the concept of the American dream, Iván Villarmea shared with me his research and some of his views on city films, and Jacline Moriceau offered me some references to urban theory. My very special thanks go to Francesc Terrades, who designed the maps of the city included in the book on very short notice and with considerable effort. I am particularly grateful to Gemma López, who kindly read my manuscript, and to Marimar Azcona for her constant help and unflinching support and for always believing in what I do, even when I don't myself. At Wayne State University Press, Annie Martin was always at hand, offering all the encouragement and advice an author could possibly ask for, and more. Barry Grant, the series editor, not only believed in my project from the beginning but also contributed to turn it into a better book.

Finally, my greatest gratitude is, as ever, to Esther, Elena, and Anita, the three shining stars in my own private Tinseltown.

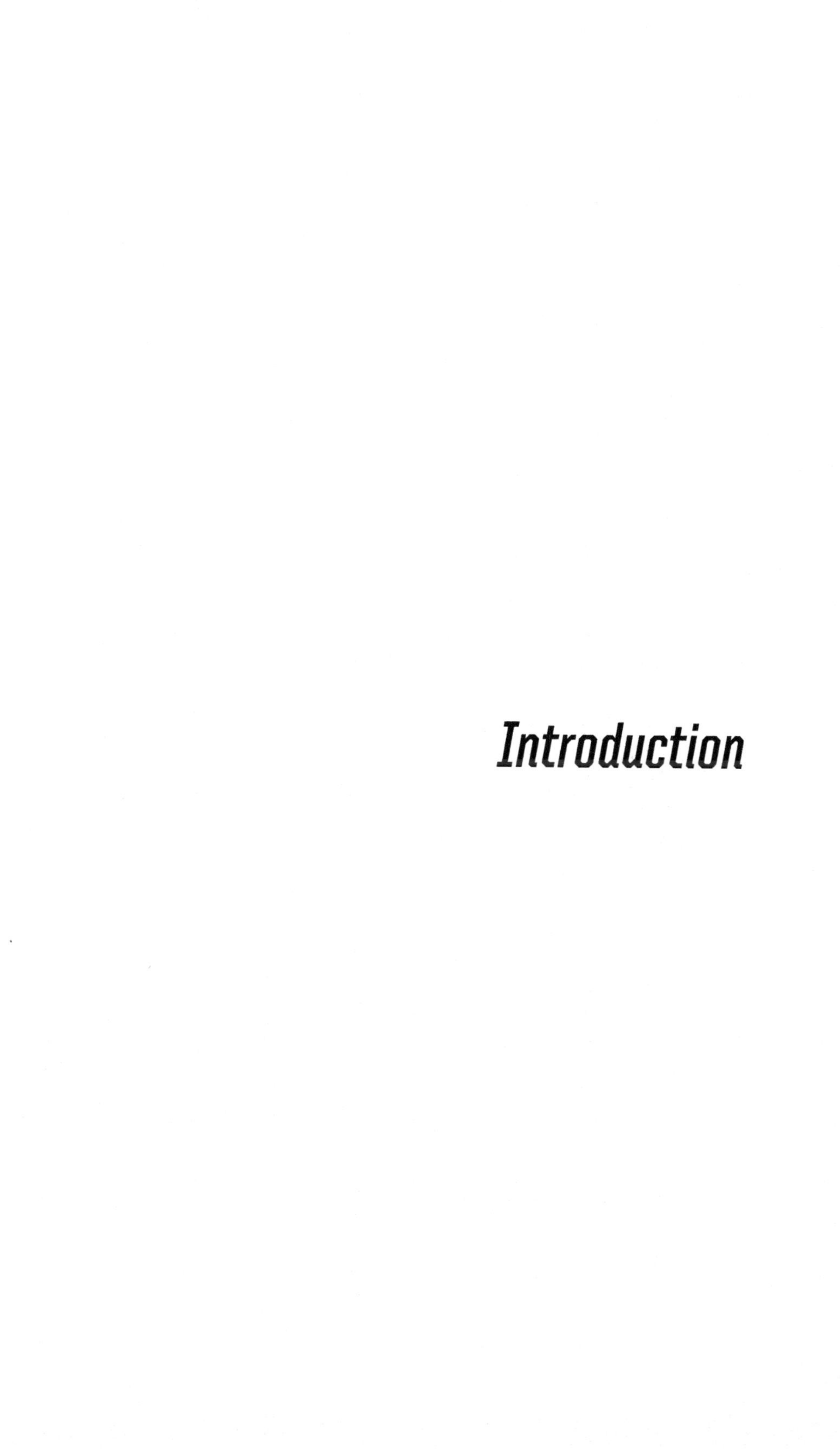

Introduction

1

The Exorbitant City

This book originates from my personal experience on first visiting Los Angeles in 2008. I stayed at a hotel in the Westwood area, and the first people I saw on the mostly deserted sidewalks of Sepulveda Boulevard were a group of Latinos sitting on a low wall, waiting for work, I suppose, mostly looking down as I walked by. A few hours later my wife and I went for dinner at nearby Norm's, a traditional Angeleno diner. Inside we were immediately entranced by the vibrancy of the place and the ethnic makeup of both patrons and workers; many of the customers were Latino, and so were most of the waiters, as were practically all the busboys and even the restaurant manager, at least on that particular day. We soon noticed that they were not all the same in terms of social class; there were categories and divisions between them, probably some Mexican Americans and others recent arrivals from Mexico or other Latin American countries. Some spoke Spanish, others English, most of them a mixture of both; some acted more "American" than others, but they all blended into the complex social dynamic of the place, which included people from many other ethnic origins, although in smaller proportions. In the following days (and years), we returned to Norm's several times. As our fascination with the city grew, the restaurant remained for us a powerful microcosm of the city, because our ensuing experiences of LA at large did nothing but confirm our first impression.

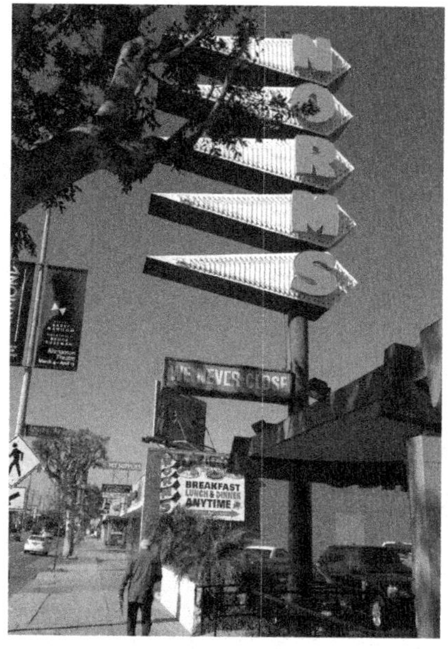

Norm's on Pico Boulevard.

What was that first impression? That for such movie aficionados and Hollywood film lovers as we are and after seeing Los Angeles in hundreds of films past and present over more than four decades, LA seemed to us an almost completely new city. This was while we stayed on the Westside and before we hit Broadway, the Grand Central Market, La Placita, and Olvera Street and before even hearing of Boyle Heights, Lincoln Heights, and all the other neighborhoods east of the Los Angeles River. Maybe LA had been different in the past but, because we had mostly avoided the freeways during that first stay, there was little we could see that we could relate to the cinematic city we were familiar with. That city was dominated by cops and gangsters, alienated heroes and smart teen heroines, Hollywood stars and fancy automobiles speeding, in recent decades, along wide and generally not too busy freeways. Of course we noticed the street signs, such as the familiar Sunset Boulevard, and we walked along the utterly unexceptional Hollywood Boulevard, visited the studios, and saw the Hollywood sign, but after a few days in the city all of these seemed relatively unimportant to LA's urban identity, or, rather, identities. Maybe Venice, Santa Monica, and Malibu were slightly more recognizable, but even in these traditional beach communities people's skin seemed a notch or two browner than in the movies, and not just because of the sun.

It was this discrepancy that first encouraged me to delve deeper into the two terms of my puzzling equation: the city and the movies. As a citizen of Spain, I was and continue to be particularly sensitive to the pervasive Spanish names and sounds of the city, to its pulsating Latino culture and communal habits, but also to what became an obsession and a paradox: the striking invisibility of Mexicans and other Latinos and Latinas on many economic, social, and political levels, given their overwhelming numbers. The movies had prepared me well for this invisibility. Contemporary films in particular seemed remarkably adept at hiding what to me soon became one of the foremost features of Los Angeles: its Mexicanness. I discovered that LA is in many ways a particular kind of Mexican city, but, at the same time, it is much more than that. It is a city characterized by a staggering diversity and by a simultaneous tendency, in many of its dominant discourses, to erase such diversity. In fact, the dynamic between visibility and erasure and its attendant fears, anxieties, and hopes came to define for me the shape of Angeleno history, politics, and social interactions. At the same time, the cinema, both classical and contemporary, could be considered a particularly powerful instrument in the construction of discourses of erasure and concomitant celebration of—to me nonexistent—homogeneity.

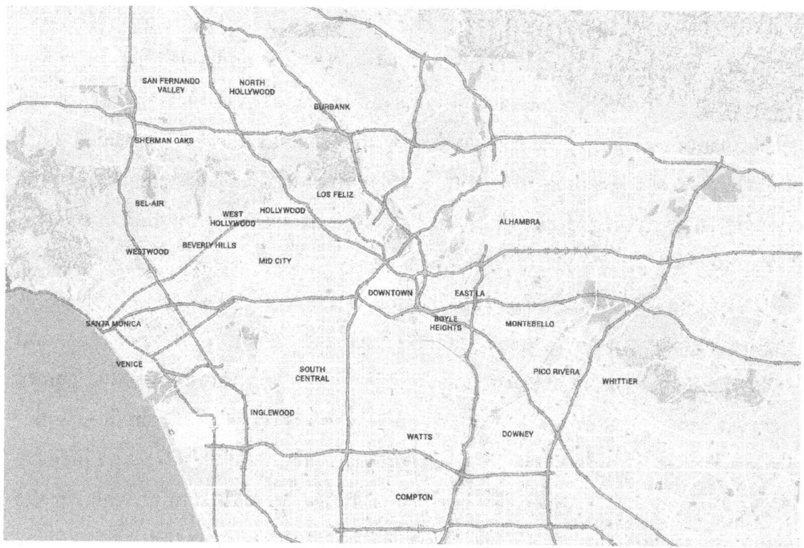

Map 1. Los Angeles and some of its neighborhoods and incorporated cities in the metropolitan area. Map by Francesc Terrades.

In recent decades many voices have been raised against the erasure of ethnic difference in dominant conversations about LA, present and past. Although the vast numbers of Latinos in the city have made their economic, social, and cultural invisibility particularly noticeable, the situation is not different for other ethnic minorities. In an interview about her novel *Tropic of Orange* (1997), author Karen Tei Yamashita explains that LA means to her a layered geography traversed every day by different people, and it is those layers, which can merge or remain distinct, that define the city (Glixman 2007). Yet many of those layers have been underrepresented or not represented at all in the literature about LA. Yamashita's novel, with seven protagonists, none of whom is Anglo, can be seen as a symptom of a shift in this trend. In the ten years between the book's publication and the interview, Yamashita herself noticed a subtle change from the narrow vision of Los Angeles and Hollywood as a racially divided city between blacks and whites toward a growing recognition of LA as a Latino city and a crossroads for global migrations (Glixman 2007). Yamashita's appreciation of social change in recent years coincides with the insights of many historians and cultural critics. In this, Los Angeles is both exceptional and representative of other social transformations in big cities around the world, with its exceptionality probably caused by the specificity of its relatively short but packed history of racial and ethnic conflict. The year 1992 was a crucial moment in this history and one that, as many observers agree, brought about a series of slow and uneven but unstoppable social transformations of the type acknowledged by Yamashita; 1992 also intensified other social changes of a less promising nature, including racial violence, vigilantism, the privatization of public spaces, and the social and economic deterioration of suburbs (Davis 1998, 360–422).

This book starts from the recognition of the centrality of 1992 in the contemporary history of the city. I seek to ascertain the extent to which changes and developments that originated around that time found their way into contemporary cinematic representations of the city. In more general terms, I explore how movies from the last two decades have engaged with urban, cultural, and ideological discourses about Los Angeles. My goal is not, however, to determine whether the movies succeed or fail at faithfully conveying a sense of the "real" city. Although my initial impression was that films had indeed failed in important ways to connect with the city that I was experiencing when I first arrived, a more detailed acquaintance with what could be described as the discursive history of LA and a greater familiarity with its topography and urban dynamics led me to modulate my views: As part of the cultural and ideological conversation, all movies provide important insights into the various ways in which LA is constructed and imagined. The views of the city that films convey are all equally "real," equally incomplete and inescapably ideological. Furthermore, the prevalence of certain perspectives over others in recent LA movies roughly reproduces the existing balance in discourses about the city outside the cinema. Our own ideological leanings may make us more sympathetic to some perceptions than to others, but that does not necessarily signify that those truths we agree with are "truer" than those conveyed by other movies. Rather, given the social and cultural complexity of Los Angeles, the movies (specifically those selected for this study, taken as a whole) manage to reproduce the variety, diversity, and heterogeneity of the city, its anxieties and contradictions, and its different ways of representing itself.

To "look for the city" in my selection of movies, I propose a change of perspective in film analysis: from the foreground, where the central characters are generally found and the main narrative thrust usually takes place, to the background, where alternative and often more significant stories and spatial configurations can be found. It is overwhelmingly in the background of the cinematic image that I find the most significant traces of the city. Like Roland-François Lack, who gets irritated when an actor is standing in front of a significant place (Lack 2016, 60), I am less interested in the people on the screen than in the places behind them. Reversing the usual critical practice, I conceive of protagonists and narratives as functions of cinematic space. In other words, my analysis looks for evidence of social and political transformations in the post-1992 metropolis in the movies' constructions of cinematic space and in their use, for this purpose, of real places and culturally constructed spaces of the city. This is, therefore, a study of cinematic space and an attempt to understand how real places and cultural spaces are transformed into cinematic space and how cinematic space produces urban discourse from the background of the stories.

Cinematic Cities, Place, and Space

Cinematic cities have never been real cities, just as film stories and characters are distinct from reality. The interests of Hollywood producers rarely include the accurate documentation of a city's demographic, cultural, and historical realities; rather, the producers tend to appropriate those urban spaces to provide audiences with entertaining and exciting stories and fictional worlds. Even ideologically committed films with social preoccupations manipulate the reality they are describing and turn it into discourse. Yet many of us have become acquainted and even familiarized with many of the cities we know through films. We will never know some cities except through the movies. Even in an age of proliferating travel options and instant communications, we are more likely than not to know cities first through cinema and other audiovisual texts. Barbara Mennel rightly points out that the cinema has been of central importance in understanding how cities are imagined (2008, 16). There is a sense, therefore, that movies bear a certain responsibility toward the images of the cities they offer.

In film studies the connection between cities and cinema can be approached within the larger framework of the analysis of cinematic space. In fiction films there are no real places, only artificial elaborations that may or may not take as their point of departure a real place. Even when they do, that real place is transformed in such a way that, from the perspective of the film text, the constructed space becomes predominant. Perhaps for this reason film theory is generally not interested in the real places that movies refer to. Discussions of cinematic space focus mostly on perception and perspective and on abstract fictional spaces and have little to say about their connections with real places. In one of the most influential such theoretical elaborations, Stephen Heath (1981) traces the construction of narrative space in the cinema back to the Quattrocento single perspective in the pictorial arts. Besides the importance of perspective, Heath considers other elements, such as movement and even sound, but his discussion remains anchored in considerations of framing, the look, point of view, and identification as the central components of cinematic space. For Heath, space can have ideological or political dimensions, but it remains a function of the narrative. As in a painting, it is created *ex nihilo*, like the rest of the constituents of the filmic text (Heath 1981, 24–52).

Other film theorists, such as David Bordwell (1988), Edward Branigan (1992), and Deborah Thomas (2001), have continued the same tradition of underplaying, if not totally ignoring, the impact of real places in movies and the power of the cinema to intervene in those places and their role in the creation of social discourse. Thus, although Thomas, for example, does take into consideration the difference between geographic space and cinematic space, her focus is on how those "real places" are transformed in the film narrative through editing, camera position, and frame composition in order to produce meaning (2001, 9–10). These meanings are never directly linked to geographic space but are situated elsewhere, within the complex dynamic of narrative form. Mise-en-scène analysis, though often dealing with elements of space, is mostly interested in the narrative and metaphorical meanings of the mise-en-scène but never in its links to the real world to which it refers. When a film such as *North by Northwest* (Alfred Hitchcock, 1959) uses well-known United States landmarks, the critical focus is invariably on what the United Nations building, Chicago's Union Station, and especially Mount Rushmore contribute to the narrative and to character construction and development rather than on what the film might have to say, through narrative, characters, and so on, about those places. In always aiming to explicate the workings of the text, film theory inevitably underplays the real world, history, and society where those texts come from and to which they return.

Yet, as Mark Shiel notes, film is more a spatial system than a textual system, and, as such, it is especially adept at illuminating the dynamics of lived spaces (2001, 6). Film spaces are never real places and there is always a process of transformation, but the film text features abundant traces of the places it transforms and recontextualizes them within its fictional parameters. Even Heath admits that at the beginning of cinema history the answer to "the question of space" in film would be clear enough: "The space of film is the space of reality" (1981, 25). For his part, Geoffrey Nowell-Smith warns that working with real materials, "which retain their original quality however much they are artistically transformed, is a privilege which filmmakers neglect at their peril" (2001, 107). The same could be said for critical accounts of films that fail to acknowledge the potential of the medium to intervene in the historical process of the construction of space, in our case, urban space. In their introduction to *Taking Place: Location and the Moving Image*, John David Rhodes and Elena Gorfinkel follow current trends in other disciplines, such as geography, philosophy, art history, and literary studies, and redirect theoretical attention in film studies from space to place (2011, x). They argue that our experience of the cinema is intimately connected to our experience of place because of the "seemingly natural ability" of the medium to record place; and, in elucidating the need to position place centrally in the analysis of cinematic texts, Rhodes and Gorfinkel agree with those who affirm that "identity is constructed in and through place" (viii, ix). They share with this study an interest in "drawing background to foreground, periphery to center" (xi).

Films, then, do not reproduce real places but, by transforming them through specifically cinematic elements such as mise-en-scène, framing, editing, and sound, they produce discourses about those real places and therefore have an important impact on our perception of those places and their history. In this respect, filmic discourses are not, at least theoretically, radically different from other cultural discourses. Cities are, as Colin McArthur explains, social and ideological and always immersed in narrative (1997, 20). Given the effervescence of urban discourse and the proliferation of narratives that attempt to make sense of cities and to control their development through mechanisms of power, cinematic urban fictions ought to be considered within the larger parameters of cultural, urban, and political discourse. Their study would surely benefit from conceptualizations of urban space from the viewpoint of urban studies, geography, and sociology, among other disciplines.

Geographers and other social scientists often start from definitions of space and place, ranging from the classic accounts of Edward Relph's (2008) authentic places and placelessness in the modern world and Yi-Fu Tuan's (1977) distinction between abstract spaces and concrete places to Michel de Certeau's (1984) notions of spatial practices that structure the conditions of social life and of space as practiced place. These spatial practices, both imposed from above and transformed and rewritten from below, are linked to Henri Lefebvre's (1991) influential insight that space is socially produced, through both discourse and social practices, and that all social relations are spatially inscribed. More recently, Doreen Massey (2005) reminds us that the spatial is always political. For her, spatialized social practices and relations are part of the mechanisms of power (Massey 2005, 167). Place, on the other hand, is the sphere of the everyday, of real and valued practices, the geographic source of meaning (5). This meaning, for Massey as for Lefebvre, is produced in the process of spatialization, and it is closely linked with time and history. Massey's link between time and space, her view of space as a meeting-up of histories (1), is an important move forward: Space is not static, but it is always involved in temporality. She laments the strict structuralist division between space and time and, more generally, the prominence that philosophers have given to time. Space can be just as exhilarating and threatening as time (59). The imbrication of space with time is particularly relevant to film analysis, both because of the nature of the medium and because of the temporality and historicity of the places spatialized by film texts.

Filmic discourses about cities are conceptually no different from other cultural discourses and therefore from other ways of constructing space. The cinema is one more cultural mechanism that is constantly at work in the creation of social space. Its goals are to turn places into spaces, even if its operations may seem more indirect than, say, those of an urban designer. Films are directly implicated in the construction of urban discourses and are enmeshed in the struggles for the control of discourse. Films transform real places, but these are similar transformations to those effected in other cultural and social texts. Our perception of those places is inevitably mediated by spatial discourses, filmic or otherwise.

In this sense, and to return to the beginning, it would not be accurate to say that Hollywood cinema has, as a whole, misrepresented Los Angeles. The more or less subjective impression that what we see upon first arriving in the city is not what the movies have led us to expect is not so much a symptom of misrepresentation as evidence that, throughout history, LA movies have been part of the construction of specific discourses about the city. Films have contributed in relevant ways to the ongoing history of the city and to the ways in which people, both Angelenos and outsiders, have experienced it, even when they have apparently failed to incorporate important aspects of its social fabric. In this context the absence of social minorities from movie screens in relation to their presence in the city is part of the history of urban discourses and part of a contested discursive space populated by power struggles and communal anxieties.

Besides, our experience of film analysis teaches that what is left offscreen is often as important as what remains in the frame. Similarly, LA ethnic and social minorities may well be important presences in cultural texts, even when, paradoxically, they are absent—or, particularly, when they are absent. Once the terms of the analysis are set, the edges of the narrative, the edges of the frame, and even the edges of the filmic canon begin to acquire a new visibility for the analyst. What had not been noticed before now stares us in the face, producing insights into the city that had previously been kept outside the field of vision.

Global Cities

The social dynamics of Los Angeles and the spatial discourses that convey the city's stories and experiences to us have certain specificities, but they are also representative of similar processes in other global cities. Edward Soja's (2000) focus on this metropolis to explain more generalized global urban dynamics is significant of the Southern California city's potential to clarify how contemporary cities function. In this sense, a book about Los Angeles must be seen within the context of the recent interest of urban theory in global cities.

Soja traces the history of cities through a series of urban revolutions, the fourth of which led from the modern to the postmodern city in the 1960s and 1970s. He calls the resulting phenomenon "postmetropolis," a concept that he closely links to Los Angeles (Soja 2000, 115). The postmetropolis is described through six urban developments, one of which is the global city or "cosmopolis," a term referring to the rise of the metropolis in a world system, signifying the intensification of globalization in the spheres of social, economic, political, and cultural relations (191).

These locations become nodal centers in a new paradigm dominated by a certain view of globalization, one in which the economic dominates over the rest, a smooth process given the aura of inevitability surrounding the discourses of late capitalism. Yet the emphasis on the primacy of financial flows and open markets is, as Doreen Massey (2005) warns us, part of the discourse of globalization. This discourse does not just state that globalization is inevitable but that only one view of globalization is possible. In reality, what passes itself off as objective description of the contemporary world is "an image in which the world is being made" (Massey 2005, 86), that is, a particularly powerful instance of the construction of space. Bringing Soja's and Massey's insights together, we can surmise that the current notions of globalization and global cities are immersed in discourse, that the dominant discourse tends to situate globalization within purely economic parameters, that other ways of looking at the phenomenon are possible, and that actual global cities like Los Angeles work on a multiplicity of levels, the economic dimension being only one of them.

Even at the purely economic level, the dominant discourse of globalization is simplistic and incomplete. In her description of global cities, Saskia Sassen (2006) argues that globalization and the globalized economy are not only about global information, instant communication, and electronic markets but also about material conditions and real people and workers, not just those in high-paying jobs. Cities are important as "real" sites of globalization, because global processes do not happen in virtual space but are very much "place centered." They are defined not only by top-level transnational managers and professionals but also by their secretaries and the janitors who clean the buildings where the new professional class works. Cities are the world of immigrants who become the nannies, domestic cleaners, and dog walkers of those top professionals, as well the assistants of the boutique shops where they buy their food in their exclusive neighborhoods, the drivers of the cabs who make their mobility possible, and, of course, their gardeners, the human figures who go a long way toward explaining the social dynamic of contemporary Los Angeles (Sassen 2006, 2). These cities are also strategic sites for the transnationalization of labor and the formation of transnational identities, but these identities conjure up a different notion of globalization: "a process that generates contradictory spaces, characterized by contestation, internal differentiation, continuous border crossings" (xxxiv).

Against the monolithic view of the global city as a financial center surrounded by a vague amalgam of urban experiences that do not matter very much and tend to be ignored or actively repressed in dominant discourses, many observers focus instead on this teeming mixture of activity, struggle, and chaos. This social accumulation goes against the city planners' blueprints of unlimited progress through the unruly everyday practices described by Michel de Certeau (1984). These practices may not always be radical or subversive, as the French thinker optimistically suggested, but they are at least unorthodox, unexpected, and difficult to contain. They are also often difficult to perceive and to understand. Ackbar Abbas calls this ineffable quality the "exorbitant city," a city that is neither graspable nor fully representable. He contrasts it with the "generic city," a term he borrows from Rem Koolhaas to refer to a city that is superficial, like a Hollywood studio lot. The exorbitant city is not defined by its physical size and population but by the complexity of historical and cultural change and movement that it contains (Abbas 2003, 144–47).

Abbas argues that the exorbitant city is representable only as the cinematic city. The instability of the cinematic image allows it to evoke most powerfully the city "in all its errancy" in a way that is beyond the possibility of stable images (Abbas 2003, 145). He is interested in the forms of desire produced by the exorbitant city and the ability of the cinema to grasp that urban eroticism, including sudden eruptions of irrational impulses and obsessions. These pulsations and urges may be quite distant from the processes that make global cities ungraspable, but they do form part of an alternative urban discourse, and they are more amenable to the type of story that the cinema has familiarized us with.

Films have been focusing on the city since only a few decades after Baudelaire walked the streets of Paris, and from the beginning they have been energized by the same curiosity that was felt by the French author's figure of the flâneur. Their fascination with cities continues unabated, as does their effect on the way cities are imagined. In the case of U.S. cities, films have often preceded other experiences of cities by outsiders. As Jean Baudrillard famously argued in *America*, the American city seems to have stepped right out of the movies (1989, 55). For this reason, cinematic images are of particular importance to make sense of the cities they evoke. Los Angeles, the hometown of Hollywood, is an exceptional case because of the importance of the film industry in its recent history and because no other city in the world has appeared in movies as often as it has.

That a person who, Baudrillard-like, has "known" the city from decades of film watching may be surprised on first visiting Los Angeles suggests that this particular exorbitant city encompasses a multitude of urban and social peculiarities, more than those contained by a single mode of representation. Alternatively, it points to the implication of films in specific urban ideologies. Cinematic images directly link with certain historical discourses on LA, whereas other voices have proven more difficult to articulate. Even the celebrated documentary *Los Angeles Plays Itself* (Thom Andersen, 2003), made up of a wide selection of clips of LA movies, may fail to convey the variety and heterogeneity that others have seen in the city, even as it denounces the invisibility of minorities in the history of cinematic representation. In general, movies, like the city, are far from homogeneous and they do provide a variety of images, even though some of them are more difficult to find than others. Given the global centrality of contemporary Los Angeles and the importance of the cinema as an urban image-generating machine, it seems appropriate at this time to attempt an exploration of the ways in which recent films have visually articulated what makes Los Angeles, in Shiel's words, "*the* paradigmatic city space, urban society, and cultural environment of the late twentieth and twenty-first centuries" (2001, 7).

A City of Superlatives

Ex-mayor Tom Bradley called Los Angeles "the crossroads city" (quoted in Kurashige 2010, 69). Some years later, the *Los Angeles 2000* report boasted that LA was becoming the "global crossroads city" (quoted in Davis 1998, 419). The city holds a privileged geopolitical position in the world, a kind of Clapham Junction, between north and south, east and west. It looks north at the powerful country of which it is the second largest city, still retaining strong reverberations of the American dream and the frontier myth, the final destination of centuries of epic migration. It looks south at a whole continent, specifically, at the country to which it once belonged and, in an increasingly pressing and anxiety-ridden sense, has never abandoned. It looks to the East Coast and the Midwest, where most of its Anglo inhabitants originate, and beyond it at their European roots; and it looks west, at Asia and the Pacific Rim, one of its main sources of geopolitical and economic power and also the origin of much of its population. As the meeting point of Mexican Americans, white Americans, African Americans, Japanese, Chinese, and Korean Americans, and many other minority ethnic groups, LA offers "the social clash that is the very hallmark of urban life" (Avila 2010, 108). As the second largest city in the United States, LA "embodies the racially and culturally diverse American metropolis" (Hayden 1995, 83). Angelenos are proud of their city's trademark diversity, and newcomers and visitors marvel at it and praise its extraordinary cultural variety.

Other cities in the United States and around the world may approximate this seemingly unstoppable hybridity, but Los Angeles leads them in the direction of the sea changes that the world's demographic makeup is undergoing, epitomizing a new U.S. geography and contributing to new definitions of what the United States means (de la Campa 2001, xviii). As Dolores Hayden foresaw in the 1990s, "A new American sense of identity is emerging as we begin to recognize a diverse society where cultural differences are respected" (1995, 237). Whatever will happen in the continent and beyond, many people feel, will happen in LA first. In Eric Avila's words, LA is a laboratory in which to observe "patterns of interaction among people of diverse cultural, linguistic, and geographical backgrounds" (2010, 96). According to Guillermo Gómez-Peña (1988, 130–31), like Tijuana, LA's poorer neighbor south of the border, what was once perceived as a social aberration is fast becoming the model of a hybrid culture.

"Fast" is another adjective that accurately describes urban and social change in Los Angeles. Although the pattern of segregated neighborhoods still applies to much of the city's urban geography, the communities themselves have not necessarily stayed put. Rather, they have followed intricate patterns of mobility around the city. Los Angeles is a city where permanence is a prized commodity, certainly something that cannot be taken for granted, as illustrated by the efforts of the Los Angeles Conservancy and other organizations to protect the city's buildings and communities from disappearing (see www.laconservancy.org). The last months of 2014 saw the beginning of significant developments concerning Norm's, the diner with which I started this book. After more than 65 years, the family of Norman Roybark, who opened the chain's first diner near Sunset and Vine, decided to sell the business (Nichols 2015). A few weeks later, the new owners were granted a permit to demolish the most iconic of the restaurants, the Norm's flagship building on La Cienega Boulevard. Many organizations and citizens, including the Los Angeles Conservancy, rallied to save this celebrated exemplar of post–World War II

Angeleno Googie architecture (Barragan 2015). When I wrote this introduction, demolition had been temporarily prevented because the city's Cultural Heritage Commission voted to designate Norm's a historic and cultural monument (Karlamanga and Reyes 2015), but, in a city in which frenetic change is a constant feature, the future of this building—imagined at the time of its construction as a monument to the urban future—is difficult to predict. The battle over the protection of Norm's La Cienega coffee shop also shows that urban discourses include preferences over what is or is not worthy of preservation and that these battles are themselves ideologically loaded. Since its creation in 1978, the Los Angeles Conservancy has been particularly active in the Downtown area. As can be seen on the organization's webpage, they have exhibited a particular zeal in reclaiming the history of Broadway theaters from the golden age of Hollywood (the 1920s through the 1940s), but they have mostly ignored the more recent past, when Spanish-language films were screened in these venues, and the Latino present. These theaters will reappear later in the study of *Mulholland Drive* (Chapter 4), but here it is important to point out that rapid transformations are consubstantial to the City of Angels and that the narratives of such changes are part of urban ideologies.

In more general terms, globalization, transnational exchanges, and cultural cosmopolitanism are today part of the social and urban core of Los Angeles. Its decentered structure, its enormous size, the difficulties in establishing its exact limits, and its peculiar social dynamic, with strongly segregated and at the same time mobile neighborhoods, all make this Californian city difficult to comprehend but fascinating to discover and also irresolvably contradictory, an urban space standing at the forefront of world social change but also struggling with enormous problems. The Los Angeles 2020 Commission starts its pessimistic report with the following sentence: "Los Angeles is barely treading water while the rest of the world is moving forward," reversing, in one fell swoop, the celebratory discourse of a city at the cutting edge of social change (2013, 1). For the Commission, job loss, rising poverty (40 percent of the population lives in misery), impossible traffic conditions, a deteriorating public school system, and underinvestment in key areas are transforming LA into a city in decline (1–3). Superlatives also characterize the diagnosis of the city, but the problems call for urgent action, according to the authors of the report.

Alongside LA's specific urban and historical profile and its huge difficulties, one more area of its social and economic activity must be added to the mix: Los

Angeles is the home of the most powerful film industry in the world, the capital of entertainment and fantasy (Posner 1997, 1). Settled in part, more than a century ago, in the suburb of Los Angeles that later gave it its name, Hollywood has dominated world cinema economically and culturally since its early years and has contributed crucially to the history of the city, its complex power structure, and its ethnic makeup; and Hollywood has lent the city symbolic meaning as the final destination of the American dream. Hollywood is an important part of the history and urban identity of Los Angeles and an important source of fascination for millions of visitors from all over the world. Los Angeles is the most often filmed city on the planet, the default cinematic city (Braudy 2010, 277): When a film is not supposed to take place in any specific place, it has probably been shot in LA; when the cinematic city is visible but not narratively important, that city is likely to be LA; when a story is told in Hollywood cinema about urban conflict, urban excitement, or urban alienation, the city that is usually taken to represent these issues is LA; and, of course, many filmic stories have the City of Angels as a more or less central narrative element—they are in more or less ostensible ways *about* LA.

Our cinematic impressions of the city are therefore a combination of the fact that LA is the home of the Hollywood industry, that it has been widely used as the urban context of thousands of films, and that in some of those films it is easily recognizable and sometimes narratively important. As a consequence of this, Los Angeles may be the most mediated city in the United States (Avila 2010, 96). Take the well-known example of *Blade Runner* (Ridley Scott, 1982), for many the paradigmatic modern LA movie. With its combination of retro-noir look and science fiction and its dystopian view of a dehumanized society dominated by incomprehensible and ruthless corporations, *Blade Runner* offers not only a powerful statement about our society but also a deep insight into what makes the city where it was shot and where its action takes place the center of modern alienation. *Blade Runner* is a good example of the pervasiveness of LA as a Hollywood narrative trope at a variety of levels and of the multiple ways in which Hollywood has contributed to the construction of LA as a global city. It is also an illustration of the predominant meanings of the cinematic city: Partly figured as a border city both visually and narratively, it privileges one of many urban experiences—that of its neo-noir Anglo alienated hero.

If we look at the history of Hollywood cinema, a number of urban images have become familiar: the bustling Downtown scene that we see in countless silent movies, the dark streets of film noir exuding postwar malaise, the urban decadence pervading numerous movies of the New American cinema of the late 1960s and early 1970s, and the postmodern metropolis of more recent movies, among others (see Avila 2010; Davis 2001; Dimendberg 2010; Silver and Ursini 2005). Individual Hollywood films portray particular aspects of the history of the city: the importance of water in the development of the global metropolis in *Chinatown* (Roman Polanski, 1974), the Catholic Church and its political ramifications in *True Confessions* (Ulu Grosbard, 1981), local politics and racial conflict in *Devil in a Blue Dress* (Carl Franklin, 1995), or the historical power of the Los Angeles Police Department (LAPD) in *L.A. Confidential* (Curtis Hanson, 1997) and *Changeling* (Clint Eastwood, 2008). In general, however, the discourse that Hollywood cinema has produced about the city is not significantly different from other dominant urban discourses. These have attempted, from various perspectives, to repress and hide the city's heterogeneity behind an airtight mask of Anglo uniformity. Braudy describes this dialectic as the basic Angeleno tension between purity and mixture (2010, 277). More specifically, Robert Gottlieb argues that the history and identity of Los Angeles combines the type of multiethnic neighborhoods embodied by, for example, Boyle Heights in the 1950s with the sustained efforts of housing developers to break up neighborhoods through racial exclusion (2007, 68–69). Rodolfo Acuña puts it more incisively: "Los Angeles boasts of being a multicultural city, but nothing is further from the truth" (1996, 14). Historians of the city explain that, since at least the postwar period, the city has become increasingly diverse even as it lays out its peculiar demographic mosaic of racially exclusive communities. Southern California as a whole may be heterogeneous, but its individual communities are essentially homogeneous (Avila 2006, 44–45). Partly because of the extremity of these tensions and the ways in which they have affected Angelenos throughout the history of the city, social conflicts frequently flare up. The latest of these explosions, in 1992, may well have been a point of no return.

The Justice Riots and After

Los Angeles went up in flames on April 29, 1992. On March 3, 1991, taxi driver Rodney King had been stopped by four members of the LAPD for speeding on a freeway and was subsequently beaten savagely. George Holliday videotaped the incident from the balcony of his nearby home (Avila 2010, 105), and his video became the first viral film on network and cable TV. LA history was being made appropriately enough on film (see www.rodneykingvideo.com.ar/). Holliday's movie may not have been a sophisticated piece of filmmaking, but it crucially contributed to converting the beatings into a turning point in the city's history. Fourteen months later, a mostly white jury in Simi Valley acquitted the four officers, and the city exploded in what came to be known as the Rodney King riots or the justice riots (Soja 2000, 465) but what some called the LAPD riots, given the central role of the local police in instigating the events. Whole areas of South Central and Mid-City, including Koreatown, and the Pico-Union neighborhood, were devastated, but the uprising also affected many other parts of town. The apocalyptic dimensions of the riots did not quite develop into the type of society depicted in *Blade Runner*, but something changed in LA that April. Mike Davis (1998) includes the riots and their consequences in his book on the natural disasters that devastated the city in the 1990s. For him, the ultimate causes of the riots—unbearable differences in income, land value, class, and race—are truly "ecological" determinants (Davis 1998, 363).

Beyond the failure of the "Rebuild LA" official initiative to reinvigorate the city and provide the conditions to prevent this type of violence from recurring (Pastor 2010, 256–57; Saul 2010, 160), the aftereffects of the uprisings were wide reaching. In materially ascertainable terms, not much has changed in the city since 1992—the economic distance has grown rather than decreased between social groups—but the less tangible social and cultural climate has moved toward a new, albeit precarious, acceptance of difference and diversity. After all, as Davis summarizes, although the focus was initially on Anglos as victims of African American rage, evidence of the involvement of Latinos and Asian Americans in the ensuing confrontations made this a riot in Technicolor (Davis 1998, 371). For Davis, the riots exacerbated existing problems: the privatization of Downtown and other areas, the fortification of gated communities, the proliferation of "social control districts," racially biased neighborhood watch programs, white violence against African Americans and other minorities, consolidation of tourist bubbles, and the growth in size and cost to the taxpayer of the prison system (366–91, 404–18). Yet, at the same time, awareness of the multiracial nature of the outburst of violence also led, first, to the social and cultural necessity of acknowledging the presence of what had remained hidden and, later, haltingly, to the incorporation of demographic realities into dominant discourses.

Sociologists and cultural theorists have often pondered this paradox since the riots. Hayden summarizes it in the following terms: "The larger urban questions remain unanswered. Is it inevitable for Los Angeles to be torn by conflicts of race, ethnicity, gender, and class? Or is it possible to argue that the citizens of Los Angeles are learning to develop an American city based on diversity?" (1995, 244). For Scott Kurashige and other writers, the diversity lesson had already begun in the aftermath of the Watts riots in 1966, with the "qualified embrace of multiculturalism" being reflected in such phenomena as the election of an African American mayor, extensive trade with Asia, and the hiring of first Japanese and later Mexican immigrants as gardeners (Kurashige 2010, 68). However, the trend had obviously not solidified enough when, twenty-seven years later, anger about racial and ethnic discrimination and social injustice as well as interethnic tension again came to the surface. In fact, the tortuous road toward acceptance of diversity in Los Angeles is a long one. As Avila contends, interethnic and racial clashes have punctuated the city's history from the beginning and never really went away (2010, 95–96). Past experience drives people to wonder when the next burst of violence will occur. For Susan Anderson, this history of violence may be the city's "perverse gift": "the city as oracle, the prophetic urban place that utters a message no one wants to hear" (1996, 357).

In many ways the recent history and the demographic evolution of Los Angeles are not so different from the paths of other U.S. cities. Hayden (1995) noted that in the largest cities the population of white citizens declined from about 75 percent to about 40 percent. The large minorities together—African Americans, Latinos, and Asian Americans—were already outnumbering the white majorities in several cities. Since then the balance has tipped further in the same direction. In a few years' time one in every two people in California will be Latino. At the same time, other minority groups, particularly Asian Americans, have continued to grow and to make their presence felt in the geography of LA, making "diversity" not just a buzzword but the central demographic and social feature for politicians, urban planners, and social workers to deal with. In Los Angeles the inevitability of diversity or multiculturalism as the only way ahead may have dawned on people in the aftermath of the April 29 events, and it has changed perceptions in ways that are not always sufficiently acknowledged. As Soja puts it, another "new" Los Angeles burst onto the scene in 1992 (2000, 396). Given the characteristics of LA, other cities in the United States and the rest of the world were looking closely.

Charles Jencks (1996) describes the "heteropolis" as "the new form of urban agglomeration that thrives on difference," one that, at a certain point in recent history, became a positive cause of economic and cultural growth. Los Angeles became "the ultimate urban bouillabaisse," with its multiplicity of urban cores, incorporated cities, major ethnic groups, and languages spoken in its schools (Jencks 1996, 47–48). Although the justice riots demonstrated the resistance of the status quo to these social transformations and amplified the conflict between the two forces, the perception is that things finally started to change slowly as multiculturalism became an important part of the everyday experience of contemporary Angelenos. At the same time, multiculturalism continues to be a useful tourist and economic hook that makes the ongoing prominence of historically powerful discourses of racialized segregation and white supremacy more palatable: We are the ultimate diverse city, even though the Anglo minority continues to hold the reins of the economy, urban development, and discourse, often in more effective and anxiety-ridden ways than ever before.

The cinema has historically felt more comfortable reproducing these dominant positions. To a large extent, this has not changed since 1992, but signs of competing perspectives also abound, and the imagination of what Davis calls "ordinary disaster" (1998, 5) remains constant. Take, for example, the film *Battle Los Angeles* (Jonathan Liebesman, 2011), a science fiction disaster action blockbuster that fits the parameters of the contemporary Hollywood product, made and marketed for a global audience. The fact that the action takes place in Los Angeles may not seem significant, yet it is inscribed within an apocalyptic discourse that is deeply entrenched in the history of the city, including its cinematic images. Further, there is a certain geographic verisimilitude in the physical journeys of the human characters around the metropolis (although, for financial reasons, much of the action was shot in Louisiana). The eerie views of Downtown may be linked to deep-seated anxieties about urban development, whereas the destruction of Santa Monica, where much of the story takes place, may target different fears about the safety of the lifestyle of the wealthy classes. In addition, although this "global" narrative could have happened anywhere in the world, even in an unspecified location, it happens in Los Angeles, with the city taken here as the center of a world on the verge of catastrophe. Finally, there is the ethnic makeup of the protagonists. Of the six surviving soldiers, three are African American, two are Anglos, including the protagonist, and one is Latina; but there are three more Latino marines, including a lieutenant who dies, and a Latino civilian, who also dies, and his son, who survives. In fact, part of the fun of the proceedings consists in guessing who will be dispensed with next and the social group to which he or she belongs. This combination of characters makes sense in a city of such ethnic diversity, but what the text does with it may point to general trends in demographic discourses that have a particular momentum in LA and to post-1992 changes in public perception about how the city ought to be represented, even in the least socially committed of movies. *Battle Los Angeles* beckons to the type of cultural analysis I pursue in this book, because it highlights the tension between continuing traditional patterns of representation and the growing presence of alternative perspectives. One could say that, from its modest cultural position as an "unthinking" product of mass entertainment, *Battle Los Angeles* is a trendsetter for the future, not least in its unobtrusive acknowledgment of ethnic, cultural, and social impurity in the city's population.

Los Angeles Films and Conglomerate Hollywood

In general terms, therefore, I argue that the justice riots of 1992 constitute an important moment in the recent history of Los Angeles, that the complex social dynamics that produced that outburst of violence brought about a gradual series of transformations in public perceptions of the city, and that these, along with clearly identifiable continuities with the past, found their way, often in heavily mediated forms, onto the cinematic screen. Through the uneven assimilation of these changes and continuities into their narratives, LA films have continued to participate in the creation of urban discourse and, consequently, in the construction of social and cultural identities.

The phrase *Los Angeles films* is used here to refer to those movies that are set in the city and contribute important meanings to its history and culture through stories that may or may not be openly "about" LA. The proliferation in recent years of audiovisual formats and platforms makes it increasingly difficult to describe what may or may not be considered a film, a movie, or an audiovisual narrative. Indeed, the boundaries between the cinema and other arts are increasingly blurry and uncertain. Contemporary artists have taken advantage of this, and, in the case of Los Angeles, what could be described as alternative views of the city have become apparent from a large and vibrant body of artistic works that often offer drastically different perspectives from those of the dominant culture, mainstream art, and, in our case, Hollywood cinema. As David James has shown, Los Angeles has a long and rich history of what he calls "minor cinemas": avant-garde, independent, and underground films, extending back to the 1920s, that often challenge the values, myths, and dreams of Hollywood and offer alternative views of the city (2005, 3). Many of these cinematic trends and movements directly address the invisibility of various ethnic and social groups in mainstream cinema and seek to counteract prevailing stereotypes and silences. The Chicano cinema that emerged as a direct offshoot of the Chicano civil rights movement in the 1960s and 1970s is one such example (Noriega 1992b, xix), but many other voices can be found in this parallel tradition. The aftermath of the 1992 riots and the rest of the period covered in this book have been particularly fertile and abundant in audiovisual texts that have openly constructed themselves in counter distinction to mainstream Hollywood.

Minor cinemas therefore might be the obvious place to look for stories and images that speak differently about the city. Digitization and the Internet have made access to many of these texts much easier than, for example, most of the movies from earlier decades explored by James, many of which can only be found in archives. Yet the question of availability and impact remains a serious consideration when assessing these materials. That they exist and even that they are accessible to those interested in looking for them do not guarantee their visibility and therefore their impact on audiences around the world. Many of them remain in the domain of a reduced niche, often almost exclusively local audiences and academics. On the other hand, I attempt to explain cinematic images of Los Angeles and the effect they have had on the ways that wider audiences, including outsiders to the city like myself, have imagined and interpreted the city. For this reason I restrict my exploration to Hollywood films, even though I am aware that the inclusion of alternative audiovisual representations would significantly alter the view. For better or for worse, "this is Hollywood."

The question arises as to what, in the second decade of the twenty-first century, constitutes a "Hollywood film." Like the city of Los Angeles, the film industry has undergone important changes recently and, as a consequence of this, what we understand by "Hollywood" may have also changed. For one thing, as Paul McDonald and Janet Wasko (2008) have argued, the Hollywood film industry—traditionally a synonym for the U.S. film industry—has become increasingly internationalized to the extent that the question of the nationality of Hollywood is becoming more and more problematic. If it ever was, "Hollywood" is no longer in Hollywood. To some extent, it continues to be based in LA, but it is also in Buenos Aires, Paris, Warsaw, Mumbai, Sydney, and Shanghai (McDonald and Wasko 2008, 6–7). On the other hand, starting many decades ago with television and continuing with video and then with an increasing number of commercial outlets, nowadays a Hollywood film is, as these authors argue, no longer only a movie but also a TV program, a digital or optical disc, or downloaded or streamed content. As a consequence of this, rather than primarily producing or even distributing films, the contemporary Hollywood industry is now in the business of exploiting intellectual property rights in an increasingly transnational context. What constitutes a Hollywood film, then, remains an open question, yet as McDonald and Wasko remind us, for moviegoers all over the world the popular Hollywood feature continues to define what they expect a film to be (5–6).

Coincidentally around the same time as the 1992 justice riots, important transformations began to gather momentum in the Hollywood industry. Tom Schatz summarizes them in the phrase "from New Hollywood to Conglomerate Hollywood," indicating a period in which a group of media giants took control of the U.S. film and television industries and became dominant in the expanding entertainment market. The film studios, however, remained at the epicenter of this industry, and more or less traditional feature films continued to be their key commodity (Schatz 2008, 25–27). The signature product of this new conglomerate Hollywood was the blockbuster, but the new companies financed a greater variety of feature films, notably those made by independent companies that, though originally operating as a response to the specialization of New Hollywood in the blockbuster in the late 1970s and early 1980s, gained an unexpected degree of visibility and financial success toward the end of the 1980s. As a consequence of this, a few years later, the Hollywood studios, now part of the larger entertainment giants, gradually bought these companies, starting with the most successful, Miramax and New Line

Cinema, in the early 1990s. By the early 2000s the incorporation of the independent cinema into the mainstream industry was more or less complete. In financial terms at least, independent cinema was not independent any more. Newly labeled indie or Indiewood, the earlier independent companies had become divisions of conglomerate Hollywood. At the same time, the movies they produced remained fairly distinct, both in marketing and in formal terms, from the blockbusters and more commercial fare.

Schatz offers a three-tier classification of Hollywood films according to the size of their budgets: (1) blockbusters largely produced by the studios with budgets over $100 million; (2) medium-size movies, produced by the studios' indie subsidiaries for around $40 million; and (3) smaller films, made by independent producer-distributors for under $10 million and sometimes much less. Today, conglomerate Hollywood remains as heavily invested in the indie movement as in the blockbuster to the extent that two Hollywoods can be said to be in place, both in aesthetic and economic terms, even though active cross-fertilization is an integral part of the structure (Schatz 2008, 31–33). The term *independent cinema*, therefore, no longer describes movies made outside Hollywood but has, in fact, become a central part of the industry (see also G. King et al. 2012; and Tzioumakis 2006).

Most of the films selected for analysis in this book occupy the central part of the spectrum in Schatz's categorization. Some, like *White Men Can't Jump* (Ron Shelton, 1992), *Collateral* (Michael Mann, 2003), and *The Soloist* (Joe Wright, 2009), though far from having blockbuster aspirations and budgets, approximate the first category and are, in financial terms, mainstream fare. *Luminarias* (José Luis Valenzuela, 2000), on the other hand, is at the other end of the spectrum. Produced independently by the filmmakers through an early form of crowdfunding, with money raised by family and friends in the LA Latino community, the film was distributed by "truly independent" New Latin Pictures. To different degrees, *Quinceañera* (Richard Glatzer and Wash Westmoreland, 2006), *What's Cooking?* (Gurinder Chadha, 2000), *Mother and Child* (Rodrigo García, 2009), *A Better Life* (Chris Weitz, 2011), and, in a different sense, *Real Women Have Curves* (Patricia Cardoso, 2002) occupy the same area around Schatz's third category. The rest are clearer illustrations of the history of "independent cinema" as it moved from the margins to the center of the industry. Although *Luminarias* may come close to some manifestations of James's minor cinema, particularly in the way it was financed, and although *Mulholland Drive* (David Lynch, 2001) may challenge Hollywood conventions in more or less radical ways, the movies I have selected are all part of the industry in either financial or stylistic terms (and often in both).

As can be inferred from the preceding paragraphs, the structure of this book revolves around close readings of individual films that, within the contemporary industrial scenario delineated earlier, articulate what I take to be important discourses on Los Angeles as well as mutated versions of the most salient traditions of representation of the city in earlier Hollywood cinema, starting with film noir. Like the editors of the new *Movie: A Journal of Film Criticism*, I defend the continuing importance of critical writing centered on textual analysis and film aesthetics (Pye and Walker 2010). At the same time, I understand this type of analysis not as an end in itself but as a way to explore the politics and ideology of the films, in this case, the ideological and cultural dimensions of cinematic approaches to the city. Other perspectives and emphases are possible, and indeed relevant for a study of Hollywood and Los Angeles. Post-1992 cinema is rather more than a selection of more or less representative movies. It is also a set of institutions and industrial practices that, like Los Angeles, have undergone deep transformations, such as those touched on earlier but also including shifting exhibition platforms and new distribution and marketing practices (Drake 2008). The discourses that Hollywood produces about the city are obviously linked with its industrial strategies, and those strategies are, in turn, affected, if not driven, by social change. I invoke such industrial considerations, particularly marketing strategies, in the following chapters whenever relevant to the analysis. Yet my focus remains on the texts. I share Richard Dyer's worry that, in the midst of the cultures of producers and the complexities of audience research, "films may get rather lost in this process" (1998, 9). Therefore the scope of my inquiry is restricted to the imaginary (cultural, ideological, aesthetic) line that links the city to the cinematic text. In a sense, the analysis moves from the city to the screen and back to the city. This underlying premise is reflected in the organization of the chapters.

The book has an introductory section and three parts. In Chapter 2 of the Introduction I examine two movies that were being made when tensions were coming to a boiling point in LA: the police beating of Rodney King, the subsequent acquittal of the police officers in Simi Valley the following year, and the explosion of urban violence that it provoked. In this chapter I look for images of those tensions in the movies coming out of Hollywood at the time and, while considering other examples, zero in on two of them for detailed analysis: *White Men Can't Jump* and *Falling Down* (Joel Schumacher, 1993). Both texts deal with the urban climate of the early 1990s in quite different, even opposed, ways, but they share a surprising immediacy in Hollywood's response to social anxieties, given their unequivocal mainstream vocation.

In Part I, I consider the history of representation of the city in pre-1992 Hollywood cinema and how post-1992 films offer continuities with earlier patterns and representational tropes. Taking classic film noir as a particularly intense flashpoint that shaped cinematic urban meanings, I single out three tropes or signifying areas that summarize classic Hollywood's approach to the city: alienation, ethnic homogeneity, and self-representation. Other meanings are certainly to be found in earlier traditions and individual texts, but the view of the city as producing alienated (male) individuals, the fantasy of white exclusivity, and the industry's fascination with itself, with its dreams, its anxieties, and its corruptions, are a constant presence in the history of "Hollywood's LA." These dominant tropes are still very much a part of the scene in post-1992 movies, and each of the three chapters in Part I focuses on recent manifestations of each trope. Chapter 3 revisits the trope of alienation through the analysis of *Collateral* as a post-noir narrative. In Chapter 4 I look at two movies that apparently perpetuate the fantasy of a white Los Angeles from within the aesthetic and industrial confines of indie cinema: *(500) Days of Summer* (Marc Webb, 2009) and *Magnolia* (Paul Thomas Anderson, 1999). In Chapter 5 *Mulholland Drive* is presented as an example of Hollywood's continuing attraction to itself. In the three chapters, however, continuities are blended with tensions and the threat of ruptures. The four texts appear fraught with counterforces that threaten the traditional hegemonies.

In Part II, I look at thematic areas that may have remained repressed under the surface before the riots but since then have gradually found their way to visibility as certain urban discourses started to change. In Chapter 6 *Devil in a Blue Dress* (Carl Franklin, 1995) is analyzed as an example of post-1992 attempts to rewrite the city's history. Specifically, the movie returns to the past of the city's racist 1950s, coinciding with the apogee of film noir in Hollywood, and excavates the social importance of the Angeleno African American community and the centrality of the LAPD in its historical repression. In Chapter 7 I analyze *What's Cooking* and *Mother and Child* as instances of a genre that gathered momentum in the 1990s, the multi-protagonist film. This genre has been seen as particularly suited to the representation of Los Angeles in its ability to narrativize diversity and encompass the postmetropolis. In Chapter 8 I visit the intensified borderliness of the contemporary cosmopolis and explore cinematic articulations of the border as a central trope of contemporary life in *The Soloist*.

Beyond the importance of 1992 as a watershed year in recent Angeleno history, there is no clearly discernible narrative of progress in recent LA movies. Competing discourses continue to appear in relation to the thematic clusters that I have singled out for analysis. Movies respond to social and cultural changes, but these responses are neither homogeneous nor consistent. The visibility-invisibility dialectic, for example, remains as uncertain and as unresolved today as it was in the 1990s. By focusing on the presence of Latinos and Latinas in post-1992 films in Part III, it may appear that I am positing some form of evolution toward a pretended fullness. This is not the case, or, at least, the road to a cinema that may begin to reflect urban statistics is still a long one. In Part III, I focus on films about Latinos and Latinas in Los Angeles because they are the starting point of this project, because their social impact on the city is undeniable, and because the four movies analyzed in this part—*Luminarias*, *Real Women Have Curves*, *Quinceañera*, and *A Better Life*—reflect what I take to be relevant issues in the life of the city not touched on in previous chapters. From the perspective of the Latino constituency in LA, these movies are not more "important" than earlier examples, such as *American Me* (James Edward Olmos, 1992) and *My Family/Mi Familia* (Gregory Nava, 1995), nor do they represent a clear and unambiguous progression in Hollywood's attitudes toward Latinos and Latinas. Rather, I attempt to highlight the relevance of Latinos and Latinas in my views of the city and its cinema. Yet this discussion is not to be taken as the culmination of a linear narrative. Like the city itself, like its network of freeways, the recent history of the Latino presence in the cinema resembles an undecipherable tangle of bifurcating roads whose structure and rationale are difficult to detect.

The cinema's urban articulations contribute in no small measure to shaping the way in which people think about and make sense of urban culture and politics. No city in the world has been seen on the screen as often as LA, still the capital of the most powerful film industry in the world and, in more ways than one, still the quintessential cinematic city. In this book I attempt to capture the ways in which the purely cinematic city, that is, the city in films, contributes to the ongoing construction of the post-1992 cosmopolis, the exorbitant city as seen on the exorbitant screen.

2

Rodney King's Los Angeles in the Hollywood Mainstream

Up in Flames

At some point in its recent history, the profile of Los Angeles in public discourse changed from being the paradigm of white U.S. supremacy to being defined as the most diverse city in the world and the harbinger of changes to come. For some, the shift in social perspective and cultural discourse came on the back of sheer demographic upheaval. Whereas in 1960, 80 percent of the population was Anglo, fifty years later, the percentage of non-Hispanic whites had decreased to less than 30 percent, with Latinos nearing 60 percent and citizens of Asian origin (10 percent) surpassing African Americans (quickfacts.census.gov/qfd/states/06/0644000.html). Yet, beyond this drastic demographic change, the history of LA has been marked by racial multiplicity and conflict ever since the city, along with the rest of California, became part of the United States in 1848 as a result of the Treaty of Guadalupe Hidalgo.

As elsewhere in America, the colonization of Southern California by the Spanish Empire, particularly Franciscan missionaries, and the later Anglo settlement brought Native Americans close to extinction. In California this process sped up after 1848: The number of Indians dropped from 72,000 at the time of the U.S. conquest to 15,000 by 1880 (McWilliams 2010, 29–46). The new U.S. city of Los Angeles soon became adept at racist episodes, starting with the Chinese massacre of 1871, when 19 Chinese American men, women, and children were murdered (most of them were hung from improvised gallows) by a mob of 500 people of European, U.S., and Mexican origin in the Calle de los Negros in the old Chinatown. Several decades later, in 1942, Angeleno Japanese Americans were officially declared "a hostile and enemy race" and interned in makeshift camps in the deserts of California and Arizona until the end of World War II (Kurashige 2010, 62, 65; G. Sánchez 2010,

141–44). During the same period, violence against Mexican Americans was also rife and materialized in two episodes: the Sleepy Lagoon murder trial in 1942 and the Zoot Suit Riots the following year, during which white sailors assaulted Chicanos in the streets of Los Angeles with the acquiescence and collaboration of the LAPD (Anderson 1996, 353; Avila 2010, 101–2; Weaver 1980, 134–41). In 1965 it was the turn of African Americans in the Watts neighborhood to confront the LAPD, following the arrest of a young man for erratic driving; residents vented their anger and frustration over police brutality against black people and the general impoverishment of the African American community (Saul 2010, 148–55; Soja 1996, 427–32). The result was 35 people dead, more than 1,000 injured, extensive damage to mostly white property, and, as Eric Avila summarizes, the shattering of the 1960s myth of Los Angeles as one big beach party (2010, 103).

Twenty-seven years later, violence erupted once again at the intersection of Florence and Normandie Avenues, in a relatively prosperous section of South Central LA, as a consequence of the acquittal in Simi Valley of the four policemen charged with brutalizing Rodney King the previous year. To some, it felt as though nothing had changed or been learned. It was one more episode fueling images of Los Angeles as the repository of "dark fantasies of race war" and anxieties of "an imminent racial apocalypse" (Avila 2010, 95–96). This time anger was directed not only toward the LAPD but also against Korean-owned businesses and Latino neighbors, who had begun to encroach on the traditionally African American communities of South Central. As Scott Saul explains, most of the people who were beaten up were Latino and Asian and at least 30 percent of the businesses damaged were owned by Latinos (2010, 158). For Elaine Kim, the riots were "a baptism in what it really means for a Korean to become American in the 1990s" (quoted in Abelmann and Lie 1995, 24). For Saul, the crucible of the riot revealed and remade the transnational aspect of immigrant identities (2010, 160). The Watts riots may have highlighted the dominant white-black paradigm of racial conflict, but the so-called justice riots of 1992 reminded observers of the range of racial relationships and tensions in Southern California.

Maybe the conclusion to be derived from this brief account of the conflict-ridden short history of the city is that, in terms of race relationships, Los Angeles is beyond hope. Edward Soja finds some of the roots of the situation in "the crusade-like mentality of [a] white, often anti-papist and racially proud Christian majority" that became the dominant social group in the city at the end of the nineteenth century (2000, 136). After the failure of Rebuild Los Angeles, a private organization, to bring a measure of social justice to the city after the Rodney King riots, LA continues to be split between extremes of wealth and poverty, the urban meeting point of first and third world (Dear 1996, 98), or, in the words of Paul Ong and Evelyn Blumenberg, a city made up of two cities, "one amazingly prosperous, the other increasingly poor in substance and in hope" (1996, 329). As mentioned in Chapter 1, the "Time for Truth" report, published at the end of 2013, saw the city as sinking into a bleak future with the unbearable burden of almost 40 percent of its population living in misery (Los Angeles 2020 Commission, 2013, 1, 7).

Yet, as Scott Kurashige points out, the 1965 Watts riots had already brought about an awareness of the city's multiracial diversity and its national and global importance, an incipient cosmopolitan city that embraced a qualified form of multiculturalism (2010, 68). This commitment to multiculturalism then produced, among other ostensible signs, the city's first African American mayor, Tom Bradley (1973–1993), and subsequently the first Mexican American mayor, Antonio Villaraigosa (2005–2013). Mike Davis, among others, has lamented that first Bradley and then Villaraigosa became representative of "liberal accommodation to an unchanging elite agenda of pharaonic redevelopment projects" (2006, 9), yet the visibility of these hitherto invisible demographic groups in recent decades was surely an index of change. Villaraigosa was succeeded at the helm of the city by Eric Garcetti, not only the youngest mayor in more than a century but also its first ever Jewish mayor, whose mother is of Russian Jewish descent and whose father is a Mexican American of Spanish, Italian, and Indigenous descent. Los Angeles is now profoundly, irremediably ethnic, and the tilting of political culture toward Latinos may have caused the politics of racial division to lose its currency (Ethington 2010, 209; Soja 2000, 289). As Avila reminds us, the city's social clash is, after all, the hallmark of urban life (2010, 108). Soja concludes that the issue is whether or not the multiethnic, multicultural society can work (2000, 289). The upheavals of 1992, which left economic and social inequality largely unchanged, also marked a turning point in the acceptance of its striking diversity.

How has Hollywood cinema responded to these changes? Historically, the movie industry sided with Anglo supremacist discourses through its own strategies of invisibility, stereotyping, and often outright racism in representations of Los

Angeles. At the same time, films, including Hollywood films, have always found ways to reproduce not only dominant discourses but also cracks, fissures, tensions, and crises in those discourses and, if we know where and how to look, alternative visions. The justice riots did not just happen spontaneously but were the outcome of long-standing social injustice and slow-brewing rage. More or less mainstream movies as varied as *Blade Runner* (Ridley Scott, 1982), *Breathless* (Jim McBride, 1983), *Into the Night* (John Landis, 1985), *Colors* (Dennis Hopper, 1988), *They Live* (John Carpenter, 1988), *The Rookie* (Clint Eastwood, 1991), and even *Barton Fink* (Joel Coen, 1991), among others, can be read from an Angeleno viewpoint as cinematic correlatives of that rage in the previous decade. More openly, *Boyz n the Hood* (John Singleton, 1991), with its bleak account of young black lives in South Central, depicts a society in the grip of violence that is crying out for drastic change or the kind of social explosion that would occur only months after its release. The film itself provoked disturbances in ghettos across the United States, anticipating in reduced form the riots of the following year. Movies may not always be as openly prescient or direct in their reaction to social events, but they are always part of the cultural and social fabric that produces those events. As such, they can function as symptoms of crises and of social and cultural transformations. Given the history of overwhelming Anglo dominance in LA films, examples like those just mentioned can be seen as symptomatic of things to come, keeping in mind that social and cultural issues most often find their way into mainstream movies in heavily mediated ways.

Although the examination of the industry's response to the justice riots and their aftermath is the subject of this book as a whole, in this chapter I focus on films that were made in Hollywood and released as the April 1992 crisis was coming to a boiling point and in its immediate aftermath. In it I explore the ways in which these movies tackled in more or less direct ways the social issues that came to the forefront at the end of April 1992.

Through the Cinematic Glass

The examples given earlier show that an impending social crisis can find its way into a movie in a variety of ways, including complete absence. Romantic comedies of the early 1990s, such as *Pretty Woman* (Garry Marshall, 1990) and *L.A. Story* (Mick Jackson, 1991), offer the viewer a fairy-tale Los Angeles, as distant from social unrest as can be imagined. In *Pretty Woman* we visit mansions in Bel Air, exclusive boutiques on Rodeo Drive, luxury hotels on Wilshire Boulevard, and even a polo club in Burbank. Despite the cautionary anticapitalist tale included in the Cinderella plot, there is nothing specifically Angeleno about the social conflict or even the seedier parts of Hollywood Boulevard, where Vivian (Julia Roberts) plies her wares. They all become part of the conventional comic space of the film. *Pretty Woman* shows a keen sense of LA geography but no intimation of social malaise.

Even more fantastically, *L.A. Story* boasts a fanciful view of the city, all palm trees and exotic plants, romantically savvy freeway signposts that direct the protagonist's love life, eccentric characters, and exclusive concentration on Westside and beachfront locations. The film's title equivocates as to the social relevance of what it is about to offer, given that it was released only a few weeks before Rodney King was chased and beaten up by the LAPD. Not that any film or cultural text should be expected to reflect what outsiders might see as socially relevant at the moment of its release. Rather, in retrospect, through its whimsical approach to the city, *L.A. Story* can be seen as one more articulation of the same social environment that would produce the justice riots the following year. Considered together with *Boyz n the Hood*, also released in 1991, the textual distance between the two films could well be seen as a fictional correlative of a comparable social disparity in Angeleno society, one that for many of its citizens was becoming untenable in its flagrant injustice. In other words, it would be inaccurate to assert that *Pretty Woman* and *L.A. Story* are misrepresentations of the city where they were made and where their actions take place. On the contrary, they were very much part of the urban discourses prevalent at the time. *Boyz n the Hood* can be considered a more realistic movie, yet the three texts taken together offer a more accurate view of the city than any one of them in isolation.

Steve Martin, who plays the protagonist in *L.A. Story*, is the link with *Grand Canyon* (Lawrence Kasdan, 1991), another movie from the same year that, however indirectly, was more openly vocal and restless about social conflict. Kasdan's film is, in fact, exemplary of the many ways in which Los Angeles has been portrayed on the screen in the period covered by this book. As an early instance of the Angeleno multi-protagonist film, which will reappear at various points in this book and will

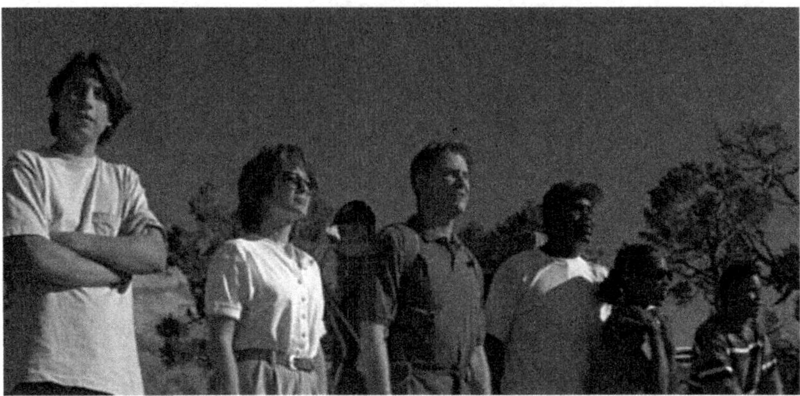

Grand Canyon: struggling for diversity.

be the focus of Chapter 7, it is also representative of the displaced and interstitial presence of ethnic diversity in Anglo-centered movies and of the growing unease about such displacements.

Coming out of a basketball game with his son, Kevin Kline's protagonist Mack makes a wrong turn and finds himself accosted by a gang of African Americans. Simon (Danny Glover) arrives in the nick of time to save them, and the two men develop a bond. *Grand Canyon* starts from this central biracial friendship and weaves a canvas that encompasses various social classes and various areas of LA, embodied in its six protagonists. Its liberal credentials are reinforced by the relative balance that it attempts to strike between black and white characters, moving carefully between acknowledgment of Anglo dominance in the society it depicts and textual equality that seeks to indirectly oppose social discrimination. At the same time, the plot offers constant examples of the rage, anxiety, blatant inequality, and urban alienation of a city on the verge of breakdown: Mack and his son, Roberto (Jeremy Sisto), are attacked by the gang, who accuse them of Anglo privilege; Mack's friend Davis (Martin) is shot in the leg and almost killed in the middle of the day in a wealthy area; Simon's teenage nephew Otis (Patrick Malone) is reluctant to abandon his neighborhood and his gang; later, his mother's house is shot up by a rival band; even Dee's (Mary Louise Parker) dissatisfaction with the pallid affair she is having with Mack is part of this extreme unease. Mack and his family appear to live in one of the most exclusive parts of the Westside, probably Brentwood, and lead a life of comfort and privilege, yet Claire (Mary McDonnell) is profoundly unhappy for reasons that are never apparent and that she cannot even explain herself. The film's topography is never clear, but Los Angeles is depicted as a city over which some unspecified malaise is hanging, even though it lacks the comparable metaphor of the medfly plague in the slightly later *Short Cuts* (Robert Altman, 1993). Like Altman's film, the narrative of *Grand Canyon* is punctuated by shots of helicopters flying across the city sky, both day and night, which highlights the permanent state of surveillance of a city always in danger. Mack, for his part, has a dream in which he flies over LA, coming in from the sea, suggesting his wish to escape from a life that leaves him as empty and as alienated as his wife.

Mack is a lawyer who specializes in immigration law, yet it is significant that we never see any immigrants in his stylish Downtown office or anywhere else in the city. The text never underlines this discrepancy, but, given the release date of the film, it is tempting to find an explanation for the depressed and hysterical city it depicts in the arrogance of a wealthy Anglo constituency for which immigrants are exclusively the reason for a good job. At the same time, films of the kind Davis makes have no other social function than to make a fortune for Anglo elites. The black-white narrative balance can be seen in this light as a way for the filmmakers to dissociate themselves from the racist social structure they are criticizing, but the binary racial structure on which this critique is based betrays the text's difficulties in understanding its own city. Other ethnic groups, such as Asian Americans and Latinos, are practically absent. One of the police officers who arrest Otis for running in his new neighborhood in the San Fernando Valley is Asian American, and the gang that briefly approaches him there seem Latino, but all these characters are peripheral to the story.

Like other multi-protagonist films, *Grand Canyon* does attempt to render the diversity of the city through a multiplicity of interwoven stories and through a variety of characters, but it forgets to even mention its largest social group. Or almost: Mack has called his son after famous Puerto Rican baseball player Roberto Clemente, and when, in the middle of her spiritual crisis, Claire finds an abandoned baby (whom she later adopts), it is a little Hispanic girl. The new demographic majorities are largely absent from the film, but they turn up, in unconventional ways, in the younger generations, pointing the way to the future.

The narrative combination in *Grand Canyon* is indeed explosive: the careful textual equality between black and white characters, the unnamed social and spiritual malaise, the persistent indications of Anglo arrogance and guilt, and the invisibility of the demographically most powerful ethnic groups together with the textual near-acknowledgment of its own limitations in this area. All these factors are indicative of a society out of joint, one that includes the film itself and its textual strategies: Kasdan's movie is both a denunciation of social injustice and a symptom of that injustice, metaphorically one of the policemen who beat Rodney King and the onlooker who videotaped the act of violence from the balcony of his nearby apartment. In this sense the film is an apt illustration of an industry openly engaged with its social environment even while producing mainstream movies with audience and critical appeal, an industry that appears to be both attuned to and implicated in the immediate social background of events that would change the history of the city. *White Men Can't Jump* and *Falling Down* belong in the same group and are analyzed here as instances of almost instant cinematic responses to the riots. Both movies were medium-budget studio productions—*White Men Can't Jump* from Twentieth Century Fox and *Falling Down* from Warner Bros.—created to a large extent around the audience appeal of their male stars, although with some differences between them. They both did well at the box office, particularly *White Men*, with an overall gross of over $76 million (according to Box Office Mojo), at a time when independent movies were at the height of their success and had started to pose a serious challenge to the type of mainstream production that these two movies represent.

The King of Mid-City

Falling Down was released in the United States at the end of February 1993, barely a month before the verdict in the retrials of the four policemen who brutalized Rodney King came out. Given the uncertainty about the outcome of the second trial and the devastating consequences of the first verdict the previous year, there were fears of further riots in the event of a second acquittal. In the end, two of the policemen were convicted, two were acquitted again, and there were no further riots. At the time, *Falling Down* hit a raw nerve with its story of "a day of fury" (the title with which the movie was released in Spain) in the life of disenfranchised white middle-class Bill Foster (Michael Douglas). Numerous groups protested the film, including aerospace workers (the protagonist has been made redundant at an aerospace plant), Vietnam veterans (a Vietnam veteran, the owner of an army surplus store, is a neo-Nazi), and, especially, various associations of Korean Americans (the Korean American shop owner who Bill visits at the beginning is depicted in negative terms, according to the associations). Korean Americans tried to boycott the film (Harmon 1993, D1; Honeycutt 1993, 81; Reinhold 1993, A11). Writing in the *Los Angeles Times*, Korean American Jeana Park cried, "I had to clench my jaws throughout the entire scene to control my horror and disappointment. They had to be joking. Rubbing salt on our open wounds for the sake of the almighty dollar" (1993, F3).

The *Los Angeles Times* ran several articles on *Falling Down* in the next few weeks after the movie's release, most of them critical of the film's depiction of the city. Although Park demanded more realistic portrayals of Korean Americans, most of the local newspaper reviewers also criticized the film's shortcomings and betrayals of urban realism. Peter King retraced Bill's long walk from Downtown to Venice and concluded that, unlike in the film, what happened to him during his walk was mostly everyday inconsequential stuff, and he suggested that the Los Angeles of *Falling Down* is "the new mythical L.A.," a myth of social apocalypse that has little connection with the city's reality (P. King 1993). Similarly, Bob Baker suggested that, after the previous year's riots, Hollywood was exploiting the city "as a pressure cooker of horrors" (1993, F1). Kirk Honeycutt joined the chorus, expressing everybody's anxieties about the movie with its release coming so close to the anniversary of the police beating and to the second police trial, as well as the lesser publicized trial of the three youths accused of the murder of a truck driver (1993, 81). In general, local writers were anxious to underplay what Mike Davis (1998) would call "the imagination of disaster" a few years later and to put the riots behind them, but they still worried that any spark (including a film) might re-ignite them. Consequently, they joined forces to persuade their readers that Los Angeles was a different city from that depicted in the movie. They saw *Falling Down* as exhibiting unusually intense and dishonest claims of realism and set out to contradict them, suggesting that the producers and filmmakers sought to exploit the troubles of the previous year for financial gain by misrepresenting the city. Amy Harmon summarized the general feeling in the title of her piece: "Fed Up with 'Down'" (1993).

The criticism sampled in the previous paragraphs, while openly adverse to the movie, reveals the type of passionate response that was probably expected by the filmmakers through their own display of narrative and visual intensity. As is often the case, critical reaction fed into their marketing strategy and was seamlessly incorporated into the publicity in the weeks and months following the movie's release, from interviews with the director and star (Andrew 1993) to contributions by Douglas's father, Kirk, in the *Los Angeles Times*, urging readers to see the movie as the "deep look at our urban society" that it was (Douglas 1993). Whether these strongly felt anxieties were a genuine and socially concerned reaction on the part of the text to a city in the grip of racial and social tension or a calculated attempt to exploit urban conflict may not be as significant as the ways in which both text and critical and audience reaction, as well as the industry's co-optation of it, illuminate a historical moment in which important changes were taking place.

The opening of *Falling Down* firmly establishes the near hysterical tone of the narrative. Total silence accompanies the first credits on a black screen. After the name of the director disappears and before the names of the principal actors are shown, the frame fades into an extreme close-up of Bill's mouth, thus initiating both our close involvement with the protagonist and the distorted lens through which we will be given access to his disturbed mind. Like a latter-day Hitchcock hero, D-Fens (as the character is also known, after the inscription on the license plate of his car) commands both our identification and our repulsion, thus ensuring that the spectator is put in a difficult emotional position that will color our response to the rest of the narrative. The close-up of the lips evokes the famous first shot of *Citizen Kane* (Orson Welles, 1941) in which the protagonist utters the word "Rosebud" before dying, thus triggering the film's journalistic investigation. Although Welles's film invokes a more distanced and intellectual relationship between hero and spectator than *Falling Down*, this initial reference will acquire a fuller meaning in the shot that closes the film, which I analyze later. For the moment, it constitutes an ironic evocation of an immensely powerful man to introduce an anonymous, powerless individual.

The tight framing of the lips is the beginning of a long take that lasts almost two minutes and that, in its complex use of frame movement, also parallels the first shot of Welles's *Touch of Evil* (1958). The shot starts with a close visual exploration of Bill Foster's face, from mouth to nose and bespectacled eyes. Then it circles slightly around and tilts up, as the character's anxious breathing is heard in the soundtrack, to suggest confinement within the double frame of the car through a high-angle shot, before momentarily abandoning the vehicle and revealing that the character is in the midst of a traffic jam. The extremely close framing distance can be seen as an attempt to probe into a sick mind, as though sustaining the illusion that the camera could indeed go inside the protagonist and learn the secret of his trouble, but its effect is, rather, one of a distorted hyperreality that formally anticipates the imminence of psychological breakdown.

The shot continues outside the automobile to offer glimpses of other people caught in the traffic jam. Colored by Bill's perspective and by the objects they carry with them, these people are turned into figures in a nightmare. We hear radio voices in Spanish and English, see a forlorn Latina child looking out the back window of the car in front, a woman applying lipstick, again in extreme close-up, children playing inside a school bus, grotesque-looking toys, men arguing on the phone, and such telling vanity plates as "financial freedom," "He died for our Sins," and the more direct "Eat Shit." The camera completes a full circle and returns to Bill's car from the back, as we begin to hear the buzzing of a fly inside. From this point on, and for most of the remainder of the scene, the text offers a shot sequence structured around eye-line matches from Bill's point of view that gradually paint the road where the characters are stuck as the hall of horrors in a fairground or, indeed, as one of the circles of hell in Dante's *Inferno*. A traffic jam may be a mundane scene, particularly in LA, but the combination of the various stylistic devices described here anticipates a nightmarish vision that will pervade the rest of the movie while simultaneously making the claims to realism that most critics decried as manipulative.

Over the course of the film we have ample opportunity to explore various parts and aspects of the city, but in this initial scene Los Angeles is defined through one of its central characteristics: the automobile as the historically favorite Angeleno mode of transportation and its conversion, in recent decades, into the object of a constant threat of gridlock. I return to the significance of the freeways in the city and in contemporary films in later chapters, but it is ironic that in *Falling Down* it is the city's impossible traffic that triggers the protagonist's initial reaction and that, in a film about a journey through the city, prompts him to choose such a fantastic method of urban travel as walking. This is not a film about freeways, and yet their cultural significance is so obvious that both traffic congestion and Bill's decision to abandon his car and walk automatically become a transparent index of a locally specific psychological and social malaise.

Given Bill's predicament—he has recently been laid off from his job as an engineer in an armaments company—the story is firmly entrenched in Angeleno history. Southern California became an important center of the aircraft and munitions industry during World War II, and this sector was badly hit by the recession and industrial transformations of the 1980s, with major cutbacks following the end of the cold war (Hogen-Esch 2010, 239). In her analysis of the effects of the loss of jobs in this period on U.S. men, Susan Faludi describes the typical "McDonnell Douglas man"—"middle-aged, college-educated, a homeowner, a family provider; a man from the company that had conquered the skies, rained bombs on the Axis, and built the beloved DC plane series as well as the feared F-15s and F/A-18 jet fighters" (2000, 62)—to try to imagine how these men must have felt when they lost their jobs in the 1970s and 1980s. In Faludi's *Stiffed* (2000), a sequel to her study of the patriarchal backlash on feminism of the 1980s, Faludi attempts to understand the widespread crisis of masculinity that triggered the sexist backlash. Bill Foster (like other characters played by Douglas in the 1980s and early 1990s) is an embodiment of this crisis. Richard Dyer sees Bill as the repository of 1990s discourses on masculinity: the angry and decentered white masculinity under threat that becomes an index of "the fear of annihilation that will be the realization of our emptiness" (1997, 222). In the opening scene, divested of job and family and overwhelmed by modern urban life, Bill abandons his car in the middle of the traffic jam, picks up his empty briefcase, and indicates to another driver that he is going home.

Home is where his ex-wife and daughter live, in Venice Beach. From Koreatown, where he starts off, he attempts the seemingly impossible task of covering the distance in time for his daughter's birthday party later in the day. By leaving his car and deciding to walk, it can be argued that D-Fens puts himself beyond the pale as a citizen of Los Angeles and takes Michel de Certeau's urban practices to an extreme. For the French thinker, ordinary citizens resist and transgress the "theoretical city" imagined and planned by politicians and urban designers by following their own paths, which do not always correspond to those constructed for them. Thus they draw their own trajectories and their own narratives and constitute what de Certeau calls the migrational and metaphorical city, a city that eludes legibility (1984, 93–95). Freeways, surface roads, and automobiles are an integral part of the planned city in LA. Despite sporadic efforts to the contrary, for decades walking has not been a "reasonable" means of urban mobility here. When he starts walking, Bill is making a statement against this theoretical city and the way it directs people's movements. He does not exactly elude legibility, because, in classic Hollywood manner, his actions and decisions are given sufficient narrative motivation, but, within the diegesis, his journey is a puzzling endeavor for those who witness his actions. This is illustrated in the first scene by the reaction of the driver who cannot understand what the protagonist means when he affirms that he is going home . . . without his car.

Faludi provides an accurate sociological context to understand Bill's frustration and the increasing violence produced by his decision to walk home. Unable to confront those who divested him of his job, he revolts against a dominant urban policy as a preamble to his openly antisocial and criminal behavior. His choice of this decidedly marginal behavior is an apt metaphor for his having become a "marginal" Angeleno after losing his very Angeleno job and after the breakup of his marriage. Even though classic cinematic precepts dictate that he will not survive the day, he accumulates enough sympathy in the course of the narrative, not least from his pursuer and eventually unwitting executor, to turn him into a victim of unbearable social pressure and injustice. This difficult balance revolves around the meanings that Douglas accumulated as a star who, at the time, seemed to specialize in portraying beleaguered masculinity in the context of second-wave feminism's demands of equality. Douglas's other roles of the period in *Fatal Attraction* (Adrian Lyne, 1987), *Basic Instinct* (Paul Verhoeven, 1992), and *Disclosure* (Barry Levinson, 1994) depict a crisis of masculinity that translates on the screen into often hysterical combinations of melodramatic identification and distance. In *Falling Down*, because of the nature of the story and the filmmakers' choice to feature the city of Los Angeles so centrally, this persona is given more precise local connotations: The male crisis is compounded by the crisis of a city with specific social tensions, with D-Fens as its ultimate representative.

The distance from Koreatown to Venice is 14 miles, but the walk is made much longer by the fact that D-Fens, perhaps echoing his mental condition, does not take a straight line. From the north of Koreatown he walks east toward Downtown and farther east to Lincoln Heights in East LA, then back west to MacArthur Park, north to Hollywood, and then through unidentified wealthy areas that might be in Beverly Hills or Brentwood west to the Oceanside. Given that in this city one is not unlikely

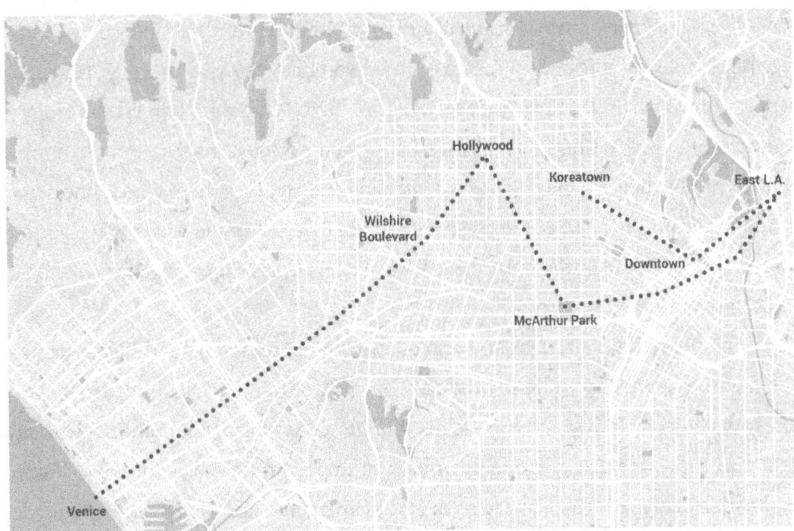

Map 2. Bill's "impossible" one-day walk from Mid-City to the ocean in *Falling Down*. Map by Francesc Terrades.

to come across streets and roads where there is nowhere for pedestrians to walk, the feat seems literally impossible. Yet Bill plods on, and the movie tags along, intercutting his progress with the much more "readable" movements of Prendergast (Robert Duvall), the police detective who drives around town in pursuit and finally catches up with Bill at the end of the Venice Fishing Pier.

Bill's progress around the city may not always be topographically clear, but the various neighborhoods he visits are all significant in terms of the city's sociological profile. His trajectory takes him from a socially depressed Downtown (where he comes across young Latino men), to a colorful ethnic neighborhood in East LA, to the equally depressed MacArthur Park, and then to gradually more wealthy areas of the Westside, including a section of Wilshire Boulevard, a golf course, and a surgeon's mansion. Although the long journey traverses various areas of the city, it is significant that a sizable portion of it takes place in Mid-City, roughly the segment of the city lying between Downtown and the Westside. Koreatown, Hollywood, MacArthur Park, and the once-affluent Mid-Wilshire corridor all figure prominently, whereas both East LA and the Westside are visited more fleetingly. The contemporary significance of Mid-City lies in the fact that, although less publicized than South Central, it became an equally hot point of confrontation, violence, looting, and police arrests during the 1992 riots. As Davis explains, the greatest density of riot-related incidents happened in this area, north of the Santa Monica Freeway, in predominantly Latino and Asian neighborhoods (1998, 371). The multiracial nature of this conflict is what made it different from other racial uprisings in the short history of the city. Bill's 14-mile-plus walk symbolizes Angeleno mobility, but his association with this particular sector of the city is also revealing. An important scene, for example, takes place outside a bank on Wilshire, in a sector of the boulevard once known as Los Angeles's Champs Elysées, which since the mid-1970s has been in decline, leading Davis to introduce the concept of "the modern high-rise ghost town" (377). In Angeleno terms, Bill embodies this decline too, and his victimization is also that of the once-affluent, mostly white Mid-City, whose explosion in the riots was the climax of a protracted and historically loaded process of ethnic multiplication.

Equally significant from a demographic standpoint are the crosscut scenes involving Prendergast and his fellow detective, Sandra (Rachel Ticotin), and Bill's ex-wife, Beth (Barbara Hershey), and his daughter, Adele (Joey Hope Singer). Beth and Adele spend the film in and around their house in Venice, just up the street from the boardwalk, but the coastal community we see here is not the center of beatnik and hippie counterculture that we can see in movies from the 1960s or the bright and carefree environment found in more recent films such as *L.A. Story* and *I Love You, Man* (John Hamburg, 2009), the successful TV series *Californication*, or even the other film discussed in this chapter, *White Men Can't Jump*; instead, it is a dangerous place colored by the imminent threat of the protagonist's arrival and his obvious intention to ignore the restraining order issued against him. By coming to Venice from the more traditionally conflictive areas of the city, Bill carries their violence with him.

Bill has lost his job, like so many white-collar workers, and this brings out his worst instincts, but everywhere he goes, he comes across people who are not too far behind him in the loss of self-esteem and self-control provoked by a sick society. At the Korean store, the shop owner is first offhand and impatient and then verbally aggressive toward him. The Chicano members of the local gang he meets first Downtown and later in East LA (although the geographic rationale is not clear here) are violent both when they attempt to rob him and later when they try to kill him. In MacArthur Park Bill is assailed by a homeless man who claims it is *his* park. On Wilshire Boulevard an African American middle-class man is demonstrating outside a bank. Bill is the only violent person at the Whammy Burger, but both the waitress and, particularly, the manager are portrayed as familiarly exasperating, the type of people who would make anybody lose their cool. Nick (Frederic Forrest), the Nazi surplus store owner, is a vicious psychopath who makes Bill look sedate in comparison. Finally, at the golf course that he is trying to cross to get to his destination, Bill meets the aggressive elderly man who, in a fit of anger at Bill's trespassing, ends up having a heart attack. As I have pointed out, most of these locations are in Mid-City, the film's urban heart, and Bill's desperate attempts to reassert the authority of the once-thriving professional Anglo man in this once-flourishing part of town can also be read as expressions of textual distress at the unstoppable transformations brought to the forefront by the summer's events. Metaphorically, Bill is the deposed king of a desolate kingdom, the part of the city that has been lost to his once-thriving now-disappearing constituency.

Elsewhere in town, though, things are not that different. Beth is verbally abused by the police officer who has come to protect her but ends up suggesting that the divorce and Bill's violence may well have been her fault. Prendergast has a vicious colleague to deal with at the station and also has to tolerate his chief, Captain Yardley (Raymond J. Barry), who despises him for not behaving aggressively, as a man should. "Real men curse," he contends. A barely contained anger pervades the city, and we feel that numerous other people around Bill are no different from him and, like him, are ready to burst into violence at any moment. This city in the throes of widespread tension corresponds to the register established in the first scene. Although distorted by stylistic means, it is uncomfortably recognizable, particularly when the justice riots were so recent and there were well-founded fears that they could return soon.

The riots, like most of the historical conflicts before them in LA, had a racial origin, but one that was, as we have seen, more multiracial than before. George Sanchez explains that, although violence originated as a response to the verdict of an all-white jury acquitting an almost all-white group of police officers (see Saul 2010, 158), the resentment of South Central African Americans was in the end mostly directed at Latino and Asian people. The LAPD was perceived as the enemy, but so were Korean business owners and Latino neighbors who were encroaching on South Central and gradually altering the demographic profile of the area. Both Koreans and Latinos were seen as threats by the disenfranchised blacks. As Saul explains, the Florence-Normandie area was a relatively prosperous part of South Central but also a "contact zone" where Latino immigrants were displacing African American residents (158). Mid-City was also a contact zone, one that epitomized urban mobility and decline, with Asian Americans both in Koreatown and in Mid-Wilshire becoming important and resented urban players and the unstoppably growing Latino population becoming a more generalized threat to the ethnic structure. Resentment against Asian Americans was an important ingredient of the riots, and it did not stop then. As Robert Reinhold explains, in the aftermath of the riots, Korean American merchants continued to be attacked and sometimes shot in the city (1993). This anti-immigrant vigilante backlash was perhaps less publicized than the easier-to-understand black-white vector, but it is essential to understanding the dynamics of what were considered the first multicultural riots.

As a timely cinematic rendering of these multicultural riots, *Falling Down* defends itself against charges of racism by suggesting a covert alliance between black and white. Jude Davies argues that there is a hierarchy of minority races in the film's ideology, with blacks being included within the circle of privilege, Hispanics allowed on the margins, and Asians firmly excluded (1995, 221). I am not so sure that Asian Americans and Hispanics in the film are treated significantly differently—the Latino East LA gang is more negatively portrayed than the Korean American store owner—but racial conflict between D-Fens and African American citizens is indeed carefully avoided. We see a furtive look of sympathy and identification between the financially "unviable" African American demonstrating outside the bank on Wilshire Boulevard and the protagonist. Later, at different points in the film, two black children show more understanding toward Bill than anybody else in the story. Comically, one of them even teaches him how to operate his bazooka at a construction site. It is as though the film is trying hard to avoid confrontation between Bill and black Angelenos in order to turn him into a spokesman for their anger too or to subliminally suggest that black and white anger is the same anger.

No such effort is made in the case of the other races. Latinos are predictably seen as reckless and ultraviolent gang members, and Asian Americans are unreasonable and unfathomable merchants who overcharge "real Americans." Both ethnic groups have their counterparts at Prendergast's police station, with sympathetic Asian American and Latino police officers, particularly Latina Sandra, but the text does not seem able to include these groups, the foremost victims of the riots, into its "circle of privilege," turning the vigilantism of the historical events into a fantastical alliance between black and white as a way to counteract the complexities of multiculturalism.

Equally significant, in terms of the film's evocation of contemporaneous events, is its positive depiction of the LAPD through the characters of Prendergast and Sandra, at a time when the institution had come under criticism for causing the riots and was literally on trial for the beating of Rodney King. There are unsavory characters at the police station, but the friendship between these two detectives is uniformly positive, the one strand of the story that is free from conflict or aggression. When we compare Prendergast's telephone conversations with his unstable wife, Amanda (Tuesday Weld), to his relationship with Sandra, we conclude that working for the LAPD is preferable to being married for a man. Indeed, at the end of the film, the old detective changes his mind and, against his wife's wishes, decides to stay on the police force instead of retiring to Arizona, as she wanted. The police force becomes the only safe space from the nightmare of desolation and despair. In this context, Prendergast goes some way toward counteracting Bill's hysterical masculinity in crisis, representing what Dyer describes as "the old everything and nothing-in-particular hegemony" (1997, 222). This ordinary whiteness, however, seems to need to adapt to new times, and the old policeman's closeness with Sandra is a significant sign of these transformations.

Sandra and Prendergast's transethnic friendship is the clearest of the generally unobtrusive instances of the film suggesting the potential of LA citizens to live together across racial barriers. In her analysis of the scenes at the Korean-owned convenience store, Davies focuses on the billboard of a woman advertising suntan lotion that helps Prendergast identify D-Fens. For her, the sign is used to proclaim an antiracist message, but this ostensible message is predicated on the manipulation of a "yellow" woman (Davies 1995, 219). In my view, the use of the billboard illustrates the profound textual ambivalence toward race, the ethnic realities of the city, and its dominant discourses. It is an index of the positive aspects of the browning of LA, its irreversibility, and its suffocating effects on the beleaguered white man (the drawing of a desperate little man trying to find his way out of the woman's bikini top). Although the advertisement is visually linked with Prendergast, it also stands for Bill's predicament and the city that he discovers as he makes his way westward toward the ocean: A "brown" woman who dominates the landscape ("white is for

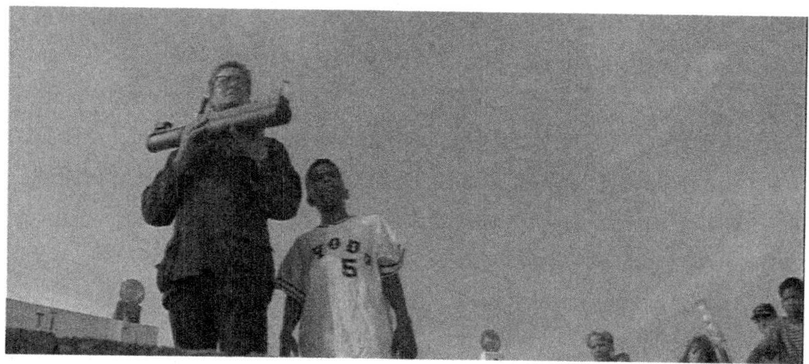

Falling Down: violence and bonding in the devastated city.

laundry," one of the slogans reads) is an index of the ethnic future of the city but also a formidable threat to the shrunken helpless white man.

More unobtrusively and less ambivalently, the African American boy who helps the protagonist with his bazooka later in the film is part of a gang of five children who think that Bill is an actor in a movie being shot on location. This multiracial group's casual presence in the narrative suggests a future in which racial conflict will become a thing of the past and human relationships will become color-blind. This is narratively as irrelevant as the Latino orange seller noticed by Elana Zilberg (1998, 188), but it is details like this, or the diversity of the patrons at the Whammy Burger, where the younger African American boy volunteers to answer Bill's question, that become an indication of the film's struggle to find a way out of the social tension of the present in the midst of its gloating in chaos and anguish.

On the opposite end of the spectrum is the white supremacist who runs the army surplus store in Hollywood. His fanaticism and bigotry provide the spectator with one of those moments in which we can sympathize with Bill and understand his violent outbursts. As John Gabriel's ethnographic research proves, the protagonist's confrontation with the neo-Nazi momentarily restores Bill's legitimacy in the minds of the spectators. For example, for one of Gabriel's interviewees, the neo-Nazi was totally different from Bill: He was a racist, whereas "Michael Douglas" simply stood up for his country (Gabriel 1996, 141–42). Episodes like this can be seen as a way to validate Bill's actions and to justify his more unpalatable excesses and therefore the film's manipulation of us into identifying with the victimized Anglo man. The text walks a difficult tightrope, both presenting Bill as a deranged and dangerous individual who cannot be recuperated into civilized society and describing him as a victim of social ills and thus a figure of identification. As an Angeleno, he is both a victim of a rampant economic crisis that affected both the working and the middle classes and a representative of the dominant Anglo majority and therefore of a history of social injustice, the most recent consequences of which were the justice riots. Bill is a victim but also part of the origin of the problem, and *Falling Down*, perhaps unexpectedly, closes with a subtle but powerful indictment of the white man.

In a film about a character constantly on the move, the most interesting frame movement comes at the very end, in the last shot: After shooting Bill at the Venice Fishing Pier, Prendergast sits next to the protagonist's wife, Beth, trying to console her. The camera tracks past them and inside the house, eventually focusing on the home movie that Bill had put on a few minutes before, when he broke into the house. This movie is a snatch from the past of the happy Anglo family together, at home by the beach, apparently a recording of better times. Yet it includes an illustration of Bill's violent temper, even in those blissful moments, and reveals Beth's worry, already then, about their future as a family. In a movie that highlights spatiality, both in Bill's relentless, though roundabout, westward movement and in the visual construction of a city dominated by violence, tension, and impending fear, the final camera movement acquires a crucial temporal dimension. The film had quoted *Citizen Kane* in its first shot and in the paperweight that Bill later buys for his daughter's birthday. It closes the Wellesian circle by emulating the earlier film's famous final frame movement. The camera travels to the past, looking for the root of the violence and turmoil that affect the city. Although over the course of the movie the growing visibility of various ethnic minorities is ambiguously linked with its present state, the origin of all this urban evil is ascribed to the white male and situated within the suburban middle-class Anglo family. Lost in a vortex of social unrest, recalling dystopian images of the cinematic past from classic noir to *Blade Runner*, seemingly wrapped up in the hero's unhinged push forward no matter what, *Falling Down* takes this moment of reflection before the final credits to apportion responsibility on the Anglo supremacists who, according to Soja and others, have dominated the history of the city.

Falling Down is an urban apocalyptic film that envisions the city, and specifically Los Angeles, as the repository of a millennial crisis. This "belch of outrage" (Baker 1993, F6) latches onto the justice riots as a manifestation of this condition and situates its story, with various racial displacements, within the tense climate that followed the Simi Valley trials and the jury's failure to condemn the brutality of the LAPD the previous year; more specifically, the film's story is situated in Mid-City, the part of town that was most savagely hit by the riots. Beyond this, *Falling Down* manages, if from an unmistakably male Anglo perspective, to suggest the city's diversity and, perhaps more important, to highlight the symbolic centrality of Anglo violence and guilt in its history. On the other hand, we have Prendergast, the LAPD officer. He may be cynical about police methods and about the city as a whole, but this honest white policeman holds the key to the future in his liberal attitude. The movie does not offer any solutions to assuage urban anguish, but it does become a powerful symptom, from the cinematic mainstream, of the social and discursive tensions besetting the city. It is a cultural text situated in the vortex of the storm.

Racial Binaries and the Brown Woman

Paradoxically, the future seems much nearer in *White Men Can't Jump*, another mainstream movie from 1992, released by its studio, Fox, only one month before all hell broke loose at Florence and Normandie Avenues. It features crossover stars Wesley Snipes, Woody Harrelson, and Rosie Pérez and a generic configuration that would become a mainstay of Hollywood cinema: the comic buddy film, later labeled "bromance" or "hommecom" (Jeffers McDonald 2007, 108–9). A pent-up anger comparable to that found in *Falling Down* can be felt throughout the narrative of *White Men*, but its comic register channels that anger in a different direction, in this case through the performance of street basketball. Although local reviewers objected to the problematic and, for most of them, misleading realist vocation of *Falling Down*, no such worries were expressed about the realism of *White Men*, which was thought to be more effortless and effective in its depiction of social dynamics. In the press release, director Ron Shelton declared that he wanted to show the real Los Angeles, "the places where people live, not the exotic postcard images" (press release, 1992), and many in the press thought that he succeeded (e.g., Carson 1992; C. James 1992). Tom Carson, for instance, sees the film as Shelton's answer to *L.A. Story* and celebrates the Angeleno realities that the other film left out. The director captures "L.A.'s affability and ramshackle grace, and the boundary-crossing intimacies at the disheveled bottom of the city's social heap" (Carson 1992, 33). In general, whether it was because of the effect of the justice riots or because the comedic register of *White Men* made it seem less threatening, reactions were markedly different from those to *Falling Down*, even though both films engaged with the city in direct ways and even though both dealt head-on with interracial relationships. In a wider sense, both films were symptomatic of ongoing social processes in LA. Their different receptions, separated as they were by the Rodney King riots, must also be seen as part of the same process of social struggle to adapt to new urban realities. Given the extreme proximity between the release date of *White Men* and the flare-up of the justice riots, it is tempting to speculate that the movie was reflecting anxieties similar to those that broke out one month later but that it was finding less violent, more hopeful ways of imagining the multicultural, multiethnic city; and it was doing so from the standpoint of some of the very neighborhoods and citizens who felt most acutely the impact of global processes and social injustice—those who, in the real city, initiated the uprising. In this sense *White Men* can be seen as a comic Hollywood counterpart to the "black cinema" that, with *Boyz n the Hood* at the front, offered a purportedly realistic denunciation of poverty and injustice in African American neighborhoods.

Part of the attractiveness of *White Men* lies in its narrative premise. As a mainstream product with a keen interest in realism, the film can be described, paradoxically, as truly fantastic in that it offers its audiences a fictional Angeleno society dominated by black men and, secondarily, women in which the white hero is practically on his own. Going several steps further than, for example, *Grand Canyon* and its efforts to counter Anglo supremacy in the movies with a difficult balance between white and black characters, *White Men* throws its white hero, Billy Hoyle (Harrelson), into an almost exclusively African American street basketball scene and leaves him to fend for himself in a racial scenario practically unknown in mainstream comedy. When they first meet, on the Venice Beach courts, Sidney Deane (Snipes) keeps repeating to Billy that it is *his* court, that the court is *his* house, that Billy is a foreigner, and that basketball is a black thing. In the film's fictional world Sidney is right and Billy accepts his position of inferiority. Regardless of narrative incident and development, *White Men* points at the potential for change of such a mobile and changing society as that of Los Angeles at the end of the twentieth century, hypothesizing that in this city, despite its loaded history, everything is possible.

On the other hand, like his namesake Bill, the protagonist of *Falling Down*, and Mack in *Grand Canyon*, Billy is one more embodiment of early 1990s white masculinity in crisis, and as such, his being surrounded by racially other characters facilitates his victimization. However, *White Men* is never willing to let its hero off the hook and is more interested in his inadequacies to adapt to a changing world than in blaming others around him for his crisis. Both Sidney, his buddy, and Gloria (Rosie Pérez), his girlfriend, are constructed as more mature and smarter characters than him, and they are, in narratological terms, his *helpers* in his learning process (Greimas 1986, 174–85). A thriller buddy film such as *Se7en* (David Fincher, 1995) features a comparable structure, with the Anglo hero (Brad Pitt) having his wife, Tracy (Gwyneth Paltrow), and an older African American detective, Somerset (Morgan Freeman), as catalysts for his moral and emotional growth, but neither Somerset nor Tracy embodies historical situatedness in the way that Gloria and Sidney do. *Se7en* is color-blind in its articulation of the relationship between the two policemen, and Tracy's femininity and role in the narrative are part of an essentialist worldview revolving around the eternal fight between good and evil. Gloria and Sidney, on the other hand, base their narrative superiority over Billy on their gender and race. Unlike *Se7en* and *Falling Down*, *White Men* announces from the beginning that the dynamics of gender and race are, in fact, what its story is about.

In this sense the movie wears its stereotypes on its sleeve. Jane Galbraith, referring to the film's poster and marketing campaign, argues that the image of a white guy and a black guy is part of a very American language, something that everybody understands (1992, 27) and that points to the centrality of stereotypes in the text. Yet, unlike the following year's *Demolition Man* (Marco Bramvilla, 1993), another LA movie that uses a white-black protagonist pair as a selling point (Sylvester Stallone and Snipes again), stereotypes are both used and constantly subverted. Aesthetically and narratively, *White Men* is very much a text of its moment, and, as Caryn James argues, it manages to capture the pulse of the times: "The film is politically correct in its attacks on stereotypes, but rude enough in its humor so that no one feels preached at; it echoes both political correctness and the anti-P.C. backlash" (1992, n.p.). Similarly, for Terrence Rafferty, racial stereotypes function as rules that are waiting to be broken, "occasions for comic anomalies" (1992, 80). In this sense, although the main characters in *Falling Down* are fully-fledged individuals whose gender and race are only a part of their fictional makeup, the three central figures in *White Men*, while attractive and complex enough in their construction, are also representatives of much larger groups: Anglo and African American masculinities and racially other femininity at a specific historical juncture. Their stereotypical dimension is particularly effective because the comic framework allows spectators the sufficient distance to recognize both the stereotypes and the ideological work that the film is doing with them.

Simultaneously, this contrived narrative structure and ideological construction is fleshed out not only in the performances by Snipes, Pérez, and Harrelson but also in a geographically and historically recognizable space, a familiar Los Angeles in which only one thing is radically unfamiliar: African Americans dominate the frame both visually and socially. In this, *White Men* is also a harbinger of the ethnic upheaval produced by the justice riots one month after its release. The economic decline of their neighborhoods and the growing frustration with their inability to see a future of racial equality prompted black Angelenos to take center stage in the riots and to assume a visibility that was warranted by the history of the city but not so much by its demography: In the 1990 census, the African American population of LA had decreased to 11.20 percent and would continue to shrink to 9.78 percent in 2000 and 8.78 percent in 2010 (www.laalmanac.com/population/po13.htm). *White Men* is, culturally speaking, almost a mirror image of the uprising, taking full advantage of the mechanisms of comedy to produce a discourse in which confrontation, resentment, and a charged history of injustice can lead to an empowering fantasy of African American supremacy. It is not just that the Anglo hero, thanks to his talent in a game long dominated by African Americans, can readily accept his inferior position while learning to navigate an initially hostile environment. More important, the text as a whole takes it for granted that in its fictional world African Americans are in charge, a vibrant if socially and economically impoverished community in which the Anglo character is an outsider. It is ironic, and part of the ideological work of the film, that for a city in which 40 percent of its inhabitants are foreign-born, an Anglo man maybe from the U.S. South (Billy tells Sidney that he played basketball at a college in Louisiana) is considered a foreigner, precisely in Venice Beach, one of the few neighborhoods of Los Angeles that is still predominantly white.

The story of *White Men* starts where *Falling Down* finished: on Venice Beach. Whereas in *Falling Down* the streets and ocean walk appear full of people, as they often are in this tourist enclave, *White Men* evokes fresh beginnings by having its hero reach Venice when all the streets and beachfront are still mostly empty, with only the occasional jogger, skater, and bodybuilder in sight, most of them black, as though to anticipate what is coming. Billy is welcomed by the sound of the Venice Beach Boys, real-life jazz musicians Bill Henderson, Sonny Craver, and Jon Hendricks, singing a capella the gospel song "Just a Closer Walk with Thee," as part of the entertainment on offer at this early hour. The basketball courts can be seen behind the singers, and Billy, who enjoys their performance, immediately associates them with the space he aspires to enter and conquer: the courts where (fictional) street basketball legends Eddie "the King" Farouk and Duck Johnson used to play. At the end of the story, Billy, forming a team with Sidney, will see his dream of challenging and beating the masters (played by college and professional basketball player Freeman Williams and singer Louis Price) come true.

The song also anticipates the importance of music in the film, which boasts an eclectic but almost exclusively African American soundtrack, including rap, rock, soul, and R&B. Centrally, the running gag between the buddy protagonists is whether Billy can or cannot "hear" Jimi (Hendrix). This starts when Sidney objects to his new friend playing a tape of the black musical legend's songs in his car. Billy insists that he can hear Jimi, by which he simultaneously means (1) that he can be a part of Sidney's black basketball world, that he too can be "black," and (2) that one does not need to be black to appreciate "black" music, and, further, (3) that by pretending to be "a chump" (i.e., white), he, as a white man, can beat black people at their own game.

This attitude and narrative dynamic transpire in the first basketball game, in which Billy's strategy appears to be successful as he takes everyone by surprise by beating Sidney twice, taking advantage of the other's feeling of superiority. Yet things are not so easy for Billy because of his self-destructive personality and his propensity to always make the wrong decision. Billy is incapable of dunking the ball (a relatively redundant ability in practical terms but one that is part of the "aesthetic" side of the sport and has come to signify black men's physical superiority) because "white men can't jump." When Sidney challenges him, he loses his bet and all the money he had just won hustling. In the final game he finally manages the dunk for their winning point against "the King" and Duck, but this also makes him lose his girlfriend, this time for good. The final jam does not even secure him a stable place in the African American community because, as Sidney says, "Hell, you can put a cat in a oven—that don't make it a biscuit." On the other hand, Sidney has enough faith in his friend to produce the above-the-hoop pass that makes Billy improve his jump to dunk the ball at the crucial moment to give them victory over their rivals.

The first basketball scene, segueing seamlessly from the Venice Beach Boys performance through a graphic match, anticipates the extent to which basketball is the center of the plot. Billy's plan to get into the game and make money is the basic hustling ploy, one that in cinema history has been used memorably by the protagonists of *The Hustler* (Robert Rossen, 1961) and its sequel *The Color of Money* (Martin Scorsese, 1986): He pretends to be a chump. In fact, he does not even have to pretend much; being white is enough for the rest of the players to laugh him off as a poor challenge. Once the game starts, though, his pretense stops: Billy is an efficient player who takes advantage of what the film seems to construe as the inability of African Americans to tell good basketball from showing off. At the same time, the film visually sides with the exuberance and energy of the Venice courts, as embodied in Sidney. Frame movement and editing constantly succeed at reproducing the idiom of the players. In other words, the text both distances itself, with Billy, from the black players' superfluous antics and visually identifies with them. Sidney's performance starts the minute Billy's ends. Billy performs outside the court, pretending he cannot play. Sidney's performance is his way of playing basketball; his game consists of decorative flourishes and constant bragging. For him there is no basketball outside the performance and the posturing. The film rejoices in it even as, with Billy, it pokes fun at it. Billy, for his part, soon learns to master the endless chatter to undermine his rivals' concentration but finds it more difficult to "look good" and change his "white" sobriety. In this he remains an outsider. The film often resorts to slow motion to insert his approach to playing into its visual style, and although this works visually, it narratively underlines the gap that he cannot bridge.

What Billy also still needs to learn is that his more efficient manner of playing does not guarantee success, nor is it necessarily better than Sidney's. Snipes's performance captures the complexities of his character's approach to basketball and to social exchanges when, after losing the first two challenges to Billy and being laughed at for what appears to be childish boasting, the frame pulls in to a close-up of Sidney sizing up the business possibilities of an alliance with the character on whom he has just unleashed countless aggravation. He is a more mature player in the broader sense. He plots to take financial advantage of the inexperienced player and hustle him even as Billy thinks they are hustling together. At the same time, he becomes, however reluctantly, the white man's aid in his attempt to "become black." Billy, for his part, needs to learn that, as Gloria cryptically explains, when you win, sometimes you lose, and when you lose, sometimes you win. In other words, he still needs to learn that in a game the final score is not always the final word and, more generally, that his binary thinking is a thing of the past and a poor tool to adapt to the modern world embodied in the film by Gloria, Sidney, and the city of Los Angeles. At the end of the film Billy has not fully comprehended what his girlfriend meant, but he is learning (he can hear the music, Sidney concludes, which does not mean to say that he can hear *Jimi* yet).

Billy knows from the beginning, or at least has a good intuition, about the magical qualities of Venice Beach, and both his brief dialogue with the Venice Beach Boys and the first pickup game confirm that he is indeed in the right place. Once the plot is set in motion, his fascination becomes focused on Sidney, and this fascination is reciprocal, though not exactly symmetric: Billy finds in Sidney a role model both as a basketball player and as the type of adult man he has so far failed to become, whereas Sidney is first curious about the white man's desire of transformation and gradually more involved in the process. He is also amused by the "ebony and ivory" team they have formed. Within its comic world, the film uses this dynamic to put forward a discourse of social tolerance, flexible identities, and interracial homosocial bonding. Its use of the city as the environment in which this social utopia can work explains the centrality of the beach community. In fact, the characters move around various inner-city locations (a neighborhood court on 22nd Street in South Central; another one in Watts, visually dominated by the famous Watts Towers; the tournament in Lafayette Park near MacArthur Park; and the Crenshaw area where Sidney and Rhonda Deane [Tyra Ferrell] live) before returning to Venice and, toward the end of the story, Santa Monica. Yet the movie manages to make all the inner-city neighborhoods look as attractive, sunny, and lively as the beach communities. In fact, somebody not paying too much attention to the specificities of the various locations, and given that the characters often return to the Oceanside, might think that the characters never leave Venice, Santa Monica, and neighboring

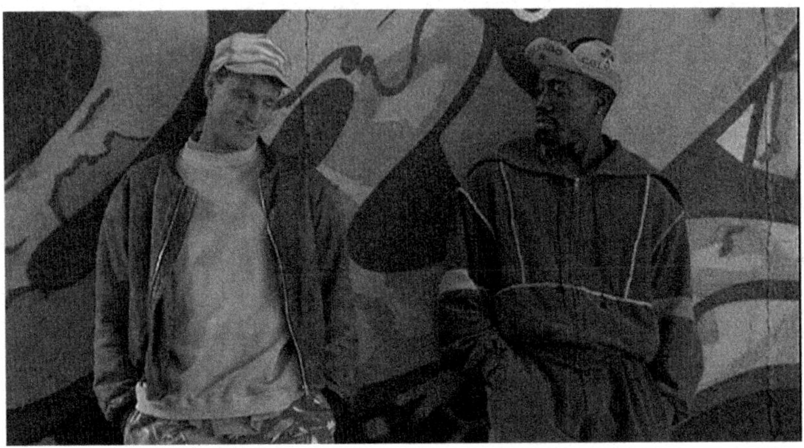

White Men Can't Jump: ebony and ivory.

areas. Everywhere is equally sunny and visualized through the energy and vibrancy provided by the game. Going against dominant discourses of the city, *White Men* is remarkably democratic in its attempt to bring into the realm of comedy areas of LA almost exclusively associated with poverty, criminality, and danger. Conversely, it could be argued that, rather than everywhere else in the space of the film being made to look like an extension of Venice, it is Venice that, with its new racial makeup, has turned into the inner-city neighborhoods without losing its sunny appearance. Like Billy, Venice has also "gone black."

The combination of acknowledgment of racial tension and envisioning of a future in which diversity can be celebrated beyond vacuous official discourses is based on the traditional dichotomy of black and white that in Los Angeles, as everywhere else in the country, is no longer operative, if it ever was. *White Men* can be related to *Boyz n the Hood* and the hood films of the period in highlighting African American experience as an antidote to a long history of white dominance. Both films articulate their respective critiques of white masculinity, however differently, on the basis of its oppression of African Americans. *White Men* constructs its racial utopia as the result of a simple turning of the social tables between white and black. Like *Grand Canyon*, its attempt at political correctness is predominantly based on racial binarism. Also like *Grand Canyon*, the racial diversity that deconstructs this binarism is also present, except that, whereas in Kasdan's movie this presence is marginal and remains practically outside the frame, in *White Men* it is embodied in the formidable character of Gloria.

On one level, Gloria's role in the film is that of the woman who highlights Billy's inadequate masculinity, just as Sidney provides the contrast to his whiteness. As mentioned, she spells out the limitations of Billy's binary approach to both basketball and relationships. Earlier she had mystified her boyfriend when, after telling him she is thirsty, she reprimanded him for bringing her a glass of water, instead of "sympathizing with her drymouthedness." Billy's world of simple solutions (a way for men to control women, according to a magazine she has read) is not good enough for her. She relates binarism to her boyfriend's inability to get on in life and his constant wrong decision making. But she is also critical of Sidney's racial binarism. When Sidney objects to Billy playing Hendrix in the car because he is white, she reminds him that Hendrix's drummer was white, that is, that Jimi himself was not as intolerant toward white people's musical abilities as he is. Given the movie's emphasis on masculinity, Gloria, along with Sidney's wife, Rhonda, provides the counterpoint within a postfeminist discourse on sexual politics. At the same time, Gloria Clemente is there to break the racial dichotomy on which the text is based. Like *Falling Down*, *White Men* posits an alliance between white and black that excludes other races and even makes them invisible. In *White Men* it is not just that Venice Beach, a predominantly white community, has become mostly black; the inner city and South Central locations show no trace of the Latino or the Asian communities that one month later would become such central players in the riots. Given that part of the pent-up anger of South Central African Americans about their living conditions would be directed against the other racial minorities whom they thought were trespassing on their territory and stealing their jobs, *White Men*, like *Falling Down*, is also utopian, although in a different sense, in its summary erasure of any Angeleno who is not white or black. Yet this attitude is contradicted by the narrative centrality of Gloria.

The presence of the "brown" woman, then, reminds us that in Los Angeles not only must black and white learn to live together and benefit from their differences and from each other's strengths, but room must also be made for brown, a skin color that, after all, constitutes more than half the city's population. Gloria's presence is a powerful reminder of the ethnic diversity and complexity of Los Angeles, a social makeup that needs to be taken into consideration before a future of social equality and justice can be envisaged. The film's ending suggests that, although maybe

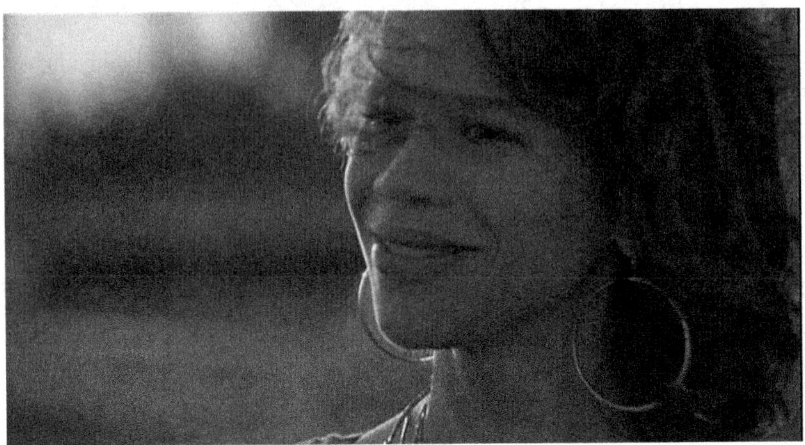

White Men Can't Jump: listen to the brown woman.

black and white, with the necessary adjustments, could in the early 1990s begin to imagine living together in the magic comic space of a film, the time was not yet ripe (both in Hollywood and in Angeleno society) to consider Latinos and Latinas on the same footing (Asian Americans are not even seen in the film). In *White Men* the future of an urban society that has learned from its past is still some way off, but at least this comic story of racial difference points in the right direction.

Even the inclusion of the Latina woman in the magic circle can be seen as just a matter of time: "If I listen to the woman, do I have to agree with her, too?" Billy asks Sidney when Gloria has just left him, to which Sidney replies, "No, no, no. You listen. That's a good enough start. I don't want to stress you out." The exchange is inscribed within the interracial homosocial bonding that makes the ending happy, even though the heterosexual couple does not end up together, but the incorporation of Gloria and the group she stands for (not only women but also Latinos and Latinas) does not seem far off: All the Anglo man has to do is understand her importance and the justice of her demands. And what both the Anglo and the African American men need to learn is the inevitability of a more complex society than the one they are learning to build together, at least in this utopian comedy. Gloria may be gone at the end of the story and Billy may not fully understand her yet, but she, along with millions of her ethnic group, is sure to come back to ask not just for visibility but also for justice and equality in their city.

White Men Can't Jump and *Falling Down* are two mainstream productions from a Hollywood industry that was on the verge of drastic changes, especially as the contemporaneous success of independent cinema was starting to bring about its co-optation by the big studios and the redrawing of the boundaries between mainstream and independent. Released just before (*White Men*) and after (*Falling Down*) the social event that marked the beginning of contemporary LA, the two films outline the industry's cultural and ideological engagement with current urban discourses. In a general sense, as cinematic narratives of LA in the early 1990s, the two films show awareness of the conflicts and contradictions at the center of those urban discourses. Their different generic registers and their different aspirations as records of reality produced drastically diverse reactions from audiences and critics. They both had different things to say about ethnic tensions and relationships and tapped into different traditions of cinematic Los Angeles, but they were both part of an ongoing social conversation that allowed people to look back at the city's darkest history and at the same time ahead to the future. In retrospect, both films offer alternative visions of the same anxiety-ridden society that produced the riots. These two movies, along with *Grand Canyon* and a few others, openly engaged with the social crisis that was about to erupt (or in the case of *Falling Down* had just erupted). Later films would reflect the resilience of traditional tropes and the industry's ability to find ways to allow alternative visions to creep in. Both tendencies would insert themselves in what might be described as a classical tradition of cinematic representations of Los Angeles. That tradition and its continuation in post-1992 movies are the subject of the two chapters in Part 1.

I

Historical Continuities

3

Alienation and Redemption in the City of Angels

A Dark City in the Land of Sunshine

The history of Los Angeles on-screen begins with the first shorts shot in Southern California toward the end of the first decade of the twentieth century (see Shiel 2012). Mark Shiel sees the slapstick comedy of the late 1910s and 1920s and the movies about Hollywood of the late 1920s and 1930s as the first two strong traditions of cinematic representation of the city. Slapstick familiarized spectators all around the world with Los Angeles, especially given that one of its main narrative tropes was the internal navigation of the city and surrounding areas (Shiel 2012, 69). For the second group of movies, however, Los Angeles was overshadowed by Hollywood, as though the rest of the city had become irrelevant (128, 195). It was only with the advent of film noir in the 1940s that movies started to take an interest in the city and to consciously and actively contribute to its history. Film noir was central to Hollywood history because it both changed the aesthetics of mainstream cinema and questioned its narrative and ideological priorities by foregrounding a gallery of unsympathetic male heroes and morally corrupt women, with often downbeat endings. It was also crucial in the development of film studies, which found in these dark worlds, ambiguous characters, and intricate narrative patterns an ideal space for the rehearsal of its successive theoretical agendas (see Naremore 1998). Sixty years after its heyday, scholarly fascination with noir continues unabated.

The movies themselves also became a central part of the history of Los Angeles and of cultural representations of the city. Mike Davis, Paul Arthur, and Foster Hirsch, among others, have pointed to the ways in which the genre and the city are inextricably intertwined (see Berrettini 1999, 74). It was in these films that the city, after decades of appearing on the screen as background or standing for urban life in general, was explicitly identified as itself for the first time (Dimendberg 2010, 350; Shiel 2012, 213). As Shiel has explained, these movies, unlike earlier ones, showed a particular interest in the specificity of the real places in which they were shot (Shiel 2012, 15), a specificity that on many occasions became part of the stories they told. The images of LA in film noir conveyed a certain type of modern urban experience in the abstract, but they also stood for the city where they were shot. From the perspective of their geographic locatedness, they, as a whole, constructed a particular discourse that would gradually become the primary cinematic view of the city. Since noir, this view has associated Los Angeles with alienation, despair, and urban dystopia.

In retrospect, this gloomy view of the city on the cinematic screen is particularly surprising given that the dominant Angeleno discourse had for decades been associated with an Edenic iconography, the romantic myth of the Spanish missions, and images of the land of eternal sunshine. For the first Spanish settlers, what was then called Alta California was imagined as an island, the stuff of utopia (Shiel 2012, 20), an "island on the land," as Carey McWilliams would later label it in the subtitle of one of the most influential studies of the region (2010). Ever since the 1880s, boosters have appropriated these images for the city's and the region's territorial, commercial, and industrial expansion. One such character was Charles Fletcher Lummis, one of LA's most important mythmakers. He was the founder of the Association for the Preservation of the Missions in 1888, a leading figure of the "Arroyo Set" that revived the region's Spanish past in architecture and the other arts, editor of the *Los Angeles Times* since 1884, and author of, among other works, *Land of Sunshine*. Lummis helped harness this fictional past of an earthly Eden populated by innocent, easy-living Indians, romantic Spanish lords and ladies, and peaceful Catholic priests to an eminently Anglo and American project of untrammeled growth, aiming first to attract tourists and then to invite massive real estate investment and development (Hartig 2010, 301; Lewthwaite 2010, 43; McWilliams 2010, 77). As Mike Davis explains in *City of Quartz*, this creation underwrote the script of the city's transformation in the twentieth century from small town to metropolis (2006, 20). Later, when citrus groves and green fields had become all but obliterated by urban and industrial development, the boosters, as Shiel put it, "pretended [that the city's] growth left Nature intact, blending urbanism and Arcadia, the modern and the timeless" (2012, 20–21).

This was still the predominant public image of the city when Hollywood became the home of the most powerful film industry in the world, yet the "land of sunshine" myth did not immediately produce a recognizable image of Los Angeles on the silver screen. Many silent movies, particularly comedies from the 1910s and 1920s, familiarized spectators around the world with the landscapes of Southern California and the streets of the booming city, but the films had little specific to say about them. The movies from the 1930s were a partial exception, but they focused exclusively on Hollywood (Shiel 2012, 128). Conversely, the city that we saw in the 1940s was as different from the sunshine myth as could be imagined: a dark city of rain-soaked streets and ominous shadows, populated by unsavory men and women seemingly infected by a moral malaise, a city without a heart, and, in the words of Raymond Chandler, "a city with the personality of a paper cup" (quoted in Kim Newman 2014, 37).

Utopia and dystopia, gloomy visions and sunny dreams (Braudy 2010, 278–79), escapist utopia or nightmare (Shiel 2012, 7), or in Davis's formulation, "sunshine or *noir*" (2006, 15) have continued to coexist as images of Los Angeles in the collective imagination. Shiel does discern in early silent LA films the dissemination of the "land of sunshine" image by the civic boosters (2012, 12), and Davis reminds us how the Lummis myth was later endlessly reproduced by Hollywood (2006, 20), but the association of the city with alienation and urban dystopia has proved particularly durable and resilient (Mennel 2008, 47). There would be plenty of sunny images of the city to come, but in movie terms the gloom came first.

At its inception, Los Angeles noir had a specific geography that for Davis and others originated in Bunker Hill, the lively working-class neighborhood that would a few years later be razed and erased from the face of the earth to make way for the new Financial District and Civic Center that constitute the familiar skyline of today's Downtown. Writer John Fante (*Ask the Dust*, 1939), painter Millard Sheets (*Angels Flight*, 1931), and later Raymond Chandler "invented" the Bunker Hill that would attract the European filmmakers with Expressionist credentials who continued to pour into Hollywood (Davis 2001, 36–37). It is an irony of the city's history that the shining state-of-the-art skyscrapers that contemporary films routinely use as shorthand for the city were built on top of the remains of the old noir city, the area where dark Los Angeles was first imagined. The old Bunker Hill no longer exists, but, if only through the lasting influence of film noir, it has left an indelible imprint on the cinematic city. In this sense the old neighborhood continues to make its presence felt in cultural discourses and to color and, some would say, threaten the gleaming buildings that stand on its material ruins. In Chapter 8 I show how a film like *The Soloist* incorporates this phantasmic presence into its narrative of urban borders, displacements, and crossings.

However, noir Los Angeles extended its cinematic topography well beyond Bunker Hill and Downtown and also associated its unremitting bleakness with the feeling of urban dispersal produced by the boosterism initiated in previous decades, which would later lead to the postmodern extended city or, to use Edward Soja's term, the exopolis. According to Edward Dimendberg, noir LA possessed a particularity that distinguished it from New York and that was located in the ubiquitous highways, suburban estates, industrial landscapes, and shopping malls prevalent in Southern California (1995, 93). The city that became cinematically consolidated through noir was formed by an assortment of relatively distant neighborhoods that reflected the rapid development of the booming metropolis. Important parts of 1940s Los Angeles remained invisible, as did most of its ethnic groups, but others became increasingly familiar to spectators, if only by name, and were associated with the stories of fatalism and despair offered on the theater screens.

One of the first and most influential noir films was *Double Indemnity* (1944), adapted from the James M. Cain novel by fellow hard-boiled writer Raymond Chandler and European émigré Billy Wilder and directed by Wilder. The story locates the deadly relationship between alienated male hero Walter Neff (Fred MacMurray) and archetypal femme fatale Phyllis Dietrichson (Barbara Stanwyck) in a precise Angeleno setting, one that denotes the size of the expanding city and illustrates noir's interest in harnessing its meanings to a recognizable and minutely staked out geography: The Dietrichsons live in a "Spanish" house on Los Feliz Boulevard, where Walter visits them on his way back from Glendale. The two lovers meet at a supermarket in Los Feliz; he lives in an apartment in Hollywood and has a friend who lives in Westwood. Mr. Dietrichson (Tom Powers) works in the oil fields in Long Beach; Walter's place of work, the Pacific Risk Insurance Company, is in the Pacific Building on Olive Street, and views of Downtown from the office windows are frequent. A truck driver with a phony claim is from Inglewood. Mr. Dietrichson leaves for his trip to Palo Alto from Glendale railway station and his body is found in Burbank; Walter takes a trip to Santa Monica, takes Lola (Jean Heather)

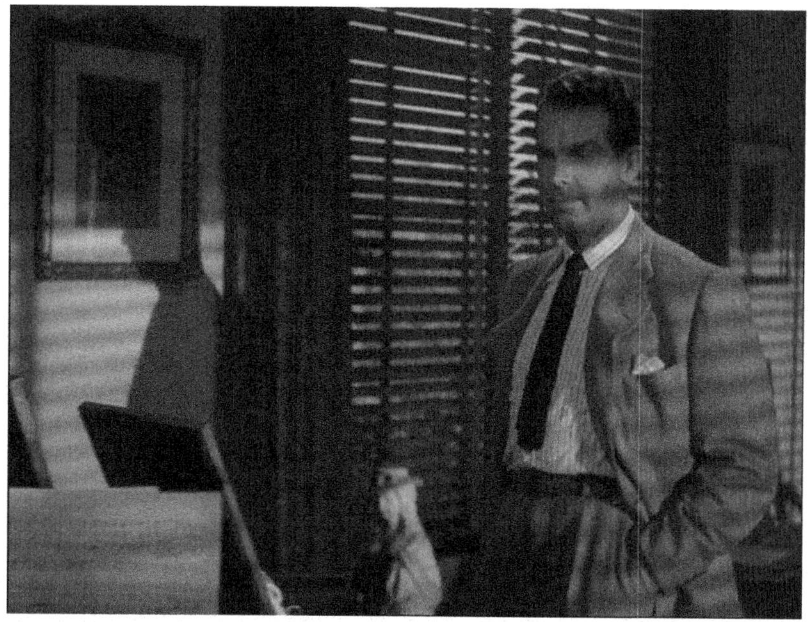

Double Idemnity: Los Angeles in chiaroscuro.

to a little Mexican restaurant in Olvera Street, then for a drive by the ocean, and finally to the hills above the Hollywood Bowl; one evening he stops at a bowling alley at 3rd and Western and later accompanies Lola to meet Zachetti (Byron Barr) at Franklin and Vermont. Zachetti lives on North La Brea Boulevard, studied to be a paramedic at USC, and at one point goes to a lecture at UCLA. The film is thick with Southern Californian atmosphere: the smell of the honeysuckle, the Spanish style of the houses, and the dust in the air as the sun hits the Venetian blinds. Walter, an insurance salesman, navigates the urban environment confidently, and the film prompts spectators to link the hero's fate to the specific places he frequents. The film never goes as far as to suggest that the city of Los Angeles is to blame for his questionable moral choices, his inevitable fate, or his alienation, but the context is there for anybody to register and recognize. In general, through the detailed geographic references and the charged atmosphere, the city of eternal sunshine is smoothly changed here into a place of "darkness, perversion, and corruption" (Shiel 2012, 222).

Later LA noir films continued to weave their urban discourses around real locations. *Mildred Pierce* (Michael Curtiz, 1945) confronts two social worlds: the affluent class represented by Monte Beragon (Zachary Scott) and the lower middle class of Mildred (Joan Crawford) and her family. These two social poles are given a concrete geography: Mildred lives in Glendale, and Monte moves between his old mansion in Pasadena and his beach house in Santa Monica. Mildred opens her first restaurant in Pasadena, but others follow in Laguna Beach, Los Feliz, and Arcadia, with the central one in Beverly Hills. Alongside its narrative of female empowerment and disempowerment the movie suggests a social Angeleno topography that speaks of Mildred's ambitions and business acumen as well as a story of class decadence and mobility in the booming town.

Mike Davis (2001) explores the centrality of Bunker Hill in *Criss Cross* (Robert Siodmak, 1949) and *Kiss Me Deadly* (Robert Aldrich, 1955), but both films feature further interesting dimensions of the protagonists' urban environment. Released in 1949, *Criss Cross* is the story of a heist in which automobiles are central, yet the Los Angeles in which the gang moves is still a freeway-free city, one that, as with the disappearance of Bunker Hill, would soon change beyond recognition because of the drastic changes in its transportation system that were about to come. In this sense, it could be argued that, beyond the destructive influence of femme fatale Anna (Yvonne de Carlo), Steve's (Burt Lancaster) dissatisfaction may be linked to anxieties about the rapidly transforming city.

Kiss Me Deadly directly links the origin of the city's generalized psychosocial crisis to the soon-to-disappear old Victorian houses, steep streets, and rundown hotels of Bunker Hill. Later, after outlining a detailed urban geography beyond Downtown, the movie locates its apocalyptic ending on the beach in Malibu, suggesting that we have reached the end of the road and that there is no escape from its deeply entrenched cold war paranoia, not even among the select beach community. Given the connotations of California as the ultimate destination of the American dream, Aldrich's movie's dystopian vocation binds the dream and the apocalypse together as though, by stopping at the Pacific shore, the apocalypse was the logical consequence of the dream.

Many other noir films took place in Los Angeles (114 between 1940 and 1959, according to Shiel 2012, 215), including "movies about the movies" (Ames 1997): *Sunset Boulevard* (Billy Wilder, 1950) and *In a Lonely Place* (Nicholas Ray, 1950). Like most films about Hollywood, Wilder's and Ray's texts offer a limited urban landscape in which LA virtually does not exist beyond the places occupied by the industry. Their stories of broken dreams and unforgiving realities are tinged with a distinctly noir atmosphere, and both of their male scriptwriter (anti-)heroes, Joe Gillis (William Holden) and Dixon Steele (Humphrey Bogart), are classic noir characters for whom the real geographic Hollywood (both Gillis and Steele live in apartments in the seedier part of the area) and Sunset Boulevard become part of the noir nightmare.

The pessimistic view of LA conveyed by film noir has been partly credited to the influence of the colony of antifascist European exiles in Hollywood that, together with the hard-boiled novelists, articulated in their stories a mood of disillusionment with the ruthless capitalism embodied by the city and its untrammeled urban and industrial development (Avila 2006, 73; Davis 2006, 21). More specifically, Shiel relates the unrest transmitted by the films to the Hollywood strikes of 1945–1947, the anti-union sentiment, and the beginning of the communist scare (2012, 243–255). Eric Avila sees noir as a cinematic expression of the displacement of New Deal idealism by a privatized conservative ethos in the wake of the cold war. The deteriorated portions of Los Angeles, such as Bunker Hill, provided an authentic setting for a midcentury malaise that went well beyond LA and affected the whole country, yet, for Avila, the films' use of views of Angeleno urban decline more specifically reflected the crisis of the local authorities' efforts to provide affordable housing for the poor: "Only a few years prior to the arrival of bulldozers in Bunker Hill, film noir had already annihilated that space in public consciousness" (2006, 78).

Film noir was therefore both historically and geographically located, and it offered meanings about the human condition that not only were spatially grounded but also remained attached to the city in the cinematic imagination. *Touch of Evil* (Orson Welles, 1958) marked the end of the classic noir period. Welles set the action of this border film in the fictional town of Los Robles, on the Mexican border, but used the dilapidated landscape of Venice for his locations, symbolically reinforcing the allegiance of the cycle to its hometown. Prophetically, Welles created a border town of the imagination without leaving Los Angeles, anticipating the importance that the city would end up acquiring as the center of the Californian borderlands. By the time of *Touch of Evil*, LA had become an easily identifiable cinematic city, not only with a detailed geography (which did not necessarily correspond to that of the real city) but also with a set of deeply entrenched meanings. Film noir declined at the end of the 1950s, but its meanings persisted and showed a remarkable capacity to adapt to new historical and local contexts. As the city continued to change exponentially and many of the real spaces of film noir became unrecognizable in a matter of a few years, the Angeleno alienated hero, and occasionally heroine, very often outsiders, became a fixture in later filmic narratives. Lobato's so-called "West Coast crime films" of the 1970s and 1980s, some of which, for example, *Point Blank* (1967), take place in Los Angeles, feature protagonists who "navigate a sun-drenched criminal megalopolis bearing little resemblance to the classic noir city" (Lobato 2008, 344), yet similar meanings of battered identity and existential anxiety continued to predominate. By then, the city had become "alienation central" (348).

An independently produced movie from the immediate post-noir period, *The Exiles* (Kent MacKenzie, 1961), is an early example of the recurrence of the imagery and discursive tropes created by noir. Like some of its earlier counterparts of the classic cycle, the protagonists of this film live in Bunker Hill, probably only a few years before the neighborhood was demolished, except that they are not the usual Anglo characters but Native Americans, in what constitutes one of the few examples of cinematic narratives featuring this ethnic group before the rise of multiculturalism (and even, after it!). These otherwise different heroes are recognizable because of the noir conventions that are used to portray them and their anxieties, as they walk past Angels Flight, the Hill Street Station, and what might be the Grand Central Market. We see them driving along the tunnel under Bunker Hill, walking on steep streets, visiting bars on Broadway, and meeting for a night out somewhere in the Hollywood Hills, from which they look at the city lights. We both acknowledge their otherness in the Anglo-dominated city and recognize their sense of alienation as cinematic Angelenos. By the early 1960s, noir had already become the default way of rendering the Southern Californian capital on-screen, no matter what else the films were about.

Two lesser-known movies directed by French filmmakers in the following years confirm the consolidation of the recognizable cinematic city: *Model Shop* (Jacques Demy, 1969) and *Un homme est mort* (The Outside Man; Jacques Deray, 1972). Both films relocate Angeleno alienation within the new context of the Vietnam War, explicitly in the first case and more indirectly in the second. In *Model Shop* we find the protagonist of Demy's earlier Nantes-based French hit *Lola* (1961), Cécile (Anouk Aimée), now working as a photographer's model in LA. She meets

George Matthews (Gary Lockwood), not a war veteran or a detective but an out-of-work architect who, like a latter-day noir hero, founders aimlessly in the city while he waits to be drafted for the Vietnam War. In *Un homme est mort* French hit man Lucien (Jean-Louis Trintignant), after fulfilling his contract early in the movie, spends most of the film running from the police and from other gangsters in the company of Nancy (Ann-Margret), another forlorn, drifting individual with whom he soon empathizes. The protagonist couples are seen as fragile victims of a cruel, uncomprehending world that threatens to engulf them. In *Model Shop* Sunset Boulevard and Venice are the specific spaces of the characters' aimless wonderings. In *Un homme est mort* the freeways take center stage and, together with parking lots, automobiles, and non-spaces such as the airport, the hotel lobby, or the bus station (Augé 1995), provide the precarious glue for a city that seems unfinished and shabbily put together, a city that privileges mobility but where there is nowhere to go. Yet in both films the spectator can strongly perceive the outsider's fascination with Los Angeles, a fascination that is intertwined with more or less specific anxieties, whether the Vietnam War or an urban space that is fast becoming the embodiment of the worst excesses of capitalism. Unlike the earlier European émigré filmmakers, Demy and Deray are only visiting Hollywood for a one-off cinematic venture, but they share their combination of attraction and repulsion.

Classic film noir ran its course in the 1950s, but it remained strong in the imagination of filmmakers not only through the evocation of its trademark alienation in movies, such as those described in the previous paragraphs, but also, a few years later, through a direct return to the pulp novels first adapted to the screen in the 1940s. The 1970s saw adaptations of Raymond Chandler's *Farewell, My Lovely* (Dick Richards, 1975), *The Big Sleep* (Michael Winner, 1978), and particularly *The Long Goodbye* (Robert Altman, 1973). In this last film detective Philip Marlowe's (Elliott Gould) alienation takes a self-referential slant that distances him from the classic Marlowes played by Humphrey Bogart and Dick Powell in the 1940s. Gould's hero is "a shabby-suited, mumbling insomniac" (Kim Newman 2014, 34) who is treated as asexual by his hippie neighbors atop the weird tower where he lives in North Hollywood and who ends up shooting his friend (the murderer) in cold blood. He parades his postmodern alienation in the North Hollywood and Malibu neighborhoods, where most of the action takes place, suggesting that noir and sunshine are not necessarily mutually exclusive.

The following year saw the release of *Chinatown* (Roman Polanski, 1974), for many the most interesting of the late noir films and a quintessential Los Angeles film. Altman's Marlowe covers a limited expanse of the city, with freeways and crowded police stations serving as the only links between the Hollywood Hills and the Malibu Colony. By contrast, *Chinatown*'s private dick J. J. Gittes (Jack Nicholson) travels extensively around Los Angeles and its surroundings, including Echo Park, both the lake and the neighborhood, San Pedro, Glendale, Brentwood, the Bradbury Building, Downtown, Pasadena, Chinatown, the San Fernando Valley, and Catalina Island. Gittes shares the nebulous anomie that had beset his forebears, but the social context for such malaise is provided here by sexual obsession and, especially, real estate greed. In its rewriting of the real story of the building of the 233-mile-long Los Angeles Aqueduct between Owens Valley and the San Fernando Valley that secured the supply of water to the city, *Chinatown* smoothly links cinematic alienation with Angeleno boosterism, adding to the growing list of causes for the noir condition, one that for many might have been the most obvious.

Alienated heroes continued to proliferate between the 1960s and the 1980s, whether in romantic comedies such as *The Graduate* (Mike Nichols, 1967) and *Into the Night* (John Landis, 1985), post-Vietnam male crisis dramas such as *Shampoo* (Hal Ashby, 1975), or neo-noir films such as *American Gigolo* (Paul Schrader, 1980) and *Breathless* (Jim McBride, 1983), an adaptation of Jean-Luc Godard's seminal homage to film noir, *À bout de souffle* (1960). The confirmation of this trait as the central paradigm of the Angeleno hero coincides in these decades with the consolidation of Beverly Hills and other affluent Westside neighborhoods, the Hollywood Hills, and the beach communities of Malibu, Santa Monica, and Venice as the cinematic spaces of the Hollywood narrative of Los Angeles, leaving huge portions of the city outside representation. It is in this limited geography that the heirs of the noir cycle parade their anomie and fatalism as the city grows incessantly around them. At the time of the justice riots, Robert Altman released what some might call the ultimate LA alienation diptych: *The Player* (1992) and *Short Cuts* (1993). In typical ironic Altmanesque mode, *The Player* revisits the "movies about the movies" genre, and, as in all of them, the city is reduced to the locations in which Hollywood people live, ignoring the millions of other citizens around them. The hero, studio executive Griffin Mill (Tim Robbins), travels from Brentwood to Pasadena, from Malibu to Palm Springs, and along the Pacific Coast Highway and San Vicente

Boulevard and visits the Hollywood Forever Cemetery and the Los Angeles County Museum of Art, but he is oblivious to anything that is not related to the business. A murder plot is superimposed on a journey of self-discovery for a typical Angeleno character who, once again, seems to have lost his way in the midst of a life of privilege. Unexpectedly, Whoopi Goldberg's Pasadena police inspector, who suspects Griffin of being the murderer, makes the only reference to the "real world," when she affirms ironically that the previous year they arrested the wrong guy—they should have arrested Griffin instead of Rodney King.

The Player's alienated single hero is replaced in *Short Cuts* by twenty-two alienated men and women in the multi-protagonist adaptation (and transposition to LA) of Raymond Carver's short stories. Here the medfly plague is the obvious metaphor for the malady that distresses the characters, particularly the men, who tend to be aggressive and violent against women, for reasons that are difficult to fathom beyond a generalized crisis of masculinity. Apart from the characteristic helicopter shots of the immense city at night, there are relatively few and narratively unimportant ostensible geographic markers or references to the actual city (Annie Ross's jazz singer says at one point, "I hate L.A. All they do is sniff coke and talk"), yet by this time the movie does not need to be more explicit: The centrality of Los Angeles is immediately noticeable in the characters' indefinable affliction, a veritable plague from which, seemingly, nobody can escape. At the same time, the city is chosen because, paradoxically, its urban and spiritual uniqueness had by the early 1990s turned it into the paradigmatic example of the global city, the location where the pressures of the contemporary experience can be felt most "naturally" and most pressingly. Once the story is over, the final credits appear superimposed on maps of the city, as though the film had been concealing the identity of its chosen space to make it look more universal, finally revealing that this story could not happen anywhere else.

Short Cuts taps into the city's capacity to represent universal meanings. A decade earlier, *Blade Runner* had become an important milestone in this tradition. Los Angeles is the absolute protagonist in this movie, even if presented as a city of the imagination, mostly created at Warners' Burbank studio. However, it displays sufficient touches of the real place to suggest the specificity of its dystopian world, a postmodern pastiche of different periods and cultures and a combination of first and third world (Dimendberg 2010, 357; Mennel 2008, 146). With the Bradbury

Building—a threatening ghost of a modernist past recast as a dilapidated technological hub—as its paradigmatic central location, space in *Blade Runner* is the predominant formal system above a relatively simple story and a set of hurriedly sketched and barely developed characters. Produced at a time when Bunker Hill was being rebuilt as a gleaming futuristic city but before the old Downtown (including the Bradbury Building) had started to undergo gentrification, what we see on the screen is a society in urgent need of the real city's favorite pastime: urban renewal. As Dimendberg has argued, this was the film that most influenced thinking about the future of Los Angeles (2010, 357), even though in cinematic terms it looked back to the past both visually and generically.

The intensely claustrophobic atmosphere once again determines the characters' behavior and the fatalism surrounding them, both in the case of its policeman of sorts (Harrison Ford) and his human antagonists, the replicants. Interestingly, the initial happy ending, which provided a way out for the protagonists, was subsequently cut in the critically preferred director's cut, underlining a cultural preference to imagine a city that cannot offer a way out to its beleaguered citizens. *Blade Runner* ratified the cultural association between then-incipient globalization and dystopia and confirmed LA as its prime location in cinematic fiction. As architecture critic Christopher Hawthorne defines it in his review of *Crash* (Paul Haggis, 2004), Los Angeles is "the only city where you can order your alienation to go" (2006, n.p.). Openly indebted to the noir tradition, *Blade Runner* showed that the real and the cinematic Los Angeles were fast becoming the spatial paradigm of times to come. However, the film's insistent Anglo-only perspective was moving further and further away from urban reality. With few exceptions, Angeleno alienation had been born and continued to develop as an exclusively Anglo state of mind and therefore ignored wide portions of the population.

Lost (and Found) on the Freeway

There are many facets to globalization and global cities. Saskia Sassen, for instance, describes global cities as strategic places for the management of the global economy (2006, 32) but also as central sites of migrant and diasporic movements and locations of a booming informal economy. She sees globalization as a process characterized by the free flow of goods and capital under an untrammeled market economy but also by contestation, difference, and continuous border crossings. For her, global cities are emblematic of this condition (Sassen 1998, xxxiv). For Soja and others, Los Angeles is the quintessential global city, the archetypal "postmetropolis" (Soja 2000).

In contemporary Hollywood cinema, the Californian city is also representative of the modern megalopolis. The cinematic tradition of Angeleno alienation has continued to be the primary, though not the only, way to understand and represent this global urban condition. Movies, which only tangentially touch on economic factors and financial scenarios, tend to focus on the consequences for individuals of pressures caused directly or indirectly by globalization. This is the case for *Collateral* (Michael Mann, 2004), a coproduction between Paramount and DreamWorks that, with an estimated budget of $65 million, drew on the star power of Tom Cruise, after his string of box office triumphs with *Mission: Impossible II* (John Woo, 2000), *Minority Report* (Steven Spielberg, 2002), and *The Last Samurai* (Edward Zwick, 2003). Cruise's casting as ruthless hit man Vincent, however, also tapped into his crossover potential and his appeal to art film audiences in two films from 1999: *Eyes Wide Shut* (Stanley Kubrick) and *Magnolia* (Paul Thomas Anderson). Cruise's hybrid appeal was also shared by *Collateral*'s director, Michael Mann, who, working in the mainstream, earned himself the label of auteur, after a string of critically successful movies, including *The Last of the Mohicans* (1992), *The Insider* (1999) and, especially, *Heat* (1995). The presence of these two figures announced that *Collateral* was a commercial movie that had important things to say and fulfilled elevated aesthetic demands. Both its aesthetic excellence and its thematic complexity were closely connected to Los Angeles.

Mann's film is characteristic of contemporary LA movies in that its alienated protagonist carries on his shoulders the weight of the postmodern urban experience. Contemporary pressures on the individual, rather than analyzed in detail, are taken for granted. For its part, Los Angeles encapsulates everything that is wrong with postindustrial capitalism. The cinematic tradition of Angeleno alienation and its smooth adaptation to the effects of global processes seem sufficient to offer the city as almost a self-explanatory paradigm of the complexities of contemporary societies: The meanings are all contained in the very mention of Los Angeles, so they do not need to be spelled out or explored in any detail. The cinematic fascination—we might even say love affair—with a mode of representation based on urban alienation has continued unabated since the time of classic noir. Today it is associated with the pitfalls of dehumanizing globalization. Simultaneously, the movie is also representative of recent LA cinema because a new urban discourse rides on the back of the alienation story, feeding off its cinematic history but moving in a different direction—the road from noir to the multicultural city.

Collateral revisits some of the territory covered in Mann's earlier *Heat*, another crime film set in Los Angeles and another movie *about* Los Angeles. *Heat* depicts a postmodern world of non-places, encapsulated in the film's opening set piece, the spot on Venice Boulevard under the exchange between the Harbor and the Santa Monica Freeways where the gang's first heist takes place; and in the final scene, in the chase on the grounds of LAX at night that is resolved among nondescript containers in the airport fields. The central score, in a bank on Figueroa and Fifth, with the Bonaventure Hotel and the Maguire Gardens in the background, and the subsequent chase around the streets and avenues of Downtown offer us a more recognizable cityscape, but this is otherwise overwhelmingly a world of automobiles and freeways and, particularly, helicopters. In some of the most characteristic shots that anticipate later framings in *Collateral* we see Vincent Hanna (Al Pacino) flying in a helicopter among the lit-up skyscrapers of Downtown with the rest of the city in the background and millions of lights surrounding his body. The sleek thieves in *Heat* cruise incessantly between industrial estates, empty lots, and designer homes, parading their despair, loneliness, and angst, a psychosocial world in which the protagonist of the later film could easily insert himself. Something similar can be said about the women, who cannot manage to lead the normal life they crave with these neo-noir antiheroes. It is not so much that *Heat* suggests that these seriously damaged human beings represent Los Angeles. Rather, they stand for a more widespread postmetropolitan condition for which a phantasmagoric LA is the natural environment. In a climactic scene, Eady (Amy Brenneman) is silently but deeply shocked when she sees that Neil (Robert de Niro) takes less than 30 seconds to leave her behind, as he said he would, even after he had just pleaded with her to start a new life with him. But this is the pathetic, updated Western code by which both policeman and outlaw live, making sense only to themselves. In *Heat* Michael Mann's LA is a place of extreme loneliness and broken souls, where there is no respite except in death, a death that even teenager Lauren (Natalie Portman) craves eagerly.

Collateral revisits this familiar landscape, but it both exacerbates and ameliorates the existential despair of the earlier film's characters. More than *Heat*, it is a film about travel within Los Angeles, and its most potent narrative and visual motif is the freeway. In the course of a single night, its two protagonists visit various locations around town. They are primarily defined by movement and by their psychological ability to navigate the freeways and surface roads of the vast metropolis. This makes them part of a globalized world and embodiments of the city. In a global world characterized by extreme mobility, the recent history of Los Angeles could be described as a quest for mobility and its urban layout as a sacrifice of more traditional urban structures for the sake of mobility. The freeways encapsulate this historical process and link it with urban alienation.

According to Robert Gottlieb, freeways are one of the three defining features of the Los Angeles region (the other two being water and cars) (2007, 11). Since the opening of the Pasadena Freeway (then called the Arroyo Seco Parkway) in 1940, a succession of massive roadways started to mushroom in Los Angeles, first linking the city with the suburbs and later, gradually, allowing citizens of middle-class neighborhoods and nearby incorporated cities to move from one to the other, bypassing the city center and the poorer areas. As the film *Who Framed Roger Rabbit?* (Robert Zemeckis, 1988) fictionalizes, the municipal streetcar system, the dominant means of urban transportation in the early decades of the twentieth century, was replaced by freeways and cars in the years following World War II. Zemeckis's movie reproduces a popular discourse according to which a combination of real estate and automobile industry interests destroyed a perfectly good rail system, the well-known Red Cars.

The freeways were a consequence of a city in love with the automobile. Carey McWilliams, writing when the freeways had hardly started to make an appearance, explained that Los Angeles had always been a city on wheels, an automobile metropolis. Even then, he was already arguing that the widespread use of the automobile had aborted other forms of transportation (McWilliams 2010, 236). Martin Wachs finds the reality more complex. In the first place, it was the streetcars, notably Henry Huntington's Pacific Electric System, not automobiles and freeways, that patterned Southern California as a horizontal city without a center. It was this urban railway system that first facilitated mobility between distant neighborhoods (by 1923 the Red Cars traveled on 1,164 miles of track extending more than 100 miles, and the smaller Yellow Cars covered 316 miles), laid out the horizontal extended city (Wachs 1996, 107–8), and attached modernity to what was essentially a means to further the primary engine of Angeleno history: regional growth through real estate interests (Weinstein 1997, 75). Second, the demise of the urban railway system had started as early as the late 1920s, with people's animosity toward the transit authorities growing during that decade; the general view among citizens was that the trains were late, the cars were filthy and uncomfortable, the drivers were unpleasant, and the owners were tyrannical. As Wachs summarizes, the street railways had become infamous and the automobile was seen as a form of liberation for commuters (1996, 118–19).

Decades later, by the end of the twentieth century, the freeways were for many the new center of the city and, as Gottlieb emphatically puts it, Los Angeles had "indeed become the proverbial string of freeways in search of a city" (2007, 175). Yet, as early as the 1980s, these urban roadways, originally designed as much for recreation and pleasure as to facilitate the movement of commuters, had turned into a nightmare of constant traffic jams and occasional Sig Alerts, turning on those occasions into immense parking lots (Gottlieb 2007, 174). In its 2013 report, the Los Angeles 2020 Commission mentions traffic as one of the worst and most difficult ills to resolve: "We are strangled by traffic—the most congested urban community in America and fourth worst in the world" (2013, 2), and it adds that none of the ambitious and expensive transit projects under way will help to solve the problem. For better of for worse, the freeway system has become not only the universal icon of Los Angeles and a dramatic metaphor for life in the modern metropolis but also a central element of the city, subject to constant criticism but an inescapable part of its everyday life. Both in practical and symbolic terms, modern Los Angeles would be unthinkable without its freeways.

The LA freeways, while reproducing the dream of mobility within the large metropolis, do not necessarily respond in their intricate layout to the frontier-expanding desire of classic American heroes. Maybe for this reason, freeways took, with some exceptions, several decades to become visible and familiar signifiers of the city. Because they differed conceptually from the myth of the road, as encapsulated in the cultural meanings of, say, Route 66 and cinematically in the road movie, they needed a new set of meanings to which to attach themselves before becoming a familiar fixture on the screens. In general terms these meanings were found in the association of the city with global processes and gathered momentum in the early 1990s, that is, in the historical period covered by this book. The alienation of the cinematic postmetropolis attached itself to the freeways.

We have seen how *Falling Down* (Joel Schumacher, 1993) opens with one of the most familiar ways in which Los Angeles freeways have been visualized in contemporary cinema: gridlock. Elsewhere in contemporary LA cinema, aerial shots of busy freeways and freeway exchanges and characters caught in never-ending traffic jams speak to fears of dehumanization, human insignificance and entrapment, and the suffocating presence of powerful forces that cannot be apprehended but control our lives. Film after film has familiarized spectators with these two images. Although the individual texts often attach specific meanings to them, on many other occasions they are just inserted as markers of the city and as indexes of the general malaise associated with the extended megalopolis. Even in a teenage comedy such as *Clueless* (Amy Heckerling, 1995), the unexpected entrance to a freeway produces immediate anxiety in the otherwise confident and carefree characters. More positive, incantatory visions of the freeways have been offered by other comedies, such as *L.A. Story* (Mick Jackson, 1991) and *I Love You, Man* (John Hamburg, 2009), but associations of the cement giants with anomie and identity crisis, as in *Somewhere* (Sofia Coppola, 2010) and *Drive* (Nicolas Winding Refn, 2011), or with urban conflict and racial tension, as in the police movies *Training Day* (Antoine Faqua, 2001) and *End of Watch* (David Ayer, 2012), overwhelmingly predominate.

Collateral inserts itself within this microhistory of cinematic articulations of the LA freeway, but, more than the films mentioned already, it places the city's transportation grid at its narrative and symbolic center. An answer to Gottlieb's "proverbial string of freeways in search of a city" or to its purported lack of identity (Lobato 2008, 347), *Collateral* finds and showcases a real city in the midst of the freeways. Driving from one neighborhood to another in the Angeleno night, Vincent, a hit man, and Max (Jamie Foxx), a cab driver, follow a complex trajectory that highlights both the topographic uniqueness of the city and its wider cinematic connotations as the world capital of alienation. The freeways define both the characters' narrative arcs and the city they travel. Their stops are all at carefully chosen parts of the city, but the freeways are the glue that brings them together and turns them into a particular urban discourse. Max and Vincent, one an Angeleno, the other an outsider, become embodiments of the postmodern city through their association with the dream/nightmare of mobility and, simultaneously, heirs of the alienated heroes who preceded them in the history of Hollywood cinema.

At the time of the film's release, critics linked *Collateral* to the noir tradition. R. Blackwelder, for example, described it as "pumped-up B-movie noir" (2004, 20), whereas others saw it as neo-noir (Kotler 2004). Critics also highlighted the city as the film's real protagonist and saw Mann as "the pre-eminent chronicler of L.A." (Levine 2004, 18), "the cinematic master poet of nocturnal L.A." (McCarthy 2004, 27), a man who has "an enormous amount to say about Los Angeles" (Atkinson 2004, 72), and "one of the cinema's great lyric poets of urban space" (G. Smith 2004, 14). The link between cinematic past and present is provided by the alienated hero: Vincent is a latter-day Walter Neff and Rick Deckard in the midst of a city that is both post-noir and post-neo-noir but that has also changed in significant ways since the times of the earlier films. His buddy of sorts, Max, is the embodiment of those social and demographic changes.

Vincent, the outsider (but then again, most people are outsiders or newcomers in LA), articulates the received view of the city in an early conversation with Max: "Tell you the truth, whenever I'm here I can't wait to leave. Too sprawled out, disconnected. . . . Seventeen million people. This was a country, it'd be the fifth biggest economy in the world, and nobody knows each other. I read about this guy, gets on the MTA here, dies. Six hours he's riding the subway before anybody notices his corpse doing laps around LA, people on and off sitting next to him. Nobody notices." This is an almost literal prolepsis of what will happen to him at the end of the story, but, beyond narrative incident, it also functions as a standard summary of the anomie that the postmetropolis inflicts on its citizens and an articulation of the blurring of the boundaries between the citizen and the urban environment, the individual and the world around him. Vincent becomes part of the engulfing and all-consuming city, a monster that annihilates and swallows the identity of its millions. This condition evokes Celeste Olalquiaga's notion of psychasthenia, a psychological disturbance in which the individual becomes incapable of demarcating the limits between his own body and the surrounding territory and becomes lost in the space beyond. This mimetic condition is characteristic of a contemporary urban culture (Olalquiaga 1992, 1–2). Vincent represents this modern disoriented individual, often incapable of establishing bonds of affection with fellow human beings, often enslaved by a set of preordained self-images that act as barriers to real communication, often brought to the verge of breakdown by unbearable loneliness in the midst of the multitude. As a psychasthenic character, Vincent does not just represent the city—he is, or becomes, the city.

The death of the striking professional killer in total anonymity, becoming an inanimate part of the city that he, in his insightful description, profoundly dislikes, turns him into the ultimate victim of the vileness of the sprawling metropolis. Before this and before the story starts, he has undergone a process of dehumanization, which is spelled out by Max much later in the film: "The standard parts that are supposed to be in people, in you aren't." As Vincent approaches his inevitable doom, Max is growing in moral and emotional stature and is ready to counter the other's psychasthenia with his own humanity, one that is born of the same postmodern urban condition.

By then, the spectator, whether or not cognizant of Mann's love of the city, has already realized that the film has not one but at least two stories to tell about LA. These can be roughly ascribed respectively to Stuart Beattie, the scriptwriter, and the director. Australian-born Beattie, whose original script was set in New York, sees the story as an encapsulation of a traditional Angeleno alienation that is constantly renewed as the city grows: "I noticed that in a city with this many people there is a distinct devaluing of human life. I began to think about what that means, and finding a way to say it in the story" (quoted in Dawes 2005, xi). Mann had a different approach in mind, one that also originated from his own experience in the City of Angels: "There's a certain romance of the city at night that I confess I'm completely vulnerable to. What happens when the marine layer comes in and all of a sudden the vapor lights bounce off the bottom of the clouds and makes a sky that looks like late afternoon in Northern Europe, and what it looks like from up there" (quoted in Abramowitz 2004, E1).

Predictably, it is this vision of wonder that predominates in critical accounts. For Ella Taylor, for example, no one working in the thriller genre "makes urban ennui look more romantic, or more intimately threatening. This is a movie that could only have been shot in L.A., with its traffic signals switching blindly above indifferent empty streets, the city painted in deep blue and black, its bone-deep loneliness relieved only by the glittering lights of Downtown office buildings and the endless suburban deserts beyond" (2004, 40). This romanticized view of the alienating city and of cinematic psychasthenia was linked at the time of release with the filmmaker's decision to shoot most of the film with high-definition (HD) video cameras, which would, in his own words, "shoot into the night" (DVD director's commentary), or, in the words of Paul Cameron (the first of two directors of photography hired for the film), allow viewers to see the action "more the way you see it by eye" and "to see into the night sky, as the horizon separates" (quoted in Goldman 2004, 49). Mann's love of the city, HD cameras, and the noir tradition became, therefore, part of the way in which DreamWorks and Paramount marketed the movie for spectators around the world as well as central ingredients of its formal structure. A cursory look at the movie's posters reveals that Cruise remained its strongest selling point, but there was enough in the way spectators were asked to approach the film generically, visually, and in terms of authorship to situate the city at the center of the narrative.

The most memorable shots of the city were made possible by digital technology and are those in which, evoking *Heat*, we see the characters, often in close-up, with the city lights and the shadowy outlines of the Downtown buildings or the half-empty roads behind them, both human figure and urban context in relatively sharp focus; but, at the same time, the city provides a sort of enchanted aura around the humans, who are both isolated and elevated by Los Angeles. Vincent succumbs to the insatiable megalopolis, but Max and Annie (Jada Pinkett Smith) are empowered by it. Although Cruise's character embodies classic Angeleno alienation, the other two are the repository of what Ramon Lobato calls "the urban sublime" (2008, 349). For this critic, both *Heat* and *Collateral* offer the spectator an aesthetic experience of urban alienation that allows us to make the city our own (350).

Max and Annie's lives and identities are affected by Vincent in a variety of ways in the course of the narrative, but they are not, like him, alienated characters. Annie has a limited presence in the film, but her two moments—a scene at the beginning and then the whole final part—are narratively central. Max, for his part, undergoes a transformation that is permanently tied to the city. To Vincent's dark and disparaging view of LA, Max opposes a much simpler opinion: "It's my home." For him, there is no disconnectedness, no overwhelming sprawl, no unbearable loneliness. His attachment to Los Angeles is stronger than it may seem at first sight, and, insofar as it is untouched by alienation, it is unusual in cinematic tradition.

At the beginning of the film Max picks Annie up at LAX and is asked to take her Downtown, to her office in a Department of Justice building. A busy woman with strong opinions, she tells him the precise route she wants him to take on surface roads, but he suggests the freeways might be faster. She mentions the traffic jams on the 110 around USC and farther north, closer to Downtown, but he seems confident that he is right and that the traffic will be heavier on the Westside boulevards. When she challenges him, he offers her a free ride if he is wrong. It is not sound business on his part, and it is almost as though he is more interested in showing off the beauty of the freeways than in earning a living. Sure enough the next long aerial shot shows, to the soft external notes of Groove Armada's "Hands of Time," a characteristic freeway exchange with the cars' headlights illuminating the darkness. The next few shots frame the two characters in medium shot inside the car with the incantatory urban lights in the background as a prelude to the dialogue during which their mutual attraction becomes obvious. Once they get closer to her Downtown destination, the dialogue is conveniently interrupted for us to admire the beauty of the skyscrapers in the dark, a fitting visual counterpart to their budding relationship, as the cab gracefully drives past them. An overhead shot of the buildings, like a symphony of urban shapes and multicolor lights, completes the ride. This is both the recognizable fascinating city of film noir and something new: an enchanted space that ascribes positive meanings to the postmodern urban condition. The freeways will soon revert to their usual connotations as soon as Vincent enters Max's cab, but through the cabdriver's presence and, one would say, the memory of Annie's ride, freeways, city lights, and buildings move away from noir and post-noir territory.

Annie, a prominent prosecutor working for the Department of Justice, has fallen for the allure of the almost magical Angeleno roads and, unexpectedly, gives Max her business card, openly asking him for a date. As she says, she has just had a vacation on the Harbor Freeway. It is as though Max has taught her to see her own town in a different light, and she, our anchor in the narrative at this point, has fallen in love with it, as we are meant to. Much later, when Vincent is coming to kill her at her office, in the darkness of the building, they are both often framed in close-up on one side of the widescreen frame with the city lights filling the rest of the screen. In a different film, maybe even in *Heat*, these framings might have been taken as part of the visual pyrotechnics of a generic thriller in its climactic scene. But here we see the city as a sheltering space that will ensure that Annie comes to no harm and Vincent gets his comeuppance. Lobato argues that the crime genre uses the dialectic of enchantment and defacement that allows us to reimagine urban space as a site of fantasy (2008, 341). In *Collateral* Max and Annie on one side and Vincent on the other represent both aspects of the dialectic. Los Angeles ends up claiming and destroying the bodies and souls of those who, like Vincent, see it as the site of alienation, but it protects and celebrates those who succumb to its powers of enchantment. This enchantment is directly linked to Mann's aesthetic fascination with the city's visual potential, but it finds a further referent in more tangible aspects of the city.

For such an abstract homage to LA, *Collateral* is unusually precise and prolific in its mapping of an Angeleno urban geography. Vincent has five stopovers planned during his night in town, to which two more locations are added in the course of the ride: the hospital where they visit Max's mother and the club where information on Vincent's last two hits has to be retrieved after Max has thrown away Vincent's briefcase. Max picks Vincent up on Spring Street, Downtown, where he has just dropped Annie, and their first destination is an address in Pico-Union, west of Downtown, a densely populated, low-income neighborhood with a majority of Latino immigrants, an area where, unlike most other parts of LA, Central Americans almost equal Mexicans in number. Their second stop is in a pointedly unglamorous area of Hollywood, between Sunset and Santa Monica Boulevards. From there they travel to Leimert Park, in South Central, a neighborhood considered a center of African American culture. Then they stop at the Martin Luther King Hospital, in South Central. The second unexpected detour happens when they have to drive southeast to the mostly Latino middle-class incorporated city of Pico Rivera, where Max meets the Mexican drug lord Felix (Javier Bardem) at a club. From there they travel to another club, this time in Koreatown, and back to their approximate point of origin in Downtown, because Vincent's last victim is Annie, who is working where Max dropped her off at the beginning of the film. In the final section of the movie the cab is replaced by the subway, and Vincent and Max travel south on the Blue Line to Long Beach.

Although it is impossible to do justice to LA's intricate and massive topography in a single film, Mann makes a believable stab at it. In an article where she traces the real locations of the movie and minutely analyzes the differences with the places we see in the film, Erin Ailworth describes *Collateral* as "a valentine to the L.A. that tourists never see" (2004, E12). More to the point for us, this is a Los Angeles virtually unknown to film spectators. The closest we get to a recognizable "movie" neighborhood is the seedy Hollywood location. The characters in *Collateral* never get anywhere near the beach neighborhoods, the affluent exclusive areas of the Westside, or the Hollywood Hills. They never even visit less glamorous but more cinematically visible areas such as Echo Park or the San Fernando Valley. The exception is Downtown, where we even get a glimpse of the Walt Disney Concert Hall and the Staples Center and where we are offered plenty of opportunities to admire the familiar skyline. The freeways remain the heart of the story, but they also work as the link between disparate and cinematically unrepresented communities that might be seen, in contrast to more habitual cinematic representations, as "the real LA."

The city that fascinates us, therefore, is not primarily the noir city, or even just the product of the special light configurations and effects that Mann so admires and so beautifully captures with his HD video camera, but the multicultural city. There are no significant Latino characters in the movie, and the only one that there is is played by a European actor (Spain's Bardem had by then displaced Spain's Antonio Banderas as the Hollywood mainstream's favorite male "Mexican"), but we often hear Spanish voices, beginning with the cab station where Max starts his day and where a Mexican mural graces the entrance and continuing with the gas station under the freeway where he fills his tank regularly and where he exchanges brief (and unfortunately incomprehensible) words in Spanish with the Latino attendant. Although there is no hint of the demographic profile of Pico Rivera in the movie, it is virtually impossible to find another LA film featuring a mostly Chicano neighborhood that is not socially depressed and life-threatening for outsiders. It is perhaps unfortunate that Pico Rivera acquires darker meanings than it has in reality, but the mere presence of the place is significant in itself, as is its contrast with Pico-Union, the protagonists' first stop and a Latino neighborhood with very different connotations. The Asian American communities of LA are made visible through the characters' drive to Koreatown, even if this area is also associated with an underworld of crime.

Traditionally African American South Central figures prominently in the film, through the visits to the jazz club in Leimert Park and the hospital further south. More important, of course, both Max and Annie are African American.

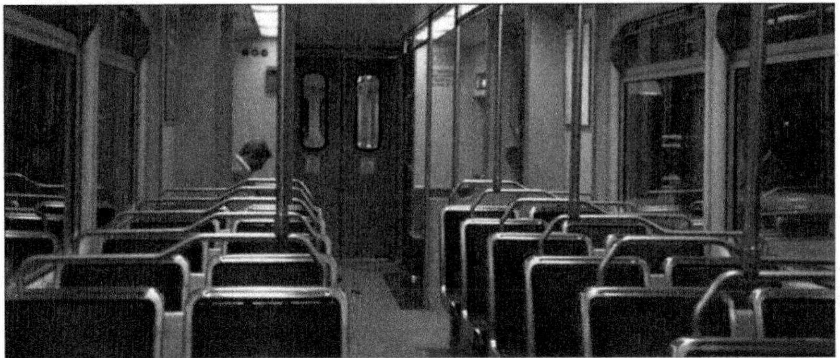

Collateral: the alienated Angeleno antihero.

Despite star power, Max is, in purely narrative terms, the true protagonist of the movie, with Vincent as antagonist. Jamie Foxx plays the Angeleno everyman who is empowered by his narrative experience, and Jada Pinkett Smith plays the contemporary educated professional woman whose ethnic origin is not an insurmountable barrier. This is a mainstream movie, with no claims to social realism or truthful representations of African American lives of the type we will find in Chapter 6. Yet it does incorporate a relatively complex racial discourse and, in its combination of casting choices and aesthetic sublimation of a Los Angeles rarely seen in the movies, it is a significant rewriting of the story of Angeleno alienation for post–justice riots times.

Through the urban experience of the two male protagonists, the film offers not only two different cities, or at least two opposite views of LA, but also two idioms of cinematic representation of the city. On the one hand, through Vincent, *Collateral* links with the tradition of cinematic Angeleno alienation and, by adapting it to modern discourses of the postmetropolis, reframes that alienation as the consequence of modern processes of globalization. In this dystopian discourse Vincent becomes the human correlative of the infrahuman evil metropolis with no hope of redemption and is eventually fused with it as the subway train rides off toward its Long Beach destination. In this context the spectator's fascination with the city as channeled through Mann's incantatory HD vision is not radically different from that of its noir and post-noir forebears, a masochistic attraction toward the devouring monster.

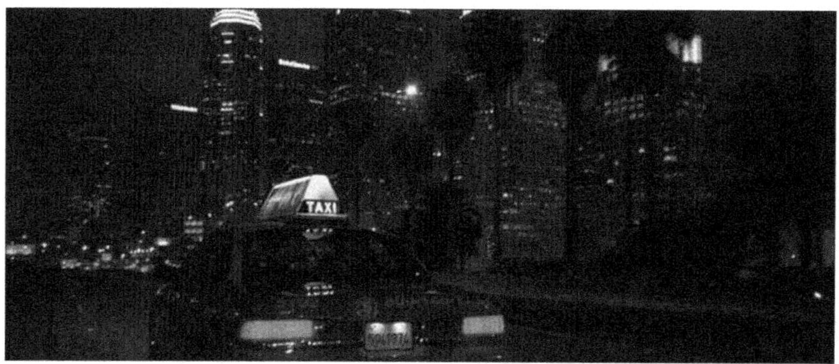

Collateral: love and enchantment in the neo-noir city.

Redemption, however, comes in the shape of Max, the classic and classically empowered hero, and his relationship with Annie, the modern professional African American woman. They represent a different LA and embody a city of diverse, though cinematically unknown, and unstoppably multicultural neighborhoods. Annie and her budding desire for Max absorb a great part of the visual beauty of the director's valentine to the city—in the couple's initial scene together, he uses the city as a weapon of seduction. The freeways, which, in facilitating Vincent's journey to nowhere or to final annihilation, further standard meanings of postmodern urban dystopia, are in their visual and narrative association with Max the symbol of a different kind of mobility: the social and cultural mobility of a city that, after 1992, realizes that it cannot cling forever to its Anglo-only past. The strategies used to sell the film largely overlooked this historical specificity in favor of revisiting more familiar noir tropes and Mann's prestige as an auteur, but this alternative presence of the city remains nevertheless its most interesting dimension as a post-1992 LA movie. It also makes *Collateral* an illustration of how, in post-1992 cinema, representations of Los Angeles combined the most traditional tropes with new ways of imagining the city.

4

Breaking at the Seams

White Los Angeles

The gentle but frightening dystopian Los Angeles of *Her* (Spike Jonze, 2013) is comfortable, neat, and tidy; its citizens are mild-mannered, cultured, and urbane but also desperately lonely. It is a city dominated by technology in which computer operating systems have acquired a life of their own and can fall in love with humans, and humans with them. They remind us of the peaceful and bored citizens of San Angeles in the 1990s dystopia of *Demolition Man*, but the most immediate referent is once again *Blade Runner* and its narrative of a dehumanized future in which feelings and emotions come from the most unexpected beings. However, behind this reference lie all the earlier and later cinematic stories of alienation that have made LA their home. Exteriors for *Her* were shot in Shanghai, and perhaps this fact accounts for the occasional Asian faces we see in the silent and orderly crowds, but the movie's Angelenos are mostly white, and all the speaking parts are uniformly white, including protagonist Samantha (Scarlett Johansson), the romantic operating system. The director explains that one of his inspirations for the world he created was Jamba Juice, the smoothie chain: very clean, brightly lit, with warm colors spelling the future for him. "In LA today things are pretty nice and easy. The weather is so nice, there are a lot of nice things that are easy to get: cups of coffee, clothes, nice food, technology which makes everything so easy" (quoted in Bell 2014, 24). Easy for some people, of course. Those for whom things are not so easy, a sizable portion of the city's population, simply do not exist in this movie. In this, *Her* is not so forward-looking. Instead it inserts itself in a long tradition of cinematic Los Angeles: the all-white city that summarily erases that which threatens its homogeneity. The absence may be becoming too glaring: Where are the brown people in *Her*'s future Los Angeles, complains Bryce Renninger (2013), who immediately notices that in the film poverty is invisible and nearly 50 percent of the population (Latinos) has disappeared. No matter what the artistic motivations may be, this type of erasure is becoming incredible. Yet it remains significant that a sizable amount of the best-known and even artistically most successful mainstream movies that take the city as their home continue to project the same image as a hundred years ago.

In this chapter I look at two specific manifestations of white LA in post–Rodney King cinema, one comic (*(500) Days of Summer*, Marc Webb, 2009) and one dramatic (*Magnolia*, Paul Thomas Anderson, 1999). Unlike the three films analyzed in Chapters 2 and 3, these two are "independent films," that is, movies that, as briefly mentioned in the Introduction, were produced by the specialty branches of the big studios. These specialty branches may have resulted from an independent company being bought by a major studio, as in the case of *Magnolia*'s New Line Cinema, one of the most successful independents of the late 1980s and early 1990s that is now part of the Time Warner conglomerate (Schatz 2008, 26); or they may be a company created by a major studio to produce indie films, as with *(500) Days of Summer*'s Fox Searchlight, established in 1994 by Twentieth Century Fox. Both movies were explicitly marketed as products of the indie phenomenon, and both tap into audience niches characterized by resistance to the clichés, predictability, and ideological conservatism of the blockbusters and other big studio fare. Yet, although the three mainstream movies included in the first two chapters manage to engage, in various ways, with contemporary urban discourses centered on the city of Los Angeles, these two art films, also very much LA films, connect more squarely with urban ideologies from the past, even if in renovated "cool" versions. The narrative of coolness is actually central to understanding what these two movies do with the city on-screen. From the perspective of the representations of Los Angeles, the discourses of mainstream and independence (Tzioumakis 2006) do not correspond to easy-to-predict ideological positions. Rather, texts need to be examined individually.

The content of this chapter reflects a dominant Angeleno discourse, both cinematic and extra-cinematic, that is more straightforward than that in the rest of the volume. As is suggested by the book title, one of the conclusions to be drawn from the study of films such as *(500) Days of Summer* and *Magnolia* is that fractures in the system remain close to the surface even in those texts that continue to harbor the fantasy of the Anglo city, because they perform the ideological operation of shoring up a social system and a discursive arena in which economic, political, and cultural power remains in the same hands. In terms of racial discourses and urban diversity, *Her* is not at all about the future but rather about the past and, to a large extent, the present. Ideologically, it can be taken as exemplary of most LA films. In imagining an all-white future for the city, it both reproduces a dominant racialized discourse and unconsciously reveals its inconsistencies and unsustainability.

Looking in the Wrong Direction

(500) Days of Summer can be read as an extended advertisement for gentrification, more specifically, the gentrification of LA's Downtown. In one brief shot from the movie we see the protagonists walking past some cheap-looking suitcases, part of the merchandise of the store that we see in the background. Tom (Joseph Gordon-Levitt) apologizes to his girlfriend Summer (Zooey Deschanel) for the drabness of the surroundings and asks her to look up at the fabulous modernist buildings instead. In this movie, this moment is the closest we get to the presence of non-Anglo characters. We might guess that this shop is on Broadway or in the nearby Garment District, that the people who work there may be Mexicans, and that its prospective customers, like most of the people walking those streets, are Mexicans too. But this is information that the movie chooses not to give us, potential figures in its narrative that it discards.

(500) Days was marketed as an offbeat indie romantic comedy, with a fragmented narrative that undercuts suspense—and anticipates an unhappy ending—and a central intimate relationship that does not work. In this it asks to be distinguished from other recent mainstream LA-based romcoms such as *Clueless* (Amy Heckerling, 1995), *I Love You, Man* (John Hamburg, 2009), and *No Strings Attached* (Ivan Reitman, 2011). In interviews, director Marc Webb and scriptwriter Scott Neustadter repeatedly explained that the script was based on the experience of rejection that Neustadter had had recently, a way to suggest that this story was closer to reality than more conventionally generic Hollywood fare (Neustadter 2009). A title card at the beginning of the movie reads, "Author's note: The following is a work of fiction. Any resemblance to any persons living or dead is purely coincidental. Especially you Jenny Beckman. Bitch." The kind of humor illustrated by this faux disclaimer is pervasive in the movie and is addressed at the 20-something demographic that constitutes the main target of the movie, as is the soundtrack.

As an adjunct to the movie, and ostensibly because Zooey Deschanel was upset about not appearing in the film's musical number, Webb and the young stars made a video featuring the song "Why Do You Let Me Stay Here?" by Deschanel's group She & Him, in which she and Gordon-Levitt perform the story of a bank heist as a dance number. The video was appropriately shot in an old bank building from LA's old financial district (see www.youtube.com/watch?v=rtVh8kVZ_XM). In a brief introduction, Deschanel invites the spectator to see the movie and uses her own "natural" appearance, her and her co-star's carefree dancing in the musical number, and the cinematic trope of the bank heist set in another Downtown modernist building to appeal to a specific audience. This is the same audience that will be amused by the web-video series *Ikea Heights*, which, apparently based on the movie's scene in an Ikea store, is included in a fan site dedicated to the movie (see www.500days.com/500-days-of-summer-blog.html). Here we can also find an interview by the blog's author with the director, links to an online contest for a prize of *(500) Days* goodie bags, announcements of the DVD and Blu-ray releases, and so on. The movie's posters feature the two young stars and the naïf drawings that the film uses to introduce new scenes to appeal to the same constituency. In general, marketing strategies and tie-ins exploited the indie credentials of Deschanel and Gordon-Levitt and, crucially, placed them in a cinematic Downtown that would have been immediately recognizable and seemingly appealing as a place to live to young, trendy, relatively wealthy young Angelenos. Coincidentally, the area was then in the process of being massively renovated, with developers hoping to attract relatively wealthy young professionals like the characters in the film. For this purpose, the movie needs to frame the area selectively and carefully. *Los Angeles Times* architecture critic Christopher Hawthorne points out how the movie looks like "an architectural guidebook come to celluloid life" in which anything that was built after 1950—that is, all of the new Financial District and Civic Center for starters—has been erased (2009, n.p.). These are important erasures and are in accordance with the movie's discursive framework, but they are not the only ones.

With its rapid development and redevelopment and its massive and often impersonal office buildings, Downtown LA represents the prototypical contemporary city. Many of the superlatives used to define it as the megalopolis of the future and the quintessential global city are visually linked to Downtown's impressive skyline and the unstoppable power with which it grew seemingly out of nothing in only a few decades. The long and slim skyscrapers, in their majesty and arrogance, stand for the absolute dominance of the new economy and also for the inhumanity of its corporate practices. For urban theorist Richard Sennett, modern capitalism is characterized by the dialectic between flexibility and indifference. Flexibility in labor relations brings about a great deal of standardization in corporations, and this applies to the buildings where people work. Modern capitalism creates "impermanent residents." The workplace must be in no way memorable for people to pass through these spaces with minimum emotional investment. This in turn creates a sort of indifference about physical space: We work here just as well as we could be working elsewhere. The paradox is therefore that a flexible social world produces social relations of indifference (Sennett 2002, 45–47).

Alongside its picture postcard quality, LA's Downtown carries with it this feeling of indifference and impermanence; the new Financial District replaced the old one some decades ago. Extraordinary modernist buildings, holding company headquarters, banks, offices, restaurants, shops, and cinemas were summarily superseded by even more impressive buildings (at least in terms of size) holding the new hub of financial power, expensive hotels, cultural centers, sports complexes, and a proliferation of parking lots. The historical lesson seems to be that these new wonders of contemporary architecture might also one day be emptied of their functions and replaced by even more impressive constructions elsewhere. This development makes perfect sense within the policies of the new capitalism, a system that offers people working spaces whose impersonality and impermanence deprive them of any sentimental ties.

At first sight, *(500) Days* has a different story to tell. Tom and Summer meet at their workplace, a greeting card company in Downtown LA. Because this is a romantic comedy and its world is a magic world, human relationships here are much warmer than Sennett suggests: Not only do Tom and Summer become intimately involved, but one of Tom's best friends also works at the same company, and Tom has friendly relationships with the rest of his co-workers, including his boss. Seeking to allay some of the anxieties of modern capitalist culture, the film counteracts the indifference inherent in a job that is seen as socially insignificant and that the protagonist dislikes (although he is good at it) with deep feelings and significant emotional and friendly ties. The filmmakers take the city of alienation and dystopia, one that fits like a glove the capitalist relationships of indifference theorized by Sennett, and magically transforms it for the benefit of the trendy but still wish-fulfillment-needing avid spectator.

This transformation is not arbitrary or gratuitous. The building blocks of the fantasy are real enough; some of the aesthetic discourses emanating from the film are linked to urban and social discourses surrounding the past and present of LA's Downtown; and traces of Sennett's alienation and indifference remain in the movie. Rather than a simple escapist fantasy, *(500) Days* is firmly grounded in social and urban realities and reveals, buried under its light surface, the tensions and struggles that have attended the formation of the city's central district. Instead of erasing the indifference of modern capitalism, the movie celebrates it by integrating it into its romantic discourse while at the same time relating it to specific aspects of the city's development. Not simply an LA of the imagination, "where all things are possible with the craft of Hollywood set designers" (Bates 2011, 18), *(500) Days* gives us an admittedly highly mediated but socially significant version of the contemporary global city. The global city is not only the sum total of its people, buildings, streets, and squares but also the sum total of the discourses that it generates. In Henri Lefebvre's (1991) terms, it is not just a real place; it is a social space, one that is woven with the threads of many narratives, including movies. In some of those narratives, like *(500) Days*, we catch glimpses of the overall structure.

In the first half of the twentieth century, Downtown LA had a quite different appearance from what the visitor sees today. Starting in the first decade of the century, a lively financial district developed along the Broadway-Spring corridor. Spring Street witnessed the mushrooming of numerous banks and office buildings, including the Los Angeles Stock Exchange, as well as hotels and restaurants, and Broadway boasted, among other amenities, a string of state-of-the-art movie theaters, where Hollywood movies were regularly premiered in glamorous surroundings. The most prestigious architects were hired to design the buildings, and quick business development turned the district into a bustling area, surrounded by popular residential districts such as Bunker Hill, Court Hill, Footmore Hill, and Boyle Heights, mostly working-class neighborhoods. The area soon acquired the appearance of the center of a big city. Photographs of Downtown streets in the early decades of the twentieth century attest to the vitality and ebullience of the then booming metropolis.

This period coincided with the consolidation of the movie industry in Hollywood to the extent that our filmic memories of cities in black and white are more

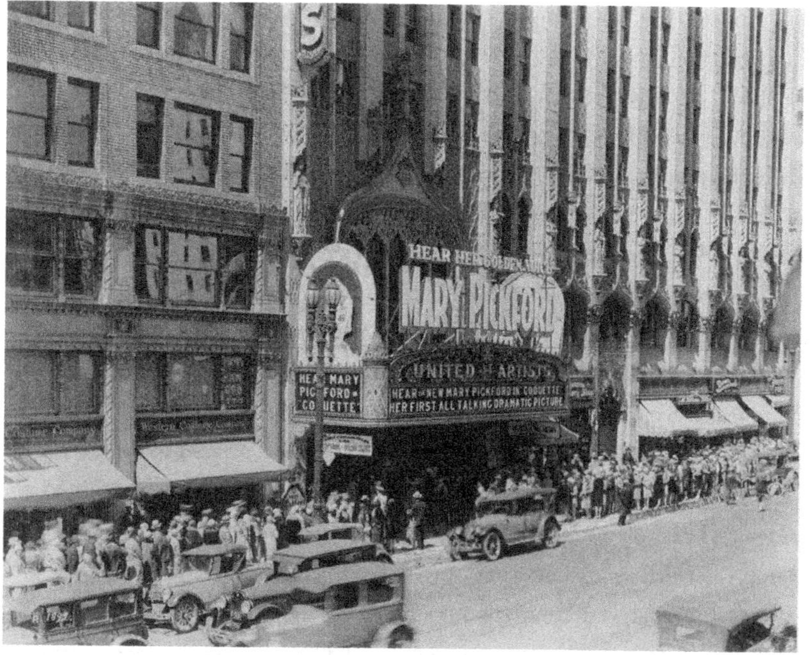

The glamour of the silver screen in the old Broadway: the United Artists Theater.

likely than not to come from movies shot in LA. It became "everyone's other city," a city in which the fictitious and the real "interweave tightly" (Braudy 2010, 271, 277). LA was a familiar feature of movie screens even though the city did not figure as itself in the narrative. Many of these locations were in fact in the Downtown area. Given the cultural centrality of the modern city in this period of history and its eventual transformation into the global city of today, it is a great paradox that those images are now little more than ghosts, images without a referent, traces of a place that is no more. Downtown was once the center of a city that has since become a city with no center.

Some of these ghosts date back to the Golden Age of silent movies. Harold Lloyd's films of the 1920s, for example, once and again reveal the comedian's fondness for central Los Angeles. Several of these movies were shot in the Downtown area and are at least partly about it. One of the most popular instances, *Safety Last* (Harold Lloyd [and Fred Newmeyer and Sam Taylor], 1923), climaxes in the famous scene in which Harold climbs to the top of a building as part of a publicity stunt for the department store where he works. Shot in several real buildings, the busy street that we can often see from Harold's precarious standpoint is none other than Broadway, and the busy crowds going about their business are LA citizens of the 1920s. Like many comedies of the decade, *Safety Last* draws its humor from the confrontation between the traditional amenities and boredom of the country, where the protagonist comes from, and the exciting and threatening city life that he plunges into in search of a better future. Downtown LA offers thrills and stimulations aplenty, and the spectator, perhaps unconsciously, revels in the exhilarating urban background as much as in Harold's comic antics. Shot in the same area, the earlier *Never Weaken* (1921) has Harold inadvertently lifted from his office by a "flying beam" from a nearby construction site. The character is predictably only interested in avoiding the fatal fall, but the spectator can simultaneously enjoy the generous views of the busy streets underneath. *Girl Shy* (Harold Lloyd [and Fred Newmeyer and Sam Taylor], 1924) tells the story of a country boy who has to go into the big city to prevent his sweetheart from marrying another man. As he races against the clock in various types of vehicles, he moves from the country to the city center through various neighborhoods, recording the variety of Los Angeles in the 1920s and its contagious energy. As much an illustration of the comedian's star persona, the movie, like *Safety Last*, becomes a celebration of his beloved city, as characteristic of the cinematic representation of the modernist metropolis as more famous texts, such as *Sunrise: A Song of Two Humans* (F. W. Murnau, 1927), *Berlin: Die Sinfonie der Grosstadt* (Walter Ruttmann, 1927), *Man with a Movie Camera* (Dziga Vertov, 1929), and the avant-garde short *Manhatta* (Charles Sheeler and Paul Strand, 1921). In Lloyd's films, as in many others, we experience the cinematic city as complex, infinitely enticing, and whole.

As seen in Chapter 3, the dream of the modernist city fell into decadence in the 1930s and 1940s, and another Hollywood cycle, film noir, came to replace it with nightmarish images of dark streets and threatening neighborhoods. These became the visual equivalent of the social alienation and malaise of the war and postwar years. Downtown and, particularly, Bunker Hill, the group of Victorian houses on a steep hill, subsequently subdivided to offer affordable housing for multiethnic working- and lower-middle-class Angelenos and immigrants, provided the real location for many of these stories, with the famous Angels Flight funicular railway becoming a familiar sight in movies such as *Act of Violence* (Fred Zinnemann, 1948), *Criss Cross* (Robert Siodmak, 1949), and *Kiss Me Deadly* (Robert Aldrich, 1955).

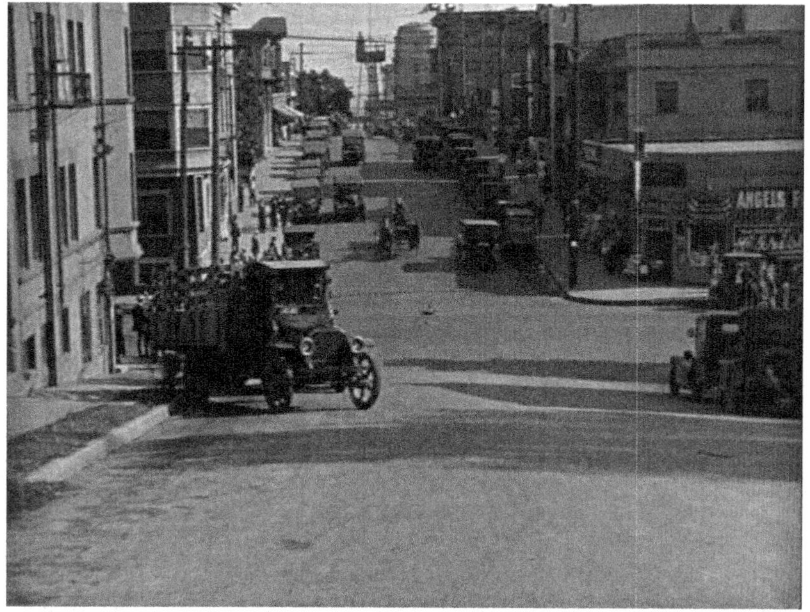

Girl Shy: Harold Lloyd and the ghosts of the old Downtown and Bunker Hill (a sign on a shop on the right reads "Angels Flight").

Angels Flight is one of the few vestiges left of the old Bunker Hill, even though not in its original location. Following a familiar pattern in the history of the city, the whole neighborhood was flattened to build the new Financial District, in what became one of the boldest and most controversial redevelopment operations ever witnessed by Angelenos. In a matter of relatively few years, high skyscrapers replaced the old Victorian houses and came to shape the familiar skyline of today's city. The successors of the modernist buildings on Spring and Broadway were enormous glass structures for banks, financial companies, and multinational business concerns, along with high-culture and religious centers such as the Music Center, the Museum of Contemporary Art, Frank Gehry's Disney Hall, and Rafael Moneo's new Catholic Cathedral. This major redevelopment, which gathered pace during the term of Tom Bradley, the first African American mayor of LA, did not just all but erase the recent past but was part of a typically Angeleno racialized discourse. As Scott Kurashige suggests, and as with the equally spectacular destruction of the relatively close Chávez Ravine, the replacement of the old Bunker Hill was inflicted in the name of urban renewal but in reality was undertaken to get rid of predominantly non-Anglo neighborhoods (2010, 66).

In the meantime, the neighboring Broadway-Spring area—the old financial district—went into decline, as city officials and real estate businesses literally abandoned the once thriving business center, leaving the beautiful old buildings in place but emptying them of their use. Mike Davis explains how property values in the old Broadway plummeted as the area's centrality for public transport made it less attractive to home owners and, particularly, as the African American and Mexican poor coming from South Central and East LA "invaded" its streets. According to Davis, what amounted to "the confiscation of the vital life activity of the center" had a double goal: "to raze all association with Downtown's past and to prevent any articulation with the non-Anglo urbanity of its future" (2006, 229). The orography of the area helped the separation, with Hill Street as a "local Berlin Wall," physically dividing the luxury and affluence of the new Bunker Hill from the ethnic bustle of Broadway, now reclaimed by Latino immigrants, at the bottom. This is how Davis explains the ideological underpinnings of the new center (writing for the first edition of *City of Quartz*): "Although a few white-collars venture into the Grand Central Market—a popular emporium of tropical produce and fresh foods—Latino shoppers or Saturday strollers never circulate in the Gucci precincts above Hill Street. The occasional appearance of a destitute street nomad in Broadway Plaza or in front of the Museum of Contemporary Art sets off quite a panic; video cameras turn on their mounts and security guards adjust their belts" (231).

The self-containment of the new Financial District, which Davis calls "a single, demonically self-referential hyperstructure" (2006, 229), is also discussed at length by Christopher Hawthorne (2010). For him, the new Bunker Hill is closed in to the undesirable life and bustle outside and at the bottom of the hill, and the very architecture of its buildings and multimillion dollar complexes is directed inward, ignoring or fortifying itself against the street. Walking in the mostly empty streets underneath the tall towers continues to be a peripheral, even unreasonable activity. An example of this is the Cathedral of Our Lady of the Angels, a building full of wonders inside but practically invisible to the pedestrian walking on the street outside (Hawthorne 2010, 486). For Hawthorne, the city's historical reliance on private urban development has shaped its structure: "It is either going to be a parking garage, ungainly and expedient and meant to be temporary, or it is going to be a gleaming collection of buildings designed by the most famous architect in the world. In that sense it is a direct reflection of the way the city's power brokers have

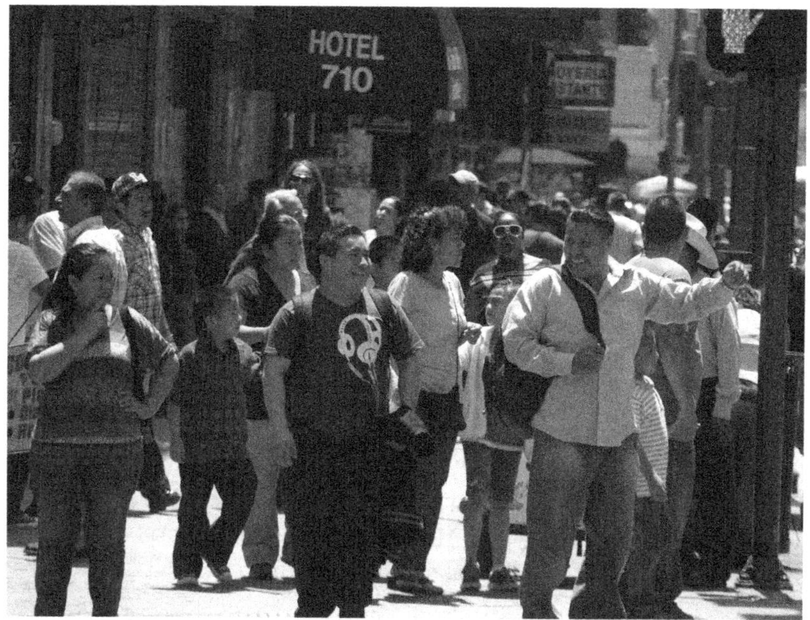

Broadway today.

long envisioned Downtown" (484). Giving private developers free rein is, for him, "a recipe for isolated monuments, for an architecture that can hardly be bothered to speak to its surroundings, let alone coalesce into anything resembling an authentic neighborhood" (492). Voicing his disappointment with Mayor Antonio Villaraigosa, Davis is less detached, bitterly attacking a policy that "promotes super-cathedrals, billionaire sports franchises, mega-museums, yuppie lofts, and drunken Frank Gehry skyscrapers at the expense of social justice and affordable housing." For Davis, this is "an evil plan to expel the majority of homeless from Downtown, in order to satisfy the greed of landowners and gentrifiers" (2006, ix).

At the same time, gentrification, a process that started in European capitals in the 1960s and spread throughout cities in the West and more recently in developing countries, reached the old Downtown area. Gentrification has come to complement the relocation of the Financial District to Bunker Hill; in recent years, the abandoned modernist buildings of the old Downtown have started to be renovated to attract new middle-class owners belonging to the managerial and professional class, artists, and intellectuals, thus pushing the poor and immigrants farther south into South Central and across the dried-up course of the Los Angeles River into East

LA. Jeremy Seabrook explains that cities are dissolving into bourgeois sites rebuilt entirely for the beneficiaries of globalization, who recolonize en masse their urban historic centers (2008, 26). Following this trend, the Broadway-Spring area, after having been taken over by the ethnic minorities and abandoned by the business elites, is now being recolonized by the middle classes, refilled where it had been emptied out. Hawthorne calculated the number of inhabitants of the district at the end of the 2000s at 39,000, modest if we think of the 100,000 people living there in the 1940s but a threefold increase with respect to the 1990s and part of what he calls a "well-chronicled rebirth of Downtown as a residential neighborhood" (2010, 482).

Yet there is a distance between the projected redevelopments and the stubborn reality. The authorities and the developers want the "undesirables" to go, but the residents have a way of refusing to move, or of returning. Mexicans continue to dominate the geography of Broadway and some of the adjacent streets. Skid Row occupies the space east of the main avenues, between approximately 3rd and 7th Streets and Alameda and Main, with 5th Street, "the Nickel," as its main artery. Skid Row is the home of the homeless, one of the most deprived neighborhoods in the whole country, yet it is across the street from the Arts District, where the new elites have been slowly moving. Next door, the Fashion District, called *los callejones* by Mexicans, is the shopping paradise of the poorer immigrant classes, with its numerous bargain stores owned by Iranians and Armenians. These are interspersed with some apparently empty buildings that house sweatshops, where undocumented Latina women, *costureras*, make clothes for paltry salaries, as though they were working in the maquiladoras south of the border. It is difficult to predict what the area will look like in five or ten years and to what extent gentrification will push all of these people and all of this variety away, but for the moment the various blocks of the urban plan have not come together properly; interferences from real life and shortcomings of the plan have delayed the desired result, with the most heterogeneous human assortment replacing for the moment the planned middle-class purity.

As we saw in Chapter 2, films may be quick to reflect some social developments and historical crises, but they are rarely receptive to such specific details of a city's history as those mentioned in this chapter. The social complexity and volatility of Downtown Los Angeles has seldom featured on-screen. In contemporary films Downtown is mostly seen from the outside, as a skyline serving as an easily recognizable index of the city, an obvious hook to help sell the city as a tourist destination and a corporate haven. From the outside, often seen at sunset or in the haze, the accumulation of skyscrapers looks not only imposing and majestic but also homogeneous, thick with the promise of humming life inside, the attractive container of a social wonder, and quite different from the dispersion, contradictions, and tensions that meet the eye of the visitor who ventures onto its streets. Hawthorne's vivid descriptions of the frustrations attending the pedestrian trying to stroll around Downtown and finding empty sidewalks and actively hostile environments, even in projects designed for community gathering and exchange (2010, 491–92), cannot be perceived from the outside in photographs, posters, commercials, or movies.

At first sight, *(500) Days of Summer* is one of several movies that attempt to fill this deficit of cinematic images of contemporary Downtown. Yet the plan seems to be to go inside the city center and reconstruct it to resemble the more familiar external view. The film does not show the architectural chaos that dominates the area, the ominously empty streets, the abandoned buildings, the half-completed gentrification, Skid Row, or the *callejones*. Inside the characters' workplaces the rooms are airy and friendly, and we often see evidence of the building's modernist past, now renovated for a business that is customer-friendly and small-scale enough to allay any fears of all-consuming capitalism; the nightmare of indifference of Sennett's modern capitalism, therefore, is turned into an attractive romantic space for the spectator. The two protagonists' apartments also look like the result of renovations of old dwellings and are often suffused in the warm colors of romantic comedy. It cannot be said that the movie is particularly interested in the streets of Downtown, and so we get only a minimum number of exterior locations. Yet the inclusion of these few locations within a coherent narrative invites us to construct an imaginary space, filling in the dots, as it were, and conferring a homogeneity that, stimulated by textual rhetoric, exists only in our minds.

At the heart of this homogenizing construction is Angelus Plaza, Tom's favorite spot in town—a location to which the film returns at several important moments and one that is also central to the story's uncertain denouement. In his spare time, Tom sits on the slope of this small park and looks at the cityscape unfolding before his eyes, admiring its beauty and harmony. To him and, by extension, to the movie, this is a magic space, one filled with immense possibility and the promise of a better, more human city. This location is threaded into the narrative and closely linked to

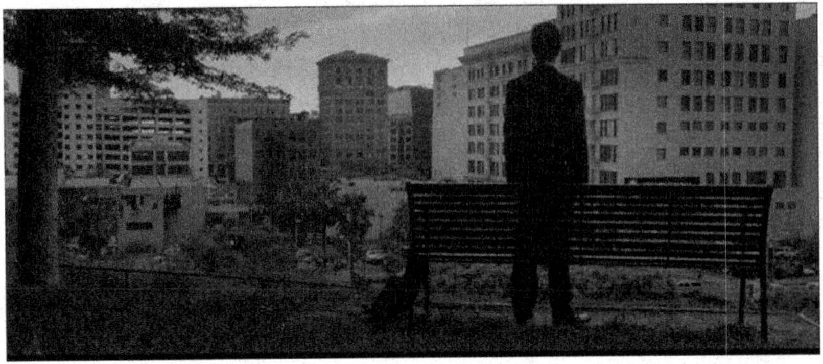

(500) Days of Summer: Tom's loving gaze at an empty city.

the hero's sentimental education, encapsulating the rocky process of his maturing gaze. Simultaneously, it stands synecdochically for the film's view of Downtown, a peaceful group of heterogeneous buildings that, oddly, make up a harmonious whole and display no tensions and, on the downside, no humanity. It is Tom's professional gaze and his love of the place that makes it all jell. In this case the process of transformation of a real place into a filmic one is both complex and significant.

The real location of this spot is Angels Knoll, a small park precariously perched above Hill Street and running alongside 4th Street, the steep road that at this point connects the old Downtown with the new. Sitting on its benches, we look east toward Broadway, Spring Street, and beyond, with the Continental Building dominating the picture. The Continental is a 1903 modernist building in the old financial district on Spring Street. Next to Angelus Knoll, on the other side, is the Angels Flight funicular, one of the most famous places and objects of tourist attraction in this part of town and also one with a long filmic history. Angels Flight runs parallel to 4th Street on the other side of Angels Knoll and connects the gallery of cafés and restaurants at Two California Plaza, one of the signature skyscrapers of the new Bunker Hill, with the Grand Central Market, across Hill Street from its bottom station. The Grand Central Market, built in 1897, is the liveliest food hall in the Downtown area, offering mostly Latino fare to a vast majority of Mexican shoppers. Renovated in the 1990s, it also attracts many tourists to its busy stalls and cafés (Hayden 1995, 118). With its vibrancy and ethnic color, it remains one of the important landmarks of the area. Further north along Hill Street is the real Angelus Plaza, a complex of five high-rise blocks housing a residence for senior citizens.

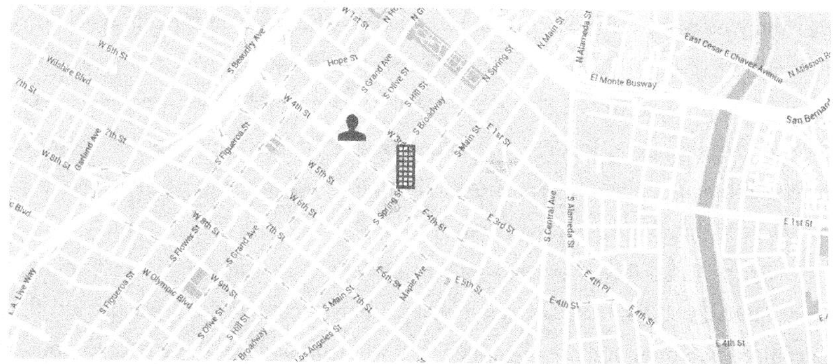

Map 3. From Angelus Plaza/Angels Knoll to the Continental Building: erasing Downtown in *(500) Days of Summer*. Map by Francesc Terrades.

Angels Knoll, like the funicular next to it, has an important symbolic function in the urban geography of the area, sitting literally on the border between the old and the new financial districts, looking down on Broadway and the old financial district and placed at the base of the imposing Two California Plaza skyscraper. It is an example of what Mike Davis calls "the third border," those invisible lines that mark areas of marginalization within the metropolis (2000, 71). The relaxed atmosphere of the place suggests the possibility of interaction and exchange between the two worlds; but the steep street that needs to be climbed to have access to its entrance represents the natural barrier that Hawthorne mentions as separating two different realities. Sitting on Tom's bench, we can embrace both sides of Downtown at the same time, but we are keenly aware of the difficulty in moving from one to the other, both symbolically and physically. In more general terms, the small park is only one of many spots in the area where internal borders can be felt between diverse social groups: the extremely wealthy financial bankers and the dejected homeless, the trendy intellectuals and middle-class loft dwellers and the undocumented immigrants, the inhabitants of the shrunken Little Tokyo and those of the new Chinatown (the old Chinatown was also moved to make room for the railway station, Union Station).

In Downtown LA moving freely from one spot to another is, for many of the people who walk its streets, much easier in theory than in practice. Take Angels Flight. Given the modest price of the ride, it is relatively easy to find various sorts of people riding the funicular as entertainment, but it is much rarer to see it being used as a way to travel the short distance from its bottom to its top, and vice versa. There are simply no reasons for the middle-class people who frequent the top to visit the bottom, and, given the prices charged at the establishments in Two California Plaza, it would be unusual to see one of the inhabitants of the bottom—mostly working-class Mexicans, undocumented migrants, and homeless people—go beyond the end of the funicular. There are no physical barriers to stop these pedestrians, but Davis's third borders are not so easy to cross.

Or take Skid Row, not far from Angels Flight. Around the corner from 5th Street on Main Street, there is a diner called The Nickel, not expensive and mostly patronized by young middle-class men and women. None of these people would be seen in the "real" Nickel, in Skid Row, going down the gentle slope that, on 5th Street, separates Main from the ironically named Wall Street, the home of the homeless, yet it is literally around the corner. Conversely, few of the inhabitants of Skid Row make it west beyond Main Street, even though there is apparently no obstacle to stop them. Around this area, Main Street is another third border, a spontaneous line of social exclusion. To sum up, Downtown reproduces in a relatively small space the social geography of the huge city: Los Angeles as a city of limitless social and ethnic diversity but not necessarily social mixture.

In the move from the world described here to the screen, a number of things have happened in the Angelus Plaza scenes of *(500) Days*. First, Angels Knoll, the park where the scenes were shot, is renamed Angelus Plaza, acquiring the name of the nearby towers. Second, Angels Flight is not visible, even though it is only a few meters away from where we see Tom sitting. Third, when Tom looks down, the framing avoids showing Grand Central Market, even though we can make out a corner of the building on the bottom left of the frame. Fourth, there is little awareness of the skyscrapers above Tom, as though that part of reality does not exist in the film's Downtown. As Hawthorne points out, these post-1950 skyscrapers and architectural wonders hold no interest for the filmmakers (2009). Finally, despite the activity at the bottom of the hill in real life, both outside the market and in the nearby establishments along Hill Street, in the film the framing is practically empty of people and cars, almost looking like a photo of a model of the buildings rather than the real buildings. With all these changes, Angels Knoll, or "Angelus Plaza," appears isolated from its surroundings, aware of neither the history of Bunker Hill where it stands, as embodied in Angels Flight, nor its present, as represented by Two California Plaza; the film is more interested in buildings than in people and actively avoids Grand Central Market and its ethnic Mexican connotations.

What is shown on the screen is a heterogeneous mixture of old and new buildings and a huge car park, all unified by Tom's loving gaze and dominated by the beautiful figure of the Continental Building in the middle of the framing. For the film the exact location of Angelus Plaza, fraught as it is with history and ideological and urban discourses, is not as relevant as the fact that it constitutes an ideal vantage point from which to contemplate the beauty of the old financial district, now gentrified as part of the "recuperation" of the old center. Everything "superfluous" has been excised. The shot of the suitcases appears three times in the film, the last two as part of Tom's memories of his affair with Summer. The first time the suitcases appear is the first shot of the sequence in which Tom shows Summer a selection of the most remarkable buildings in the old financial district. Tom is not interested in the street level, as we hear him explain in voice-over, and asks his girlfriend to look up. He prefers the tops of the buildings, with their beautiful decorations. In the Angelus Plaza sequences the movie is not interested in the street level either. This Downtown contrasts vividly with the external shots of the skyline that other films have used as shorthand for LA, but it has one thing in common with them: Although different, it is still the city as architecture, not people—unlived urban design.

By linking Tom, Summer, and his middle-class and professional but cool and easygoing friends with the old buildings, *(500) Days* becomes an animated advertising prospectus for gentrification, partly addressed to the Angelenos who were targeted in the marketing campaign. There is no reference to the destruction of the old neighborhood of Bunker Hill, no hint of the more aggressive aspects of the new economy as embodied by the state-of-the-art buildings on the top of the hill (surprisingly for an architect), and no acknowledgment of the homeless on Skid Row or of the Mexican immigrant culture than pervades the street level of Broadway and that would be immediately accessible to Tom if only he thought of looking down at the Grand Central Market.

There is no reason why the filmmakers should incorporate these aspects of the area either. Erasures, displacements, and transformations of the type described here appear in all films and cultural texts. As I argued in the Introduction, it is not my aim to suggest that *(500) Days*, unlike, say, *White Men Can't Jump* or *Collateral*, fails to capture the real city, in this case, the real Downtown. In fact, the movie powerfully reproduces an important part of Downtown, one that is concomitant with dominant discourses, especially with those promoting gentrification. This is another Lefebvrian symbolic appropriation of space, one that is true to certain views of the city and, in that sense, is based on powerful realities. At the same time, however, moving from Lefebvre to de Certeau, the rest of the area, rather than disappearing, remains in place, lurking under the surface and waiting to be unearthed by the viewer who may recognize the discourses at work and therefore the experiences they leave out. In promoting one particular view of the city, *(500) Days*, like other films, also reveals other, contesting views.

The actual Downtown displays the contradictions of competing discourses and heterogeneous urban development plans. The silence and motionlessness that dominate Tom's ideal urban design both correspond and do not correspond to the impression that visitors receive if they choose to wander around the area. Walking in the Bunker Hill financial district around the time the movie was made, particularly outside office hours and on weekends, is like walking in a ghost town: no people in the streets, no restaurants or cafeterias open, not even many cars in the eminently drivable roads. Broadway, on the other hand, and other parts of the old Downtown are always bustling with activity. If we walk a little farther north, to the site of the old pueblo of Los Angeles, particularly on weekends and special festivity days, the concentration of people around the touristic Olvera Street and the Church of Our Lady Queen of the Angels, the old church erected in 1822 and still going strong, is extraordinary, even more remarkable if we contrast it with the emptiness of Temple Street and Grand Avenue, around the new Catholic cathedral. These are all Downtown experiences that are not seen in *(500) Days* but gather at the edges of the screen. The shot of the suitcases is a small symptom of this massive offscreen space. It is a reminder that there is more to Downtown than the film has chosen to reveal and becomes an index of its conscious repressions, not there to show anything but rather to point at what is purposefully not being shown.

As mentioned earlier, among the ignored locations is the Grand Central Market. Its absence in the Angelus Plaza scenes becomes even more remarkable at the end of the film. Once Tom has realized that Summer is not coming back to him, he decides to make a change in his life, leave his job, and pursue his career as an architect. In the final scene we see him attending an interview at an architects' studio, and there he meets another interviewee and potential rival for the job, Autumn (Minka Kelly). The fact that Angelus Plaza is also *her* favorite spot and that she had noticed him there before suggests a compatibility that opens the door for a tentative happy ending. Angelus Plaza had all the makings of the magic space of romantic comedy, but Tom was literally looking in the wrong direction. With Autumn the distinctive new space in which the two characters meet also acquires those positive connotations.

This scene was shot at the Bradbury Building, another well-known and immediately recognizable building in the Downtown area, completed in 1893 and adding to the other buildings of the old financial district that have been incorporated into the area's gentrification plans. For a film that, in a typically postmodern fashion, displays a wide knowledge of the history of cinema, it is quite fitting that it should end at this location. The Bradbury Building has a long history of appearances in Hollywood movies, particularly in thrillers and film noirs, from classic instances of the genre such as *The Unfaithful* (Vincent Sherman, 1947), *Shockproof* (Douglas Sirk, 1949), *D.O.A.* (Rudolph Maté, 1950), and *M* (Joseph Losey, 1951) to *Chinatown* (Roman Polanski, 1974), *Wolf* (Mike Nichols, 1994), *Blade Runner* (Ridley Scott, 1982), and *The Artist* (Michel Hazanavicius, 2011). Ridley Scott's neo-noir science fiction film contributed in large measure to the common view of Los Angeles as a dystopia of the future, embodying the idea of contemporary urban alienation, and the Bradbury Building's conspicuous presence became an integral part of it. *(500) Days of Summer* proves particularly adept at erasing the dark connotations of this site as a film location and at transforming a previously threatening space into a friendly one, substituting harmony, beauty, and hope for its earlier meanings.

But there is another interesting fact about the real Bradbury Building, and that is its exact geographic location, on Broadway, across the street from the Grand Central Market. Emotionally, Tom has moved a long way, but physically he is barely five minutes away from his favorite place. The Bradbury Building is almost visible from Angels Knoll. The quickest way from one to the other is by crossing Hill Street from the bottom of Angels Flight and then walking through the market. This spot, however, remains outside the frame, its absence even more conspicuous in the final moments. It could be argued that the very visibility of the Bradbury Building in this final part of the film immediately conjures up certain meanings for those who know where it is situated. However, within the text those meanings are absent; in the text the Bradbury is just another beautiful modernist building, one with rich cinematic connotations. Much more striking than Tom and Summer's previous workplace, it automatically becomes part of the movie's spatial scheme, perfectly congruent with the construction of a still mostly empty modernist Downtown, free of history and free of some of its more important contemporary meanings.

Mark Shiel argues that early Los Angeles films have the ability to act as traces of times and places long since erased, but the films at the time sought to erase traces of previous societies (2012, 18). This operation is still being performed by contemporary movies. When looking at such films as *Safety Last!* or *Girl Shy*, we may mourn the passing of an era in which Downtown was dynamic and forward-looking in social terms, characterized by lively boulevards with abundant traffic, sidewalks full of people, busy trams, and glamorous cinema palaces. Given the deterioration and decay of Downtown in subsequent decades, Lloyd's films trigger nostalgia for the past. *(500) Days of Summer* is a postdecay film, congruent with an urban-political-ideological attempt to recuperate Downtown through its traces of the past—the modernist buildings on Spring Street—but this exercise in nostalgia is also politically fraught because it seeks to remove the exceptionally varied and in its own way vibrant Downtown of today. This is an operation aimed at erasing poverty, the *callejones*, sweatshops, the Nickel, even the new tourist-oriented Chinatown and Olvera Street, Little Tokyo, and the masses of brown people that populate many of its streets. What is left from this disturbing agglomeration is some briefly glimpsed cheap suitcases.

In its confluence with the views of the gentrifiers, Webb's movie suggests what portions of Downtown Los Angeles should be preserved, which ones should be renovated, and which ones are expendable, an operation that echoes the work of the Los Angeles Conservancy, which boasts on its webpage a list of the historic buildings, with its own social and political connotations, that it has targeted for protection (including the signature Norm's La Cienega restaurant) (see www.laconservancy.org/). These are all ideological operations, which, in the case of *(500) Days*, are congruent with an all-Anglo view of the city and therefore, in spite of its indie credentials, with a long history of heavily racialized mainstream representations. At this point, the indie romantic comedy becomes indistinguishable from the fashionable dystopia of *Her*.

A more specific historical change, which occurred after *(500) Days* was released, has made the movie even more fantastic in its articulation of the social and geographic space of Downtown LA. The bench in Angels Knoll from which the movie constructs, through Tom's loving gaze, its vision of an ideal (and ideally gentrified) Downtown is not accessible anymore. Because of budgetary cutbacks, Angels Knoll was closed in 2013, with no foreseeable date for reopening (Ginsberg and Baum 2013). Given that Tom's perspective is indispensable to understanding the filmic space and that this space is based on a careful use of framing to leave out those aspects of the area that would contradict the textual view, it can be argued that without access to this vantage point, *(500) Days*' Downtown vanishes into thin air . . . except in the movie, which remains an important document of urban discourse.

Down in the Valley

The San Fernando Valley, situated north of the Santa Monica Hills, has long been part of the Los Angeles metropolitan area, most of it administratively belonging to the city but also including incorporated cities such as Burbank, Glendale, and San Fernando. Its history over the last century or so has been tied to that of the metropolis, but it has also developed its own particularities and urban (or suburban) personality. Given that Hollywood straddles the Hills and that, since their settlement in Southern California, film companies have often resided in the Valley, it is not surprising that it has regularly featured in LA films. This situation remains unchanged today, with Burbank, Studio City, and North Hollywood, all in the Valley, being important centers of the industry in the twenty-first century. Apart from films specifically set in the Valley, such as *Fast Times at Ridgemont High* (Amy Heckerling, 1982), *Valley Girl* (Martha Coolidge, 1983), *2 Days in the Valley* (John Herzfeld, 1996), *Boogie Nights* (P. T. Anderson, 1997), *Things You Can Tell Just by Looking at Her* (Rodrigo García, 2000), and *Down in the Valley* (David Jacobson, 2005), many other LA films have featured the area prominently; among the most famous are *Chinatown* (Roman Polanski, 1974), *Earthquake* (Mark Robson, 1974), *La Bamba* (Luis Valdez, 1987), *Grand Canyon* (Lawrence Kasdan, 1991), *Short Cuts* (Robert Altman, 1993), *Pulp Fiction* (Quentin Tarantino, 1994), *Crash* (Paul Haggis, 2004), and *Valentine's Day* (Garry Marshall, 2010), but there is also a long list of lesser known movies.

Clueless (Amy Heckerling, 1995), one of the most popular LA comedies of the post–Rodney King period, can be more accurately labeled a Beverly Hills film. At one point in the plot, Cher (Alicia Silverstone) goes to a party in the Valley. On her way back, she is abandoned by her ride and stranded in North Hollywood, where she feels out of her element. While she is calling for a taxi on her cell phone, she is assaulted and robbed by a man who then asks her to lie down and count to 100 to facilitate his escape. A hilarious dialogue ensues with Cher trying to explain to the thief that she cannot possibly lie on the ground because she is wearing an Alaïa dress, "like a totally important designer," to which the man, unreasonably, replies, "and I will totally shoot you in the head." In this movie a North Hollywood location is imagined by the teenage protagonist as hostile territory. Although only 10 miles away from her home, the Valley might as well be a different planet for her, full of danger and people with incomprehensible values.

This view of the Valley is not the dominant one, neither in urban discourses nor in the cinema, and is part of the movie's comic exaggeration in the construction of Cher's character. The earlier *Valley Girl*, a teen comedy from the 1980s, is more representative of meanings associated with the area. In it a group of middle-class Anglo teenagers from the Valley imagine Hollywood as a den of iniquity and the source of unspeakable dangers, and the boy from Hollywood, played by Nicolas Cage, is a threat to the peace and respectability of the Valley. Released the year after *Clueless*, *2 Days in the Valley* also constructs its space as a haven. One of the protagonists, Van Nuys policeman Alvin (Jeff Daniels), considers his neighborhood a "nice place to live" and does not want to see it corrupted with the social and urban practices of other parts of the metropolitan area. He targets a massage parlor employing undocumented Asian workers. This is the type of import from the other side of the Hills that he wants to keep away from his constituency. Despite the generic combination of crime movie and comedy, the Valley is mostly pictured in this movie as a succession of clean sunny streets and peaceful communities, with Mulholland Drive as the frontier with the undesirable metropolis. *2 Days in the Valley* offers a distinctive Valley atmosphere that openly contradicts the connotations of the place in Heckerling's *Clueless*.

However, the instability introduced by *Clueless* in the cinematic characterization of the Valley and replicated, to some extent, in the generic mixture of *2 Days* reflects the complexity of the social layering of the metropolis and the subtleties in the combinations of social class and ethnicity in contemporary Los Angeles. The

San Fernando Valley remained an agricultural region until the 1920s, when the city of Los Angeles spread north of the Santa Monica Hills and south to the Port of San Pedro as part of the consolidation of its sprawling, polycentric character (Soja and Scott 1996, 6). Attempts in the 1940s to rationalize the unstoppable thrust of real estate speculation came to nothing, and by the early 1960s the Valley had become "a paved-over 'undifferentiated slurb' of nearly one million people" (Davis 1996, 169) attracted by the presence of high-tech industrial developments and more competitive property prices. Starting in the 1950s, conservationist movements sprouted in parts of the Valley, led by those who wanted to keep the area as a relatively undisturbed suburban-rural environment and who opposed progress at all costs (Scott 1996, 281). Decades later, these concerns morphed into the so-called slow-growth movement, which, according to Davis, has entirely legitimate concerns, such as a declining environment, growing traffic, and continuing real estate development, but also displays unsavory racial and ethnic attitudes and open hostility toward young Latino and Asian people. Many of the slow-growth leaders also occupied key positions in the fight against school integration in the early 1970s (Davis 2006, vii–viii). Rodolfo Acuña goes so far as to describe the San Fernando Valley as the center of LA nativism and anti-immigrant hysteria (1996, 139).

The uneasy combination of slow growth and ethnic exclusivity that is at the bottom of the relatively subdued social tensions of recent years can be incorporated in relatively unthreatening ways into comedies, such as those mentioned earlier, while remaining safely hidden under the surface. Melodramas repress these meanings in more openly unsettling ways. *Safe* (Todd Haynes, 1995) is an independent melodrama with a feminist sensibility that embodies traditional Angeleno alienation in its female protagonist, affluent middle-class homemaker Carol White (Julianne Moore). Carol lives with her husband and stepson in a prosperous area of the Valley and seems to have it all: a big house, a Latina maid, friends, parties, and a comfortable life. Yet she starts being afflicted by a mysterious illness—nose bleeds, palpitations, seizures, dizziness, breathing difficulties—a condition that the text asks us to relate to the precariousness of her white feminine identity. Various areas of the Valley are featured prominently in the first part of the movie, including several shots of the freeways. No direct links are offered between Carol's symptoms and the place where she lives, but the movie chooses the San Fernando Valley rather than any other Southern California location as the space of its story of female alienation and beleaguered identity in a white middle-class milieu. At one point, Carol's stepson reads to his parents part of the essay he is writing for school: LA has become the gang capital of America, and more and more Chicano gangs are coming into the valleys and white areas of LA. Nothing is made of this supposed research and the spectator may soon forget this scene of everyday family life, but the moment might also remain in the mind, a hint of the social anxieties lurking beneath the story of patriarchal repression of female identity.

Safe can be seen as an immediate predecessor of *Magnolia*, a more ambitious melodrama of middle-class alienation set in the San Fernando Valley, both having in common the presence of Julianne Moore in protagonist parts. Like *Safe*, *Magnolia* was primarily marketed by its indie studio New Line Cinema as a film directed by P. T. Anderson, a young auteur. After achieving considerable critical success with his previous feature, *Boogie Nights* (1997), a fictionalized account of the adult movie and video industry in the Valley in the late 1970s and 1980s, Anderson was hailed as a promising indie writer-director, a label that has since been reinforced by the enthusiastic reception of his subsequent movies, particularly *There Will Be Blood* (2007), *The Master* (2012), and *Inherent Vice* (2014). Most reviews of *Magnolia* centered on its auteur as the target of both praise and occasional disapproval, as in the cases of Luke Thompson's "Not-So-Magnificent Anderson" (1999, 40) and Stephen Farber's "Their Reputation Precedes Them, Alas" (2000, 4). In any case, critics approached the movie—which was a relative box office flop with an estimated budget of $37 million and a lifetime gross in theaters of less than $23 million (according to the IMDb)—through reference to features characteristic of "serious" auteur cinema, particularly its complex narrative structure.

Associated with such labels as "smart film" (Sconce 2002), "the polyphonic film" (Bruns, 2008), "millennial film" (Lane 2011, 9), and others, the three-hour-long *Magnolia* was also seen as a concentrated and subversive TV soap opera about gender politics and, more specifically, the crisis of masculinity (Dillman 2010). Secondarily, critics also mentioned that Anderson is a native of the San Fernando Valley—like *Safe*'s director Haynes—as a way to underline the importance of the movie as a depiction of the area. Jeffrey Sconce, for instance, described *Boogie Nights* and *Magnolia* as "operatic odes to the San Fernando Valley" (2002, 350); David Denby titled his review of *Magnolia* "San Fernando Aria" (1999, 202); and Janet Maslin wrote about "an orchestrated symphony of LA stories" (1999, E15). These labels, like those mentioned earlier, point to the magnitude of the canvas of contemporary life attempted by Anderson and to its generic profile: *Magnolia* covers twenty-four hours in the interconnected stories of a group of Angelenos caught in a web of intense suffering, acute family conflict, and overwhelming alienation, one that is often described through such musical terms as *symphony*, *opera*, and *aria*.

The musical metaphors are particularly apt in a movie that is also seen as a musical, because both the instrumental score and the numerous songs, most of them performed by Aimée Mann, are central to the construction of conflict and character development and to the generation of intense affect (Lane 2011, 79). Mann's songs, nine in total, structure the film and play a prominent part in those scenes, central to the narrative, in which the text intertwines the story lines of its characters. Christina Lane goes so far as to assert that the singer shares with Anderson authorship of the movie (2011, 82). She also echoes James Hunter's insight that Mann's voice grounds the film geographically, capturing "the nerve endings of the city" (Hunter 2000, 115). With songs that reflect "the distressed soul of a great American city" (Olsen 2000, 27), *Magnolia* not only articulates a precise Angeleno geography but also describes the city through music. On the other hand, the centrality of music in both structural and thematic terms highlights the visibility of the melodramatic register used by the movie to construct interpersonal relationships—because the *melos* is a constitutive ingredient of the genre—resulting in a broad canvas of a contemporary city in the throes of acute and unresolved anxieties. Released six years after *Falling Down*, *Magnolia* conjures up a different array of cinematic, cultural, and industrial elements than the earlier film to paint a similarly pervasive millennial social and spiritual malaise. The small section of the San Fernando Valley where the action takes place serves as a microcosm of this near-apocalyptic worldview.

In a sense, the visibility of the score suggests a metaphorical struggle for authorship between Mann, Anderson the scriptwriter, whose presence can be felt particularly in the various montage sequences that punctuate the movie and highlight its climactic points, and Anderson the director, whose visual style is characterized, for example, by an extremely visible mobile camera. This mobile camera, like the montage sequences, links the characters and narrative threads and points to a looming, inchoate presence, alternately weighing down on the characters or providing them with a way out of their afflictions. This textual presence becomes almost visible at two moments: when the characters—or perhaps the actors momentarily abandoning the characters—start singing along with the extradiegetic voice of Mann performing the song "Wise Up" and when a biblical rain of frogs besets the characters and brings about a tentative dénouement to their acute emotional crises. It is almost inevitable to glimpse the movie's composite auteur behind these flourishes, but in a book on Los Angeles it is equally tempting to feel in them the presence of the city itself.

In contrast to the visual and aural mannerisms and the emotional roller coaster, the San Fernando Valley is pictured as a relatively peaceful, uneventful suburb of the metropolis, even though the persistent rain evokes the Angeleno streets of film noir. In the first sequence after the opening credits, it is still sunny in the Valley, but the harmony is almost immediately disrupted by Donnie (William H. Macy) crashing his car into a shop window, his psychological disturbance openly affecting urban equilibrium. Elsewhere in the narrative, the unsubstantiated menace of "the Worm," a criminal who prowls the streets of the Valley, committing murders, attacking policemen, maybe also kidnapping children, confers an atmosphere of constant threat and danger to the filmic space and constantly taunts the spectator with the possibility of an explanation for the uneasiness we are made to feel, an explanation that never materializes. This mysterious presence can be seen as a shadow cast on the movie by the classic cycle, embodying the sense of impending doom that cinema history has inherited from it.

Although most of the action takes place indoors—in houses, apartments, stores, and television studios—some of the real locations in the Valley are relatively familiar. They are all in an area 16 miles from east to west and 10 miles from north to south just over the Hollywood Hills from the Los Angeles basin, covering parts of North Hollywood, Burbank, and Reseda. Maybe disconcertingly, they construct a believable space for the relatively extreme and even fantastic proceedings (McFly 2013). Central among these locations is a road intersection between Laurel Canyon Boulevard and Victory Boulevard, near the Valley Plaza shopping center. The location first features, briefly, as a transitional shot between the "Wise Up" montage sequence and the next scene. Here it appears as a deserted rain-soaked spot that both evokes such film noirs as *Double Indemnity* and anticipates the movie's final section. The next time this intersection appears, it shows four of the protagonists—Donny, Rose (Melinda Dillon), Claudia (Melora Walters), and Jim Kurring (John C. Reilly)—crossing paths as they drive to their various destinations shortly before the frog rain. The text returns to it once more, shortly after, when the ambulance carrying Linda (Julianne Moore) capsizes during the supernatural event. In general, the location works as an index of the story's locatedness both in a cinematic LA and in a "real" suburban section of the city and as a symbol of intercrossing lives and therefore of interconnectedness between humans in the inhuman metropolis. Although they are not aware of each other's presence in the same spot, the common space strengthens the impression of linked identities.

Every time the film visits this location, the spectator can briefly read the street sign of the boulevard the cars cross as they drive from north to south or from south to north, seemingly along Laurel Canyon. Although the real street may well be Victory Boulevard, the sign we see reads "Magnolia," a parallel thoroughfare a few blocks further south and the street that gives the movie its title. The title suggests that the multifaceted action we are going to witness takes place specifically along this well-known boulevard. The title shot includes a magnolia flower opening its petals in time-lapse photography, with a flashing map in the background, probably of the San Fernando Valley. This approximately 12-second-long shot, constructed through a series of special effects, anticipates the overwrought formal style of the almost three hours to follow, but it also links the flower with the boulevard around which the story will take place. The superimposition of flashing map and blooming flower points to the structure of a narrative that gradually unfolds layer after layer to offer a symphony or a polyphony of characters and stories, all of them geographically grounded. As the shot progresses, the frame seemingly pushes in to an increasingly closer view of the flower until we feel as though we can see the veins in the petals, which are then made to coincide with the streets and avenues of the map, even as Mann's music evokes, as mentioned, the emotional nerves of the city. The later shot of the street intersection and the Magnolia sign can be seen as a "realistic" counterpart of this title shot, with the boulevard as the main artery through which the tortured life of the Valley runs.

For Angelenos, Magnolia Boulevard has specific connotations that are closely linked to the Valley as a whole, its relaxed atmosphere, and its connections with the film industry. It is the widest avenue that runs parallel to the Hills and the closest to Hollywood. Like many of the boulevards in the city, it crosses several different neighborhoods. In Burbank it runs past many of the studios, both majors and independents, including soundstages, postproduction facilities, and other industry buildings. West of North Hollywood, it becomes more residential, often with a visible Jewish imprint and home of the most affluent section of the Valley. Magnolia Boulevard features in songs, jokes, and other popular manifestations of local life. It is not only a synecdoche of the Valley but also, like other famous LA roads, a symbol of Angeleno identity. In the exopolis, the city with no center, these never-ending avenues, especially those running from east to west, stand for the thin thread that joins together human beings who otherwise have no link, the local signifier of social life and social interaction. Since at least *Sunset Boulevard*, Hollywood has taken advantage of the psychosocial meanings of its roads, and the years around the turn of the twenty-first century saw at least two other major films with evocative road names, both close to Magnolia: *Mulholland Drive* (David Lynch, 2001), which is the subject of Chapter 5, and *Laurel Canyon* (Lisa Cholodenko, 2002). *Magnolia* activates all these meanings simultaneously.

At the same time, there are differences among the boulevards: Magnolia is not exciting like Sunset, intriguing like Mulholland, or alternative like Laurel Canyon. It is peaceful and perhaps a little dull, a place where nothing much usually happens. The location of the road intersection in North Hollywood that features centrally in the film lends credibility to the industry associations of most of the characters—in general terms, we could say that they work east and live west of this intersection. More abstractly, it seems particularly apt that the movie's focus on suburban alienation should converge in the name of a famous avenue; like these names, it evokes a city in which human relationships are always precarious. Finally, the connotations of suburban bliss and/or monotony are ironically contradicted by a story that delves beneath the apparently uneventful surface. All these meanings become more complex because the title shot explicitly links the local street with the flower.

Associated with the Southern states of the Union and with their history, the magnolia is a white flower that metaphorically turns the city on whose map it is superimposed into a white city, suggesting that those veins to which we are going to have privileged access and that keep the city alive are exclusively those of its Anglo population. The connotations of this beautiful signifier of whiteness are borne out by the movie: Going against the demographics of the Valley but not against the cultural connotations of the boulevard and its links with the entertainment industry, all nine central characters and most of the secondary ones are white. One of them, nurse Phil Parma (Philip Seymour Hoffman), works on shifts, but he remains in

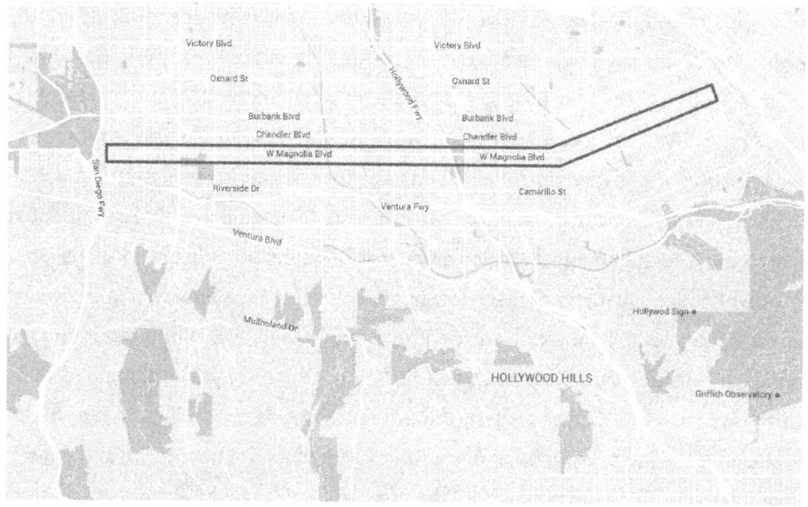

Map 4. Magnolia Boulevard in the heart of the San Fernando Valley. Map by Francesc Terrades.

the Partridge mansion for the twenty-four hours of the diegetic time. He appears to alternate in his job with another nurse whose name is Juan (Juan Medrano). We see Juan leave the house when the film starts, and we see him return later to start his new shift, but Phil tells him that he would rather stay by Earl's side himself and sends him home. In these two brief moments we do not even catch a glimpse of Juan's face, and Medrano certainly did not become a more bankable actor after this movie. Yet, in terms of racial politics, his is a structuring absence. He can be seen as the equivalent of the absent Grand Central Market in the framings of the old Downtown from Angelus Plaza in *(500) Days*. The profound crisis outlined by the narrative of *Magnolia* is an exclusively Anglo crisis, focused mostly on the affluent professionals of the entertainment industry but extending also to such working-class personages as Phil and policeman Jim. *Falling Down* encapsulates variations of the same "white crisis" in its protagonist and the policeman chasing after him, but it allows a certain degree of diversity to surround them as they move around the multiethnic city. *Magnolia*, like the flower, keeps its array of human figures immaculately white, yet, like flowers in time-lapse photography, they are quickly withering and decaying.

We are left with a cinematic San Fernando Valley and a Magnolia Boulevard that have been thoroughly whitened for the occasion and with a movie that self-consciously uses a melodramatic register and a sumptuous formal style to convey historically specific anxieties about whiteness, smoothly inserting itself into the history of cinematic representation of Los Angeles and indirectly into post-1992 urban discourses: The film adds to the dominant tendency of all-white representations of the city in the history of cinema while reproducing the social scenario that brought about the justice riots. Published two years before *Magnolia* was released, Richard Dyer's *White* not only theorizes the discourse of whiteness and its presence in films but also documents a particularly dense breaking point in the social history of the white race. Dyer argues that white has been seen as the nonrace, as the human norm: "Other people are raced, we are just people" (1997, 10). White is nothing in particular—it is an empty signifier that represents the human condition and that which is normal (1–7). Dyer suggests that whiteness needs to be made strange, to be racialized. He relates the classical discourse of whiteness to imperialism and enterprise. Westerns, for example, narrate the construction of a white national identity defined by white men in the face of an indigenous ethnic Other (35).

The history of Los Angeles is part of this history of the construction of a nation on the basis of the expulsion of the indigenous Other but also of the immigrant Other. LA cinema has significantly contributed, from the heart of the industry, to the perpetuation of the ideology of whiteness. However, as argued in this book, 1992 heralded a breaking point. The crisis narrated in *Magnolia* can be seen as the result of the confrontation between the awareness of the inevitability of that breaking point and the ongoing march of supremacist discourses, a type of discourse with which the San Fernando Valley is not unfamiliar. Frank T. J. Mackey (Tom Cruise) is the most visible and outrageous exemplar of this historic tension, and his hysterical response to women's demands for equality, including sexual equality, is a comic rendition of the end of an era. Ostensibly, patriarchy is the target of the film's critique, but, as the movie makes clear through the casting of the African American character of Gwenovier (April Grace) as his interviewer, his race is also part of the equation. In a movie about a race on the verge of annihilation, Frank is its most outspoken representative.

In his analysis of contemporary science fiction films such as the *Alien* series and *Blade Runner*, Dyer also notices the articulation in these texts of powerful cultural anxieties about white nonexistence. He encapsulates this in the conclusion of his reading of *Moby Dick*: "To be white is to be a thing of terror to oneself" (1997, 212). In *Magnolia* this terror, vaguely identified in purely plot terms with the Worm,

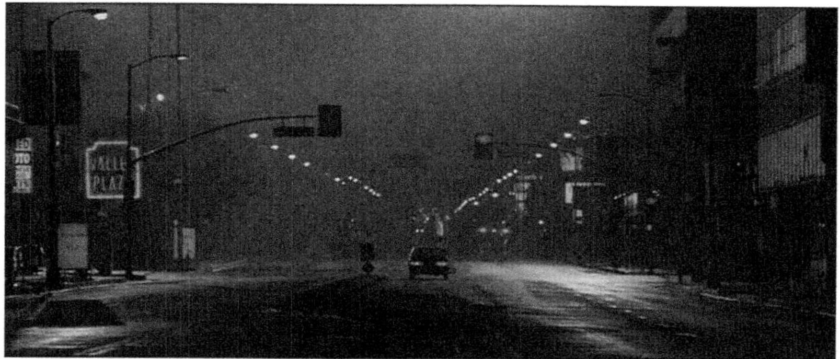

Magnolia: back to the all-white noir city.

is ubiquitous. Inside the mansions of the affluent and the apartments of their traumatized children, the terror is linked to various forms of deterioration of the discourse of whiteness described by Dyer: the unspeakable sexual excesses of the older generation of men, their failure to conform to the notion of self-control in mind and body, the hysterical reaction of white men to the threats of feminism, and a generalized inability to perpetuate traditional patterns of behavior. In a film that is characterized by its self-consciousness as an artifact and as part of the history of cinema, the whiteness it obsessively flaunts is made strange, both in its excesses and in the excess of its representation. In the inexorable downward spiral outlined by the film and the portentousness of the filmic construct, the spectator senses an epochal ending: These paragons of the white race are speeding toward oblivion. The precarious thread on which some of them survive reminds us that something has to change drastically for any kind of future to be envisaged. The solution lies in the city itself and in the type of diversity that *Magnolia* both rejects and yearns for.

The only two nonwhite characters of any relevance that the film allows some visibility are worth mentioning. Gwenovier, the journalist who interviews Mackey, is less interested in finding out information about him than in exposing that his identity is based on a series of lies about his past, notably about his relationship with his father. Being, as an African American, an outsider to the world of the film, she finds it relatively easy to deconstruct his masculinity and to tear down his mask of sexual prowess and arrogance. Once she starts her interview, we learn to interpret his performance of masculinity at the men's seminars and in the video clips as a thin gloss that barely hides his crumbling identity. She is our anchor in this particular strand of the plot, and, given her race, she invites us to look at the character as outsiders too.

Dixon (Emmanuel Johnson) is an African American child who comes up to Jim Kurring to volunteer information about the murders and about the Worm and to offer clues important to solving the case in the form of a rap song. More concerned with the child's foul language than with his interpretation of the mysterious events, Jim dismisses his help to his own detriment and, one would say, to the detriment of his race. Later, Dixon finds Linda dying in her car, after her attempted suicide, and both steals her money and saves her life by calling an ambulance. His response may appear contradictory to some, but it is the response of another outsider to the white middle-class world of *Magnolia*. Together with Stanley Spector (Jeremy Blackman), Dixon is the only child with a relevant part in the story and therefore the only hope of a new beginning. He helps spectators distance themselves from the emotional ride, like Gwenovier, a Brechtian element in a text that elsewhere demands from us intense levels of identification. They help us realize that, for all the geographic locatedness and all the accuracy in the evocation of Magnolia Boulevard and of Angeleno road culture, this is an incredible and socially unfeasible picture of the Valley at the end of the twentieth century and that, for all its art cinema pedigree, it inscribes itself within discourses that are losing valence in the contemporary city.

(500) Days of Summer and *Magnolia* are two different instances of the discourse of independent cinema, offering themselves, respectively, to a demographic of wealthy 20-somethings who like to see themselves as progressive and alternative and to a cinephile audience that appreciates the formal imprints of important artists. Yet in both films the fantasy of a white Los Angeles continues to run strong.

The two films represent a still powerful tendency inside and often outside Hollywood cinema. At the same time, their generic differences and their textual features highlighted in the preceding analyses suggest important nuances and frequent contradictions within the discourse they represent. The romantic context of *(500) Days* and its bittersweet approach to contemporary intimate protocols are the ideal channel for the celebration of a process of gentrification that is crucial to understanding the complexities of early-twenty-first-century Downtown. This is predicated on the displacement of all but Anglo characters from what in reality is an extremely diverse neighborhood. Although the text does not consciously call our attention to this erasure, ethnic diversity is glaring in its invisibility, the ideological operation becoming counterproductive in its extremity. The current inaccessibility of the bench from which Tom imagines his architect's dream of LA unexpectedly becomes a fitting metaphor of its evanescence.

Melodrama works differently. It is a mode that both demands strong identification and, in its narrative excess, simultaneously elicits reflexive distance. Under the general umbrella of postmodernism, many of its contemporary cinematic instances are openly self-conscious. Such is the case of *Magnolia* and its construction of a similarly incredible all-white San Fernando Valley. By the end of the twentieth century the ideology of white superiority had become fragile and the transparency of whiteness an illusion. The whitening of the Valley in Anderson's operatic canvas cannot go unnoticed anymore. Melodramatic excess, here crucially enhanced by the soundtrack and specifically by Aimée Mann's songs, is compounded by textual self-consciousness in the choice of narrative structure, formal "thickness," and explicit references to cinema history. This makes the construction more obvious and what is left out even more visible. By locating the anxieties, fears, and unspoken terrors in this particular area of Southern California, with its recent history of racial tension and nativist tendencies, *Magnolia* explores the end-of-century malaise of a white race that sees itself in danger of annihilation. The narrative complexity and formal frenzy of the proceedings, anticipating the biblical plague in the last half-hour and evoking the torrential rains and the final tornado that consumes the fictional town of Macondo in Gabriel García Márquez's *One Hundred Years of Solitude*, conjure up the powerful image of a civilization coming apart at the seams.

5

Tinseltown

Near the beginning of *Mulholland Drive*, sunny Betty Elms (Naomi Watts) arrives at LAX with two suitcases full of dreams of success and fame in the movie industry, thus joining the long list of young hopefuls who have been attracted to Hollywood for almost a century. After leaving the airport, Betty's first steps in Los Angeles are conveyed by a sequence of shots that include some palm trees from the moving perspective of the taxi, a crane shot of the Hollywood sign, and a series of shot/reverse shots as she walks into the apartment complex where her Aunt Ruth (Maya Bond) lives and where she is going to reside. The address she gives the cab driver, 1612 Havenhurst, is a West Hollywood address, just around the corner from Sunset Boulevard at the eastern end of the Sunset Strip and across the street from the renowned Chateau Marmont Hotel.

The selection of shots to convey her cab ride is significant: a luminous climate at the welcoming airport, the sight of palm trees, and the scent of movies summarize the type of Angeleno experience that Betty is interested in and determined to have. This synecdoche is exemplary of how the city is perceived from the perspective of an aspiring star. For Betty, nothing beyond the movie world—both the industry and the fantasy of living in a movie—matters, and the movie suggests that this is part and parcel of Hollywood's approach to its urban environment. Emulating, for instance, Griffin Mill in *The Player* (Robert Altman, 1992), Betty becomes on arrival not so much a citizen of Los Angeles as a denizen of Hollywood, and she illustrates how, for the Hollywood community, there is not much to say about the city beyond its immediate cinematic environment. The contemporary postmetropolis would be incomprehensible without taking into account the place of the entertainment industry in its history, cultural heritage, and social fabric, but it is much more than that. The Hollywood sign that figures prominently in this movie is both an apt icon of the city as a whole and a reminder, from its almost Olympian heights, of the danger of reducing the metropolis to its movieland connotations.

As a fictional character, Betty is the inheritor of earlier movie protagonists such as Peggy Pepper (Marion Davis) in *Show People* (King Vidor, 1928), Mary

Evans (Constance Bennett) in *What Price Hollywood?* (George Cukor, 1932), Vicki Lester (Janet Gaynor) in *A Star is Born* (William Wellman, 1937) and the later versions of the story, and the unnamed girl played by Veronica Lake in *Sullivan's Travels* (Preston Sturges, 1941). She embodies the myth of Hollywood as a particularly enticing variant of the American dream, the dream of classlessness whereby anyone can become, in this particular version, not the president of the United States but something even better—a film star. But the aerial shot of the sign, given the ominous notes of the Angelo Badalamenti score that accompany it, the previous scene with the car accident, and the fact that David Lynch is the director, also conjure up the image of Peg Entwistle, the real-life starlet who, according to Hollywood lore, committed suicide by jumping off the H of the Hollywood sign in 1932, when her dream of success turned sour. Entwistle went down in industry history as the sad starlet, the young woman hopelessly seeking fame in Hollywood or, as scriptwriter Ben Hecht defined the term, "any woman under thirty not actively employed in a brothel" (Braudy 2011, 92). Betty is both Peg Entwistle and Vicki Lester, and the movie's narrative division into two parts conveys the indivisibility of the two sides of the coin: the gifted performer who is justly discovered and the bitterly disappointed woman whose dream ends in tragedy.

In this chapter I address the third recurrent feature of traditional cinematic representations of Los Angeles that continued to be visible after 1992: Following alienation as the default state of mind of cinematic Angelenos and the dominance of white Los Angeles comes Hollywood's fascination with itself, its own narratives, and its own myths. Given their familiarity with their part of the city, it is a small wonder that filmmakers and studios have often turned themselves into the subjects of their own narratives. Originating, as Christopher Ames points out, in efforts to help self-promotion and Southern California boosterism (1997, 7), these films have come to constitute a full-fledged genre with its own conventions, its own stories of naïveté and cynicism, of glamour and sordidness, of power and humiliation, and its own history and evolution. *Sunset Boulevard* and *In a Lonely Place* have already been mentioned at the intersection of the genre with film noir, 1950s versions of the dark side of the dream, but other movies from the same period, such as *The Bad and the Beautiful* (Vincente Minnelli, 1952) and *What Ever Happened to Baby Jane* (Robert Aldrich, 1962), tell comparable stories. These stories deal with starlets seeking fame and fortune, stars meeting tragedy and decline, filmmakers ruthlessly struggling for success, and screenwriters, often with personal problems, trying to make a living in the Hollywood jungle (Ames 1997, 9–10). The genre has adapted and morphed in various ways, suggesting that, whatever historical vicissitudes and changes the city has undergone, the dream of Hollywood with its attendant miseries lives on and continues to exert its powerful draw on audiences. Movies such as the ironically named *L.A. Story* (a 1991 film, directed by Mick Jackson, about the entertainment industry that calls itself a film about Los Angeles) and *Barton Fink* (Joel and Ethan Coen, 1991) are immediate precedents of *Mulholland Drive* in their open use of fantasy to convey the experience of Hollywood. *The Player* adopts a more realistic and cynical angle on the same topic, as does, almost two decades later, *Somewhere* (Sofia Coppola, 2010), whose story of Angeleno alienation among Hollywood stars takes place across the road from Betty's residence at Chateau Marmont.

These are only a few examples of a genre that does not show signs of exhaustion, as illustrated by such disparate instances, generically, narratively, and industrially, as *Bugsy* (Barry Levinson, 1991), *Get Shorty* (Barry Sonnenfeld, 1995), *Boogie Nights* (Paul Thomas Anderson, 1997), *The Limey* (Steven Soderbergh, 1999), *Bowfinger* (Frank Oz, 1999), *Kiss Kiss Bang Bang* (Shane Black, 2005), *The Holiday* (Nancy Meyers, 2006), *The Black Dahlia* (Brian de Palma, 2006), *For Your Consideration* (Christopher Guest, 2006), *The Artist* (Michel Hazanavicius, 2011), *Seven Psychopaths* (Martin McDonagh, 2012), *In a World . . .* (Lake Bell, 2013), and, of course, *Inland Empire* (2006), Lynch's extremely cryptic follow-up to *Mulholland Drive* and his latest theatrically released movie to date. For all the assortment of stories and registers they offer, these movies, released in the cultural climate of the 1992 events and their consequences in the recent history of the city, betray, with a few exceptions, a parochial view of Los Angeles. Apart from some scattered moments, the movies suggest that for Hollywood it is always business as usual, no matter how much the city around it may be changing. The industry continues to be an airtight social, racial, and economic balloon.

The genre's vitality, therefore, is not historically specific; rather, it responds to Hollywood's unrelenting desire for self-examination and, as Ames summarizes, the public's hunger to see behind the scenes (1997, 6). Betty's first steps in the story seem to confirm that *Mulholland Drive* is also attuned to the genre's historical resistance to include in its fictional worlds social changes in the metropolis. This brings it closer to the two movies discussed in Chapter 4. Yet further analysis will show that this both is and is not the case. It is, in the sense that for the movie's imagination there is no LA beyond Hollywood. It is not, because the city's changes do find their way into the story in interesting ways. However, for a film that, in line with its critical prestige, has been painstakingly scrutinized by the academic institution, it is equally striking that there is a practically unanimous critical blindness to this incursion of recent local history into the Hollywood cocoon.

In Dreams

The production history of the movie is well-known. The film was originally created as a pilot for a TV series that was rejected by ABC and later picked up by French producers Alain Sarde and Pierre Edelman. Sarde and Edelman matched the original investment for additional shooting and postproduction to turn the pilot into what eventually became a theatrical movie (McCarthy 2001, 15). The resulting patchwork, which, according to Graham Fuller, may be "the most audacious salvage job in recent Hollywood history" (2001, 14), consists of a story that starts with a car accident on Mulholland Drive and ends at a Downtown midnight vaudeville theater/nightclub called Silencio, or maybe in the following scene back at Aunt Ruth's house in West Hollywood. Then, a much shorter story follows, with approximately the same settings and the same actors but with the actors playing different characters, who have names that intersect with those of the characters in the first part: Betty becomes Diane, the woman whose name Rita (Laura Elena Harring) had remembered and who was later found dead on her bed in the Sierra Bonita apartments; Rita becomes Camilla Rhodes, a successful actress and Diane's ex-lover, and so on. If we take the moment when Rita opens the blue box and the camera takes us inside it with a fade-out as the dividing point, the two parts stand approximately at 110 minutes and 30 minutes, respectively. Yet, because the second part thoroughly reframes what happens in the first, critics and commentators have tended to place the same importance on both. Rather than the two parts, in this section of my analysis, I would like to focus my attention on the transition between the two.

Descriptions of the plot tend to explain the first, longer story as a dream of Diane's during the second story, which, despite its narrative discontinuities and temporal fragmentation, constitutes the movie's "reality" and is a framing narrative. The brief shot of a dark red sheet along which the camera glides, seemingly trying to discover the sleeper lying underneath, placed between the jitterbug contest of the credit sequence and the first Mulholland Drive scene, is taken as a cue to the fact that what comes after is a dream narrated within this framing narrative, the dreamer being the person under the red sheet (Fuller 2001, 14). Yet most commentators appear to agree that this strict separation does not really work with the film deconstructing its own narrative structure (Andrews 2004, 34; Hudson 2004, 17; McGowan 2004, 68; Kim Newman 2002, 51; Vass 2005, 17–18). This blurring of boundaries does not invalidate, in their view, the importance of the two-part narrative but rather complicates the neat split that spectators, in their longing to disentangle a Lynchian plot (his previous movie, *Lost Highway* [1997], featured a similarly split narrative), might find after an initial viewing. They try to warn against the danger that, after making the effort of giving some coherence to the resistant text, we will abandon the further work of interpretation and affective response demanded by the movie. Yet the narrative structure, as it stands, persists, and the sudden dissolution of the story into the dark depths of the blue box and its reappearance, considerably changed, on the other side, as it were, of the looking glass makes spectators wonder about the power of the nightclub to trigger such a radical change or, if we accept the oneiric logic, to wake the dreamer up.

At the seam between the two stories stands the scene at Club Silencio and the second instance of lip-synching to a Roy Orbison song that we find in Lynch's oeuvre after Ben's (Dean Stockwell) performance of "In Dreams" in *Blue Velvet* (1986). The song this time is "Crying," not the original version but a Spanish version ("Llorando") sung by Mexican Rebekah del Río, who, playing herself, lip-synchs to her own voice on the stage. Donning heavy makeup, which includes a silvery tear, del Río faints on the stage halfway through the song, apparently from the intense emotions it conjures up, as her prerecorded voice continues to resonate in the theater. She also provokes real tears in Rita and Betty, who have come to Silencio at 2 o'clock in the morning after Rita has pronounced the club's name several times in her sleep. Apparently looking for a handkerchief to wipe her tears, Betty opens her purse and finds instead the blue box. The story is swallowed by the box and disappears, leaving everything unresolved. When the box falls in Diane's bedroom, on the other side of the seam, the new story begins.

Rebekah del Río's nickname in the story is la Llorona de Los Angeles. La Llorona is, along with la Virgen de Guadalupe and la Malinche, one of the three central icons of femininity in Mexican culture. The legend, with many reincarnations in various Latin American countries, tells the story of an indigenous woman who falls in love with a Spanish nobleman. The man abandons her and marries a Spanish lady, as a consequence of which the woman goes crazy, drowns her three children in a river, and commits suicide. Afterward, her ghost, not allowed to enter heaven, wanders endlessly looking for her children and crying in the night. For Gloria Anzaldúa, la Llorona is a descendant of Cihuacoatl, the serpent woman of Aztec folklore, the goddess of the earth, of war and birth, who wears a white dress with red and black decorations. She cries and screams at night, as though demented. She brings mental depression and sorrow, and she is the first one to predict that something is going to happen long before it happens (Anzaldúa 1999, 57–58). In one of the few critical references to this character in the context of the film, Kim Newman places la Llorona at the center of the narrative, providing the "prevailing spirit of the film" (2002, 51), and finds various versions of la Llorona in the rest of the story.

By relocating this mythical character in Southern California, the film evokes, if only briefly, the myth of Aztlan and puts the Angelena Mexican woman in the limelight, nodding to the silent majority in the metropolis on which Hollywood movies, particularly Hollywood-on-Hollywood movies, have traditionally turned their backs. Del Río is one of several characters who make a brief appearance in the film and whose role remains unexplained and undeveloped, yet her narrative position at the end of the first story and her extraordinary performance demand critical attention. Given that the film's structure offers the two stories successively rather than simultaneously, the Silencio scene can be seen as the hinge on which the two turn and the glue that holds them together. Because in narrative terms the events at the theater provoke the abrupt end of the first story and its transformation, almost as though falling from the sky, or at least the ceiling, into the second one, the scene bears closer scrutiny.

Jennifer Hudson (2004) explains the defiance of traditional logic posited by the text through reference to Julia Kristeva's *chora*, the presymbolic realm related to the mother, the bodily space shared by mother and child where semiotic traces predate symbolic signification. The *chora* is experienced by the subject as desire, the

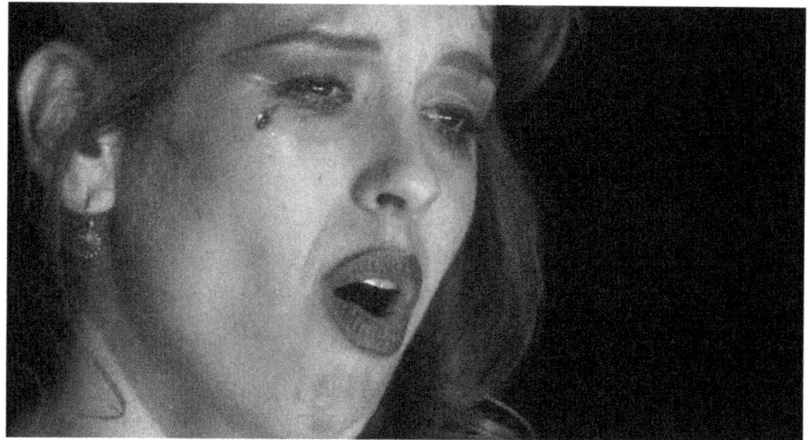

Mulholland Drive: la Llorona in Tinseltown.

uncanny, or the mystical; it reverses coherence and defies logic (Hudson 2004, 19). For Hudson, Club Silencio evokes this semiotic *chora* as a site of linguistic deferral and difference, emotional pulsions, and linguistic nonsignification. Here the master of ceremonies (Richard Green), a sort of magician who speaks indistinctly in Spanish, French, and English, utters various statements about the prerecorded unreality of the proceedings ("No hay banda"—"There is no band") that for Hudson highlight the fact that at this point language, or the seemingly arbitrary mixture of languages, fails to describe or construct reality. She makes much of the fact that when del Río sings "Crying" in Spanish, the spectators do not understand the words, yet, like Rita and Betty, they have no problem identifying with the emotions, crying itself, or even the semblance of crying through the painted tear on the singer's face, becoming a language, the language of the semiotic *chora* (23). There is no ostensible reason for the tears; the characters and we are just deeply moved at a primal level.

The apparently arbitrary mixture of languages spoken by the master of ceremonies (in native English, not-so-native Spanish, and more dubious French) and the difficulty of making some sense out of what he is saying bear Hudson's interpretation out. The play with recorded sounds, whether musical instruments or the roar of a storm, and the insistence on their unreality reinforce the point. Rita and Betty are moved by the show from the beginning, and Betty even goes into a tantrum on hearing the storm, even though we are warned that it is a recording, a sound effect. Yet the act is not the same from beginning to end. It has two parts, the second one starting when a man dressed in a red suit (Geno Silva) introduces Rebekah del Río, this time in impeccable Mexican Spanish. To say that the spectators do not understand the words sung by la Llorona is perhaps too much to presume. In the first place, Orbison's song is popular enough, even though the Spanish version may defamiliarize it, and no doubt many English speakers will remember the original words as they hear them in Spanish; and second, millions of spectators around the world will indeed understand Rebekah's crystalline Spanish. Betty and Rita certainly seem to, because they too start crying as the performer sings her story of unrequited love, one that affects both of them directly. The film underlines this rhetorically, alternating the extreme close-ups of Rebekah with matching reverse shots of the two protagonists in the dark, also in close-up, from a variety of angles, as though trying to explore the reasons for their grief. Even though this scene follows the sexual consummation of their mutual attraction, their response to "Llorando" seems to come from a deeper consciousness, from a different story, in which love between them has turned into jealousy, frustration, and despair. At this point both appear to be the victims in this alternative story, which will soon unfold in front of our eyes.

At the same time, Rebekah's powerful and plaintive voice evokes the desperate screams of la Llorona and the prescience of the serpent woman of the Aztecs, anticipating the intensity of the suffering that will come between the two lead characters. The deep red of her thickly applied lipstick and the visibility of her red and orange eye shadow, setting out the darkness of the running eyeliner and the silvery tear and matching the ruby earrings, gives Rebekah the appearance of an admittedly sad and exhausted but proud Aztec princess, placing her in a position of power also constructed through her heartbreaking voice. Here la Llorona reigns supreme and exerts her apparently irresistible influence over those around her.

Beyond the variety of languages on offer, Mexicanness is dominant in this scene, as befits its location. In deciding to visit Club Silencio, or, rather, in being mysteriously drawn to it by a dream, Betty and Rita venture in the old financial and entertainment section of Downtown, specifically Broadway, the same general area in which *(500) Days* takes place. The scene was shot at two different theaters on Broadway: The Palace for some of the exteriors and The Tower for the interiors (this theater is especially a familiar presence in Hollywood movies; see the webpage "Historic Los Angeles Theaters," sites.google.com/site/Downtownlosangelestheatres/

tower). They, and the fleapit constructed out of them by the film, evoke the history of the area, its glamorous connection with the golden age of Hollywood in the classical period, its decline, and its later takeover by a Hispanic population. The choice of location for this crucial scene can be read as a reminder of the blindness of recent Hollywood movies, including Hollywood-on-Hollywood movies, to historical developments in the city. From the point of view of the predominantly Anglo film community, Club Silencio is unsavory and threatening, but it is also a quintessentially Lynchian space, where unnamed primal forces beyond our consciousness control our lives. These forces appear to be all the more threatening because of their ethnicity. At the center of this story of fantasy and desire in Hollywood stands the invisible Mexican population of the city. In directing us to look beneath the surface, as Lynch's earlier *Blue Velvet* had done, the director finds the heart of Los Angeles in the desperate cries of la Llorona. Given the history of Hollywood's narratives about itself, this is truly the return of the repressed.

This revelation may shed some light on the proceedings. *Mulholland Drive* is, according to many critics, Lynch's most located movie and, for most of them, his most detailed study of Los Angeles and his most explicit take on the industry (Fuller 2001, 16; Hoberman 2001; Levy 2006; McCarthy 2001, 24). For Philip Lopate, the movie describes the insularity of the Southern California film community (2001, 48), and for Kristin Hohenadel, in her article "Real L.A., the One That's Lived In," it is one of those rare movies that show us the distance between Los Angeles and Hollywood. It gives us a sense of the centerless metropolis, with its high hopes and its bright façades, its banal coffee shops and parking lots, a city "between the euphoria of possibility and the misery of defeat and Apocalypse" (Hohenadel 2001, n.p.). In Hohenadel's account *Mulholland Drive* is a film about both the city and the industry, highlighting both the interconnectedness and the distance that sometimes exists between the two. Like *Magnolia* with its multiple interconnected Valley narratives and its Aimée Mann soundtrack, this movie offers a recognizable and iconic urban geography to convey the fascination and the fantasy of the Hollywood experience, both from the point of view of its fictional denizens and from that of the global spectator. As in *Magnolia*, the complex narrative structure is part of the textual look at the city and the centerlessness of the urban experience. In *Mulholland Drive* the story folding onto itself suggests the role of fantasy in conceptualizations of LA and the ineffability of the City of Dreams (Aoun 2003, 204). More unusually, at the very seam where the narrative folds and retraces its steps stands the mythical Mexican icon and the Aztec goddess. Resisting obvious signification and unveiling the hidden portal to the urban fantasy, the brownness of the fold comes as a revelation for those who care to look.

Passing

Rebekah del Río embodies la Llorona, who, with the aid of the blue box, ushers in the story of unrequited love and despair that replicates her song and dramatically changes our interpretation of what has gone on before. She is a formidable Mexican presence who deeply affects all those who hear her, but she is not the only one, or the most important, in the movie. Unremarked by most, Rita/Camilla, the movie's coprotagonist, is also Mexican. The two young women's trip to the nightclub at 2 o'clock in the morning is triggered by Rita's dream, maybe her second dream of the story. First in her sleep, after her sexual encounter with Betty, and then seemingly awake, she repeats the name of the establishment, Silencio, seven times as well as two of the phrases that will later be uttered at the club: "No hay banda" and "No hay orquesta." These are the only Spanish words that the character speaks in the course of the narrative, and, in the way she pronounces them, they are the only explicit indication that she may be a native speaker of the language. Her name in the framing narrative, Camilla Rhodes, does not help with her ethnic identification, nor does particularly Laura Harring, the name of the actress.

Nevertheless, Harring is a Mexican actress. Born in Sinaloa, she was the first Hispanic woman to become Miss USA in 1985. Shortly afterward, she became a countess through a brief marriage to a German aristocrat. Both Naomi Watts and Laura Harring were unfamiliar faces in the industry when they were cast as protagonists in the movie, and both made a strong impression, but whereas *Mulholland Drive* became Watts's breakthrough moment and launched her star career, Harring's profile remained low and she played mostly secondary parts in unmemorable movies and TV shows. Given the two actresses' stunning performances here, it is significant that the two careers have since then been so divergent.

In the movie it is equally striking that Rita/Camilla's ethnic origin goes practically unnoticed. We first see Rita after the credit sequence, which includes various shots of a car gliding along the bendy road to the tune of Badalamenti's haunting score and a characteristic night shot of the LA basin, as seen and experienced from Mulholland—"the diamonds tossed in black velvet" (Thomson 2001 n.p.). As soon as the credits are over, but still within the same scene, we move to the inside of the car with the first shot of Rita, a 10-second close-up, still accompanied by the movie's signature melody, thus including the new character in the incantatory world constructed by the sequence. From the beginning, before we know her name or who she is (we never really actually find out who she is in this first part of the narrative), she is visually associated with the road and therefore with the film's title. She is, like the road, constructed as somewhat otherworldly, as part of a story that, however precise and familiar the location, is presented as existing in an alternative world.

In cinematic terms the obvious referent for our first impression of Rita is the femme fatale of classic film noir. More than one critic has related Betty with Nancy Drew, the feisty young heroine of the popular mystery novels; Harring as Rita has been compared with Ava Gardner, who jumped to stardom after her part as Kitty Collins in *The Killers* (Robert Siodmak, 1946) (Dargis 2001; Fuller 2001, 14). The similarities are obvious, and the inscrutability of Rita's character, who conveniently loses her memory after the car accident, brings her close to the femme fatale, a cinematic type who, because she is always seen in the movies exclusively from the viewpoint of the male protagonist, is usually indecipherable and comes out as unstable and fractured in her characterization (Gledhill 1980, 18).

Mulholland Drive underlines the Angeleno specificity of the protagonist by associating Rita with the mountain road of the title, the 21-mile-long winding road that stretches along the top of the eastern part of the Santa Monica Hills, looking south onto the Los Angeles Basin and north onto the San Fernando Valley. The movie explicitly sets it in contrast to the nearby Sunset Boulevard, a much straighter road that, although of approximately the same length, covers a much longer stretch of the city, from Downtown to the Pacific Ocean. Philip French, in his review of the movie, compares the two and explains that Mulholland Drive is "altogether darker" and, evoking Ken Schessler's novel *This Is Hollywood*, "redolent with evil, haunted by the sad and bad spirits of the stars and starlets who have been murdered, committed suicide or participated in orgies in the past century" (2002, n.p.). Mulholland

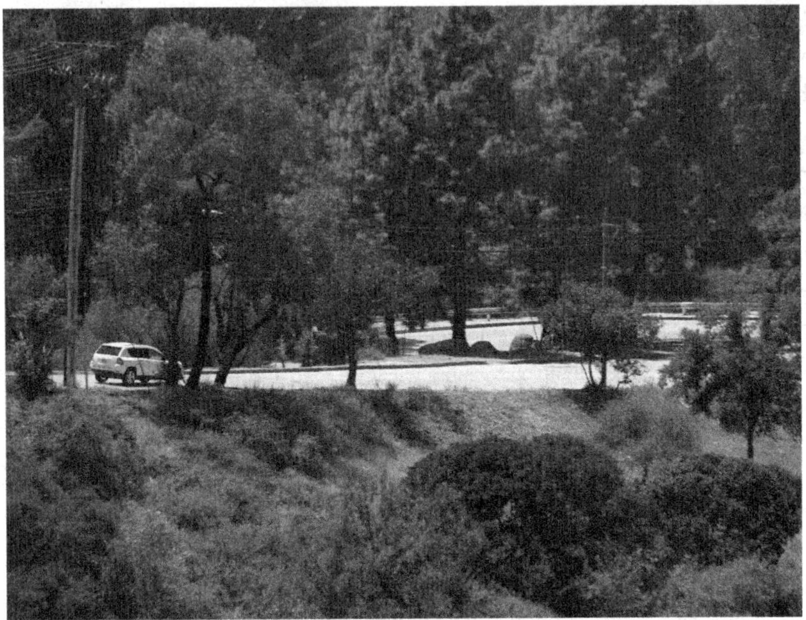

Mulholland Drive: the long winding road.

Drive is the place where locals and visitors go to enjoy the spectacular views of the city at night and the site of the mansions of some Hollywood stars, but, as it winds its way westward toward the ocean, it becomes a dirt road, a place where David Thomson, in another review of the movie, would not recommend picking anyone up (2001). The chilling corral at Beechwood Canyon, where film director Adam (Justin Theroux) is threatened by the creepy Cowboy (Lafayette Montgomery), evokes this seedy and ominous atmosphere, even though the scene was shot at Sunset Ranch near the eastern end of Mulholland and just below the Hollywood sign. Apart from the connotations of danger and darkness and the potent parallel between the zigzagging road and the zigzagging plot of the film, the road also calls attention to the real person after whom it is named: William Mulholland, the Belfast-born engineer who built the city's water infrastructure in the first decades of the twentieth century by polemically constructing the 233-mile-long aqueduct from Owens Valley northeast of LA and securing the city's supply for years to come (Erie and MacKenzie 2010, 219–20; Hise 2010, 409–10). For Thomson (2001), what makes this reference relevant to Lynch's film is that Mulholland, like Lynch, was a designer of dreams.

Armed with all these resonances and associations, Rita starts her bumpy narrative journey, one that will eventually lead her to not one but two destinations: Club Silencio and, like many of her noir forebears, very probably death in the second segment. The two men who are apparently taking her to an unspecified evening party or event (she is wearing a black cocktail dress) unexpectedly stop the car and ask her to get out, the confidence transpiring from her first close-up now turning into helplessness, but then some boisterous kids who are racing along Mulholland crash into the stopped automobile and cause a fatal accident. The car is in flames but Rita has survived the accident. She stumbles out of the car and, in a state of shock, crosses the road and heads south down the hill. For the first time after the brief title shot, the subjective camera is activated. We get two more shots of the diamonds tossed in velvet, but this time from Rita's perspective. Although her aloofness, provoked by the accident, and the mystery of her identity keep her close to the femme fatale, the strong identification with her viewpoint distances her from the classic stereotype, who is rarely given the subjectivity of the look. The alternation between mobile camera shots of what she has in front of her, even sometimes imitating her physical movement with its shakiness, and reverse shots of her progress down the hill continues until she reaches her destination: Aunt Ruth's house near Sunset, where she will soon meet Betty. This pattern firmly establishes Rita as the protagonist, and it is reinforced when, after Aunt Ruth leaves the house, she relaxes and falls asleep, the next sequence ambiguously cued as though it were her dream.

Alongside the stylized views of the city, the hallucinatory score that is reprised after the accident, and Rita's ethereal appearance, the narrative makes a point of not letting us forget exactly where we are in purely geographic terms. Locations are surprisingly precise at this point: The character crosses Franklin Avenue and then reaches Sunset Boulevard, and both times we get shots, from her perspective, of the exact addresses. Taking these into account, we can infer that the accident took place near Runyon Canyon Park, a favorite weekend destination of Angelenos who want to escape the pollution and traffic of the metropolis and go for treks in the mountains. If Rita walks more or less in a straight line, from that approximate location until she hits 7200 Sunset, then she has trekked more than 2 miles downhill, to which we have to add another mile or so walking west along the boulevard until she reaches Aunt Ruth's house. This distance of more than 3 miles is, in film terms, both big and small. By traveling from the meandering dangers of Mulholland to the more welcoming straightness of Sunset—although Sunset also has its share of unsavory areas—Rita moves from the darkness of the inhospitable road toward the relative safety of West Hollywood. At the same time, the proximity between the two roads in the general topography of the city and the association of both with the history of Hollywood keep Rita's long walk contained within a single space, that of the film industry's Los Angeles, the familiar city of dreams.

When asked about his favorite Hollywood movie, Lynch often mentions *Sunset Boulevard* (Aoun 2003, 136; Hohenadel 2001; Nochimson 2002, 39). *Mulholland Drive* can be seen as Lynch's own version of the Billy Wilder movie, the two roads not so distant from each other from the perspective of the Hollywood denizen. Rita, therefore, brings the two locations together and, in infiltrating Betty's new home, she also incorporates the twisting road and its resonances as part of the movie's gaze at Hollywood. The fact that the Hollywood sign, both a signifier of the dream and of its concomitant nightmare, is part of the sequence that conveys Betty's first impression of the city also anticipates the proximity between the two roads and the two protagonists and the doubleness of the vision of Hollywood that they encapsulate. In a sense, then, Rita, like Betty, *is* Hollywood, an egregious amalgamation of many of the ingredients that feed into the Hollywood-on-Hollywood film.

When she wakes up the next day and meets Betty, who has just arrived from the airport, the dark lady does not remember anything. When pressed to reveal her name, her look falls on a poster of *Gilda* (Charles Vidor, 1946) on the wall and she tells Betty that her name is Rita, like the star of that film, Rita Hayworth. On one level, this new cinematic reference confirms the association of the character with the femme fatale of film noir. Furthermore, unlike Elsa Bannister, Hayworth's character in the following year's *Lady from Shanghai* (Orson Welles, 1947), Gilda is less the inscrutable predator that drives men to perdition for no discernible reason and more the melodramatic victim of a patriarchal world and the objectified woman, exclusively there for men's erotic pleasure, both dimensions coming together in the scene in which her lover, Johnny Farrell (Glenn Ford), slaps her across the face. Our experience of Rita so far comes closer to Gilda than to Elsa, although in the second part of the narrative, when the emphasis on her look and her subjectivity all but disappears, her capricious and callous behavior toward her ex-lover aligns her much more clearly with noir's traditional dark ladies.

There is, however, another dimension to the character's choice of name. Rita Hayworth, whose real name was Margarita Carmen Cansino, was born in Brooklyn of a Spanish father, Eduardo Cansino, a professional dancer, and an Irish mother. A dancer like her father, she started her movie-acting career as Margarita Cansino, then shortened her name to Rita Cansino and finally changed it to the Anglo Hayworth—based on Haworth, her mother's maiden name. This change of name, along with various alterations to her physical appearance, watered down her half-Spanish origin and turned her into a glamorous Hollywood star, the "love goddess," hardly distinguishable in ethnic terms from the other Anglo stars of the time (Shipman 1989, 290–91). Yet, as Adrienne McLean and Priscilla Peña Ovalle have pointed out in their studies of the star, Rita's Hispanic dimension was never forgotten by the public and was regularly invoked by studio marketing. According to McLean, Margarita Cansino was always present as part of Rita Hayworth's star persona, her ethnic background remaining present throughout her career as a prominent element of her star appeal (2004, 31–32). McLean suggests that, even as she became "Americanized" physically, the meanings associated with her ethnicity remained in place (55). Peña Ovalle concentrates on Hayworth's racial mobility, a product of the combination of the whitening brought about by her well-publicized cosmetic changes and her nonwhiteness epitomized by her dances. For her, Hayworth is an example of "the Hollywood Latina's in-betweenness" and its relation to the reconstruction of U.S. national identity during World War II. Peña Ovalle explores the malleability of an image that incorporated Spanish, Irish, Mexican, and "American" meanings. Hayworth's Europeanness made her "nonwhiteness" assimilable in a way that was not available to other Latina stars, such as Dolores del Río and Carmen Miranda (Peña Ovalle 2011, 73–74). Although Peña Ovalle puts more emphasis than McLean on Hayworth's Americanization, she concurs that Margarita Cansino's ethnicity was never lost during her time as a Hollywood star (80). Rita Hayworth, therefore, became a signifier of the constructedness of both stardom and racial identity, a process that was public and was incorporated into the star text. It was an act of passing that, in calling attention to itself, undercut its own effectiveness but at the same time remained successful.

The decision of the amnesiac protagonist of the first part of *Mulholland Drive* to name herself after Hayworth taps into the complex meanings of the star's ethnicity and Americanization. It reinforces Rita's ethnicity even as it underlines its invisibility. With the exception of a few brief mentions (Lopate 2001, 47; McCarthy 2001, 24), the significance of Hayworth's otherness in the movie and Rita's own ethnic marginality have gone unnoticed; commentators replicate the invisibility of her Mexicanness in the plot, no matter how many times she later utters the word "silencio" in a recognizable Mexican accent. It is not that the movie goes to any particular lengths to construct the disguise. Rather, it is as though, in a complex postmodern fashion, it brings the character's ethnicity to the fore in order to admonish spectators that, even though it is there for us to grasp and interpret, we will not see it; the act of passing is located more in a cultural blindness to difference than in the text itself. Peña Ovalle, while agreeing with McLean about the lingering visibility of Hayworth's ethnic origins, reminds us that today Rita is rarely remembered as Latina (2011, 72). It is as though, in linking Lynch's Rita to Hayworth, the film is capitalizing on this erasure. It seems to be saying to us, "Look, one of the protagonists is Mexican, but you have not even noticed."

Visually, the text underlines the crucial moment of Rita's provisional acquisition of an identity by means of a complex double mirror shot, in which three images of women are included: the character, her reflection in the mirror, and the poster of *Gilda* doubly framed inside the little magnifying mirror. The framing shows both Rita and her mirror reflection looking in the same direction toward Rita Hayworth, tracing a trajectory that leads to the borrowed identity. The shot deconstructs human identity by equating its constitution with a game of mirrors, and, in its composition, it simultaneously suggests the irresistible attraction of becoming somebody different or, maybe, just somebody. From the perspective of the spectator, we look at Rita (or Camilla, or Laura, the actor) in the process of acquiring a new subjectivity, but, through multiple framing, we are also made to look at ourselves and at our own willingness to change identities through the cinematic experience. It is significant that the final destination of the character and the spectator's look at this point is a star whose process of fabrication as such was famous and public. The visual logic of the shot in *Mulholland Drive* leads from the spectator to Gilda/Rita Hayworth through a hall of mirrors and a sequence of different identities and highlights the role of the classic star in the (post)modern narrative. Having survived her first moments as an amnesiac, Rita starts a process of becoming a gradually stronger and more attractive person in the story, a process that will culminate in her and Betty

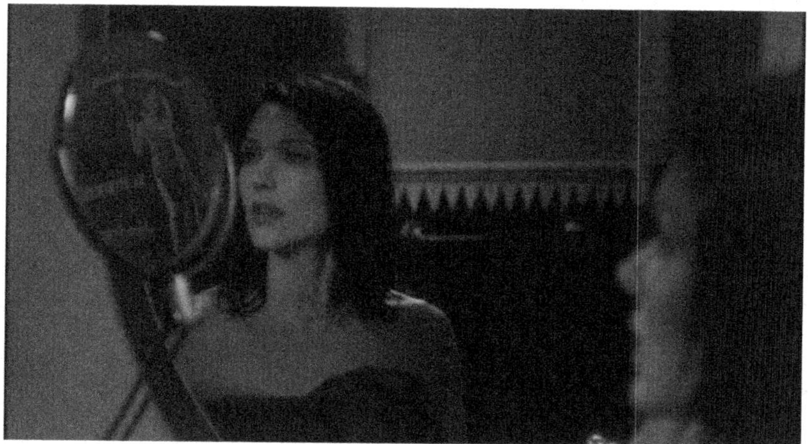

Mulholland Drive: multiple framing and the hybridity of identity.

falling in love. Her new personality starts at the moment of the naming, one that, as we have seen, also highlights her ethnicity.

Knowing her name, even though we know that it is a false name, helps spectators continue to closely engage with the character through the rhetorical mechanisms of framing used in the film. Until this point, the narrative has alternated between scenes focusing on Rita and those focusing on Betty, and it continues to do so, but increasingly the two women are also shown together, sharing the process of unraveling the mystery of Rita's identity and the money she finds in her purse. As part of this investigation, Rita and Betty visit the Sierra Bonita apartments, where Diane, the name that Rita vaguely remembers from her past, may live. This scene culminates in the discovery that Diane is dead and that her corpse is festering in her apartment. The subjective camera pattern that the film has been using consistently to convey both characters' experiences, and also, occasionally, those of other secondary characters, is again employed to present their joint subjectivity, the ambivalent sunny starlet and the dark lady becoming one as points of spectatorial engagement. What they briefly and shockingly see inside Diane's room is a foray into the alternative universe that will be the space of their next story, and this is a moment they both experience simultaneously and that the spectator is prompted to experience through both of them. In a more classical manner, their later response to Rebekah del Río's song and fainting at the club is also a simultaneous experience, the sequence consisting of shots and reverse shots in which the reverse shots frame both women, mostly in two-shots or framings that move from one to the other, looking offscreen toward the stage. Both the Sierra Bonita and Silencio scenes are climactic moments in that they incorporate portals into the alternative universe that their narrative trajectory is gradually leading them to. Both times, the text constructs a single subjectivity, with only slight variations, for the two women. What are the consequences of this blending for the construction of social identity, especially in a movie in which the subjective camera carries as much weight as the oneiric atmosphere?

Critics have mobilized another filmic reference in the scene of the sexual encounter between Rita and Betty: Ingmar Bergman's *Persona* (1966) (Andrews 2004, 36; Hudson 2004, 22; Laine 2009, 326 and *passim*; Levy 2006). The reference becomes visually explicit in the sequence that follows their sexual encounter, when Rita starts repeating the word "silencio" in her sleep. At this point, Lynch offers us a sequence of three shots, all from a close distance. The first shot is a lateral close-up of the two women lying in bed, Rita on her back and Betty on her side looking toward her friend, with Rita's face in focus in the foreground and Betty's out of focus in the background. The second shot is a high-angle extreme close-up of Rita's eyes. The third returns to the framing of the first but with Rita out of focus and Betty in focus. Shots 1 and 3 are taken to reproduce the famous scene in *Persona* in which the two women, Alma (Bibi Andersson) and Elisabet (Liv Ullmann), blur into one woman on the screen. Betty and Rita do not quite achieve the same visual fusion—the framing positions them as mirror images of each other—but the similarities with the Bergman moment are striking.

This scene follows the aforementioned discovery of Diane's body at the Sierra Bonita apartments. The two friends see the corpse simultaneously, but it is Rita who appears to be most affected: She runs out of the house and screams in horror. The volume is turned off at this point, as though no microphone could possibly capture her reaction. We are offered instead a momentary doubling of the image, the physical film shuddering. Rita's reaction is so extreme that it is unrepresentable in conventional ways and so penetrating that it affects the very being of the story, its physical existence, threatening, as in *Persona*, to dissolve the celluloid, although here all we get is the tremor and the double image. When the screen shudders, the world of *Mulholland Drive* is violently shaken. In the violence and unfathomability of her scream, Rita, the sophisticated and aloof amnesiac, becomes la Llorona, anticipating the mythical woman's later incarnation in Rebekah del Río. The extremity of the moment is strongly evocative of the demented laments of the prescient woman, who, from the deepest recesses of her unconscious and with the help of her twin soul Betty, will upturn the narrative trajectory and generically reveal the dark side of the Hollywood adventure. Rita's silent scream and Rebekah's performance are comparable in their intensity and in how that intensity brings the narrative and the spectators closer to the hidden knowledge of the second part of the plot. They are both recreations of the serpent woman and the triggers of the seam that gives meaning to this cryptic story.

As a consequence of her shock, Rita is next seen cutting her hair and donning a blond wig that makes her look more like Betty. This unexplained and inexplicable decision brings the two closer together, ushering in their sexual encounter. At the same time, the cosmetic operation brings us back to Rita Hayworth and the importance of her hair in the transformation of her image on the road to stardom. Peña Ovalle points out that dying Hayworth's hair from dark (Margarita's natural lighter hair had already been darkened to turn her into Rita Cansino) to auburn was a good business decision, blond being, as it were, out of her reach because of her ethnic history. This transformation was even narrativized in her breakthrough movie, *Only Angels Have Wings* (Howard Hawks, 1939), when, on being reunited with her character Judy again after having lost touch for a while, Geoff (Cary Grant) says, when he sees her hair, "I thought it looked different." For Peña Ovalle, "the scene signifies Hayworth's reentry into Hollywood as a siren with a makeover" (2011, 76–77). Still identifying with the star from whom she has taken her name, Rita incorporates Betty's blondness into her identity, continuing a process of self-fabrication that is marked by the shocking blending of the dark Mexican Llorona and the blond all-American girl next door. Going beyond Hayworth's "acceptable mobility" but taking her inspiration from her, Rita comes to embody a monstrous hybrid with whom we are forced to identify.

The road from the discovery of the corpse to Rita and Betty's bed is not easy to fathom in a cause-and-effect narrative but seems straight enough in Rita's dream. It is, like Mulholland Drive, a bendy and dangerous road that evokes the city's traumatic relationship with ethnic hybridity. This is a history that the movie highlights and openly revises. The road also leads, as we have seen, to the Mexican fleapit on Broadway and to the side of the city that narratives about Hollywood have consistently ignored. The screams, laments, and singing of la Llorona can be interpreted as a call of attention to what remains hidden but drives not only the individual psyche but also the social group, in this case, the city of Los Angeles. That Rita's ethnicity is so unobtrusive despite its conspicuousness is part of the film's engagement with the history of the Hollywood-on-Hollywood film and, through it, with the historical blindness of the industry to its social and cultural environment. That her scream and Rebekah del Río's song wield the power to dissolve the narrative and send it into a new dimension may also be an indication of historical changes that, after 1992, cannot be held at bay for much longer. Her strong, although, in femme fatale fashion, impenetrable subjectivity becomes merged with that of the Nancy Drew/Peg Entwistle Anglo starlet, articulating an unusual metaphor for the future of an industry that, like the dominant discourses in the metropolis, must learn from the surrounding diversity. Rita Hayworth's journey from Latina starlet to all-American femme fatale in *Gilda* and especially *The Lady from Shanghai* helps unfold these hidden meanings even as she stands as a reminder of continuing cultural invisibility. The starlet and the neo–femme fatale are two types that *Mulholland Drive* easily complicates and problematizes with the help of the two performers, but as symbols of the history of Hollywood, they become apt ingredients of the movie's reworking of the genre and their coming together is a celebration of difference but also of the hidden history of the city.

The celebration, of course, is not complete, and the final half-hour of the film tears the two women apart, probably sees them both dead, and perhaps explains the horrible lament of the prescient Mexican goddess at the nagging realities of the industry and, specifically, of the Hollywood-on-Hollywood movie. The invisibility of the Mexican woman in *Mulholland Drive* is a reminder of the continuing insularity and relative impermeability of the industry to its urban environment. Hollywood makes films about the city with which it is familiar. This city, carefully reconstructed in Lynch's movie, is only a small part of Los Angeles. When Hollywood makes movies about itself, the insularity becomes more intense. From *The Player* to *Somewhere* this is still largely the pattern in post-1992 movies. The fact that the most prestigious of the recent offerings of the genre breaks this pattern and even addresses the unsustainability of such insularity is, in the final analysis, as significant as the fact that, despite or perhaps because of its justly attained canonicity, nobody has noticed it.

II

The Legacy of the Riots

6

Out of the Past

At one point Hollywood started to look at the past of Los Angeles. Karen Voss, looking back from the late 1990s, noted the increase of mainstream "history of Los Angeles narratives," a trend that for her started with *Chinatown* (Voss 1998, 157). Whereas most of the movies discussed in this volume deal with the present, in this chapter I focus on post-1992 movies that return to LA's past to explore the ways in which the city that gradually emerged after the riots was cinematically reconstructed in relation to its more or less recent history. More specifically, I focus on *Devil in a Blue Dress* (Carl Franklin, 1995), a filmic reconstruction of African American life in the late 1940s in the City of Angels.

The LAPD, with its heavy responsibility in the 1992 riots and later events and its decades-long infamous record of corruption, repression, and disregard for human rights, might have been expected to become one of the favorite objects of post-1992 cinematic explorations of the city's past. From the beginning, the LAPD has been an unusually repressive force, with numerous notorious incidents to its name. Victor Jew (2010) links the first racialized disturbance in LA history—the so-called anti-Chinese massacre of 1871—with the anti–Mexican American beatings of 1943, the Watts uprising, and the riots of April 1992. All four events had in common a violent investment in whiteness and the presence of law enforcement at the epicenter of the troubles (Jew 2010, 111). The subsequent chronicle of the Angeleno police force includes the harassment of ethnic minorities and other groups, for example, hippies in the 1960s (McBride 2010, 337) and left-wing activists; the ill-reputed "Red Squad" was instituted in 1933 by Chief James E. Davis to investigate and control radical activities, strikes, and riots. This unit was still in existence under Chief William Parker (1950–1966), who used it as part of his program of law enforcement (Davis 2006, 114; Ethington 2010, 206).

But the links between the LAPD and African Americans are particularly traumatic and have been sustained throughout the city's history. As Mike Davis asserts, at least since Parker became chief, the African American community has regarded the police as an occupation army, a feeling reinforced by Daryl Gates's (1978–1992) later excesses (2006, 271, 277). Scott Saul concurs and relates the fear of racial mixing to the force's use of aggressive, high-tech methods and their independence from civilian control, particularly under Parker and Gates (2010, 155). Susan Anderson concludes that the political fates of black Angelenos and the LAPD have always been closely intertwined (1996, 352). After 1992 the LAPD continued to be immersed in continuous scandals, which eventually led the Department of Justice to find a "pervasive pattern of constitutional-rights violation" and to force the LAPD to accept a different status (Saul 2010, 160–61).

Hollywood was reluctant to endorse this change of perception. As we have seen, *Falling Down*, produced immediately after the riots, presents an urban dystopia from which only two brave and honest police officers can be saved. The movie draws from a long tradition of popularity of police procedural narratives in the industry. When, after the riots, Hollywood started to look at the past of the LAPD, the attitude was equally celebratory, through movies in which courageous, if sometimes, flawed individual officers become a more familiar representation of the force than its bureaucratic or political machine. From *Mulholland Falls* (Lee Tamahori, 1996) to *The Black Dahlia* (Brian de Palma, 2006) and *Gangster Squad* (Ruben Fleischer, 2013), the police protagonists of these films are unambiguously upright citizens and proficient professionals whose heroic deeds never begin to reflect the darker historical realities of the institution. *Mulholland Falls*, for instance, features a violent special crime squad in the 1950s that answers only to their immediate superior and commits all sorts of excesses, ostensibly to rid the city of gangsters coming from Chicago and various East Coast cities. Answering only to one boss is shorthand for untrammeled violence and disregard for basic citizen rights. The title of the film is not the name of a place but the phrase that describes the policemen's favorite practice, which we witness in the movie's first scene: They drag undesirable citizens to a specific spot on Mulholland Drive from which they push them downhill as a warning to leave town immediately. As played by Nick Nolte, Chazz Palminteri, Chris Penn, and Michael Madsen, all actors often associated with gangster roles, the four policemen are never less than heroic and are constructed as figures of identification for the audience.

Something similar happens with the evocation of another special team in *Gangster Squad*, a movie in which even Chief Parker (Nick Nolte again) becomes a courageous citizen as he struggles to get rid of a historical figure, gangster Mickey

Cohen (Sean Penn), with the help of his gang. After watching these movies, all of them more or less loosely based on "historical facts," spectators get the impression of an impeccable and gallant history. The project at work in them seems to be one of recuperation of the institution in the face of public disapproval after the riots: In their narratives, the LAPD's violent, undemocratic methods are understandable and inevitable. It is public opinion that needs to change. An exception in mainstream Hollywood is Clint Eastwood's *Changeling* (2008), which retells the real case of a woman in the 1920s who, in the times of Chief James Davis, is ruthlessly harassed by the LAPD when they replace her missing child with an impostor and she refuses to accept the scam. Justice is done in the end, the truth shines through, and there is no exoneration of the execrable behavior of the institution. Yet most post-1992 mainstream historical movies about the LAPD do not follow this path.

It is equally noticeable that none of these post-1992 historical movies, including *Changeling*, appear to be interested in reflecting the impact of the LAPD on the city's African American community. Their plots construct an almost exclusively white city in which all characters, victims, perpetrators, and law enforcers are racially homogeneous. From this perspective these revisions of history, rather than exploring the numerous controversies affecting the institution, appear to use the LAPD as an excuse to produce fantasies of whiteness in the face of diversity and multiculturalism, a project that aligns itself with the project of those in charge of the police force. Mike Davis describes Chief Parker as a puritanical crusader against race mixing (2006, 294), and these revisionist movies appear to be engaged in the same crusade.

Consequently, for those interested in finding cinematic accounts of the history of African American Angelenos, movies about the LAPD should have been but are not the right place to look. Of course, many gangster and police films feature African Americans, first exclusively as gangsters. *Colors* (Dennis Hopper, 1988) is an example of a prestigious, "independent" movie in which, under the impressive presence of the Watts Towers, the two white policemen are the heroes and the blacks are divided into members of two gangs: the Bloods and the Crips. Gradually, later movies incorporated black Angelenos who are corrupt (*Training Day*, Antoine Fuqua, 2001) or upright members of the police force (*Crash*, Paul Haggis, 2004). However, with the exception of narratives that, like *Boyz 'n the Hood* and, to a lesser extent, *Menace II Society*, adopt the point of view of the African Americans attempting to survive in the midst of gang warfare, none of these films are interested in exploring urban realities. Even presenting African American Angelenos exclusively through their experience with street gangs may be, as Davis suggests, part of a neosupremacist strategy that pigeonholes this diverse community in an impoverishing and damaging background. For Davis, the gang scare became in the 1980s "an imaginary class relationship, a terrain of pseudo-knowledge and fantasy projection" (2006, 270). As a consequence of this and of the city's war on drugs, African Americans, particularly young males, were openly demonized as a group and subsequently indiscriminately harassed by the police (284). Given that Los Angeles has the highest concentration of high-income blacks as well as the highest concentration of low-income blacks in the United States (Anderson 1996, 338), the predominant association of African Americans with a generic confrontation between citizens on either side of the law enforcement line results in a discursive manipulation and simplification of the community, one that consciously seeks to ignore its social and cultural complexity.

But these films set their stories in their own present time. The movie with the highest industrial and critical profile among those dealing with the past of the LAPD has not been mentioned yet. *L.A. Confidential* (Curtis Hanson, 1997) was one of the most popular LA movies of the 1990s. Set, like the later *Gangster Squad*, within the early 1950s struggle between the LAPD and Mickey Cohen, Hanson's movie does feature the force's corruption and unrestrained violence in its plot, but it focuses on its trio of protagonist policemen who, with their heroic actions, manage to cleanse the institution of its cankers. These heroes are a pathologically ultraviolent cop (officer Bud White, played by Russell Crowe), an ambitious careerist (Sergeant Ed Exley, played by Guy Pearce), and an adviser to a *Dragnet*-like TV program, Sergeant Jack Vincennes (Kevin Spacey), who is more interested in celebrity than in police work. Their final sacrifice or triumph, as the case may be, is a discursive way of making us accept their objectionable methods and the LAPD's general approach to law enforcement. There is no hint of criticism or irony in the construction of these powerful individuals. Second, as Mark Ramsey affirms (in Shefrin 2005, 174), *L.A. Confidential* is the whitest movie of all time, with all the significant parts, whether bona fide law enforcers, corrupt policemen, or outlaws, played by Anglo actors and only a group of young black men in secondary roles and a young Latina woman (Marisol Padilla Sánchez) making a brief appearance as a rape victim to

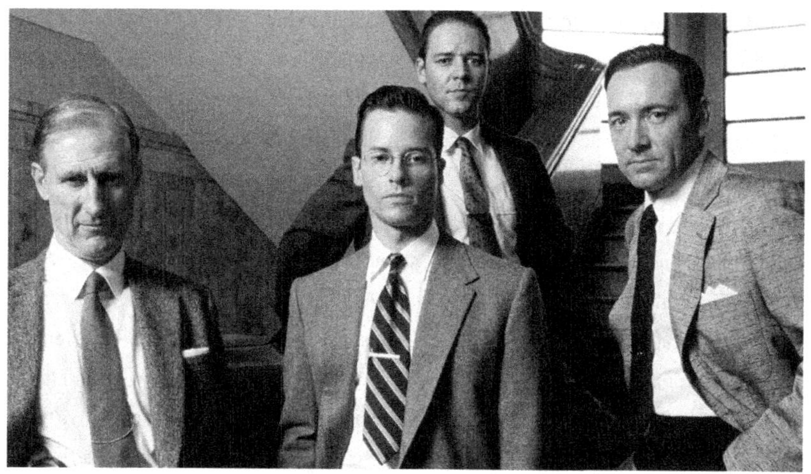

L.A. Confidential: "the whitest movie of all time."

pallidly fill the "ethnic quota." Comparing *L.A. Confidential* with *Chinatown*, James Naremore criticizes Hanson's movie as an exercise in nostalgia (1998, 276), a description that, in terms of urban discourses about the city's post-1992 identity, could be applied to any of the LAPD movies mentioned.

Naremore refers to *L.A. Confidential* in his book on film noir as part of what he calls "the noir mediascape" (1998, 254) and considers *Devil in a Blue Dress* a more accomplished contemporary instance of the genre. Most critics and reviewers have, in fact, framed their discussions of both films within the generic framework of noir or neo-noir, and in some cases they have been considered together, as in Elana Shefrin's significantly titled "*Le Noir et Le Blanc*" (2005). The parallels between the two are striking: Both are movies from the mid-1990s released by major studios (Columbia-TriStar in the case of *Blue Devil* and Warner Brothers for *L.A. Confidential*) with similar budgets ($27 million for Franklin's movie and $35 million for Hanson's, according to the IMDb); both are based on novels published in 1990 and written by noir Los Angeles–born authors (James Ellroy for *L.A. Confidential* and Walter Mosley for *Devil in a Blue Dress*); and both tell stories set in Los Angeles around the same time, the postwar years. As Shefrin explains, both movies draw on noir traditions, aim for visual authenticity in the reconstruction of the city's past, and make truth claims about the city's past (2005, 172–74).

In Chapter 3 I focused on alienation as the most important legacy of classic film noir from an Angeleno perspective, but a more obvious legacy of noir is noir itself, or neo-noir, as some critics label it, when, after some fifteen years dead, it was resuscitated in the early 1970s (see Naremore 1998, 10–11; and Rich 1995). *Chinatown* marked not only the beginning of Hollywood's interest in recreating episodes of Los Angeles history but also the starting point of neo-noir, preceded the previous year by Robert Altman's parodic take on a Philip Marlowe story, *The Long Goodbye*. Many other instances would follow, including *Body Heat* (Lawrence Kasdan, 1981), *Blood Simple* (Joel and Ethan Coen, 1984), and even *Blade Runner* (Ridley Scott, 1982). By looking at such movies as *Kill Me Again* (John Dahl, 1989), *The Grifters* (Stephen Frears, 1990), *Guncrazy* (Tamra Davis, 1992), *After Dark, My Sweet* (James Foley, 1990), *One False Move* (Carl Franklin, 1993), *The Last Seduction* (John Dahl, 1994), and *Devil in a Blue Dress*, B. Ruby Rich affirmed that by the mid-1990s "film noir [was] back with a vengeance" (1995, 6). She characterizes neo-noir as a return to the irrational universe of noir's "demonic narratives," "for the cultivation of our own *fin-de-siècle* nightmares." Neo-noir is over-the-top, flashy, and self-conscious and is populated by "irresistibly sexy and inexplicable evil" women and dumb men (Rich 1995, 6, 8). Naremore notes the ubiquity of the term *neo-noir* and relates it to his central idea about film noir—that rather than a style or a group of films, noir is primarily a discourse, a set of arguments and interpretations that shape commercial strategies and ideologies (1998, 10–11). After the hiatus of the 1960s, cinematic and critical conversation about film noir reopened and retook center stage.

Given the central role of film noir in the construction of cinematic Los Angeles, it is no surprise that the renovated genre would return, once and again, to its home city. *L.A. Confidential* and *Devil in a Blue Dress* are two such examples. In the 1940s and 1950s, noir offered radically novel representations of LA and, in the process, solidified a cinematic image on which many later movies would build, reproducing it or transforming it. In looking back at the city through its generic lens, noir proved itself capable of underlining (in the case of *L.A. Confidential*) and actively engaging with (in *Devil in a Blue Dress*) its blind spots. It has always been a paradox of critical vocabulary that there is no connection between "film noir" and "black cinema" (see Diawara 1993). As Justus Nieland sums it up in the title of his essay on *Devil in a Blue Dress* and Franklin's earlier movie, *One False Move*, these movies are "race noir" (1999, 63), or, in other words, they "make noir really noir." The dark city acquires in these movies a different shade of dark. It is this *noiring* of noir and, in the process, of Los Angeles that makes *Devil in a Blue Dress* a relevant movie and one that opened an avenue that, at least in the twenty years or so that have since elapsed, has not been traveled again. From an Angeleno perspective, the result is a city that is both familiar and defamiliarized, one that history has described to us but that, in contemporaneous movies like *L.A. Confidential* as much as in classic noir, has remained, well, in the dark.

Noir Home Owner

Devil in a Blue Dress explicitly presents itself as a Los Angeles movie, from its emphasis on visual authenticity (Shefrin 2005, 173) to the attention it pays to sociohistorical aspects of the city in the postwar years (Berrettini 1999, 74). The first shot confirms the filmmakers' intention as the camera gracefully cranes from a lovingly reconstructed establishing shot of Central Avenue in 1948 to "Joppy's Bar," on the first floor of a building at the corner with 34th Street, next to the "Central Meat Market," and frames from behind a man sitting by the window. The street is extremely busy and everybody—men, women, and children—is African American. In terms of generic expectations, the beginning is ambiguous because the internal voice-over narration by the protagonist, Ezekiel "Easy" Rawlins (Denzel Washington), evokes the well-known classic noir convention, but visually the movie seems more interested in offering us a glimpse of what South Central might have looked like in 1948, when the action takes place, than in recreating more stylized and ominous noir cityscapes. Once we are taken inside Joppy's, where a few men are drinking and smoking, we feel more at home as far as noir conventions are concerned, especially when Easy's voice-over tantalizes us with the beginning of a familiar mystery plot, except that it is told with a novel inflection—that of his African American accent.

The title sequence places the story to come within a precise African American urban milieu, with the credits unrolling over "Bronzeville at Night," a 1949 painting by Archibald Motley. The canvas shows a nighttime urban scene, originally in Chicago, but Franklin, as he explains in the DVD commentary, thought it could do for Los Angeles as well. In the soundtrack, we hear "West Side Baby," by T-Bone Walker, representing contemporaneous "shout and jump" music, a precursor of the rock and roll of the following decade that was born precisely around Central Avenue in LA.

The first scene segues from the title sequence, keeping the pace slow and translating the thick atmosphere of the credits into the density of life in the colorful street.

The film's opening portends a sense of new beginnings for African Americans in the city, a celebration of the thriving black business district and jazz culture of Central Avenue around 1948 (Voss 1998, 170), one firmly based on historical evidence. The film, says Naremore, celebrates "the resilience and tenacity of the postwar black community" (1998, 252). Its fictional world contrasts vividly with the Crenshaw and Compton of *Boyz n the Hood*, released four years earlier. In the earlier movie, these neighborhoods, which Furious Styles (Laurence Fishburne) wants to keep African American as a way of preserving black Angeleno identity, seem to be beyond recovery. Ominously, two police officers mention in passing a disturbance on Florence and Vermont, anticipating the urban troubles that would soon explode in the real city. *Boyz n the Hood* is born out of the same desperation about life in Los Angeles from which the justice riots would follow, whereas *Devil in a Blue Dress* returns to a moment in which history might have taken a different direction. As Shefrin argues, the story takes place within the African American experience of vacillation between segregation from and integration into mainstream white culture in the mid-twentieth century (2005, 174). However, this is only the establishing shot and the story has not even started. Once the detective plot gets into full swing, the film explores the foundations of the ephemerality of the black version of the Southern California dream (Davis 2006, 296). Mark Berrettini summarizes, "What is shown at the film's conclusion is a good moment in Easy's life and in the history of LA, but, after all, it is only a moment" (1999, 86).

At the outset, Easy is not a private dick, like the Sam Spades and Philip Marlowes of earlier noirs, but a machinist at an aircraft company, originally from Texas, who drives a Pontiac and owns a house in a quiet but lively new housing estate south of Downtown, probably in the Watts area. By the end of the movie, he seems to have made up his mind to continue his fledgling career as a detective. In the original novel this constitutes the open ending that made possible a long series of subsequent detective books (twelve to date). In the first installment, as in the movie, Rawlins represents the many African Americans who, attracted by the oil and aircraft industries, migrated to Southern California from Texas, Louisiana, and other Southern states. As Lawrence Culver explains, these people were drawn by the prospect of a better life that included decent jobs, cars, and, despite the restrictions, homes (2010, 426–27), goals that were not unlike those of middle-class and working-class Anglos from the same regions of the country. Easy decides to take on the investigative job that is offered to him at Joppy's because he has just lost his position at the aircraft plant (incidentally, like Bill Foster in *Falling Down*, although not the same type of job) and he is already two months behind with his mortgage. He does not have a wife or children but feels he is entitled to his small portion of the American dream. He is a good illustration of Mike Davis's perception that Los Angeles home owners love their children but they love their property values more (2006, 153). Easy Rawlins could be defined as a desperate home owner.

Joppy (Mel Winkler) introduces Easy to Albright (Tom Sizemore), the mysterious man who offers him a job, as one of the few African Americans who own a house, paying his mortgage every month, "just like y'all folks," meaning, of course, white people. Not being particularly interested in property ownership, Albright does not think anything of it, but for a black working-class Angeleno, or any black Angeleno, in the postwar years, having one's own house was no easy proposition. Davis (2006, 162–65) describes how the Anti-African Housing Association had been campaigning for a restrictive agreement to exclude nonwhites since the 1920s and 1930s. Every attempt by an African American to purchase property in a residential area had traditionally met with resistance or outright aggression from Anglo residents. This attitude was generally supported by developers, who refused to sell houses in privileged locations to blacks, even if they had the money to purchase them. In 1948 the Supreme Court ruled against this type of restrictive covenant, and later, in 1950, California's Alien Land Law was repealed. Yet developers continued to exclude nonwhites, and Anglo home owners continued to resist living in the same neighborhoods as nonwhites. In fact, white home owners were, throughout the twentieth century, instrumental in the consolidation of incorporations, a phenomenon to which I return in Chapter 8, as they sought to protect their privileged communities.

Eric Avila (2006) explains how suburbanization in the 1950s produced a new urban geography in the city based on a harsh contrast between white and black. As African Americans migrated to cities such as Los Angeles, the separation between black cities and white suburbs increased. The perimeter of the metropolis increased exponentially as an expanding generation of suburban U.S. citizens left the downtown areas looking for "homogeneity, containment, and predictability"

(Avila 2006, 6). This process became known as white flight, and it resulted in the fragmentation of an increasingly diverse population into a long series of exclusive communities, the uniformity of which vividly contrasted with the heterogeneity of the city as a whole. The development of Orange County after the war, as explained by Avila, is a good illustration of this process (44–45). Although film noir did not, as a whole, feature black characters, it did offer a bleak portrait of urban decadence. These filmic fictions articulated a social state of mind that produced white flight from the city centers, leaving behind what Avila calls, after a 1970s song by George Clinton, "chocolate cities" (65).

Susan Anderson (1996) also discusses the historical importance of the color line in housing—the strict housing segregation that became consolidated after the 1930s migration of blacks and whites from the South. As the population of black Angelenos grew from 7,599 in 1910 to nearly 200,000 by 1950, the color line became more visible and segregation stricter, despite legislation to the contrary. Anderson exemplifies this with the episode known as the 92nd Street Outrage: African Americans Mr. and Mrs. Lee Lofton bought a house in the Good Year Tract on East 92nd Street and were subsequently sued by neighbors for being "other than Caucasians"; they were harassed, eventually evicted, and forcibly taken to jail after they refused to leave their property (Anderson 1996, 344). It was as a consequence of this and similar cases that, ten years later, the Supreme Court ruled against restrictive covenants and declared them unconstitutional. As Karen Voss explains, the growing African American population of the city was boxed in around Central Avenue with nowhere to expand, except into Little Tokyo when Japanese Americans were taken to internment camps during World War II (1998, 170).

It is within this historical background that Easy is willing to first risk his job when he demands better pay and then, after losing it as a consequence of his demand, takes Albright's offer to investigate the disappearance of the missing woman. As an Angeleno, he understands the importance of home ownership, particularly for a black person. In the novel the first-person narrator makes explicit what is only implied in the movie: "The thought of paying the mortgage reminded me of my front yard and the shade of my fruit trees in the summer heat. I felt I was just as good as any white man, but if I didn't even own my front door, then people would look at me just like another poor beggar, with his hand outstretched" (Mosley 2010, 16). For Easy, his small property is a symbol of social justice, and his difficulties holding on to it a reflection of the long road to equality for African Americans.

The woman he is looking for is Daphne Monet (Jennifer Beals), the fiancée of mayoral incumbent Todd Carter (Terry Kinney). Monet disappears a few days before the plot starts. Albright is looking for a black man to carry out an investigation he does not feel capable of pursuing himself, precisely because of the color line. Given that Daphne "has a predilection for the company of Negroes," he thinks somebody like Easy will have easier access to the areas of the city where she might be found. The private detectives of noir fictions are particularly adept at navigating the city, capable of accessing parts that are beyond everyday visibility and even readability. In a noir film in which, practically for the first time in the genre, the city includes African American neighborhoods, it seems reasonable to surmise that the black protagonist might find it easier to get to the bottom of the mystery of the missing woman. Yet, in the course of his quest, Easy discovers, among other things, the power and the asymmetry of the color line in Los Angeles.

His journey around the city first takes him to an illegal club at 89th and Central. He moves effortlessly in the packed nightlife of the streets of South Central as well as inside the club, where most people are African American. But when his inquiries direct him to the Malibu Pier, things suddenly change: A white woman strikes up a casual conversation with him, and immediately several young white men materialize out of nowhere and threaten him. His mistake is simply being there, in a part of the city where people of his race are not welcome. He is momentarily saved by Albright, but from that moment on, both Easy and the spectator become aware of the proliferation of barriers to his mobility around the city. His nickname might, in fact, be read as a signifier of the contrast between the ease of his movements in the areas of the city that he knows and the constant discomfort and impending danger he encounters when he moves outside them. This extreme unease reappears when he is summoned to the Ambassador Hotel on Wilshire Boulevard by Daphne and has to sneak in through the back door because African Americans are not allowed in restricted areas of the establishment. When a few minutes later Daphne asks him to accompany her to an address in Laurel Canyon, she asks him, as they drive in the dark past a police car, if he is nervous. We hear his voice-over: "In a white neighborhood, with a white woman in my car. No, I wasn't nervous. I was stupid." The white world is for the protagonist, as Naremore concludes, a dangerously alien territory (1998, 250).

Conversely, Easy's dearest possession, his house, is constantly trespassed by other, generally white, people, particularly the LAPD, who seem to be forever looming close to him, waiting for his next mistake to arrest him. Easy's sense of security in South Central is a mirage. As the plot unfolds, he discovers that he has been framed by Joppy, his own friend. He seems at home at the illegal club where he first goes looking for Daphne, but a few hours after his tryst with Coretta (Lisa Nicole Carson) she is found dead and, in a typically noir implacable logic, he becomes the prime suspect in her murder. This makes him easy prey for the racist LAPD and the gangsters looking for Daphne. The movie carefully outlines an urban topography that is defined by race but at the same time suggests that the whole city is a potential trap for an African American citizen. Easy's mobility is seriously impaired, and his desire to settle down in his own property and in his own neighborhood is just as precarious. He cannot move around the city without putting his life at risk, but staying at home appears to be equally dangerous. Not unlike his Anglo ancestors from the noir movies of the 1940s and 1950s, he embodies an embattled masculinity, but one that, in Franklin's movie, is explicitly racialized.

Devil in a Blue Dress attempts to recuperate the midcentury noir city for its black dwellers and, in bringing to the surface what had remained invisible in the classic movies, unveils a cinematically unfamiliar urban space, but one that has a real existence in history. As a consequence of his noiring of noir, Franklin brings to the foreground the importance of real estate ownership in the drawing of racial lines in Los Angeles and the difficult predicament of potential African American home owners. Simultaneously, given that mobility within the city was about to change drastically with the construction of the grid of freeways that would crisscross it (the Pasadena Freeway had opened in 1940 and would be given its first extension in 1953), the film underlines the risks of such mobility for the racial minorities in the city. Easy Rawlins is not unlike his Anglo noir predecessors in experiencing the city as fraught with constant danger to themselves, whether in their offices and homes or as they travel through the city, but *Devil in a Blue Dress* recontextualizes this sense of pervasive menace and historicizes it as a specific African American experience. The protagonist is convincing as a noir hero precisely because he is a black man in a white city.

Mixing and Passing

After being released from jail, we find Easy walking along a bridge over the Los Angeles River at night. He is accosted by several men in a car and forced to get inside. There he meets Todd Carter's rival at the mayoral election, Mathew Terell (Maury Chaykin), who is mysteriously cruising the night accompanied by a young Latino boy, Jesús, whom he introduces as his adopted son. By this time the plot has thickened considerably and it is uncertain what Terell's role will be in the narrative. Later, as the story unravels the complex net of political and moral corruption that besets the noir city, it is revealed that Terell is a pedophile and Jesús is one of his victims. The boy materializes precisely when Easy is on the bridge, either walking toward or coming from East LA. What he is doing in that part of town is not clear, but this is one more thwarted crossing of his in the course of the story. Anglo Terell, for his part, has, metaphorically, no difficulty making a crossing to satisfy his sexual excesses, one that brings to the fore the racialized underside of the city's power dynamics. That we come across this character for the first and almost only time as he crosses the bridge that joins the Downtown area with the Mexican neighborhoods suggests the unspoken racial stratification of the cinematic city. Furthermore, and although both liaisons are not comparable, it is significant that in the story's imaginary, the two powerful candidates are sexually involved with people from a different race. It is as though a sexual link with the racial Other has become an unspoken sine qua non for local Anglo politicians.

Unlike Terell's crossing, however, Carter's is unintended, provoked as it is by Daphne's concealment of her racial identity: Daphne Monet is not Anglo, as everybody in the film thinks. She is really biracial Ruby Hanks from Louisiana, the daughter of a Creole mother and a white father. This characterizes her as a heroine of melodrama. Like other "tragic mulattas" in film and literature, for example, Peola Johnson (Fredi Washington) and Sarah Jane (Susan Kohner) in the two filmic versions of *Imitation of Life* (John M. Stahl, 1934; and Douglas Sirk, 1959), all Daphne wants is, in Easy's voice-over words, a place to fit in. Once her ruse is discovered, there is no such place for her in Los Angeles and she leaves the city. The possibility of integration will have to wait.

Ed Guerrero (1996) affirms that the miscegenation evoked by Daphne was as potent and socially charged an issue in the United States at the time of the film's

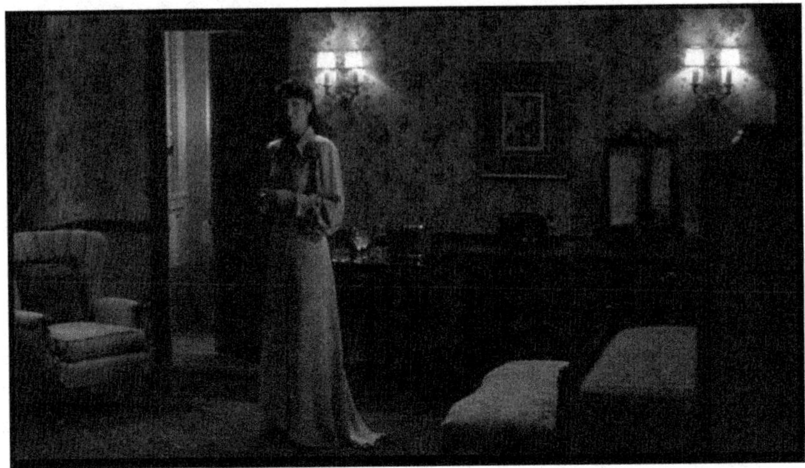

Devil in a Blue Dress: Daphne, or the public construction of racial identity.

release as it was in 1948, when the action takes place, but it was obviously not potent enough to guarantee the movie commercial success, probably because of the social climate in which the film was released, with the O. J. Simpson trial occupying the main headlines. Guerrero praises the main actors' performances, except in the case of Jennifer Beals, whose acting he finds flat (40–41). For Manohla Dargis, on the other hand, the problem is the movie's "curiously misjudged" casting option (1996, 38), by which she means that Beals could never pass as white and bears the signs of her biracial identity too evidently in her physical appearance. The mystery is understandable in the novel, in which we do not see her, but does not make much sense in the movie with this particular actor playing the part of Daphne. Dargis's is a strong point, yet it is curious that hardly anybody else followed her in objecting to Beals's part as the "passing mulatta" (Nieland 1999, 74). This may point to a certain relaxation in the cultural meanings and limits of whiteness in the 1990s and, as a consequence, to a less resistant attitude in the United States toward the idea of miscegenation. According to this rationale, spectators may have accepted the narrative conceit as part of the past that the film evokes but are less sensitive to what, in a cultural climate of strong rejection of miscegenation such as the late 1940s, may or may not have been perceived as white. As Berrettini perceptively argues through the analysis of the photograph of Daphne with Todd Carter in the newspaper, Daphne is white because she is publicly perceived as white, and neither Albright nor Rawlins nor anyone else, including her boyfriend, thinks of objecting to this description until she tells them otherwise (1999, 75–77). The same might be said about the film's critics and spectators in the 1990s, whose culturally determined willing suspension of disbelief leads them to accept Beals as white until her character reveals her "secret." This would probably contradict Guerrero's insight and point to a reduction in the cultural valence of racial mixing in the 1990s with respect to previous decades and to a simultaneous awareness of the crucial role it played in the historical construction of U.S. identity and, in our case, LA culture.

Whether or not these speculations can explain 1990s reactions to the movie, they provide a context to Daphne's presence in it and to the construction of her identity as an embodiment of both the recent history of the city and its post–Rodney King present. After she discloses the truth of her mixed race and, as a consequence, is rejected by her powerful fiancé, Easy's voice-over, drawing on the classic trope of the tragic mulatta, summarizes the end of her dream of belonging and also the unviability of the African American dream of equality: "She was still convinced, though, that her Negro blood didn't matter now that Terell couldn't use it to keep the man she wanted to marry out of the mayor's race. She was in love and couldn't see for dreamin' any better than the rest of us, I guess. 'Cause even though we had fought a war to keep the world free, the color line in America worked both ways and even a rich white man like Todd Carter was afraid to cross it."

Daphne's vulnerability in the story derives, therefore, from her straddling of the city's color line. As Justus Nieland affirms, the mulatta body is the place where racial boundaries collapse. He borrows from Homi Bhabha the insight that her racial indeterminacy challenges the efficacy of skin color as a signifier of cultural and racial difference (Nieland 1999, 63, 68). For Nieland, this makes her accessible to the depredations of those belonging to the dominant race, but at the same time it makes her dangerous because she threatens to usher in a different understanding of color lines and, in the sexualized world in which both the tragic mulatta stereotype and Daphne exist, she activates a different economy of desire. Daphne makes only three relatively brief appearances in the movie: when she summons Easy to the Ambassador Hotel and asks him to take her to the place in Laurel Canyon, when she breaks into his house and reveals to him and to us her hybrid identity, and when he rescues her in Malibu and takes her first to Carter's mansion and then to her brother's house. Until she "confesses" to Easy that she is biracial, she, acting as a white woman, constantly flirts with the protagonist. Although he resists her overtures and her innuendo in a way that, for example, he had not managed to do with Coretta previously, he is obviously not immune. Evoking, as Berrettini (1999, 76) points out, Barbara Stanwyck's performance in *Double Indemnity*, Daphne makes an immediate impact on the not-so-impassible private dick, for whom her whiteness is both a source of fascination and, following his recent experience on the Malibu Pier, a source of precaution. Similarly, Todd Carter has fallen in love with her because she is white, as the photograph in the newspaper sanctions. Yet it could be argued that her secret identity is also part of the attraction she has for both men: Todd may love her because, as a white woman, she is different. Easy may detect in her different whiteness—her off-whiteness—a promise of accessibility for the African American man.

Once she turns into a woman of mixed race, through the mere act of speaking it (no documental evidence seems required), Todd, given his social position and also his conservativism, has to reject her, but a barrier has fallen for Easy. Returning to find her a few days after dropping her off at her brother's house, he admits that he is excited at the prospect of seeing her again and is subsequently disappointed that she has disappeared. Unlike in Mosley's novel, there is no sexual consummation between the two characters, and this is evidence, according to Naremore (1998, 252), that the color line may have affected the film itself. Yet Daphne's mixed racial identity has also placed her in a desiring space in which she can break racial barriers. As Voss (1998, 173) argues, Daphne's biracial identity points to the possibility of integration of African American and white LA.

Daphne's disappearance from the film indicates the potency of miscegenation in postwar LA, but for contemporary audiences her trajectory in the movie suggests the precariousness of the color line, both its continuing validity and its cultural deterioration. It is this dynamic between possibility and impossibility, between resilience and decline of a traditional racialized cultural economy, that may be speaking, through its complex historical reconstruction, to post–justice riots Los Angeles. That Beals can be simultaneously accepted as white and as biracial without much commentary, even with a certain indifference toward her plight, underscores both the difficulties and the inevitability of change. *Devil in a Blue Dress* is, in this sense, a film about both the recent past and the immediate future. This future is subtly beckoned in the final scene.

After Easy discovers that Daphne has left town, a dissolve of his car to a headline in a local newspaper that announces that Carter is back (after Terell has been exposed as a pedophile) marks the transition to the movie's final scene. Easy is back in his house in Watts, watering his front lawn, as a police car with two Anglo police officers inside drives ominously by. Easy's expression portends his awareness that nothing has changed in his life, even though he has managed to survive the present adventure and paid the latest monthly installment on the mortgage. He confesses to his friend Odell (Albert Hall) that he is not interested in finding another job. Instead, he is thinking of becoming a private eye and investing in real estate, both relative acts of social passing, given, on the one hand, the whiteness of cinematic noir detectives and, on the other, the historical restrictions suffered by African Americans in the housing market. That an African American may want to play such a black-unfriendly market looks like open defiance of the city's ideological structure on the hero's part. Even as Daphne concedes defeat at her admittedly more drastic attempt at whiteness and even as the narrator "wisely" acknowledges the impossibility of her dream in a racist society, Easy nevertheless plans to follow her example, maybe as a tribute to her daring.

Unlike other movies mentioned at the beginning of this chapter, the LAPD takes a secondary role here. In *Devil in a Blue Dress* they are not particularly corrupt, just violent and cavalier about curtailing the rights and liberties of African Americans. It is as though their historical role as a tyrannical and pseudofascist force is so well established that it does not need to be explained once again and can just be taken as a given. Yet the reappearance of the police in the final scene suggests some supplementary meanings. Easy's fulfillment of his agreement with Carter provisionally guarantees him immunity from the police. At the story's end, however, the policemen are still visible, closely watching him, like tireless birds of prey. For a few seconds and five shots, the two officers and Easy are locked in an exchange of looks that indicates that the film's central conflict has not been resolved.

The sequence is put together by a series of eye-line matches that privilege Easy's look but equally underline the impersonal surveillance to which he is being subjected. The exchange consists of three shots of Easy, at progressively closer distances, and two countershots of the car. In the second shot of the protagonist, Washington's minimalist acting style conveys acknowledgment of their presence and their mission with an almost imperceptible nod in their direction. The third

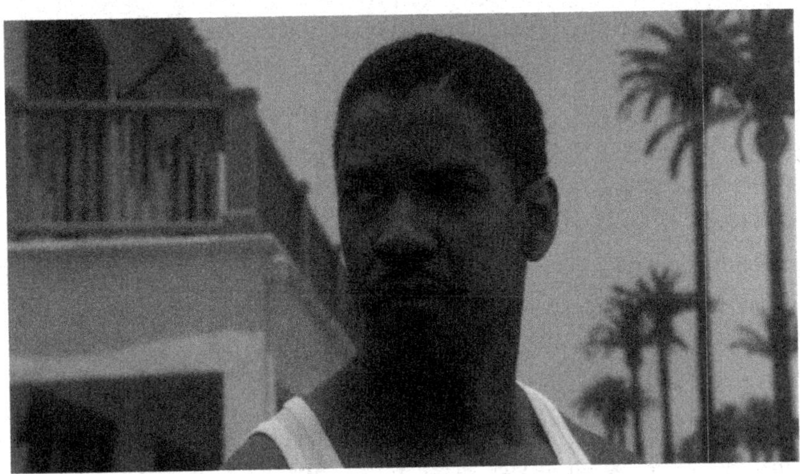

Devil in a Blue Dress: the defiant African American look.

shot, a close-up of his head following the trajectory of the car, expresses defiance. The movie's pace has slowed down to emphasize the narrative importance of the moment. It is at this point that Easy spells out to Odell his plans for the future. The impression is that the LAPD is somehow aware of these plans and of the subversion of the racialized status quo that they contain and that it is warning the aspiring detective that it is not going to allow any transgressions. Easy's brief nod suggests that he knows that the LAPD knows but that he is going to carry on regardless and that the struggle therefore continues. It could be argued that Washington's performance here as a calmly defiant African American is historically inaccurate, but it does evoke, for example, the attitude of the protagonists of Chester Himes's novels, especially his first one, *If He Hollers, Let Him Go* (1945).

Because the story of *Devil* is roughly set at the beginning of Chief Parker's long term as head of the LAPD, this standoff between the black hero and the policemen signals, in historical terms, the beginning of a long period of conflict and repression. Parker, who would during the Watts uprising notoriously describe rioters as "monkeys in a zoo" (Avila 2010, 103), considered himself a crusader against racial mixing. Appropriately, Daphne, the dangerous product of racial mixing, has been excised from Parker's city. Under different circumstances she might well have been standing next to Easy in the front garden, turning his property into a family home. This is, at some level, part of what may be going through the character's mind and conveyed through his rebellious look. His decision to, as it were, keep her spirit alive is also included in the exchange of looks of the sequence. The LAPD detectives, for their part, remind Easy that they will continue to police the racial boundaries, keeping those who, like him, threaten to demolish them under tight control.

In a sense, then, *Devil in a Blue Dress* turns out to be, after all, part of the historical examination of the LAPD that was to be expected from cultural texts after the force's participation in the 1992 riots. The movie ostensibly seeks to recuperate a part of the lost history of the city by appropriating film noir, one of the cinematic forms that had contributed to the invisibility of African American life. An exploration of the LAPD is not explicitly included in its ideological agenda, yet it finally becomes an important narrative element. At the same time, by strengthening in the final scene the opposition between the repressive institution and the African American hero, the movie indirectly highlights the centrality of Daphne in its discursive structure. The tragic mulatta, the well-known stereotype of the recent past, embodies in the 1990s the potential of a city that, given its profound demographic changes and the events that they unleashed, is ready to bring about the collapse of the urban boundaries so carefully constructed by generations of Anglo elites, with the aid of the LAPD, among others. Taken together with its companion piece, *L.A. Confidential*, *Devil in a Blue Dress* is representative of the discursive space that Hollywood is ready to occupy through its relatively novel interest in excavating the city's past. The two movies provide an insight into the new urban dynamics at work after 1992: The postmetropolis vacillates between recuperation of Anglo pride (and of the historical role of the LAPD) and celebration of the invisible place of racial minorities in the city's history and acknowledgment of their demands for a more visible part in its immediate future.

7

The Plot Thickens

Multi-Protagonist LA

Certain LA movies, for example, *Falling Down* (Joel Schumacher, 1993) and, to a lesser extent, *Collateral* (Michael Mann, 2004), touched a raw nerve among Angelenos, provoking a controversy that transcended the film community and eliciting commentary and discussion in purely Angeleno terms. Unlike hundreds of other movies that set their action in LA, these films are seen as being about the city and inevitably project an image of it that its citizens find inaccurate and often damaging. *Crash* (Paul Haggis, 2004) is another case in point. Ostensibly a melodrama about the state of racism in the city (and in the United States in general) in the aftermath of the 1992 riots, Paul Haggis's movie divided film aficionados, critics, political commentators, politicians, and LA citizens. Was the film a fair portrayal of the racial conflict lurking beneath the multicultural surface of the city or just a collection of stereotypes passing as the real LA, wondered Cara Mia DiMassa (2006, A23) in the *Los Angeles Times*. For DiMassa, the movie became a Rorschach test of Angelenos' opinion of their city. Although it was almost instantly attacked by many cultural critics and political activists, some of the city's most distinguished representatives praised it unconditionally, including then recently elected mayor Antonio Villaraigosa and LAPD chief William J. Bratton (DiMassa 2006, A1), who were more interested in the message of reconciliation and hope for the future suggested by the movie's resolution.

Particularly vocal in its critique of the movie was *Los Angeles Times* columnist Steve Lopez, who would himself four years later become the coprotagonist of another important LA movie, *The Soloist* (see Chapter 8). In a series of articles published after the movie's release and its subsequent Academy Award nomination for best movie of 2004 the following year, Lopez protested that the city was far from the dangerous battlefield pictured in *Crash*. Repeating similar arguments to those offered on the occasion of the release of *Falling Down*, Lopez wondered in these columns why "is it that out-of-towners can't resist the chance to cheer the long-awaited Los Angeles apocalypse?" (2005, B1). The city *is* divided by race and ethnicity but no more than other cities, and Lopez finds it to be in fact "one of the more successfully integrated cities in the world" (2006b, B1). In his *Times* article he was particularly critical of the Academy members who voted *Crash* best film of the year, calling them "kabbala and Bikram yoga practitioners" who hardly ever venture beyond Robertson "except to hand out Oscars or cruise for hookers" (B1) and accusing them of knowing little about the real experiences of Angeleno citizens. Although agreeing that the polyglot city abounds in instances of disenfranchisement, bias, and friction, Lopez asserted that it also offered "more opportunity for the kinds of real encounters that lead to greater tolerance and understanding." As an example of this, he concluded his third article with the signature of a reader: "From a Los Angeles Chinese-Jewish couple, whose neighbors are Korean, whose landlord is Armenian, who live down from a Sikh temple, whose dry cleaner is an African American and who never venture WEST of Robertson (except to eat Japanese or Persian)" (S. Lopez 2006a, B7).

I have quoted some of Lopez's views on the movie and his city not only because of his opinions about the enormous distance between the "real LA" and the city he finds depicted in *Crash* but also because of the accuracy of his delineation of the cultural debate in Los Angeles after 1992, between the city's diversity and multicultural environment on the one hand and the ever-growing proliferation of racial and ethnic enclaves on the other, a city where people from all around the world live close to each other but not always, or not generally, *with* each other. The part played by members of the Academy in Lopez's indictment is routinely extended to the whole of the Hollywood community, linked by family and business relationships and friendships to Angeleno life yet largely oblivious to the social changes happening around them and largely ignorant of the social dynamics of their own city.

Crash is part of a group of contemporary movies that feature several protagonists and several plot strands, often taking place in a big city and generally intersecting at various points in the narrative. In our increasingly multidimensional and multivocal societies, these movies are seen as a generic configuration that harbors the potentiality to articulate such contemporary experiences as those repeatedly described in discourses about Los Angeles. As María del Mar Azcona (2010, 19) explains in her book-length study of the genre, which she labels multi-protagonist films, these movies have always existed both in and outside Hollywood, but they started to visibly multiply in the 1980s, precisely when economic, social, and cultural globalization was becoming a visible influence on the lives of millions of people around the world. I am following Azcona's nomenclature here, but the variety of labels that have been ascribed to these movies in the last fifteen years or so attests to the critical and academic interest they have raised: ensemble and mosaic movies (Tröhler 2007), complex narratives (Bordwell 2006; Metz 2006), network narratives (Bordwell 2006), multitrack plots (Metz 2006), polyphonic, parallel, daisy chain, hub-and-spoke plots (Ramírez Berg 2006), hyperlink films (Quart 2005), and fractal films (Everett 2005), among others. Among the conventions of the genre, Azcona highlights the proliferation of protagonists and story lines, the tendency of these texts to concentrate more on characters than on action, their reliance on coincidence and chance and on group dynamics over traditional cause-and-effect relationships, the centrality of interconnectedness in an increasingly interconnected world, and the complexity and multisidedness of the issues dealt with. This assortment of characters, story lines, and points of view aspires to provide a more faithful representation of a complex human reality than would be possible with a single narrative plot. The movies prompt viewers to look for a different logic, one that often derives from the surplus of meaning produced by the proliferating parallels and contrasts between the different story lines and characters rather than from the individual narrative arcs (Azcona 2010, 7, 37–42).

Most multi-protagonist movies, particularly those in which the various narrative threads share a single space, are set in cities, and among these cities Los Angeles is the most familiar spatial presence, to the extent that this group of films has also been labeled "LA ensemble" (Hsu 2006, 134). Because the industry is based in the city that epitomizes the effects of globalization on urban structure and growth and because the postmetropolis/exopolis resists easy explanations, it is small wonder that the daisy chain plots of many multi-protagonist movies have found their natural space in Los Angeles. If no traditional narrative can hope to incorporate the multiplicity of this city, here is a genre that offers multiplicity as its central structural paradigm. If the progress forward toward a resolution of the conflict of traditional stories is particularly inadequate to reproduce the absence of linearity of LA life and its ineffability, here is a genre that, while remaining relatively close to the mainstream, says that traditional cause-and-effect relationships are not the best way to convey contemporary experiences. Instead, it offers narrative lines that, rather than move forward, tend to expand and spread out in all sorts of directions, like the maze of freeways that simultaneously encapsulate the nature of movement in the city and hamper surface mobility in many of its poorer neighborhoods.

Not all multi-protagonist movies can be said to fully realize this potential. *Magnolia* (Paul Thomas Anderson, 1999) is an LA ensemble movie, yet its principal goal is not to reproduce multiplicity or diversity in the city. Rather, it continues to imagine LA exclusively as the socially and ethnically homogeneous hometown of the entertainment industry. Similarly, *Short Cuts* (Robert Altman, 1993), for many one of the central exemplars of a genre that some have called Altmanesque films, is, for all its proliferation of Angeleno characters and stories, equally uniform and equally blind to the multicultural realities of its city. *Grand Canyon* (Lawrence Kasdan, 1991), another early LA multi-protagonist movie, does allow for greater diversity in its interwoven stories, but its wealthy Anglo protagonists remain firmly at the center of the plot and its multistrand structure does not begin to reflect the conflicts, interactions, and coalitions that were at the time of its release coming to a head. *Crash*, in tackling the issue of racism head on and in offering a more balanced cross-section of Angeleno society, represents a step forward with respect to earlier efforts, yet its multi-protagonist approach to racism and interethnic conflict in LA has been challenged from various quarters. A particularly damning critique of the film was offered by Hsuan Hsu (2006, 144), whose main argument is that the movie reduces the realities of racism to interpersonal relationships, thus hiding its more important institutional, legal, and historical aspects. This is a general analysis that can be applied to most multi-protagonist movies, including what for Hsu is the subgenre of the ensemble film set in LA, a genre with four entries, the four movies mentioned in this paragraph: *Grand Canyon*, *Short Cuts*, *Magnolia*, and *Crash*.

The emphasis on interpersonal relationships that we find in multi-protagonist movies is, according to Hsu (2006), a limitation rather than an asset of the genre as a viable representation of the ethnic complexities of such urban centers as Los Angeles. In fact, *Crash* becomes a reactionary and insidious text in its privatization of race. Like *Crash*, the LA ensemble film in general focuses exclusively on interpersonal, sexual, and psychological issues. A more accurate exploration of the complexity of life in the modern metropolis would require an account of the social, political, economic, and geographic conditions that keep people apart. Moreover, these films betray the white male, presumably liberal, perspective of their directors, who exclude most ethnic and demographic groups and claim to represent race through a few token, generally African American, characters (Hsu 2006, 134–36). This is not even the case for *Short Cuts*, which eschews characters other than white almost completely, but seems to be the strategy used in *Grand Canyon* and, to a lesser extent, in *Magnolia*, whereas *Crash* incorporates greater variety but still maintains the centrality of the male Anglo perspective. Hsu, like Lopez, maps the theoretical debate in forceful terms. For him, multi-protagonist movies are feeble attempts to hide the continuing dominance of the white male hero behind an appearance of narrative complexity; and, in the case of LA, they substitute intense interpersonal relationships in a city where connections are difficult for a deeper exploration of the causes of social inequality and segregation.

Whether or not we accept Hsu's general point about the inadequacy of the movies' emphasis on the individual, his list of multi-protagonist LA movies must be enlarged. In the post-1992 period we need to also include at least *Pulp Fiction* (Quentin Tarantino, 1994), *2 Days in the Valley* (John Herzfeld, 1996), *Boogie Nights* (Paul Thomas Anderson, 1997), *Jackie Brown* (Quentin Tarantino, 1997), *Things You Can Tell Just by Looking at Her* (Rodrigo García, 1999), *The Million Dollar Hotel* (Wim Wenders, 1999), *What's Cooking?* (Gurinder Chadha, 2000), *Happy Endings* (Don Roos, 2005), *Friends with Money* (Nicole Holofcener, 2006), *The Informers* (Gregor Jordan, 2008), *Crossing Over* (Wayne Kramer, 2009), *Mother and Child* (Rodrigo García, 2009), *Valentine's Day* (Garry Marshall, 2010), *Girl Walks into a Bar* (Sebastián Gutiérrez, 2011), and *The Bling Ring* (Sofia Coppola, 2013). This longer list offers examples of more varied structures than the four core cases mentioned by Hsu and constitutes a more workable sample of the variety and heterogeneity of multi-protagonist LA movies.

In this chapter I explore the LA constructed by the multi-protagonist genre. Although I find the movies discussed by Hsu relevant for this purpose, and *Crash* in particular as a crucial post-1992 Los Angeles movie, here I want to move away from the more obvious examples and focus on two relatively minor movies with two divergent generic registers: the comedic *What's Cooking?* and the melodramatic *Mother and Child*. Both movies had modest budgets, placing them in Schatz's third class of contemporary Hollywood fare, were produced independently, although Sony Classics picked up *Mother and Child* for U.S. distribution, and yielded similar results at the box office, slightly above the $1 million mark (according to the IMDb).

The two also share the relative outsider status of their filmmakers. *What's Cooking?* was co-written and directed by Gurinder Chadha, a woman of Indian origin who was born in Kenya but has lived in London since childhood (and is a U.K. citizen). Her co-writer is her husband and regular writing partner Paul Mayeda Berges, a Japanese American Angeleno. *Mother and Child* was written and directed by Rodrigo García, the Bogotá-born son of Colombian novelist Gabriel García Márquez. If, as Hsu contends, LA ensemble films invariably convey the male Anglo perspective of the filmmakers, regardless of their narrative variety, what happens when the filmmakers are not white males but part of the very minorities that the movies discriminate against? Do the emphasis and the ideological focus change in significant ways depending on the ethnic identity of the artists, or is the pattern more structural, more entrenched in the culture, and therefore independent of the ethnic and national identities of the filmmakers?

The Other European Gaze

In a brief interview included in the DVD extras, Chadha describes *What's Cooking?* as the kind of film about Los Angeles that she had never seen before. On going to LA to promote her first feature, *Bhaji on the Beach* (1993), she saw a different city from what she had experienced in the movies, and her second feature came out of her desire to turn that discrepancy into a film text. For this she chose a multi-protagonist canvas, a structure that she has not repeated in any of her subsequent movies, even though all of them, like *Bhaji*, are about intercultural clashes and transnational experiences. The multi-protagonist genre is therefore a one-off in her cinematic career. Azcona (2010) tentatively includes Chadha's movie in the subgroup of mosaic films, a form that started to proliferate in the 1990s. Mosaic films feature a set of characters with little connection to one another, at least at the beginning, even though they cross paths over the course of the story and their story lines become more or less intertwined, mainly through coincidence. Although this label may usefully capture the distinctiveness of a movie like *What's Cooking?* the differences among the instances from the 1990s that Azcona includes in this group highlight, as she argues, the difficulties inherent in any categorization (2010, 21–22).

The structural tension that Azcona finds in mosaic movies between narrative segregation and intermittent interconnection of plot strands captures an important dimension of the urban dynamics of the postmetropolis, at least as a discursive formation of the multicultural era. Coincidence, the narrative resource that many critics have complained about in connection with *Crash* and other multi-protagonist movies but one that Azcona (2010, 37) places at the center of the conventions of the genre, can also be seen as a powerful metaphor for the randomness and unpredictability of social relations in a city such as LA. As a mosaic movie, however, *What's Cooking?* has at least one important limitation: It does not deal with isolated individuals and their difficulties to connect with other people. Instead of individuals, the multiple plot affects four families. The close-knit intragroup links are their members' primary antidote to the ravages caused by the city. What characterizes Chadha's LA is not traditional or neotraditional Angeleno alienation but rather ethnic segregation. The movie's main conceit and the core feature of its comic space is the fact that the distance between these diverse communities is more apparent than real. This is not only because interethnic links proliferate as the story develops but also because, unbeknownst to the spectator and to the characters themselves, the four families live in adjacent houses, occupying the four corners of the intersection of two streets.

The families are Hispanic, Jewish, African American, and Vietnamese American, and each is culturally defined through their more or less stereotyped response to the social and cultural changes around them. The Vietnamese American family is depicted as the most traditional, bewildered by social and cultural transformations that they do not understand and averse to interethnic intimate relationships and the prospect of hybrid families. The Hispanic family is relatively more tolerant toward ethnic difference, although its members are not particularly enthusiastic about understanding those outside their community beyond comically inexact clichés and they remain patriarchal and sexist. The Jewish parents are incapable of coping with their daughter's sexual orientation and her pregnancy outside heterosexual wedlock. The African American family is beset with pressures from gender and intergenerational conflicts that are loosely related to institutional racism. The rift between parents and children is common to all four families, although it is less obvious in the Hispanic corner. The younger generation, although not immune to making mistakes, is characterized by greater tolerance toward the Other and becomes the motor of change.

Narrative progress and narrative arcs are limited in multi-protagonist movies. Given the average length of most feature films, the proliferation of stories makes the time devoted to each individual story much shorter, and therefore character development is more problematic. For this reason, movies such as *What's Cooking?* often resort to stereotypes and quick methods of characterization, both for individual people and for groups, a strategy that the genre shares with comedy and that is therefore essential in the movie. It is, as Azcona (2010) reminds us, in the multiplying interconnections and parallels between the different strands that we are more likely to find not only what is distinctive about the genre but also narrative complexity and thematic reverberations. The movie intensifies this dimension of the genre by cutting rapidly between stories, with generally no more than two or three minutes devoted to each of the four stories before moving on to the next one. As a consequence, the individual stories are slight. The narrative is more interested in the intertwining of the plots than in letting each individual story develop at its leisure. In *What's Cooking?* this is not just an arbitrary conceit or an exclusively comic device but a strong structural correlative of the dynamic between urban segregation and interconnection that, in the movie's discourse, characterizes contemporary lives in LA.

When Chadha points out that the city she found when she traveled to Los Angeles was not what she had expected from her movie experience, she means the baffling diversity that the cinema has failed to capture. It must be as a response to the Anglo-dominated stories that preceded this movie that none of the four families in the plot are Anglo and that, for once, Anglo characters are displaced to the margins of the narrative. It could be argued that the Jewish family stands for whiteness, but the movie does not present it as such, drawing from the historical ambivalence of Jews toward white assimilation, specifically in Los Angeles. Eric Avila (2006), for example, explains how Jews "became white folks" in the aftermath of World War II and how in LA many moved from the more "ethnic" Eastside, particularly Boyle Heights, to the Westside, including affluent communities in Beverly Hills, Bel Air, Brentwood, Pacific Palisades, and parts of the San Fernando Valley, while some of them became instrumental in the real estate development of postwar suburbia. Hollywood facilitated this "Jewish whitening" because most of the studio moguls who had moved from the East Coast to Southern California in the first decades of the twentieth century were European Jews. Avila notes how Jack Warner established a strict whites-only hiring policy at Warner Brothers and, later, in the 1960s, how Jewish millionaire Mark Taper contributed $1 million to the building of the Music Center Downtown, thus bringing Eastside WASP wealth and Westside Jewish wealth together in a drive to upgrade the cultural profile of the city (Avila 2006, 15, 43–44, 61–62). As Philip Ethington (2010, 202) argues, this process was possible because in LA "ethnic" groups such as Italians and East European Jews were endowed with a social mobility that was denied to nonwhite racial groups. Still, the whiteness of "ethnic whites" has historically been questioned by nativist Anglo Americans (Culver 2010, 426). American Jews, like Italian Americans, have often occupied a gray area in the Southern Californian mix, while at the same time remaining a large and culturally distinctive and visible ethnic group. The size of the Jewish population of the city is in itself striking; with more than 600,000 Jews at the beginning of the twenty-first century, Los Angeles was, ahead of Jerusalem, the fourth largest world city in terms of the number of Jewish inhabitants (LeElef 2001).

Local ethnic history, therefore, reinforces the movie's choice of the Seelig family as one of its four "ethnic" groups, despite the white identification of such relatively high-profile actors as Julianna Margulies and, especially, Kyra Sedgwick, who play, respectively, Carla and Rachel, the lesbian couple. Curiously, most of the cast in this story, including Margulies and Sedgwick but also Lainie Kazan and Maury Chaykin, Rachel's Angeleno parents in the movie, and Estelle Harris, as Fairfax born and raised Aunt Bea, are East Coast Jewish actors. Something similar can be said about the Avila family, whose central figure, Elizabeth, is played by New Yorker Mercedes Ruehl, whose Hispanic roots are Cuban. Cuban-born Victor Rivers plays her ex-husband, Javier. Their daughter, Gina Avila, is played by Isidra Vega, also from New York. Given that LA's diversity is matched only by its demographic mobility and that a large part of its population was born outside the city, these casting choices may be acceptable. Cubans and Cuban Americans, for instance, have a visible presence in Southern California, if not comparable to Florida or New York. Still, the Avilas are supposed to be Mexican American, and the Seeligs Angelenos. Casting is most problematic in the case of the Vietnamese American Nguyen family, whose members are played by Chinese Joan Chen (as Trinh Nguyen) and Chao Li Chi (as her father), Cambodian François Chau (as Trinh's husband, Duc), and Virginia-born Korean American Will Yun Lee (as son Jimmy). When the men in the Avila family try to bond with Jimmy by mentioning legendary Hong Kong stars Bruce Lee and Jackie Chan, Jimmy tolerantly accepts the attempt and does not mention that he is Vietnamese American and not from Hong Kong, but actor Lee must have felt amused at acknowledging the other characters' ignorance, because the movie reproduces a similar attitude in his own casting. Although such casting decisions as those described here are usual in Hollywood movies and although the history of U.S. cinema abounds in much more outrageous discrepancies between actor and character, they are particularly visible and problematic in a movie that attempts to capture the realities of ethnic diversity in Los Angeles and makes the celebration of this diversity its main discursive goal. Greater accuracy would have been preferable.

The exact location of the area where the four families live is not explicitly mentioned in *What's Cooking?* but briefly glimpsed street signs place it at the intersection of Kelton Avenue and Tennessee Avenue, in a Westside neighborhood west of Century City between Pico and Olympic Boulevards and Westwood and Sepulveda Boulevards. It is not a strongly marked location in terms of Angeleno topography, but it encapsulates a generic Westside not-particularly-wealthy middle-class neighborhood, crossed by long narrow avenues framed by palm trees and built with a mix of vaguely California-style houses. Given its lack of specific ethnic features, Kelton and Tennessee can be constructed by the filmmakers as an LA spot where interethnic proximity is possible and even likely. After all, moving to the Westside from communities east of the Los Angeles River or from South Central can be construed as a historically accurate aspirational move for upwardly mobile families—not everybody can move directly to Hancock Park, Beverly Hills, Bel Air, Brentwood, or Pacific Palisades. In revealing that the four houses are so close at the end of the story, the movie makes this closeness its central discursive point and underlines both the unlikelihood of such a coincidence in LA and the fact that it can nevertheless happen—a confirmation of the dynamic between segregation and interconnection that defines the experience of the city put forward by the movie through its multi-protagonist structure.

This spatial coexistence is an important plot element that the narrative keeps hidden until its climactic moment, but it makes sense in a film whose structure is mostly devoted to establishing constant formal parallels between the four stories and to the frequent diegetic intersections between all or some of them. For instance, a scene at LAX, where Audrey Williams (Alfre Woodard) goes to meet her mother-in-law, Grace (Ann Weldon), has her cross paths inside the airport with Rachel Seelig and her "roommate" Carla. The characters, not knowing each other, are not aware, but the narrative highlights it for us. A few minutes later, members of the Avila, Seelig, and Williams families are all shopping at the same supermarket at the same time, and the movie rhetorically emphasizes this proximity by means of framing and camera movements that link them together. Elizabeth Avila, a school teacher, goes to the Nguyens' video store, where she sees Joey, the youngest son of the Vietnamese American family and one of her pupils. She is briefly introduced to Duc Nguyen, but neither of them is aware that their older children, Gina and Jimmy, both studying at Berkeley, are a couple and, in fact, at this point, traveling south to spend Thanksgiving with the Avila family. Gina and Jimmy must know that they are neighbors in LA, but they hide this information both from their families and from us. As part of the opening scene, the kids at the school put on a play to celebrate Thanksgiving, with Elizabeth "directing" them and both the Nguyens and Audrey in the audience.

These moments are characteristic of mosaic films, the intersections often being casual, coincidental, and irrelevant in terms of narrative development, yet structurally they are important nodes that emphasize the "small world phenomenon" (Azcona 2010, 35–36). *What's Cooking?* like many other multi-protagonist films, revels in moments like these that highlight the potential for interconnectedness of traditionally alienated Angelenos. In general terms, however, the movie prefers to let the four stories run simultaneously and cuts constantly between them, emphasizing their commonalities, especially those centered around food and cooking. Thus turkeys seem to go in and out of the oven at the same time, the various families are watching the same program on TV, blessings commemorating the pioneers and giving thanks to the Native Americans happen simultaneously, and so on. Sometimes, frequent cutting between stories is so fast that they become montage sequences of the various houses or the various side dishes prepared by the women in each of the families. The abundance and deliciousness of the ethnic foods that accompany but overwhelm the common turkey is a thinly disguised metaphor for the text's comic point: The bringing together of such variety will make the city stronger. Even crises such as the arrival of Elizabeth's fellow teacher Danny (A Martínez) at the party, the collapsing of the table at the Williamses', and the news that Rachel is pregnant at the Seeligs are made to rhyme, with the gun being shot at the Nguyens' as the culmination of the climactic scenes. In general, the text is more interested in the potentialities of these rhymes and coincidences than in the outcome of the individual stories.

The narrative moves from relative ethnic segregation to growing interaction. At the outset the members of each of the four families come together for a common celebration, Thanksgiving, one that links them as U.S. Americans but amusedly emphasizes the many specific ways in which the celebration can be carried out—that is, the many ways of being "American." The celebration is a good excuse to bring everybody to their own kind and to reinforce the solidity of the individual ethnic group. Yet the "purity" of the individual communities is compromised from the beginning. The traditional views of the Nguyen family, particularly of the two parents, are obviously not shared by the younger generation: Jenny (Kristy Wu) has an Anglo boyfriend and Jimmy a Hispanic girlfriend. These are the two most obvious interethnic relationships in the movie. Their younger brother, Gary (Jimmy Pham), however, is more drawn toward gang life, precisely as a way to protect the group from external attacks. The movie highlights the contrast between both attitudes by having the parents be initially opposed to Jenny's liaison but then bringing them to understand how much more serious Gary's situation is and, indirectly, how misguided their anxiety about miscegenation is and how familiarity with other ethnic groups might prevent Gary's predicament.

At the Williams household the perspective is different. Ron (Dennis Haysbert) works as an assistant to Anglo governor Rhodes (Frank Novak), and he sees his promising political career as evidence that compromising with those in charge (the Anglo-dominated institutions) is the way for African Americans to thrive in the community. He favors assimilation over confrontation. His conflict with his son Michael (Eric George) revolves around this issue. Michael, who, at the beginning, has embarrassed his father by being involved in a mildly violent protest against the governor (with his father present), later accuses Ron of selling out and justifies his decision to enroll in an African American university rather than the most prestigious (and much closer) UC Santa Barbara as a way to remain alert to the constant injustices dealt to black people in the country. The Williamses have white guests, the only case (apart from Jimmy's presence at the Avilas') in which people from a different race are invited to one of the houses. This form of interaction is not exactly endorsed by the text, because it seems based on Ron's political ambitions and desire for assimilation, something that does not fit exactly within the film's ideological remit. Curiously, the Jewish family is the only one that remains wholly contained, because Carla, the outsider, is also Jewish. When Rachel discloses at the meal that she is pregnant and that the donor is their guest Jerry (Andrew Heckler), who is gay, Aunt Bea provides the comic punch line, releasing the tension with her question "Is the baby Jewish?" No mixing at the Seeligs for the moment.

This asymmetry in the approaches of the four stories toward segregation and interrelations counterbalances the movie's fondness for connections between them. Generic and structural considerations never keep *What's Cooking?* far away from stereotypes, even if these stereotypes are parodied or revised in various comic ways. As Charles Ramírez Berg (2002) reminds us in his exploration of Hollywood Latino stereotypes, the original meaning of the term, as coined by cognitive psychologist Walter Lippmann, was value-neutral. Negative and damaging stereotyping came later, but the psychological mechanism itself is not necessarily aggressive or diminishing. We all need stereotypes to help us make sense of the world around us (Ramírez Berg 2002, 14). In certain contexts, stereotypes can serve a constructive function if they are used reflexively to convey the contradictions behind them. A reliance on stereotypes is, as we have seen, habitual in multi-protagonist movies, where it is not individual features but the result of the combination of stereotypes that matters. This reliance on them steers a text such as *What's Cooking?* away from realistic forms of representation. In fact, it could be said that, as in *Magnolia* and, in a different sense, in *Mulholland Drive*, the textual take on the city resides in the film's form: Rather than attempting a slice of life narrative, the film draws our attention to the way in which it combines familiar views in a complex way to project both the energy and unpredictability of the postmetropolis—not a society that can be explained away with a few brushes or with realistic concentration on isolated individual experiences. As Margrit Tröhler argues (in Azcona 2010, 21), *What's Cooking?* makes good use of the potential of the genre and its rhizomatic quality—a structure without a center in which hierarchical organization gives way to arbitrary and open connections. The narrative may seem predictable, but the constant links throw the ideological discourse in different directions, offering as a result an irregular canvas that resists tidy decodifications. The ending may offer a more or less conventional resolution, but the beginning is more representative of the film's "messy" use of generic mechanisms.

Anticipating all the later moments mentioned in the preceding paragraphs and, more important, the film's stylized comic structure, the title sequence of *What's Cooking?* introduces the various plots simultaneously but is more interested in conveying a more abstract picture of the urban space in which the stories develop. Here the protagonist is the city, and the narrative excuse used to introduce us to its variety and energy is, significantly for LA, a bus ride. I have described the four protagonist families in *What's Cooking?* but there is a fifth family that is missing from my description: the smiling Anglo family with which the movie starts after the first few credits on black lead. A detail shot of a turkey being carved becomes, as the frame pulls back, a family group with smiling faces and white skin that encapsulates, in the celebration of the very American holiday, the traditional view of the country, one that has been dominant throughout most of LA history and throughout the shorter history of Los Angeles movies. The accompanying slow rendition of the American anthem emphasizes the iconicity of the image. But then the wholesome picture is revealed to be part of an advertisement on the side of a Metro bus. As the music suddenly changes to a more lively Latin rhythm, the bus drives off and we are given access to its interior. This interior is portrayed as the flip side of the smiling family. We are first offered a close-up of the Sikh driver. Next to him is sitting a middle-aged white man who lifts his eyes from the newspaper and looks offscreen toward the back of the bus. The subsequent eye-line match reveals a full bus, with many people in animated conversation; we see two Indian women wearing saris (one of them played by the director herself), a Hispanic family, two women wearing African clothes, various Asian or Asian American people, and one or two white men and women. The main focus of the sequence, however, is on Jenny and her boyfriend, Luke (Chad Todhunter), passionately kissing in close-up. The atmosphere in the bus is festive, and nobody seems to notice or care. As the rest of the credits unroll on-screen, shots of the bus riding past various neighborhoods alternate with the school play and the incident with Governor Rhodes. We see the bus traveling across Broadway, past a section of Fairfax, and then through Little Tokyo, Boyle Heights, above a busy freeway outside Downtown, what looks like Lincoln Heights, Chinatown, the Farmer's Market again on Fairfax, and Mariachi Plaza, again in Boyle Heights. The sequence does not make any sense geographically and editing puts together a bus ride that would be impossible in real terms. The goal

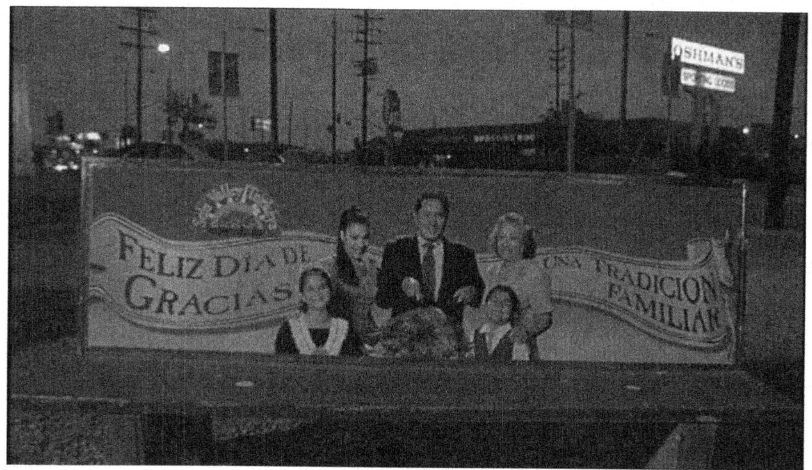

"Feliz día de acción de gracias": the heterogeneity of the multicultural city in *What's Cooking?*

here is not topographic accuracy but the conveyance of a mood that combines the "ethnic" rhythm of salsa music with the variety of locations that stand for the multicultural canvas of the city.

The ride ends, as far as the film is concerned, with some of the passengers getting off the bus. As the human figures leave the frame and the soundtrack returns to the mellow version of the national anthem, another sign is disclosed on the ground, almost identical to the one on the side of the bus, except this time the five-member family (two parents, two children, and a grandmother) is Hispanic and the legend is also in Spanish: "Feliz día de gracias, una tradición familiar," coinciding with the director's credit superimposed on the image of the smiling family. This superimposition, like the rest of the five-minute-long credit sequence, anticipates the textual gaze: a contemporary postmetropolis where being American means something different from what dominant discourses, both filmic and extra-filmic, have been telling us for decades. It conveys the perspective of the outsider, who, before visiting the place, had expected, from her experience of many cultural texts, including films, a very different, more homogeneous city, one with a different sound. That this multicultural city should "colonize" such a marked Anglo American historical celebration suggests both the pervasiveness of a transformation that, to external eyes, had remained relatively hidden and the apparent ability of the city to adapt.

What's Cooking? is not the best known of Los Angeles multi-protagonist movies, yet in its combination of the genre's conventions with a comic register, it encapsulates a contemporary commitment to a partly utopian perspective on the post-1992 city, one that, simultaneously, is grounded in an assortment of urban realities as discovered by an outsider. Casting limitations partly undermine the textual plea for a more profound understanding of the Other and weaken its efforts at authenticity and honesty, but the combination of an uninhibited and productive use of stereotypes with the potential for rhyzomatic complexity and messiness of the multi-protagonist canvas allows the movie to relocate the gaze to a vantage point from which geographic, social, and ethnic conflicts and tensions still seem fully operative and inequality seems stronger than ever, but even they cannot contain the comedic energy and vibrancy of the multi-protagonist city.

Alienation and Multiplication

Unlike Gurinder Chadha, Rodrigo García can be considered a regular of the multi-protagonist movie, having directed four films in this format: *Things You Can Tell Just by Looking at Her* (2000), *Ten Tiny Love Stories* (2002), *Nine Lives* (2005), and *Mother and Child* (2009), his latest one to date. He has also contributed the segment "La Séptima y Albareda" to the portmanteau film *Revolución* (2010), a Mexican movie made up of ten shorts directed by different filmmakers commemorating the centennial celebration of the Mexican Revolution. García's four features offer variations on the genre but also share common structural characteristics and have other similarities, the most striking being that their protagonists are almost exclusively women. The actions of these movies take place in Los Angeles, but none of them are specific about location, except that we know that the characters in *Things You Can Tell* all live in the San Fernando Valley. In *Mother and Child* the most we get is a vague reference to a restaurant in Burbank, a beautiful Californian sunset seen from the interior of a Downtown lawyer's office, and a view from the condominium where Elizabeth (Naomi Watts) lives, which places the condo near the ocean in one of the beach communities. The homogeneity of García's multi-protagonist world is further reinforced by the fact that the same actors tend to reappear in his films, including Glenn Close, Kathy Baker, Holly Hunter, Amy Brenneman, Miguel Sandoval, Elpidia Carrillo, Lisa Gay Hamilton, and Elizabeth Peña. Because the movies are visually consistent and their female protagonists belong to a relatively similar social class and live in similar Angeleno surroundings, we almost expect characters from one film to reappear in the others, and, with certain variations, it could be argued that they do, under slightly different guises and identities. The relatively restrained and unspectacular coincidences that the films incorporate in their structures make these connections between texts more likely. They also work together to create a geographically generic but socially and psychologically powerful view of the life of contemporary middle-class Angelenas.

Mother and Child can therefore be seen as a slice of García's Los Angeles, a city of clean suburbs, lonely individuals, and alienated women who may or may not find comfort in interpersonal relationships, within or outside the family. These women are the sisters of *Safe*'s Carol White, even if the somatization of their anxieties is less extreme. In the history of Los Angeles cinema, they are the female inheritors of the male protagonists of film noir and the rough contemporaries of D-Fens, the man deprived of his traditional masculinity in *Falling Down*, of Vincent, the hit man in *Collateral*, and of the men in the entertainment industry featured in *Magnolia*, among many other examples of male alienation. Contemporary life in the postmetropolis and changed social protocols have thrown these women into disarray. The women in *Mother and Child* appear to be caught between their careers and traditional female roles. Alienation is the habitual outcome of this quandary, and reaching out to those around them, although full of difficulties, is the only way out of it.

The Los Angeles pictured in *Mother and Child* is therefore a different city from the one in *What's Cooking?* The earlier movie celebrates strong family and ethnic groups and their growing capacity to interact with each other. *Mother and Child* is a story of isolated individuals who are not defined by their ethnic or social group or by any sense of belonging. They do not represent larger groups but rather the ravages of loneliness in the modern city. *What's Cooking?* uses a stylized narrative structure that revolves around ethnic and racial as well as gender and age stereotypes to convey a certain ideological discourse. *Mother and Child* is a more ostensibly realistic narrative, one much less reliant on social stereotypes, in which connections, interactions, and parallels work at the level of the individual.

What the film lacks is a visible space. In a commentary on *Children of Men* (Alfonso Cuarón, 2005) included in the DVD extras, Slavoj Žižek praises Cuarón's movie for the dominance of the background over characters and story. All movies can be said to strike some sort of balance between foreground and background, but audiences and critics have mostly focused on the foreground to the detriment of the characters' environment and the story's setting. This is a book about the construction of space and the cinematic reconstruction of place, and therefore its focus tends to be on the background. Yet the construction of space does not just include the setting. It can be argued that when we shift the point of view and put space before characters, the characters also become part of the space, a function and an ingredient of its articulation. Unlike *Children of Men* for Žižek, in *Mother and Child* and in all the other García multi-protagonist movies, character predominates over background, but the women and, secondarily, the men who populate the stories become the signifiers of space. The multi-protagonist canvas offers its view of the city through the conscious deployment of isolated individuals in its multistranded plot. It is the characters and the narrative structure that convey a particular sense of the city, one that, in a radically different way from *What's Cooking?*, also deals with the important transformations taking place in contemporary Los Angeles.

Mother and Child opens with a prologue from the past: a series of shots with two teenagers about to have sex, the girl pregnant in a house full of other girls in her same condition, and the birth of her baby. The ellipsis marked by the subsequent fade-out encompasses thirty-seven years. The fade-in to the present shows the same female character, Karen (Annette Bening), now a 51-year-old nurse who lives with her elderly mother, Nora (Eileen Ryan), whom she takes care of. It is gradually revealed to us that Nora, given her daughter's age when she became pregnant, decided to give the baby up for adoption. This baby is now Elizabeth (Naomi Watts), a 37-year-old lawyer. The two women live in Los Angeles, but they have never met or made any attempt to do so. Yet their lives and identities are defined by this traumatic moment. Karen has never recovered from her loss and has turned into a withdrawn woman, forever ill-tempered, with serious problems interacting with other people, especially men. Elizabeth is presented as professionally ambitious and personally cold and calculating. The movie alternates between scenes featuring each character. As the story develops, both women decide to seek the other out, but they never manage to meet. Into the mix is soon added Lucy (Kerry Washington), a young married woman who cannot have children and has decided, with her husband, to adopt a baby. Nora dies half an hour into the film, and she is replaced at the end by her great-granddaughter Ella (Juliette Amara). Ella is of mixed race and represents

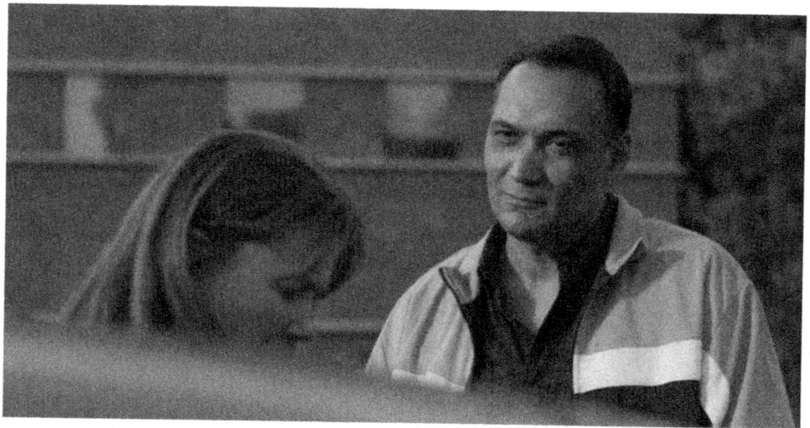

Mother and Child: the characters are the city.

the fourth generation of women in the film. When she is given to Lucy through adoption, she becomes the link that joins the various plot strands together.

In this initial description, the plot appears to be relatively linear. As García himself argues, this is not exactly the stuff of multi-protagonist movies. Soon, however, we realize that part of the distinctiveness of this movie resides in the way in which it keeps introducing interesting secondary characters. Its strategy of bringing the camera close to its human figures and the simplicity of its mise-en-scène facilitate an intense focus, if sometimes only brief, on most characters, even those with relatively small parts. Karen is first seen at home with her mother, where she has the help of Sofía (Elpidia Carrillo), who often has to bring her daughter Cristi (Simone López) with her to work. The first time we see Elizabeth she is applying for a job at a law firm and being interviewed by her future boss, Paul (Samuel L. Jackson), with whom she will soon become personally involved. Simultaneously, she is having sporadic sex with her married neighbor Steven (Marc Blucas), whose wife, Tracy (Carla Gallo), is pregnant. At the same time, Karen meets Paco (Jimmy Smits) at work and, although her aggressive temperament makes it difficult for them to become close, they eventually get married. Both Paul and Paco have daughters from previous marriages. Maria (Tatyana Ali), Paul's daughter, finds out that Elizabeth is pregnant, some months after the latter has terminated her relationship with Paul. Melissa (Gloria Garayúa) wholeheartedly welcomes Karen into her family and plants in her mind the idea of seeking out her long lost daughter. Both women have small but essential parts.

Ray (Shareeka Epps) is the 20-year-old pregnant woman whose baby will initially be given in adoption to Lucy, even though her mother, Leticia (Lisa Gay Hamilton) would like her to keep it. Lucy's mother, Ada (S. Epatha Merkerson), provides strong support to her daughter, first when Lucy's husband, Joseph (David Ramsey), changes his mind and tells his wife that he wants a baby of his own (which, since she cannot bear children, means the end of their marriage), then when Ray changes her mind after giving birth and decides to keep her newborn daughter after all, and finally when Ella becomes Lucy's adopted daughter and Lucy finds it hard to adapt to motherhood. Ada owns a local cake shop, where Lucy also works, and she offers a pointed social contrast to Joseph's parents, who are much wealthier. Other important characters are Sister Joanne (Cherry Jones), who negotiates adoptions for Lucy and Ray and who, unsuccessfully as it turns out, mediates between estranged Karen and Elizabeth for their reunion; Tom (David Morse), Elizabeth's father, with whom Karen has a rather frustrating one-night stand in a motel; Dr. Sloane (Amy Brenneman), Elizabeth's gynecologist, who becomes the target of the protagonist's rage when she finds out that she is pregnant; Amanda (Elizabeth Peña), who agrees to hire Elizabeth in her modest business when the latter gives up her job at Paul's law firm; and Violet (Britt Robinson), the young blind woman who befriends Elizabeth on the roof of their block of apartments.

As these twenty-odd characters are gradually added to the plot, Karen and Elizabeth do not necessarily recede into the background, but the narrative space becomes more crowded. Mother-daughter (and occasionally father-daughter) relationships start to proliferate and bounce off each other to provide a wider canvas and a box of resonances within which we can frame the central relationships. Moreover, the plot is energized by the successive additions, both expanding in different directions and advancing toward an inexorable end to which many of these characters will have crucially contributed. It could be argued, therefore, that *Mother and Child* is a multi-secondary-character movie, not just because there are a lot of important secondary characters but especially because they have a similar function to that played by more conventional protagonists in other instances of the genre. More important for the purposes of this chapter, these quietly introduced men and women, as they gradually populate an initially barebones plot, take the part of the almost absent background space of the movie and end up standing for the city where they live. In other words, in *Mother and Child*, as in García's other multi-protagonist stories, the characters, and here, particularly, the secondary ones, and the structure *are* the city.

What, then, is this city like? In general terms, it starts with three Anglo women from the same family, but almost immediately Latino and Latina and African American citizens become more visible and, crucially, unsettle the separation between races. The film is also perceptive in its delineation of social differences between and within the three ethnic groups, also suggesting a social mobility that is more or less fluid depending on the group: It is easier, for example, for Anglo Elizabeth to occupy a higher social rung than her mother than for Latina Melissa to improve significantly on her father's social stance—the possibility of upward mobility between generations is often considered a given among white Angelenos and U.S. Americans but not among Latinos. Among the relatively numerous African American characters who populate the plot there is a relatively wide spectrum, ranging from Joseph's wealthy family and Paul's prestigious position as the senior partner in a law firm, through Lucy and Ada's small-business status, to Ray and Leticia's working-class identity. Among the Latinos and Latinas the plot moves between the modest professional positions of Paco and Amanda and Sofía's lower social status as a housemaid. There are no exceptionally wealthy or homeless people in the story. *Mother and Child* is not interested in the growing gap between the rich and the poor that financial capitalism has produced, particularly in the postmetropolis. Rather, it focuses on the multiple differences and nuances existing in the middle section of the social spectrum and on how these, along with those of race and ethnic group, define the experience of living in Los Angeles. Although Karen and Elizabeth remain the plot's central characters and their relationship is its main driving force, it would be hard to argue that their narrative weight reinforces Anglo supremacy in the representation of the city. Rather, they offer a starting point for the multi-protagonist genre to do its work and eventually deny the simplicity that kicks off the story.

Nothing is simple in the postmetropolis, and the gradual deployment of multi-protagonist conventions narratively mirrors the social transformations of post-1992 Los Angeles. It is unfortunate that in going beyond historically dominant all-Anglo LA and also beyond the traditional reduction of the racial spectrum to black and white, the film stops at three groups and does not find, among its two dozen important characters, room for Asian Americans and other ethnic groups that have become visible in Angeleno society. It appears that, outside conscious efforts at racial and ethnic multiplicity, as in the case of *What's Cooking?*, even multi-protagonist movies can only aspire to point to Los Angeles's social complexity rather than fully display it.

One of the movie's posters suggests its generic allegiance by encasing the title in a grid of eighteen vignettes that feature some of the principal characters (only nine of them) once or twice. If we look closely, however, many of the vignettes, although formally separated from the rest for the sake of the symmetry of the design, spill into those next to them to show couples rather than individuals: Joseph and Lucy, Karen and Paco, Karen and Nora, Elizabeth and Paul, or Lucy and Ella. This arrangement suggests not only diversity but also mixture, including but not limiting itself to interracial mixture. This design elegantly encapsulates some of the directions taken by the narrative. Ella is the final result of this trajectory, and not just as Elizabeth and Paul's biological daughter. She also becomes the final instance of the complexity of the interpersonal relationships constructed by the film.

Shortly after her mother's death, Karen discovers a necklace that belonged to Nora hanging from Cristi's neck. Reflecting social prejudices against Latinas and maids, she immediately assumes that the girl stole the jewelry from Nora. She confronts Sofía with her suspicion, but Sofía explains that Nora gave the necklace to Cristi as a present. Because the object had belonged to Nora's mother, Karen is understandably distressed and finds it hard to accept that her own mother would choose to pass it on to the Latina girl rather than to herself. She may well be right to question her mother's decision because, after all, her own inability to connect is the consequence of her separation from her daughter at birth, which was Nora's decision. In any case, her failure to inherit the family heirloom marks the beginning of an emotional transformation, bumpy though the ride turns out to be. Gradually, Karen, Sofía, and Cristi get closer and, after Karen's marriage to Paco, Cristi becomes the closest Karen finds to a daughter, reading books to her and celebrating her birthday as a family. Cristi's possession of the necklace intensifies her bond with Karen, thus ensuring the family line broken by Nora's decision. What Nora has accomplished, consciously or not, is to expand the notion of family beyond blood ties. When Sofía and Cristi move to Corpus Christi, the girl gives the necklace to Karen, who has now become worthy of it. The new family is broken, but the seed for its

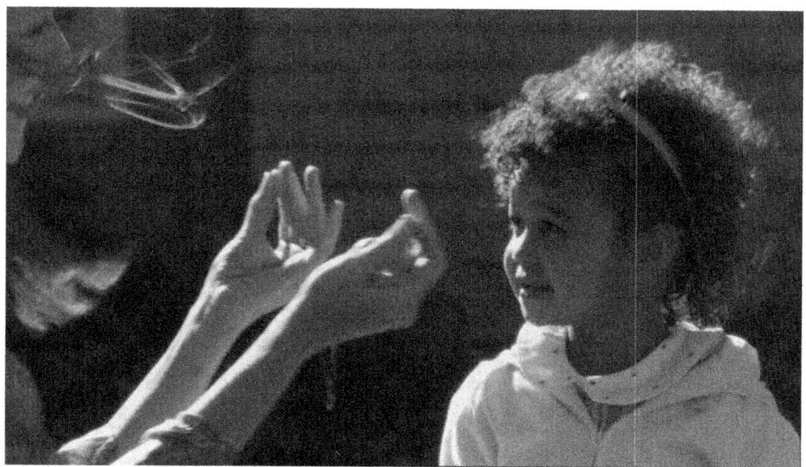

Mother and Child: Los Angeles written on the body of little Ella.

continuation has been planted. Encouraged by Cristi's gesture and also by Melissa's advice, Karen decides to try to find her daughter. At the end of the movie, she, in turn, passes the necklace on to her granddaughter Ella, the object's final recipient in the narrative. Thus Karen becomes part of the new family formed by Lucy and her adopted daughter, Ella.

The necklace links not only various generations of women but also various ethnic groups. Furthermore, as it is exchanged between various characters, it delineates the different types of families and emotional attachments that can be formed in the contemporary city. Although offering an impressive assortment of biological and adoptive mothers and daughters, *Mother and Child* does not envisage these bonds as the only possibilities and enlarges the options through many of the alternative relationships that are struck in the course of the narrative. Karen's attachment to Cristi, which does not in any way exclude Sofía, is a particularly apt example. Given the necklace's symbolic importance, it is fitting that the necklace concludes its roundabout journey in Ella's possession. The toddler that we see running around Lucy's garden at the end of the movie is herself the most potent symbol of the multicultural city, not only because of her mixed race but also because of the dense network of interpersonal exchanges among the various characters of which she becomes the center. Ella encompasses in her little body the striking variety of the Californian metropolis. She is one and many, much like the plot that is coming to an end.

Mother and Child was going to be the second feature produced under a five-film deal struck between Focus Features, the specialty branch of Universal Pictures, and Cha Cha Cha Films, the company created by Mexican directors Alfonso Cuarón, Guillermo del Toro, and Alejandro González Iñárritu (Shaw 2013, 2, 181, 288). It came after *Rudo y Cursi* (Rough and Corny; 2008), directed by Alfonso's brother, Carlos Cuarón. In 2013, after several years of silence, it was announced that the company was closing down without producing any of the other three movies, the ones that the "three amigos" themselves were going to make for their own company (Badillo 2013). In fact, although Cha Cha Cha is listed as one of the production companies for *Mother and Child* by the IMDb (see www.imdb.com/title/tt1121977/companycredits?ref_=tt_ql_10), it does not appear in the credits. In the DVD interview, García suggests that Everest Entertainment became, along with Mockingbird Pictures, the sole producers. However, Iñárritu is listed as executive producer and del Toro and Cuarón appear in the final acknowledgments. Beyond the vagaries of the movie's production, its association with the three Mexican directors, particularly with Iñárritu, is relevant here. Although different from Iñárritu's films, especially in visual terms, García's movies display an allegiance to the same cinematic form. *Mother and Child* is significantly close to *Biutiful* (2010), the first film in which the Mexican director worked with a single-protagonist formula. Its central character, Uxbal (Javier Bardem), appears in practically every scene, yet, like *Mother and Child*, the film excels at constructing a canvas of Barcelona as a contemporary multicultural city through its secondary characters and the manifold stories with which Uxbal's almost-linear narrative intersects (Azcona 2015).

The parallels and differences between the films of the two directors illustrate the suppleness of the genre in which they have worked, their popularity in a certain type of world cinema, halfway between the mainstream and more alternative forms of production, and the visibility of certain transnational Latin American directors in it. García's idiosyncratic use of the form to offer a consistent view of contemporary Los Angeles constitutes only a small sample of the genre's articulations. The personal and artistic hybridity of his cinematic voice replicates that of the thus far invisible majority of Angeleno citizens and problematizes Hsu's association of the genre with an ongoing Anglo perspective in its construction of a contemporary LA. Together with Gurinder Chadha's take on the city from a more outside but equally hybrid position, *Mother and Child* represents a significant contribution to the slow and fragmentary adaptation of the film industry to the post-1992 social and cultural changes in the city. Alongside its realistic register, *Mother and Child* incorporates into its structure a metacinematic commentary on the history of representation of the city in the movies; its all-Anglo starting point is deceptive, and the subsequent development and branching-out of the plot acknowledges the irreversibility of urban transformations. As in *What's Cooking?* the impossibility of doing justice to the exorbitant city is evident in some of the most visible limitations of the texts, but the incorporated visibilities are equally striking. More than the geographic confluence of the four families at the end of Chadha's movie, Ella's condition as *mise en abyme* of the plot and even of the postmetropolis remains a powerful index of the incommensurability of the city that she represents.

8

Bordertown

Bordertown (Archie Mayo, 1935) is, to my knowledge, the only Hollywood movie to date that starts in the same location where the city of Los Angeles began: El Pueblo de Los Ángeles, more specifically La Placita and La Iglesia de Nuestra Señora Reina de los Ángeles. By the time the film was made, the center of the Southern California capital had long been displaced south, first to Pershing Square and the old financial district and then to the new Downtown, even as the economic engine of the "city without a center" kept moving west toward the ocean. Although not far from Broadway and Spring Street, this "sacred and contested space" (Estrada 2008) became peripheral and irrelevant in the demographic development of the city and was transformed into a historical park and a tourist site that includes the Plaza, the church, Avila Adobe, Pico House, and Olvera Street (Hartig 2010, 303–4). In Mayo's film the pueblo is pictured as the spiritual epicenter of an already marginal barrio, socially and culturally distant from the affluent districts where the social elites live. *Bordertown* is, according to Ramírez Berg, the first Hollywood sound film to deal with a Mexican American's attempts to partake in the American dream (2002, 113). It is also one the first to make the borderliness of Los Angeles visible and to weave it into its plot. This borderliness became a significant ingredient of the city's contemporary identity in post-1992 LA.

The action moves between Los Angeles and a casino town south of the border, which could be Tijuana (a fictional newspaper briefly glimpsed is called *El Heraldo de la Frontera*). This southern place is a border town not only because it is physically in Mexico but also because everything is possible there: Johnny (Paul Muni), the protagonist, can become rich, and the wife of his boss-then-partner, Marie (Bette Davis), can fall in love with him even though she is Anglo and blonde (and trash too, as she herself explains). It is a new frontier town, once the frontier has completed its journey west, where civilized laws do not apply and where social and cultural boundaries are relatively easy to cross. Johnny, however, has his eyes on LA socialite Dale Elwell (Margaret Lindsay), someone far above his station, as she makes him understand when he proposes marriage. In this sense, the movie's LA is a harsher

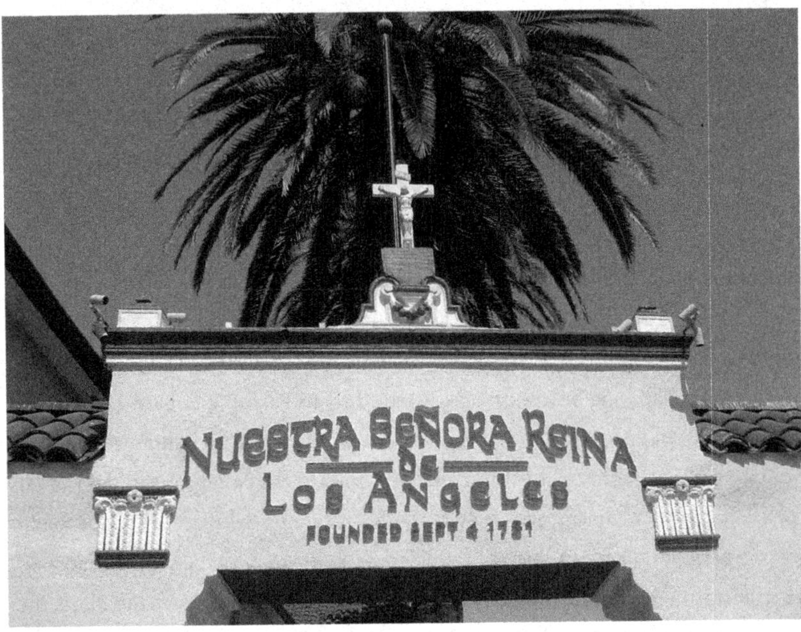

Where it all began: the Church of Nuestra Señora Reina de Los Angeles in La Placita.

border town, where internal borders are more airtight than in Tijuana. Johnny can cross boundaries and reach for the American dream by traveling south, but the much shorter journey to the Westside proves impossible to complete. In the end, he decides to return to "his people," that is, to the LA barrio where the story started. The Mexican quarter in the northern city proves to be the beginning and end of the Mexican American's social and economic aspirations, as though the old pueblo had continued to be Mexican and to be beyond the border even as the United States grew around it. This assimilation narrative (Ramírez Berg 2002, 113–16) highlights the porosity of certain borders and the impenetrability of others, even though they are not officially recognized as such or even visible. *Bordertown* is also the first film that draws an unbroken line between Los Angeles and the material *frontera* and articulates some of the particular borderly features of the city.

Johnny's experience in Los Angeles anticipates Mike Davis's (2000) concept of the third border, a term that we came across in the analysis of *(500) Days of Summer* (Marc Webb, 2009). According to Davis, Latino Angelenos find themselves daily challenged by the urban design and municipal policies in the global metropolis where they are a demographic majority. When Latinos cross into the United

States, the border follows them wherever they go. The third border is the invisible line that they come across every day in their intercourse with other communities, a reminder that their lives are under constant scrutiny and that, despite the apparent freedom of movement within their cities, there are many barriers that are difficult, if not impossible, to negotiate (Davis 2000, 71). Los Angeles is an eminently third-border city. It is crossed by invisible lines that restrict the social interactions of its citizens and that for a long time have reminded successive waves of immigrants that they are still in the borderlands they thought they had left behind, even when, as in the case of Johnny in *Bordertown*, they were born in the United States.

Insisting on this repressive dimension of intra-urban border ideology, Camilla Fojas labels Los Angeles "Schizopolis" because of the relentless way in which it destroys and divides souls as part of "the borderizing psyche" of the United States (2006, 7). In her analysis of *El Norte* (Gregory Navas, 1983) and *Star Maps* (Miguel Arteta, 1997), Fojas notices that the main characters in these movies manage to cross the border into the United States only to be "borderlined and broken down" in LA. Fojas links the city's status as a global city to its proximity to the border. For her, Los Angeles is a border city, one that "harbors the border as part of the experience of its topography" (8). That is, LA is twice a border city: first, because it is a global city, and second, because it is close to the border. She concludes that the city is a space of exclusion, more stringent as such than the boundaries of the nation. What she calls "exclusionary anxiety" is the driving force of urban border policies and practices.

Davis and Fojas extend to the postmetropolis the perspectives of those like Benjamín Alire Sáenz, a Tijuana-based writer, who summarizes his position thus: "I live on the border between México and the United States. I sometimes sneer (perhaps unfairly) at Latinos who think the border is only a metaphor. What is so radical about using a very material culture as a literary device to describe an individual's psychological state? I know border culture intimately, the anxieties and mistrust that the very fact of living here raises in people. But I refuse to romanticize my culture" (quoted in Palaversich 2003, 119). For Davis and Fojas, urban borders work primarily as sites of exclusion and oppression. As with the material border between Mexico and the United States, however, urban borders have other dimensions, and movies offer multifarious experiences, which are not always oppressive and destructive.

Davis's third border evokes Homi Bhabha's third space, even though both concepts differ substantially in their respective contents. For Bhabha, the third space, a theoretical and abstract concept, is a cultural space where incommensurable differences are negotiated, creating "a tension peculiar to borderline existences" (1994, 218). To substantiate this tension, which produces hybridity in a transnational world, Bhabha quotes Guillermo Gómez-Peña, a Chicano artist who has spent his life highlighting the productive nature of borders and their production of hybrid identities. Gómez-Peña describes the hybrid artist as "an insider and an outsider, an expert in border crossings, a temporary member of multiple communities, a citizen of two or more nations" (1996, 12). For Bhabha, similarly, third spaces are productive because they "open out," remake boundaries, and expose the limits of any claims to the singularity of difference (1994, 219). That is, borders as third spaces facilitate cultural exchanges, question exclusionary difference, and create more interesting, more modern, more complex identities. Borders are at once material and cultural, the experience of migrants and the condition of all modern subjects.

Gloria Anzaldúa conceptualizes the borderlands in a similar way, as liminal spaces in which the breaking down of immigrants and border citizens goes hand in hand with the creation of border identities, where conflict exists alongside exchange, and the physical borderlands coexist with the psychological, sexual, and spiritual borderlands (1999, 19). Her borderlands are close to the "contact zone," a term coined by Mary Louise Pratt. For Pratt, contact zones are "social spaces where cultures meet, clash, and grapple with each other, often in contexts of highly asymmetrical relations of power" (1991, 34).

More recently, Anthony Cooper and Chris Rumford have argued that the border is "the prime site for connecting individuals to the world" and to each other (2011, 262). For them the border can be thought of as a "quilting point" that makes connectedness possible (262). For Néstor García Canclini, the migratory flows from Latin America to the United States have turned border areas between Mexico and the United States into centers of modern culture. He describes cities such as Tijuana and New York as the greatest laboratories of modernity (García Canclini 2001, 283–86). These dynamics are not hindered but rather facilitated by material borders: "The wire that separates Mexico from the United States can be considered the principal monument to border culture" (292).

Borderlands, contact zones, and quilting points are concepts that facilitate the relocation of border dynamics in the metropolis. More explicitly, José David Saldívar, for whom border or *frontera* culture is an enormous "desiring machine," includes Los Angeles in the extended U.S.-Mexico borderland (1997, 95). In the version of the borderlands that emanates from these writings, the repressive and the exclusionary are balanced out by the productive and even the revolutionary, the dividing line by the contact zone, and the lethal fence by the quilting point, all constrained by liberating desires (Schimanski and Wolfe 2007b, 9), suggesting, on the one hand, the power of the identifications, anxieties, and desires created by borders and, on the other, their centrality in a city like Los Angeles. What Chris Rumford calls "borderwork," that is, people making, shifting, and dismantling borders (Cooper and Rumford 2011, 264; Rumford 2008, 248), is a central feature of Los Angeles as a postmetropolis.

New spaces for hybrid identities and communities are opened even as others are closed; the diversity discourse becomes predominant even as Anglo rebordering practices abound. In the postwar period the Los Angeles urban region became increasingly diverse, but individual communities became more homogeneous. The region was fragmented into a sprawling agglomeration of racially exclusive communities (Avila 2006, 44–45). Whole neighborhoods have been displaced and dispersed, as in the cases of Chávez Ravine, Chinatown, Bunker Hill, and massive parts of Boyle Heights, producing what Rodolfo Acuña describes as the constant fluidity of urban dynamics (1996, 19). In the process the overarching principle of an urban layout based on exclusionary and bordering practices has remained intact. Urban borders are never fixed and immutable, but at any given moment they define the experience and often the identity of Angeleno citizens. Bordering processes in Los Angeles therefore partake of all the dimensions of borders described by theorists: Symbolic or conceptual borders coexist with material borders, and linear borders coexist with border spaces or borderlands (D. Newman 2007, 27, 35; Schimanski and Wolfe 2007b, 13). In LA these concepts are not mutually exclusive; rather, multiple experiences of border crossing define to a large extent life in the contemporary postmetropolis.

With exceptions like *Bordertown* or, indirectly, *Touch of Evil* (Orson Welles, 1958), Los Angeles films have traditionally ignored the city's borderliness and its citizens' borderwork. Yet post-1992 films have increasingly incorporated exclusionary urban practices and Davisian third borders into their constructed spaces. In *White Men Can't Jump* (Ron Shelton, 1992), for instance, Sidney advises Billy, in friendly but aggressive banter, to make sure that he crosses La Brea before sundown, because he would not be able to survive east of that boulevard, thus splitting the city in two, one (the west side) Anglo-dominated and the other (Mid-City, Downtown, East LA, South Central) hostile and dangerous for the white protagonist. As we have seen, the film in general proposes a fantasy of African American control of Anglo communities such as Venice and Santa Monica, but at other times it returns to more realistic awareness of social divides and border-enforcing strategies. *Falling Down* (Joel Schumacher, 1993) and *Collateral* (Michael Mann, 2004), in different ways and for different purposes, feature heroes who can negotiate urban borders even as they make them visible to spectators and underline their importance in the urban layout and social imaginary. The multi-protagonist films discussed in Chapter 7 routinely feature boundaries as part of their generic specificity.

In general, as the city's social and ethnic diversity finds new ways onto the silver screens, third borders and other intra-urban demarcation lines proliferate. As they mushroom through the cinematic geography of the city, these borders acquire different meanings that underline the multivalence of the concept in the postmetropolis: They might be restrictive or constructive, real or metaphorical, barriers to communication and movement or spaces where strong urban identities are formed, extensions of the southern border or practices that are specifically related to real estate and urban renewal practices. Whereas such movies as *Crossing Over* (Wayne Kramer, 2009) explicitly address the dimension of Los Angeles as a border town, bordering experiences are visible in a great diversity of movies, more often than not those that reveal a keen sense of the city's social geography and urban layout. *The Soloist* (Joe Wright, 2009) is one such example. This movie focuses on Skid Row as the product of a series of exclusionary urban practices and the Downtown area as crossed by a series of invisible boundaries. Given its spatial specificity, this movie can be taken as a companion piece to *(500) Days of Summer*, bringing to the fore part of what the other film had repressed in its comic fantasy: the centrality of borderwork in the Downtown area.

On the Edge of the Nickel

Whereas in other U.S. cities historical skid rows have been disappearing through urban renewal, the Angeleno Skid Row district has remained relatively intact.

According to Jennifer Wolch, this has allowed many homeless to stay on their home turf, where they have better access to and knowledge of available social services (1996, 402). Such institutions as missions and shelters are an integral part of the everyday living dynamics of the homeless and play a central role in the amelioration of their wretched conditions. Workers in these community centers often find themselves in disputes with city authorities and with organizations representing real estate interests. In the first decade of the twenty-first century, for instance, controversy raged around the rights of the homeless to sleep in the streets of Skid Row, which became the target of the city council and the LAPD's enforcement of municipal laws and plan to clean up the streets in preparation for urban development. In 2006 the American Civil Liberties Union sued the city of Los Angeles on behalf of six homeless people and demanded that they be allowed to sit, lie, or sleep on pubic sidewalks on Skid Row. The court ruled in favor of the ACLU, and a precarious compromise was reached, stopping at least momentarily the city council's plans. Although some journalists and activists saw this as a small victory and respite for the 4,000 homeless then living on Skid Row against real estate plans to gentrify the area, others saw the court ruling and the compromise as an invitation to drug dealers, passing as homeless, to take control of the neighborhood (Hoffmann 2007; Moore 2007; Westwater 2006). This court case put the focus on the complexities and peculiarities of the Nickel and the individual stories behind the court case.

The Soloist is based on the real story of one of these people, cello and violin player Nathaniel Ayers, as it was brought to the public's attention by *Los Angeles Times* columnist Steve Lopez, the same journalist whose opinions on *Crash* have already been mentioned in this book. Lopez met Ayers in 2005 in Pershing Square and subsequently wrote a series of articles in his column about him, later collecting them into a book, *The Soloist: A Lost Dream, an Unlikely Friendship, and the Redemptive Power of Music* (2008). *Erin Brockovich* scriptwriter Susannah York turned the book into a screenplay, which was directed by British filmmaker Joe Wright, known for his film adaptations of the novels *Pride and Prejudice* and *Atonement*. *The Soloist*, with Jamie Foxx playing Ayers and Robert Downey Jr. as Lopez, was produced by DreamWorks, which had recently been purchased by Universal, but was distributed in the United States by Paramount, from which DreamWorks had broken away. According to the professional press, when pushed by its parent company Viacom to delay the release from awards-season November 2008 to April 2009, Paramount forfeited a great deal of the movie's chances of success at the box office (A. Thompson 2008). With a considerable budget of $60 million, two bankable stars (Foxx and Downey), and a social agenda as part of its remit, the movie was a relative flop at the box office, according to reviewers, because of the middle-of-the-road position it occupied in the complex industrial panorama of the early-twenty-first century. As Todd McCarthy explained in his review, the movie fell between the cracks "both creatively and commercially" (2009, n.p.). As a good illustration of the dangers of a different type of borderland—the boundary between mainstream and independent—the crossover aspirations of *The Soloist* left it in no man's land, a relatively accurate correlative of the area of the city where its action takes place. In a sense, the industrial fate of the movie echoes the consequences for Downtown of the gentrification process analyzed in the study of *(500) Days of Summer*. In *The Soloist*, however, we find a different articulation and appropriation of the urban space of Downtown.

The action of the movie, filmed entirely on location, takes place mostly in the Downtown area, and some of its most memorable scenes are set on Skid Row, making *The Soloist* the first commercial movie to feature this cinematically forgotten part of town—a movie that aspires to mainstream its social commentary on the neighborhood. The story underlines both the street life of many of its dwellers and the central role played in the community by the missions and other organizations that serve the interests of these people. The Lamp Community, one such mission, appears centrally (www.lampcommunity.org/), as do the Los Angeles Times Building, Pershing Square, the Walt Disney Concert Hall, and other Downtown locations. As I argue later, the movie constructs its space both in realistic and metaphorical terms.

In my analysis of *(500) Days*, I suggested that Hill and Main are two examples of the many third borders that crisscross the relatively reduced area of Downtown Los Angeles. Hill Street, especially as it runs past the entrance to the Grand Central Market, separates the new Financial District from the Mexican-dominated Broadway area. Main Street marks one of the current edges of the newly gentrified old financial district and provides an invisible yet functioning and in many ways strict barrier between the renovated modernist buildings and Skid Row, which literally starts on the other side of the street. Whereas *(500) Days* ignores the specifics of its chosen location, *The Soloist* weaves its story around these separations. In this sense the two films offer spectators different kinds of utopias: Webb's is the utopia of a gated-community sensibility that has managed to expel the Other; Wright's is a new version of the American dream in which internal borders and gates can not only be overcome but also turned into veritable contact zones. That both movies exist at relatively distant points of the Hollywood industrial continuum—*(500) Days* offering itself as an indie movie and *The Soloist* packaged as a crossover product with mainstream potential—suggests the complicated and often paradoxical workings of ideology in Hollywood. It also reminds viewers that marketing and textuality do not always go hand in hand ideologically.

Among the many demarcations produced by the crisscrossing of social realities and historical layers in Downtown, Wright's film selects the east-west axis to deploy its filmic space and, using three buildings as reference points, articulates a social world divided into three subspaces: the Lamp mission and the surrounding streets on Skid Row on the eastern edge, the Walt Disney Concert Hall and Grand Avenue to the west, and the Los Angeles Times Building in the middle. This spatial deployment leaves out much more than it includes, especially subdivisions along the north-south axis, but it does offer a valuable insight into the urban dynamics of the area. Two more real locations, both situated in the middle section of this geography, also carry crucial meanings in the story: Pershing Square, south of the newspaper building, and a tunnel underneath Grand Avenue, close to Walt Disney Concert Hall.

The present Los Angeles Times Building was inaugurated in 1935 and stands at the northern edge of the old financial district along the Broadway-Spring corridor. It replaces the old building that, in one of the best-known episodes of Angeleno history, was bombed in 1910 (Ethington 2010, 195). From its slightly detached vantage point, it has witnessed the decline of the old Downtown, the emergence of the recreated Bunker Hill with its gleaming skyscrapers and cultural centers, and the more recent gentrification of Spring Street and the surrounding area. Looking west, and within the distance of a short but steep 10-minute walk, the building overlooks the Walt Disney Concert Hall, one of the four buildings of the Los Angeles Music Center, designed by Frank Gehry and inaugurated in 2003, and the home of the Los Angeles Philharmonic Orchestra. It is one of the most distinctive and representative sites of the new Downtown, raised on the old location of the Bunker Hill neighborhood. Looking approximately southeast from the Los Angeles Times Building, at

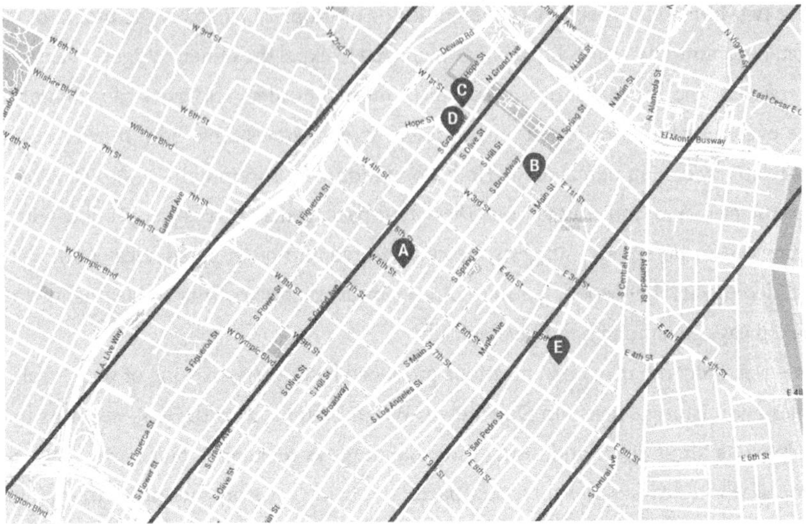

Map 5. *The Soloist's* Downtown and its three spaces: the new Bunker Hill to the west, Skid Row to the east, and the Broadway-Spring corridor in the middle. The film's central locations are (A) Pershing Square, (B) the Los Angeles Times Building, (C) Walt Disney Concert Hall, (D) a tunnel under Bunker Hill, and (E) the Lamp Mission in the Nickel. Map by Francesc Terrades.

a slightly longer distance, is Skid Row. Within this specific geography, Main and Hill Streets provide the separating lines between the three zones. Both physically and metaphorically, Steve's workplace and the concert hall are much closer to one another than Skid Row is to either of them, yet the hill that separates them makes the distance more noticeable.

In *The Soloist* Steve Lopez stands for the cultural elite of the gentrified old Downtown, and this makes his proximity to the Gehry building unproblematic, whereas his interest in looking east separates him from many of those occupying the top of the hill. As a well-known columnist of the powerful newspaper, inner borders are not operative for him; as a person with a Spanish surname, he may evoke the practical difficulties of the Latino constituency to move uphill beyond Hill Street. Conversely, as a socially minded journalist attuned to the predicament of the homeless and the poor citizens of Skid Row, he ventures beyond Main Street and into the Nickel, not without reservations and a feeling of danger.

The Soloist conveys the realities of this striated geography and the huge social distances between close locations. Like any visitor to Skid Row, the movie marvels at the unlikeliness of such obscene social differences within such close distances and at the looming presence of the proud and arrogant buildings of the new Financial District from the street level, where the homeless live. At the same time, the film focuses on two characters (based on real people) who manage to perform borderwork that questions social barriers and escapes urban blueprints. A brief transition sequence halfway through the film conveys an important part of the geography that I have just described and the position of Nathaniel and Steve in this geography.

After learning about the homeless man's passion for classical music and Beethoven and guessing his virtuosity as a musician, Steve uses his contacts to get his new friend and himself access to a rehearsal of the Los Angeles Philharmonic at the Walt Disney Concert Hall. Steve tries to persuade Nathaniel to attend, but Nathaniel refuses unless he can bring along his trolley with all his belongings, which he never leaves behind. Reluctant to miss an opportunity that may change Nathaniel's life, the journalist decides to indulge him and to help him push the trolley along the one and a half miles, mostly uphill, that separate the Lamp mission from the concert hall. They are pressed for time and have to run to avoid arriving late. In the meantime, at the Los Angeles Times Building, Mary Weston (Catherine Keener), the newspaper editor and Steve's ex-wife, looks out her office window and happens to see the two men running uphill. There are four transition shots between the scene at the Lamp mission and the arrival of the two men at Walt Disney Concert Hall: Mary looks offscreen to the right in close-up; an eye-line match shows us the two men running in a long shot from her perspective; then the close-up of Mary is repeated; and finally a wider shot of Nathaniel and Steve follows, the frame now tilting up to disclose the monumental structure of the building toward which they are heading.

This transition sequence suggests some of the central meanings of the story. On the one hand, we have the mediating position of Steve and the newspaper, here embodied in Mary, between east and west, poverty and high culture, and, by extension, the middle section of the film's Downtown geography mediating between the two poles. On the other hand, the two shots of the men running along the mostly empty streets (as indeed often is the case in this area of Downtown) conveys their determination to cross borders, their flouting of official blueprints and unwritten urban protocols, and their relative comfort as lonely inhabitants of these urban and, at first sight, desolate borderlands. The road may be steep and uphill and their

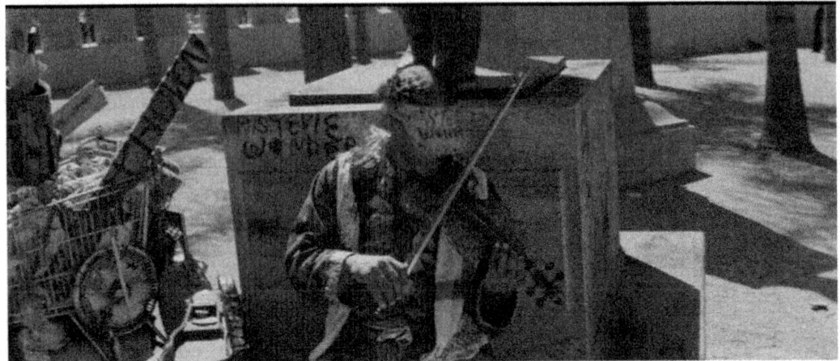

Under the shadow of Beethoven: Steve and Nathaniel meet in the Downtown borderlands in *The Soloist*.

figures together may strike an odd note in the surroundings, but, according to the film's discourse, the intricate crisscrossing of inner boundaries that is Downtown LA can also be turned into an urban contact zone. In pointed contrast to the gated-community nature of much of the city's layout and the inward-looking morphology of many of the Downtown complexes, as discussed by Christopher Hawthorne (2010, 484–92), the filmmakers here make the most of the particular design of Gehry's building, surrounded by circular ramps that give visitors the illusion of accessibility. In reality, these ramps only circle the outside of the building, and it is only Steve's contacts that facilitate their final access to the high sanctuary of culture inside. In any case, the brief sequence both turns the physical geography of the area into part of its social narrative and suggests the potential of border crossers to rewrite urban blueprints in ways similar to those theorized by de Certeau, thus calling attention to the malleability of this fraught area.

Steve first meets Nathaniel in Pershing Square, where he first hears the sound of the two-string violin coming from the location of Beethoven's statue. Before this we hear a tourist board narration of the history of the place through the earphones of a group of tourists. The park was a settler camp southeast of the city around 1850. It subsequently became a park but has had a long controversial history and several renovations, the latest attempting to keep the homeless out. Today, Pershing Square is not a particularly inviting feature of the city, even though such beautiful buildings as the Biltmore Hotel, on its west side, remind onlookers of a more glamorous past. The park also offers a privileged vantage point to understand the area's topography. A brief uphill walk along 5th Street takes the not very frequent stroller to the famous

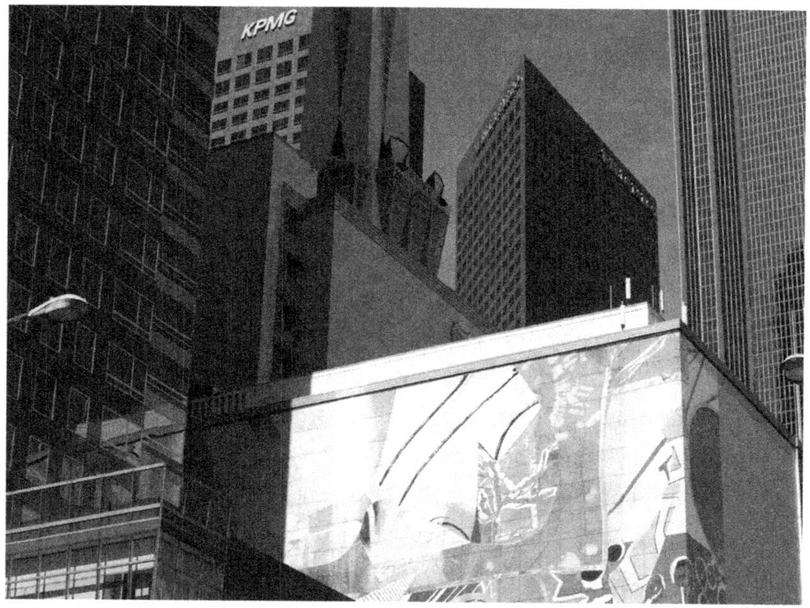

Looking at the new financial center from Pershing Square.

Bonaventure Hotel, which Fredric Jameson (1984) discusses as part of his theory of postmodernism and which remains a representative feature of the new Bunker Hill. A not much longer walk along the same street or, on the southern edge of the park, along 6th Street but in the opposite direction takes us straight to the Lamp mission in 15 minutes. It makes sense, therefore, that the two protagonists should meet here. Situated in the same middle section of the film's Downtown as the newspaper headquarters, Pershing Square provides a meeting point between tourists and the homeless, between Mexican citizens and the culturally and economically privileged.

The visual rhetoric at this point, with the mobile frame focusing on Steve as he follows the unusual sound of the two-string violin, suggests a brief journey of discovery, maybe the local journalist's first real insight into the lives of his Downtown neighbors. Nathaniel's constant and rapid chatter and the information about his life that he offers in this first conversation immediately arouse Steve's and the spectator's curiosity. The camera's circling movements around the characters and the statue evoke the creation, at this early stage, of a bond between the two men, with Beethoven, "the leader of Los Angeles," as Nathaniel calls him, the park's palm trees, and the briefly glimpsed surrounding buildings as facilitators. Pershing Square is therefore an early contact zone or quilting point, a microspace of the borderland where the three disparate communities, as represented by the three spaces into which the text structures the real Downtown, can come together in an exchange that, at the microlevel of the everyday, may well change history.

Steve and Nathaniel's second, and more important, meeting place is a tunnel underneath Grand Avenue and Third Street, near Walt Disney Concert Hall, where in the midst of the noise of the passing cars and the pigeons and within view of the looming skyscrapers through the opening above, Nathaniel is trying to "find Beethoven." Steve sees him by chance in a scene that starts with a bird's-eye view of a busy freeway, where we find Steve driving to work. Getting off the grid around Staples Center, he soon finds himself in the neighborhood of the Bonaventure, Walt Disney Concert Hall, and, indeed, the Los Angeles Times Building. Yet traveling along the tunnels underneath Bunker Hill, he unexpectedly comes across Nathaniel, who explains to him that this particular environment encapsulates the best of Los Angeles, the place where everybody smiles, unlike his hometown Cleveland, and the home of Beethoven. Later, when Steve brings him the cello that has been donated by a retired player, Nathaniel insists that this is where he should play, rather than at the Lamp mission, where Steve wants him to go for safety reasons. For Steve, helping his friend means taking him off the streets, finding somewhere for him to live, and helping him lead what he considers a normal life. He appreciates Nathaniel's street performance but would like to see him play in the "proper" context, as part of the official culture. In fact, before the final credits we learn that the real Mr. Ayers is now sleeping inside, is a member of the Lamp Community, and continues to play the cello and other instruments. In the film, however, he resists the journalist's efforts.

Nathaniel takes possession of the road underneath Bunker Hill as his performing space and his home. We see him put his life at risk to pick up from the road surface a cigarette butt that someone has dropped from a car. He will not have Beethoven played in an untidy and degraded environment. When Steve meets him in this location, he often feels that he is trespassing on the other's private space. For Nathaniel, God inhabits this place. Like any performer but also like any citizen, according to Michel de Certeau, Nathaniel feels he is within his right to make the most unlikely part of the city his own. In this he reminds us of Manzanar Murakami, one of the main characters in Karen Tei Yamashita's *Tropic of Orange*. Installed in an overpass on the Harbor Freeway, probably not far from Nathaniel's location but above the traffic, the eccentric Japanese American ex-surgeon conducts the traffic below as though it were an orchestra, turning in his mind the sounds of the city into a "beautiful noise." In their analysis of Yamashita's novel, Jesús Benito and Ana María Manzanas (2011) see this strand of the plot as Murakami's occupation of the LA symbolic space. For them, the freeway overpass is his dwelling in the full sense of the term, but a dwelling not connected with stability and permanence in the Heideggerian sense but with the constantly changing and infinitely modulated flows of the city. Unlike the nineteenth-century flâneur, Murakami is a "sign in the middle of mobility, signposts, and changing landscapes" and claims residency on the overpass (Benito and Manzanas 2011, 55–56). For these authors, Murakami is a narrative index of the radical transformation of the space of the postmetropolis carried out by the novel and an egregious example of the homeless people's appropriation of the freeway (64). *Tropic of Orange* transgresses, through the mode of magical realism, official and authoritative urban discourses. Nathaniel and *The Soloist*, on the other hand, are more interested in inhabiting than in transgressing, in colonizing borders than in bringing them down, and although the parallels between the two characters are noticeable, the differences are equally apparent.

Whereas Murakami conducts and the traffic beneath him becomes his orchestra, Nathaniel is a soloist, less interested in harmonizing the sounds of others than in finding his own sound within the constant din of the city. Topographically, Murakami stands above the freeway, whereas Nathaniel has his dwelling outside the cement monsters and underneath the surface roads. The homeless musician, standing at the base of the new Downtown, is looking to capture in his defective violin and later in his magnificent cello the echoes of the ghosts of the past, of the old Bunker Hill neighborhood that was sacrificed for the sake of progress and replaced by the imposing but lifeless shrines of late capitalism and officially sanctioned high culture, of which the Walt Disney Concert Hall is a prime example.

Nathaniel is reluctant to associate himself with the great music hall; he even fails to deliver when he is given the chance to offer a recital. One would say that the ghosts of the neighborhood's past provide a more apt environment for Beethoven than the respectful silence of the music hall. He seems to admire the state-of-the-art buildings that he can see from his hole, but he is an outsider to the pleasures and comforts they provide and represent. To him, the tunnel is, like Pershing Square, the whole space of Downtown, a borderland full of possibilities. He excels as an urban border crosser, but he must be allowed to negotiate the urban borderlands on his own terms. If borders are, for Cooper and Rumford, quilting points, Nathaniel is a consummate quilter and a representative of the mobility and membrane-like quality of borders. In a sense, by inhabiting the underworld, Nathaniel avoids the blueprint of the surface, but he also selects particularly operative hot points in the lattice of urban borders that characterizes Downtown, making them his own borderlands. More than Pershing Square, Nathaniel's tunnel is a contact zone, not so much a border that can or cannot be crossed but, in Cooper and Rumford's (2011, 265) articulation, a border from which we see, a vantage point to observe the city—with Nathaniel—in a fresh manner.

Borderwork and Film Style

The text of *The Soloist* supports its bordering sensibility through its visual rhetoric. The alert spectator would have become familiar with Joe Wright's visual flourishes in his two adaptations of English novels, particularly the spectacular long take in the scene at Omaha Beach during the invasion of Normandy in *Atonement* (2007). Although the stylistic strategies are different here, the British director reserves his cinematic virtuosity in *The Soloist* for two moments. One is the second tunnel scene. Nathaniel starts playing the beautiful third movement of Beethoven's String Quartet no. 15 and, as Steve closes his eyes and starts taking in the music, the tunnel is transformed. In this sequence the camera comes closer and closer to Nathaniel's face as he becomes submerged in the music and the sounds of the traffic around him recede. After several push-ins on the musician's face, conventionally suggesting a textual attempt to understand his talent, the strategy suddenly changes. As the music continues and a full orchestra, replacing the quartet, comes in along with the soloist, the film offers a frontal long shot of the two characters facing each other from the other side of the road and immediately starts moving left toward the car and up to the intersection of Grand and 3rd Street above, approximately following with a crane shot the flight of a group of pigeons. A sequence of shots following the flight of the birds takes us past the Downtown buildings to a shot of the Los Angeles River as a bird flies under one of the bridges, an overhead shot of a huge Downtown parking lot, and, finally, a busy freeway interchange, a shot that rhymes with the first shot of the scene, except that this time, like the traffic under the overpass in *Tropic of Orange* in Murakami's mind, it has been transformed into a ballet by Nathaniel's music.

The sound of the quartet has become identified with the pigeons and the beauty of Beethoven's music with the fluidity of the camera as it soars above the surface and then glides, unhindered, past various Angeleno locations. By constantly alternating these aerial shots with close-ups of the two men, the camera also includes them in this brief fantasy of harmonious and free movement. It could be said that Beethoven's piece, as performed by Nathaniel from the hole underneath the hill, has transformed the city. Yet the sequence does not seem so much a counterpoint to the grim reality below. Rather, it is an extension of the way the protagonists construct the city from their borderly position in the tunnel. The growing attachment between Nathaniel and Steve does not make boundaries disappear; their attachment grows out of those boundaries and outlines an alternative blueprint for the third-border-crossed metropolis.

The second virtuoso moment takes place in the Nickel. As darkness falls over Skid Row, Steve leaves the Lamp mission and gets into his car, ready to go home. In the last second, however, before turning the key in the ignition, he looks out his windshield at the teeming street outside and decides to get out of his car again and join the still threatening-looking crowds. This is an unexpected decision and nothing in Robert Downey Jr.'s performance suggests his reasons. A low-angle tracking shot pulling in toward the character, however, tells us that something important is about to happen. The middle-class Angeleno intellectual, as much the product of the city's particular topography as the homeless individuals who surround him, decides to imitate the street musician and become part of the Other's space, to become, like him, a border crosser. From this point on, the stylistic work in the scene is directed at emphasizing the transcendence of Steve's gesture and how his decision changes our perception of this "undiscovered country." He is then quietly joined by Nathaniel, and soon they are laying down the plastic, cardboards, and dirty foam mattresses to settle down for the night on one of the crowded sidewalks, within close view of the neon sign of the Rosslyn Hotel, situated on Main Street and 5th Street, just outside the Nickel.

As Nathaniel explains to Steve that the homeless around them are also God's children and the strings of another Beethoven string quartet begin to rise in the soundtrack, the camera pulls in on the journalist's face, signaling that when the next cut comes, we are going to share his perspective. What we see next is Skid Row transformed by this new vision. The first of two slow and meditative tracking shots starts with a follow focus of a huge rat hurrying across the street from Nathaniel and Steve's improvised bed to the nearest gutter. Then the camera picks up a young man walking toward a truck from which some volunteers are handing out packaged dinners. Next, the frame is lifted from street level to a relatively close overhead shot as it glides past the dozens of improvised cots where the men and women are settling down to sleep. A cut discloses the neon legend on the wall of the Lamp mission, "the wages of sin is death," and then, moving round the corner and up, the frame continues to encompass the patchwork of makeshift beds outside the mission from a gradually longer distance, evoking the famous crane shot at the train depot in *Gone with the Wind* (1939), when Scarlett discovers the size of the depredations of the Civil War. These are a different kind of depredation. Cinematic rhetoric conveys the new vision of the border crosser. All the time Nathaniel is reciting the Lord's Prayer, which, in the soundtrack, is interrupted by an excerpt of Steve's column in the *Times*: "Every night, my friend Nathaniel tucks his instruments away and lays his head among the predators and hustlers, among the fallen drunks sprawled in the streets, as rats the size of meatloaves dart out of the drains to feed off the squalor." Nathaniel finishes his prayer and the sequence ends with his words: "I hope you sleep well, Mr. López. I hope the whole world sleeps well." Skid Row is still, at this point, a ruthless reminder of a society that has lost its soul, but at the same time it has been transformed.

We are still only halfway through the film, and the second half features Steve's relatively successful efforts to integrate Nathaniel into society. Through the ups and downs of their fraught relationship, Steve returns to the Lamp mission, particularly to bring Nathaniel's sister, Flo (Lorraine Toussaint), to visit him from Cleveland. In the final sequence we see Steve sitting on the pavement outside the Lamp mission, blending in with the surroundings, and Nathaniel finally attending a concert at the Walt Disney Concert Hall (Beethoven's Ninth Symphony, of course), accompanied by his sister, Steve, and Mary. Both men's urban spaces have been enlarged by their relationship and by the strength they have derived from each other's company to negotiate borders, turning them to their own advantage and

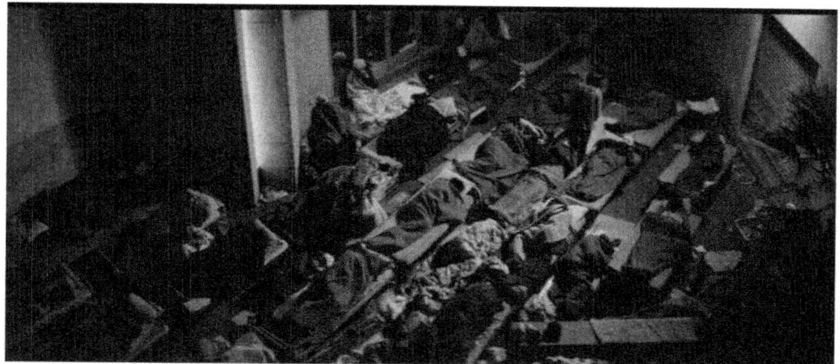

The Soloist: The Nickel transformed by the look of the border crosser.

that of the people around them, including Lopez's readers. In the meantime, Mayor Villaraigosa (Marcos de Silvas) has entered the plot. Standing outside the Lamp mission, he acknowledges the city's shame at the dimensions of poverty—"Los Angeles has the ignominious distinction of being the homeless capital of the nation"—and announces an injection of money to palliate the destitution of the area. The actual destination of the funds is not explored in the film, which is more interested in celebrating the newspaper column's and, by implication, its own power to awaken consciences.

This real-life story has not made the conditions that produced a place like the Nickel disappear. In fact, as accounts of gentrification and municipal policy prove, urban changes, particularly urban renewal, have a way of working against those for whom they appear to be intended. What *The Soloist*'s proximity to reality does, not only in its rendering of a "real-life story" but also in its attention to geographic detail, is bring into the cinematic mainstream aspects of Los Angeles that the industry has mostly ignored or even, as in *(500) Days of Summer*, consciously attempted to erase. Specifically, it is a sophisticated account of the borderliness of the postmetropolis as encapsulated in the geographically reduced but socially representative space of Downtown and its complex web of internal borders. These boundaries, which have grown out of a rich history of exclusions, erasures, renewals, and successive urban blueprints, tell stories of Fojas's borderizing psyche and Davis's third space but also of borderwork, the incessant activity of people who, like the protagonists of this film, make, shift, and dismantle borders, to use Cooper and Rumford's conceptualization. The city mayor is a marginal presence in *The Soloist*, which, like most

Hollywood films, is more interested in the vicissitudes and the agency of individuals than in institutions.

The Soloist explores both the exclusionary and the fluid features of urban borders, their resilience and malleability, and the ability of some individuals—urban border crossers—to use them productively, even as their identities remain powerfully shaped by the anxieties and social injustices they generate. In Los Angeles, the border town, the quilt town, the seams between the patches continue to define urban policy and development, but they also bring together richly diverse social groups, each with their own stories and their own ways of inhabiting the city. At such charged boundary points as Nathaniel's tunnel or Pershing Square, border experiences proliferate that, in the midst of crisis and even decline, continue to define Los Angeles as, to paraphrase García Canclini, a privileged laboratory of transnational and cosmopolitan identities.

III

The Brown City

I started this book with what I described as the striking invisibility of Latinos and Latinas, particularly Mexicans, in the cinematic history of representation of Los Angeles. This invisibility is not specific to the cinema and continues to be lamented in Latino and Chicano studies (see López Calvo 2011, 85). According to Mike Davis, it extends to other cultural areas and academic endeavors, such as "high-end" urban studies, another discipline that has largely failed to grasp the importance of this "minority-majority" in LA and other U.S. cities (2000, 9). More generally, for Rodolfo Acuña, the negation of the Mexican presence in Los Angeles history and in the city's contemporary reality is a major feature of dominant discourses in the metropolis (1996, 209).

Demographic data are too overwhelming to be ignored. In 1960 whites were 81 percent of the city's population. In the 1990 census, for almost 3.5 million people, there were already more Hispanics (40 percent) than Anglos (37 percent), with 13 percent African Americans and just under 10 percent Asian Americans and Pacific Islanders (Hayden 1995, 83). According to the 2010 census, the population grew only slightly to just under 3.8 million, out of which almost 50 percent were Hispanics, 28 percent whites, 11.3 percent Asian Americans, and 9.6 percent African Americans (quickfacts.census.gov/qfd/states/06/0644000.html). Los Angeles has for a long time been the second largest Mexican city in the world (it is also the second largest Armenian, Filipino, Salvadoran, and Guatemalan city). In 2000 California became the second state, after New Mexico, in which whites are a minority (Davis 2000, 2). Thirty-five percent of the population of California (more than 37 million, according to the 2010 census) is of Latino origin, mostly Mexicans, and in the greater metropolitan Los Angeles area there are 4.6 million Latinos, or 46 percent of the total population, 38 percent of whom are foreign born, mostly in Mexico (López Calvo 2011, 12). Given that many Mexicans and Latinos are officially invisible, because they are undocumented, the consensus is that well above half of the population of the city and the county are Latinos (some say two out of every three individuals) and that, projecting demographic trends to the near future, by 2020 Latinos will be the majority in the state of California. If we took U.S. Latinos to be a separate nation, they would be the fifth largest nation in Latin America, and by 2050 they might become the third largest (Davis 2000, 15).

The Mexican presence in Los Angeles has always been demographically important. The city was predominantly Mexican until 1876, when the transcontinental railroad reached the city and Anglos from the eastern and midwestern regions started to flood in; after that, Mexican immigration increased again at the beginning of the twentieth century, and by 1930 Mexicans were already the largest minority. This combination of history and recent developments has led many to express their anxieties, sometimes in loud and violent terms, about the *reconquista* of the city and the state by Mexico. Fear of Mexicans has been, as Robert Gottlieb asserts, an on-and-off feature of the city's history, at least since the first massive Anglo migrations of the 1880s, often acquiring nativist and class dimensions (2007, 259). Davis uses these fears ironically to conclude that the "Anglo conquest of California in the late 1840s has proven to be a very transient fact indeed" (2000, 59). This combination of history and seemingly unstoppable demographic expansion has set alarms ringing, and, apart from ascertainable cases of white flight, first from the city to certain suburbs and more recently to other states, rising hysteria can be perceived at all levels: from hysterical English-only linguistic policies at schools to nativist pronouncements about the risks of being overpowered by the "sleeping dragon." Davis quotes Dr. John Tanton's anxiety-ridden and menacing words: "To govern is to populate. In this society where the majority rules, does this hold? Will the present majority peaceably hand over its political power to a group that is simply more fertile? . . . As whites see their power and control over their lives declining, will they go quietly into the night? Or will there be an explosion?" (2000, 141–42).

The recent diversity of the city's demographic makeup is in fact nothing new and goes back to its origins. As we can read on a memorial plaque in La Placita, among the 44 men, women, and children sent by Felipe de Neve, the Spanish governor of California, to establish a pueblo in 1781 to strengthen Spain's position in the territory, there was only one Spaniard. The rest were Indians, blacks, mulattos, and mestizos; the married couples featured various ethnic combinations between the husband and wife, and none of the twenty-two children had any hope of a claim to racial purity. Los Angeles has always been a hybrid city and a city of migrations; these features have shaped its urban identity in many ways while at the same time spawning a culture of hostility toward immigrants (Gottlieb 2007, 258) and a myth of racial purity. Despite the political and economic power that white people started to wield about one century later, this hybridity has continued to characterize the city, as much in terms of its population as its culture and even its architecture.

Yet the discourse of racial homogeneity has dominated Angeleno history. As Dolores Hayden asserts, pop culture offers an urban landscape "where Disneyland, swimming pools, and freeways are icons and people of color are invisible" and where the major ethnic groups have been dispossessed (1995, 86–87). For many people around the world, Los Angeles is "the glamorous world of Hollywood stars, life in the affluent western districts, hardboiled crime fiction, and the disaster novel" (López Calvo 2011, 175), along with, as we have seen, apocalyptic views of the future metropolis and stories of the white man's alienation. Despite being located in Los Angeles, Hollywood has, with some exceptions, ignored the existence of Mexicans, Chicanos, and Latinos and other ethnic groups and largely continues to do so.

Given the segregated nature of middle-class life in Los Angeles, a person could live in the city for many years without ever visiting South Central, East LA, or, despite their proximity to the glimmering Financial District, Skid Row or even the Garment District or the Flower District in the Downtown area. These are all areas with a large population of Mexicans of various social classes, from the dispossessed of Skid Row, through the predominantly recent immigrant population of many parts of South Central, to the relatively affluent middle classes of Montebello and Pico Rivera, and to the working-class areas of Boyle Heights and other neighborhoods of East LA. The cinema rarely ventures into these areas, and when it does, Mexicans fail to materialize, as though, emulating the story of Sergio Arau's satire in *A Day Without a Mexican* (2004), some extraterrestrial power had made all those with Mexican roots evaporate. But Mexicans and Mexican culture are present everywhere in the city and also in the Westside, even in the affluent districts of Bel Air, Beverly Hills, and Hancock Park, where many of the film stars live, or the beach communities of Venice Beach, Santa Monica, and Malibu.

The Great Wall of Los Angeles is an example of the difficulties encountered by Latino culture to become part of the mainstream. This work is a half-mile-long mural located in the San Fernando Valley, on the wall of the Tujunga Wash, a flood-control channel of the Los Angeles River, a location that is part of the visual and cultural impact of the mural. First-time visitors to the city are often surprised and dismayed at the present appearance of this river, once a central feature of the Los Angeles Basin. The stream was encased for most of its length in an artificial armor of concrete in the 1940s to prevent floods and to foster industrial development in the booming city (Davis 1996, 164–66) and is now little more than a trickle in a desolate dried-out course. It parallels the freeways above, and together the river and the freeways explain the history of urban development in the megalopolis. Judith Baca, the coordinator of the Great Wall project, explains that, given the historical and symbolic importance of the massive engineering operation that tamed the water artery for the sake of real estate interests, the guiding metaphor of her project was that the mural be "*a tattoo on the scar where the river once ran*" (2002, 25; emphasis in original). More than 400 young people, between age 14 and 21, many of them referred by the criminal justice department, worked on the mural, considered the longest in the world, on several successive summers in the late 1970s and early 1980s (SPARC 2014).

More than thirty years old and well-known and admired by the Chicano community, the mural portrays the history of the city from the perspective of its ethnic minorities, starting with prehistoric animals and the Chumash Indians and ending with the Olympic Games of 1984. For José Luis Gámez, the *Great Wall* is, along with other Chicano murals, a representation of political identity, a reminder of an *other* LA, and part of an attempt to confront dominant narratives (2002, 101). Beyond ethnic identity, the mural is an impressive visual record of the untold history of the city, including the vicissitudes of Native Americans, African Americans, Dust Bowl immigrants, Asian Americans, Mexicans and other Latinos, Jews, gays and lesbians, citrus field workers, and other "minorities," and it provides a potent counterpart to the official history symbolized by the channeling of the Porciúncula River, on which the city was founded.

An often-mentioned panel in the mural, both in connection with the impact of freeways and with the destruction of Chávez Ravine, is the "Division of the Barrios," a section that represents the Chávez Ravine episode with freeways encircling and dividing members of a Chicano family (Avila 1998, 22; Parson 1993, 345). Yet the *Great Wall* does not figure in any of the tourist circuits or among the most popular sites of the city. For example, a voluminous and trendy tourist guide for visitors of the region, *The Rough Guide to Los Angeles and Southern California*, does not mention it once in its more than 400 pages, let alone selecting it among its "21 things not to miss" (Dickey 2008, 11–16). Google maps does not even recognize it by name. Giving voice to those who were for a long time silenced and standing as a milestone of popular Angeleno art, the *Great Wall* somehow has not managed to make it into

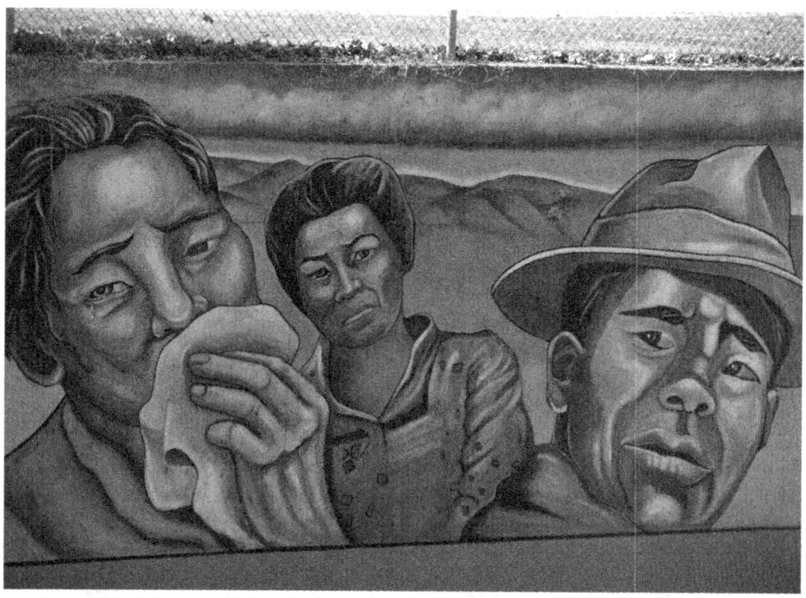

The invisible city: a section of the Great Wall of Los Angeles.

the mainstream. Today visitors to the Valley Glen neighborhood where it is located can enjoy the whole length of the mural at total leisure without sharing it with the crowds that, for instance, fill the relatively nearby Hollywood Boulevard, with only the occasional homeless person sleeping by the side of the dry canal or maybe a child playing along the equally empty park strip alongside it.

The difficulties of this masterpiece of popular art to reach the mainstream of Angeleno discourse can be extended to most Chicano art, including cinema. So-called Chicano cinema is by and large the most reliable body of films where the external observer can find the visibility that most other movies have denied Mexicans and Mexican Americans, as well as Mexican culture, in the course of history. For the most part, only Chicano scholars have explored these films. Often focusing on political activism, Chicano scholars have often sidelined the quest for the mainstream of its cinematic representations. One of several exceptions is Charles Ramírez Berg's *Latino Images in Film* (2002), which brings together the work of Chicano filmmakers and the study of Hollywood images of Chicanos. Like José Limón (1992) before him, Ramírez Berg uses the lens of stereotyping to explain the construction of Latin America and its inhabitants and of Latinos in the United States (Latinism) as a form of justification of U.S. imperialism (2002, 4).

Chon Noriega, in the introduction to his edited work *Chicanos and Film* (1992b), selects three areas of study: (1) the representation of Chicanos and Chicanas in Hollywood and Mexican cinema, (2) the continued growth and diversification of a Chicano countercinema, and (3) the emergence of Chicano film criticism. Noriega asserts that a "Chicano film" is a film by and about Chicanos (1992b, xi, xix). The challenge for this type of cinema is, as for Baca's work, how to reach the mainstream, and the need, in Noriega's words, to "get in and dirty your hands" (xxi). The problem, however, arises when not even Latino audiences have access to (or are interested in) Chicano countercinema and when the usual channels of production and distribution become virtually closed to Chicano filmmakers. Ramírez Berg points out that the divide between Chicano films and the mainstream started to shrink in the 1980s, with what he calls second-wave cinema. Noriega also sees films like *La Bamba* (Luis Valdez, 1987), *Born in East L.A.* (Cheech Marin, 1987), *Stand and Deliver* (Ramón Menéndez, 1988), and *The Milagro Beanfield War* (Robert Redford, 1988) as an indication of the irreversibility of this trend (1992c, xi), but the process has been much slower than could be anticipated twenty years ago. Now, as then, self-produced images of Latinos in the United States encounter constant obstacles to breaking into Hollywood (Noriega, 1992a, 147). The accessibility of complex images of Chicanos and Chicanas continues to be a key issue and one that applies equally to Latino images of Los Angeles.

My concern in this book has been with the ways in which the city speaks about itself through Hollywood movies, what it says and what it hides about its contemporary signature diversity. In the final part of the book I focus on how the community that constitutes half of the population of the city and of the metropolitan area is made visible in post-1992 movies, whether or not these texts can be considered Chicano cinema (most times they clearly are not). As I argued in the Introduction, these images of Chicanos that are not immediately forthcoming in the mainstream can be found more readily in alternative traditions and in other contemporary media. Because what has traditionally been considered cinema has become intertwined with other visual art forms and because the boundaries are increasingly porous, it may seem limiting to restrict my analysis to only Hollywood. Chicano scholars have actively engaged and continue to engage with these alternative representations, many of them directly connected with Los Angeles. Yet most of these cultural texts continue to have a limited reach outside specific interest groups, whereas Hollywood, through its successive metamorphoses, continues to hold a particular power to shape the collective imaginary. Furthermore, given that many of the alternative traditions of representation are created in conversation with the Hollywood tradition, it seems relevant to ascertain the extent to which that conversation has contributed to transformations in Hollywood images. Is, as Acuña argues, Hollywood still one more instance of the more general negation of the Mexican presence in Los Angeles history (1996, 209), or are things changing? The answer to this rhetorical question is not straightforward and depends very much on our perspective. The status of the *Great Wall* in urban artistic and touristic discourse can be seen as an apt metaphor for the restricted visibility decried by Acuña and many others. On the other hand, and to continue with the metaphor, Baca's mural is there for everyone who wants to see it. Something similar can be said about the type of films that I analyze and refer to in this final section of the book: They may well not constitute a consistent and visible body of work within the Hollywood mainstream, but, unlike most Chicano countercinema of the 1970s, they are easily accessible. Together they offer evidence, however fragile, of Hollywood's growing interest in the Latino market after the 2000 census.

In terms of cinematic history, the movies considered in this final part must be linked to Ramírez Berg's second wave, which includes the films mentioned earlier and others, such as *Zoot Suit* (Luis Valdez, 1981), *El Norte* (Gregory Nava, 1982), *The Ballad of Gregorio Cortez* (Robert M. Young, 1982), *American Me* (Edward James Olmos, 1992), *My Family/Mi Familia* (Gregory Nava, 1995), and the films of Robert Rodríguez, starting with *El Mariachi* (1993). At the time, these films pointed to the impact of Chicano and other Latino political and cultural movements on a national redefinition of citizenship in a multicultural society, as Kathleen Newman has argued (1992, 60), or what, in Angeleno terms, many have called the browning of the megalopolis. This change has continued to produce, among other things, popular and official manifestations of fear and anxiety, such as the 1994 California Proposition 187 (López Calvo 2011, 9). This proposition, also known as Save Our State (SOS), aimed to ban undocumented immigrants from public education and health and other social services and was found unconstitutional by a federal court. Second-wave Chicano cinema and this nativist law were divergent cultural manifestations of the same phenomenon.

Several decades later, the multicultural society has turned into a buzz phrase, not only in Los Angeles but also across the country, and Latinos and Latinas have become an even more visible factor of this epochal turn. Yet Hollywood and the Anglophone mass media are still accused of stereotyping and ignoring complex Latino images. Writing specifically about Los Angeles, López Calvo laments that images of Mexicans continue to be mostly of maids and nannies for women and gardeners and gangbangers for men (2011, 13–14). I share López Calvo's frustration but attempt to frame it within a larger gallery of cinematic images of the city. Given the exponential growth of the Mexican and Mexican American population and the ensuing proliferation of Mexicanness in LA in the post-1992 period, Mexicans are also part and parcel of the dynamics at work in contemporary cinematic discourses on the city. As with the rest of the films analyzed in earlier chapters, the films discussed in the last two chapters offer insights into wider cultural urban discourses that, in this case, are not dominant but exist in the same ideological space as more powerful ones. The struggle for visibility of Mexicans and Latinos in cinematic representations of the city cannot be understood independently from other forces playing in the representational arena.

In Chapter 9 I look at two movies from the early years of the twenty-first century that, in quite different ways, open new avenues of representation for Chicanos, in particular, Chicanas, reflecting cultural changes in the city and U.S. society in general. *Luminarias* (José Luis Valenzuela, 2000) and *Real Women Have Curves* (Patricia Cardoso, 2002) can be seen as celebrating the new millennium by imagining a new way of conveying Chicana experience that openly counteracts traditional stereotypes. The two movies in Chapter 10, released some years later, illustrate the new mainstream-indie dynamic in Hollywood and the struggles of recent Chicano cinema to find its place along this industrial spectrum. *Quinceañera* (Richard Glatzer and Wash Westmoreland, 2006) and *A Better Life* (Chris Weitz, 2011) reflect the challenges posed from within the multicultural city and the multicultural industry to the very concept of Chicano cinema. They also differ notably from earlier representations of Chicano history, such as those found in *American Me*, *Blood In Blood Out* (Taylor Hackford, 1993), *My Family/Mi Familia*, and the TV movie *Walkout* (Edward James Olmos, 2006). Like *Tortilla Soup* (Maria Ripoll, 2001), *Under the Same Moon* (Patricia Riggen, 2007), *From Prada to Nada* (Angel Gracia, 2011), and *Mosquita y Mari* (Aurora Guerrero, 2012), they tend to use mainstream genres and/or the conventions of independent cinema to depict contemporary Chicano life in the postmetropolis that Latinos have so crucially helped to shape.

9

Browning the Millennium

High on the Hill in the Border City

Luminarias is a Mexican restaurant located on a hillside at the edge of the city of Monterey Park, which borders unincorporated East LA and the city of Alhambra; it overlooks a maze of freeways, including the San Bernardino Freeway, the Long Beach Freeway, and the El Monte Busway. It is not far from the middle-class enclaves of Montebello, Pico Rivera, and San Gabriel and only a short drive away from the traditional centers of Mexican life in East LA, Boyle Heights, and Lincoln Heights. The San Gabriel Mountains serve as scenic backdrop. For several decades the restaurant has been a place of reunion for middle-class Mexican Americans and students from the California State University campus across the freeways. Cal State is one of the higher education institutions in the United States that award most of its degrees to Hispanics, and it is the top institution in California to do so; it was also the first university in the country to get a Chicano Studies Department, in 1968.

Luminarias is a border location. In terms of urban policy, both the freeways and the historical phenomenon of incorporation are part of its representativeness as an Angeleno setting. Municipal incorporation is the process by which a community constitutes itself as a city. According to Tom Hogen-Esch (2010, 234), there are 181 independent cities in Southern California (the so-called five-county region) with 88 in Los Angeles County alone. Since California became a state in 1850, the trend, especially in Southern California, has been toward local government fragmentation, with the exception of the consolidation of the City of Los Angeles between 1915 and 1930. Incorporation has been a strategy for class and racial segregation, tax privilege, and untrammeled real estate development. Lack of political clout and economic privilege has so far prevented large areas such as East LA and the San Fernando Valley from becoming incorporated. Thus, whereas most of the communities east of Downtown are segregated, the largest one but also one of the poorest,

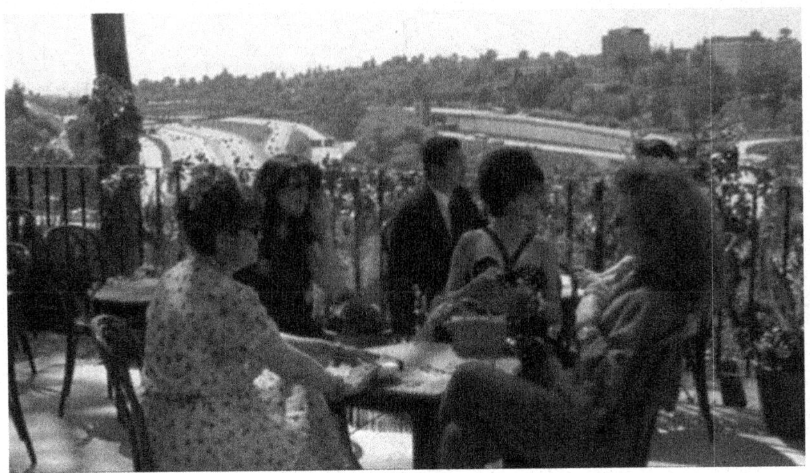

Luminarias: the liminality of the Mexican restaurant in Monterey Park.

East LA, remains a part of the City of Los Angeles. West of Downtown the situation is more puzzling: West Hollywood (like Beverly Hills) is a city, whereas Hollywood is part of LA; Santa Monica is a city, but Venice Beach, next to it, is not; Culver City, right in the middle of the metropolis, is not part of LA but an independent city; north of the Santa Monica mountains, Burbank is a city, but most of the San Fernando Valley is not.

Incorporation has promoted a model of incoherent town planning and fragmented growth that has made implementing social urban policies particularly problematic. Although incorporation has been considerably more difficult since 1992, it has been responsible to a large extent for the apparently haphazard and internally segregated social structure of Los Angeles. Historically, many incorporated cities in Southern California have been enlarged walled communities designed to protect their wealth and to prevent African Americans and successive waves of immigrants from entering and settling down. They have also been at least partly responsible for the racial segregation of the city, often pushing racial minorities toward specific neighborhoods in the unincorporated areas. On the other hand, as Hogen-Esch points out, the incorporation of areas with an immigrant majority may be a promising sign to understand the future of Los Angeles (2010, 244). The mostly non-Anglo middle-class incorporated cities around Luminarias, as well as the revived campaign to incorporate a city of East Los Angeles, are examples of this trend.

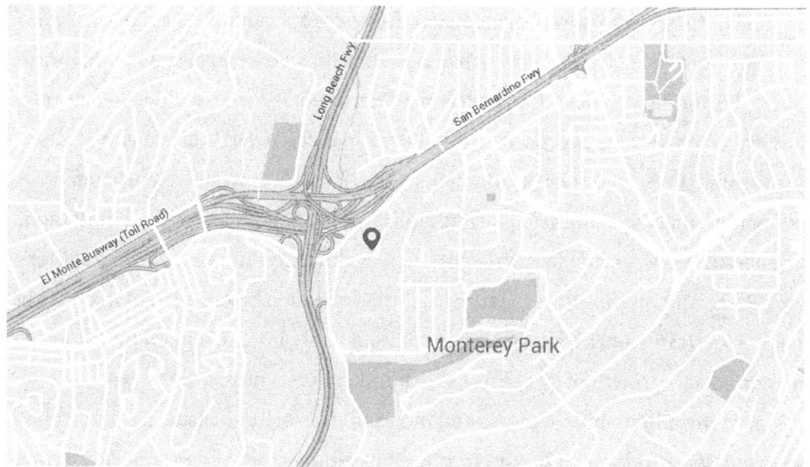

Map 6. The location of Luminarias Restaurant at the edge of Monterey Park, overlooking a freeway exchange. Map by Francesc Terrades.

As I argued in Chapter 3, freeways are a central fact of Angeleno life and a potent symbol of the city and of the postmetropolis, yet from the beginning they have also constituted an element of racial segregation. Apart from dealing a fatal blow to the Downtown area, the freeways, like incorporation, divide communities even as they purport to make communications between them easier. Boyle Heights, for instance, has 15 percent of its total surface taken up by freeways (G. Sánchez 2010, 136). Thousands of poor families were evicted from their homes as the massive infrastructures were built, and many poor neighborhoods started to live under the shadow of the cement monsters. Eric Avila (1998) argues that the origin of the freeways can be found, even if only indirectly, in the growth of Latino and African American neighborhoods such as Boyle Heights and Watts. This growth provoked white flight from the Downtown area to the urban fringe, where new communities sprouted, insulated from the racialized masses of the inner city. For Avila, this was part of the city's history: an attempt "to preserve southern California's legacy of building separate and unequal communities" and a strategy to further the production of "white space" (1998, 16). The freeways wreaked havoc on East and South Central Los Angeles. By the end of the century, as Wachs summarizes, they had destroyed the sense of community, cutting swatches out of the urban fabric and raising barriers to community cohesion by creating enormous discontinuities within the city (1996, 131).

The history and social dynamics of Los Angeles cannot be properly understood without the specificities of urban design produced by freeways and incorporation. Historically, incorporation has made it difficult for Hispanics to integrate into Angeleno society, and the freeways have often destroyed their neighborhoods. At the same time, cases such as Montebello and Pico Rivera, both incorporated cities demographically dominated by middle-class Hispanics, illustrate the limitations of generalizations, particularly in such a socially fluid city. The nearby cities of Monterey Park, Alhambra, and San Gabriel, all three of which have a current majority of Asian American citizens, many of them middle class, are also a good indication of the remarkable growth of this ethnic group in LA in recent years.

On the other hand, freeways and incorporation are two instances of the presence and social relevance of inner borders in global cities. Freeways allow travel between distant neighborhoods while making access difficult within the neighborhoods they cross, which often coincide with the neighborhoods where immigrants live. Incorporation draws boundaries, sometimes almost as visible as the fence on the U.S.-Mexico border, but mostly invisible. This institutionalized, though far from airtight, practice of urban boundary drawing is largely designed to uphold economic privilege and Anglo supremacy. It clashes with the hybrid identity of Angeleno Latinos and has a huge impact on their everyday lives.

From its elevated vantage point, Luminarias encapsulates a different perspective on the border city. It is both witness to the centrality of freeways and incorporation in the city's urban structure and a modest manifestation of the urban borderland, where social and cultural exchange is possible outside dominant urban strategies, or rather, as an unexpected side effect of those strategies. High on the hill in Monterey Park, Luminarias stands as a metaphor of the unsolvable duality of the city: its diversity and hybridity and its exclusionary and discriminatory realities. The global city as urban borderland reveals itself distinctly at this restaurant. More important for the purposes of this chapter, the global city is here seen from a Chicano perspective, highlighting the importance of bordering practices and border culture in the urban Chicano experience.

Luminarias is also the central location of the film of the same name, released in 2000. The movie was directed by José Luis Valenzuela, written by Evelina Fernández, and produced by Sal López through the company created for the occasion, Sleeping Giant Productions. Valenzuela, Fernández, and López are also the three founding members of the Latino Theater Company, which is based in LA. The theater company was established in 1988 and is committed to producing plays that present the everyday lives of Latinos in the United States to their own community and to a broader cultural audience and that counter the stereotyped and impoverishing images of them offered by the mainstream. The movie originated from a short directed by Valenzuela, *How Else Am I Supposed to Know I'm Still Alive* (1992). Sony Pictures became interested and asked the filmmakers to develop a project for a feature film. They pitched *Luminarias* and Sony liked it, but then *Waiting to Exhale* (Forest Whitaker, 1995) came along and the studio preferred it. Whitaker's film had big stars and it was about African Americans, who were more bankable at the box office than Latinos. Valenzuela, Fernández, and López then turned the story into a play, which they produced with their company in 1996. Later, they decided to make the film independently and raised the money for it through an early form of crowdfunding with private contributions from family, friends, and members of the Chicano community in Los Angeles and other places. Produced on a shoestring budget and distributed by New Latin Pictures, a small company that specializes in Latino films, *Luminarias* became a modest success, playing at various festivals around the world, having a relatively wide theatrical release, and later selling to HBO and several networks. In LA it opened on forty-five screens on May 5, Cinco de Mayo, the day of Mexican heritage and pride celebrated across the United States.

Luminarias is a romantic comedy dealing with the love lives and sexual entanglements of four middle-class Mexican American women. Reviewers highlighted the production details, particularly the then unconventional money-raising process, and celebrated the movie for showing a dimension of U.S. life so far absent from the screen, but they often also criticized the film for its relapse into stereotypes and a schematic narrative (Honeycutt 2000, 11). Kevin Thomas (2000), for instance, referred to the film as a "classic women's picture with a Spanish accent," but he also praised it for offering a fresh perspective on women's universal concerns while not cowering from the long-festering prejudice of Latinos toward Anglos. Lorenza Muñoz (2000) argued that *Luminarias* breaks new ground also within Chicano cinema, a cinema dominated by politically committed documentaries and by men (F6). *Variety* dwelled on the movie's agenda of breaking away from stereotypical representations of Latina women and the usual images of gang mothers, hookers, or maids and called attention to the special position of Chicanos in U.S. culture, "sandwiched between their Mexican roots and the Anglo culture in which they live" (Rooney 1999, n.p.).

As the reviews suggest, *Luminarias* is a film with a political agenda. It attempts to counteract cultural, particularly cinematic clichés, about the Chicano and Latino community in the United States, in particular Los Angeles. In its focus on middle-class Mexican Americans it advocates the recognition of a complexity in their everyday experiences that is systematically denied by the mainstream media. The casting of Chicano actors ensures the credibility of its discourse on ethnicity and difference, with a particular emphasis on linguistic singularity. In the process the film constructs a strong sense of identity that is shared by all its characters and that is epitomized by its central location in the interstices of the peculiar urban space created in the city by freeways and incorporation, that is, an urban border identity: Valenzuela's film creates an Angeleno Chicano community living—and in this case thriving—on the borderland. The movie, as a cultural text, demands recognition of a frequently snubbed social group, but in the process it becomes a manifestation of the urban borderland as an engine of complex twenty-first-century identities. As such, it is, no less than *The Soloist* (Joe Wright, 2009), a border film, but one with a Latino inflection. Given its symbolic central location—the Mexican restaurant on the hill—the film is a privileged example of Cooper and Rumford's call to look from the border in order to acquire a new cosmopolitan perspective (2011, 265).

This liminal position makes U.S. Latinos in general and Mexican Americans in particular unique, and Los Angeles is an apt urban environment to observe this border phenomenon. Valenzuela, Mexican born but a resident of California for more that forty years, echoes W. E. B. Dubois's (1994) concept of double consciousness to describe the African American experience when he explains that Chicanos are not half-Mexican and half-American—they are fully both things at the same time (José Luis Valenzuela, personal communication, May 16 and 24, 2012). Their children have grown up living simultaneously in two worlds. They are "American," but if you go to their houses, everything is Mexican culturally. At the end of the day, they also identify themselves as Mexican. Their identity is based on a delicate balance between the two poles, both strong forces pulling at them (Valenzuela, personal communication, 2012). Beyond its ostensible desire to counter Anglo stereotypes of Mexican Americans, *Luminarias* offers a vivid picture of this double identity, of a profound brand of cultural and personal hybridity that for this social group has been a fact of everyday life for more than a century. It also suggests the centrality of Los Angeles in contemporary transnational and cosmopolitan discourses. In *Luminarias* the global metropolis and the Latino metropolis intersect in the fictional space of the Mexican restaurant.

At first sight, what is most striking about the movie is that its four female protagonists are all prosperous middle-class professionals, businesswomen, and artists. They live in expensive houses, tastefully decorated apartments, and designer buildings that bespeak their social status. This flaunted prosperity has the obvious goal of affirming that such women do exist in the Latino community and that "Mexican American" is not synonymous with poverty, violence, lack of education, and prostitution. At the same time, the film situates its characters and their ideological positions in relation to a more or less precise Angeleno geography. Irene (Dyana Ortelli), who dates only Latinos and mistrusts Anglos, owns a clothing store in East LA, apparently in Boyle Heights, and lives nearby, in the traditional heart of the Mexican city. Sofia (Marta Dubois), a therapist with a successful professional practice, is more open to relationships with other ethnic groups and is often accused by her friends of selling out. She lives in an affluent neighborhood somewhere on the Westside. We do not know exactly where Andrea's (Evelina Fernández) posh abode is supposed to be either, although the real house where it was shot is in Whittier, in East LA. Although the exact location of the loft where Lilly (Ángela Moya) lives and works is not specified, it very much looks like the gentrified section of Downtown. Andrea aligns herself ideologically with Irene and is in fact the text's main mouthpiece of Chicanos' conflicted relationships with Anglos, whereas Lilly is ideologically closer to Sofia and advocates interethnic bonds.

The city constructed by the film is crossed along its north-south axis by La Cienega Boulevard (slightly farther west than La Brea, the symbolic dividing line in *White Men Can't Jump*). Beyond La Cienega is the Westside, associated with Anglo privilege and therefore alien and even hostile to the Chicano community; east of the boulevard is home. The real geography of the city is more complicated. Such wealthy enclaves as Hancock Park (predominantly Jewish), West Hollywood, and the famous Rodeo Drive are located not west but east of La Cienega, and, in any case, in today's metropolis the Mexican presence can be felt across the board, from the Pacific Coast to the San Gabriel Mountains. On the other hand, Mid-Town, the large section of central Los Angeles between La Cienega and Downtown is occupied by neighborhoods linked with other ethnic minorities: the huge Koreatown, Little Armenia, Thai Town, MacArthur Park, and many others. Still, the long boulevard that stretches from south of LAX to the Sunset Strip is used, in the movie's ideological structure, as a border between two different worlds.

For Andrea and Irene, the fact that Sofia has moved out of East LA, her "natural home," is a betrayal of her principles and her identity, and she is rebuked by her friends for never crossing this third border again to visit her Mexican mother. Irene, on the other hand, is proud of being faithful to her roots and remaining in Boyle Heights, proving that an LA Chicana can become successful and thrive on the social scale without "betraying" her identity. Like Irene, Andrea, although living in obvious comfort, continues to be part of her own community, as can be seen in the scene of the barbecue party at her parents' house. This scene celebrates the close-knit quality of the traditional Mexican family, with Andrea's boyfriend, Joseph (Scott Bakula), providing the outsider's perspective to introduce the spectator into the community. The ideological center of this gathering is provided by Andrea's brother Jesús (Cheech Marin), an eccentric character who looks like an old homeboy but is really a professor at UCLA. Jesús offers Joseph an ambivalent welcome and his nephew Joey (Fidel Gómez), Andrea's son, some advice when Joey reacts with hostility toward his mother's new boyfriend. Marin's character, with his characteristic and carefully modulated mixture of English and Spanish when he speaks, displays a combination of Chicano militancy and pride and capacity for reconciliation, thus representing the complexity of Chicano identity—he seems to have come to terms with the doubleness of the Mexican American experience. Marin's filmic persona contributes the appropriate connotations to Jesús's ideological role in the film: As a crossover Chicano actor who acquired visibility in the mainstream (one who, metaphorically, also crossed La Cienega), he has at the same time remained faithful to his roots and supportive of the Chicano community.

Against this backdrop, the film's conflict is presented as a struggle between acceptance and rejection, diversity and ethnic exclusivity, U.S. and Mexican American identities. The generic conventions of romantic comedy are used to frame this dynamic within the realm of intimate discourses. Starting from opposite positions, the development of the plot makes the four friends change or modulate their ideas and finally allow their desire, which in romantic comedy must always be paramount, to reign supreme (Deleyto 2009, 30–38). But sexual desire here comes close to the liberating desires of the border mentioned by Schimanski and Wolfe (2007b, 9). The fascination exerted by these women and by their expressions of sexual desire is intimately linked to the spectators' familiarity with their urban Chicano border identities.

Valenzuela explains that the filmmakers chose the generic framework of romantic comedy as an ideological weapon. What makes humans different from animals is their capacity to reason and to love. In the eyes of those in power, minorities are not completely human unless they are shown falling in love and engaging in intimate relationships. Therefore the type of narrative offered by this film is an instrument of empowerment for those who are still seen as not quite fully human (Valenzuela, personal communication, 2012). In romantic comedies, love has the power to transform people and make them better individuals. In *Luminarias* this transformation takes place within the context of the existence in the Chicano community of prejudices bred from many years of oppression and injustice. The romcom structure is superimposed on the debate among the four friends to suggest that the way ahead for Chicanos, and in this case for Chicana women, lies in the acceptance of the Other and the breaking down of barriers, no matter what the historical discriminations and the real political and social situation may be. Sofia, in her obsession with passing as Anglo, has forgotten her roots ("I've been trying to fit in with white people for so many years; I even started to resent who I am," she confesses) but ends up marrying Pablo (Sal López), an undocumented immigrant from Mexico who reminds her of her historical origins ("I don't know if I'm in love with Pablo for who he is or because he reminds me of who I am; it's like I'm falling in love with who I am"). Her wedding provides the traditional romcom celebration and happy ending. The party at Luminarias that closes the story reinforces the productive dimensions of the borderland and the potential of Los Angeles to carve out spaces for new identities in the interstices of its historically loaded demography.

Andrea's narrative evolution is bumpier and more difficult to resolve. Her intimate relationship with fellow lawyer Joseph is constantly challenged by her rage, a communal feeling that Chicanos have and that comes from "way back," as she explains to her son Joey. Compared to her macho, womanizing husband Joe (Robert Beltrán), Joseph is a caring, affectionate boyfriend, but his Jewishness is too imposing a barrier for Andrea to overcome easily. At the final wedding party, there is a tentative, precarious reconciliation, but their future together is uncertain, to say the least. As a character of romantic comedy, Andrea learns to see her resistance to white people as a limitation not only to fulfillment in love but also to the development of a sense of Chicana identity for the future, but she cannot yet go beyond this recognition. In a sense, though, the resolution of her narrative predicament is displaced onto her son Joey, who is initially against Joseph because he is not a member of the Chicano community, like his father, but whose new girlfriend, Laura Johnson (Aiysha Sinclair), turns out to be, to his mother's delighted surprise and admiration, African American. The discourse of love is therefore superimposed on and ultimately subordinated to the exploration and celebration of the contradictions and subtleties of Chicano and Chicana identity and the wish, even for such a modest independent production, to reverse the cinematic invisibility of the Mexican American community and to put it on the map.

The symbolic importance of La Cienega Boulevard has already been explained, but other parts of the city's urban layout are also highlighted, notably the freeways. Shots of these roads frequently punctuate the action. In *Luminarias*, as, for different reasons, in *Falling Down* and *Collateral*, the freeways are part of what the story is about. For example, the scene in which Irene and her brother Carlos/Carmela (Geoffrey Rivas) are walking along the street in Boyle Heights arguing about his sexuality starts with a shot of a freeway taken from a bridge above it. This stretch of freeway reminds the viewer of the overwhelming presence of these roads in the lives of Mexican Angelenos, a proliferation that was not designed to make communications easier for them but rather for those of other, more privileged neighborhoods. Yet in this scene the textual attitude is not critical but rather celebratory. The shot is accompanied in the soundtrack by lively Latino music. The dissolve with the next shot of the street in Boyle Heights associates the energy of Mexican American life, as represented here by Irene and Carmela's brisk walk and lively argument, with the constant movement of cars on the freeway. It inaugurates a sequence that revels in East LA energy and color. The movie seems to suggest that, although the freeways may have contributed to the production of inner borders in the city, there are productive dimensions to the resulting borderlands.

Unlike more mainstream movies, then, the presence of freeways is not so much alienating and apocalyptic as demonstrative of Angeleno, particularly Mexican American, society. Seen from a comedic Latino perspective, that which makes the city unlivable and alienating can be turned into an integral part of its power. The film shows Latinos, used to being discriminated against and trampled on for so long, appropriating the historically hostile space and making it their own.

This takes us back to Luminarias, the restaurant. A significant scene in this respect takes place there in the daytime. The four friends are sitting outside, with the freeways and Cal State visible in the background. As in the previously discussed shot, the constant traffic provides a counterpoint to the friends' discussion of their love lives. Whereas in an earlier restaurant scene they had discussed men from various races and ethnic groups in general, in this scene their conversation is more focused on their current affairs: Lilly is about to meet Lu's (Andrew C. Lim) parents, Andrea is trying to negotiate her professional life and her incipient liaison with Joseph, and Sofia reveals to her friends that she has been seeing Pablo, the waiter, who, even as they talk, is serving them margaritas. At this point in the narrative, it becomes clear that their romantic entanglements are to be seen as a metaphor for the Latino-based cultural and racial hybridity that the text proposes as representative of the city. This hybridity is not without problems: The rage against Anglos that generations of Chicanos have harbored as a result of decades of oppression, injustice, and invisibility and the particular type of racial prejudice that has originated from it shape their social interactions, including intimate relationships and sexual protocols.

At the same time, however, the energy displayed by the four friends is also an indication of the vigor of a community that is coming to terms with the momentum of its awakening and their singular power to redefine what it is to be American in the twenty-first century. The freeways behind them, with their combined meanings of constant movement and social disruption, provide not only the appropriate visual environment for the friends' predicaments but also an accurate reminder of the urban layout of the city that, because of its history and its geographic position, is seen as a workshop from which this new identity is emerging. In other words, the freeways in Valenzuela's film are part of a whole, a visible ingredient of a city in the throes of oceanic changes. Unlike in earlier, more mainstream films, the freeways in *Luminarias* are a contradictory signifier of both energy and alienation, that is, of the harsh and extreme type of urban experience that Angeleno Chicanos have been used to. It could be said that in learning to survive these experiences, these citizens have become stronger and more adept at transforming their exclusionary dimensions into more constructive meanings. At Luminarias the four friends demonstrate that they are comfortable in an urban environment that others find oppressive and that they can navigate better than most.

Also visible in this scene, beyond the freeways, is the edge of official East Los Angeles, the territory that, despite its proximity, legally belongs to a different city. There are many senses in which Luminarias and the city where it is placed, Monterey Park, are indeed part of East LA, like Whittier, the other city in which important parts of the film were shot. Incorporation has greatly influenced urban developmental patterns and has affected, like the freeways, Latinos in important ways. Yet the urban borders that incorporation draws have proven to be as permeable and even fruitful as the material border between Mexico and the United States 135 miles farther south. In the film incorporated Monterey Park, with its middle-class associations and its recent history of fluid ethnic shifts, is a symbol of Chicano upward mobility, and Luminarias is the ideal location to tease out this potentiality. At the same time, the presence of East LA, as seen from the restaurant, is equally important not only as a reminder of where the characters come from but also as a declaration of new urban centralities. Downtown LA, where for instance Andrea has her professional office, is also visible at certain points in the movie, but, in the text's unwritten urban hierarchies, it is secondary to East LA, the lively historical center of the Mexican American community.

In any case, the expansion of Mexican LA to the Downtown area is not an invention of the filmmakers but a reflection of real urban developments of the kind that incorporation and kindred practices such as gentrification try but do not manage to prevent altogether. For instance, Lilly's loft Downtown is both an example of the area's gentrification and its Mexicanization; the Chicano artist is simultaneously embodying successive urban waves. Lilly also links, with her presence, the two sides of the Los Angeles River. In the Luminarias scene, with East LA in the background and Downtown farther west, with the busy freeways beneath signaling a form of victory of the resilience of Chicanos and other Angeleno minorities, the comic action taking place in the foreground is significantly reframed: As important as love stories may be in Latinos' quest for equality and visibility, the comic scenario of the struggle for acceptance of the Other, in the face of prejudice and ingrained rage, acquires supplementary meanings. What is being played out against the backdrop of freeways and incorporations is the future of a hybrid city, one crossed by many inner borders with, for once, the Chicano community at its center. These borders are seen as generators of powerful group identities and as engines of utopian social change.

Under the Shadow of the Maquiladora

Luminarias stands as an example of a Latino-oriented movie that acquired a certain degree of visibility in Los Angeles and at film festivals, but it did not find mainstream distribution despite its relatively conventional narrative. Alone, the adroit use of the generic conventions of romantic comedy to convey the normalcy of Latino life in the city was not enough to reach wider audiences. The case of *Real Women Have Curves* (Patricia Cardoso, 2002) is different. TV pay channel HBO had just created a Latino division and *Real Women* was going to be the second film they produced (Riley 2002). This was an indication of a desire on the part of producers to attract Latino audiences. After collecting an audience award and a special jury prize at the 2002 Sundance Film Festival for its two female protagonists, America Ferrera and Lupe Ontiveros, as well as other accolades, *Real Women* became the cable network's first theatrical release ever (Harris 2002, 1; Kaufman 2002, 124). As a consequence of this, the movie, apart from its successful presence in the festival circuit, was released commercially around the world, in such countries as the United Kingdom, Italy, France, Israel, Spain, Mexico, and Argentina, as well as the United States. Doubling its estimated $3 million budget at the domestic box office, *Real Women* became not only a modest financial success but also a critical success (according to the IMDb and Box Office Mojo). One isolated example is clearly not enough to set a trend, and examples of earlier Latino-oriented movies that broke barriers have been mentioned before. Nevertheless, the movie's production and distribution history illustrates both the industry's renewed attempt to reach out to Hispanic audiences and a relatively straightforward crossover performance at the box office.

The film was praised for its authenticity in portraying its East LA Latina characters, a segment of the population not frequently found in films, avoiding stereotypical images and defying popular notions about immigrant families (Goodridge 2002, 19; Harris 2002, 1; Meyer 2002; Puig 2002). The film was deemed a crowd pleaser with commercial potential (Riley 2002). Critics mostly focused on the central mother-daughter relationship and the complexity and credibility of the central performances, with several newspaper spreads on both Ferrera's fledgling career and Ontiveros's long-overdue recognition as a top-class actor (L. King 2002; Painter Young 2002). Given the journalistic discourse of authenticity that was common to most critical responses to the movie, audiences were also, if not always directly, primed to look at its depiction of place in a specific way. As we will see, however, the realism of East LA became part of the creative tensions in the text.

The critical response, which predictably also emphasized issues of the female body and female objectification by the dominant culture, matched the ostensible goals of the filmmakers. Latina visibility, authenticity, and complex character construction were particularly relevant for a movie that, as in the case of *Luminarias*, explicitly set out to counter dominant images. The film is based on a play by Chicana writer Josefina López, who co-wrote the screenplay. López describes what she does as "Chicano theater" and "Chicano Cinema" because her works are attempts to show the reality of her people, to tell their stories, and "a refusal to be dismissed, and also to reject the lies about the Latino community" (Urtiaga 2016, 266). In this sense, it was crucial for the filmmakers to offer images of the barrio that deconstruct the stereotypes of dangerous neighborhoods dominated by gangs and squalor. With the help of production designer Brigitte Broch, habitual collaborator of Alejandro González Iñárritu's movies, the filmmakers used what they considered real images of Boyle Heights, where most of the film was shot, as weapons against invisibility. López explains how this part of Los Angeles is always portrayed as an ugly, dirty, and gang-riddled neighborhood and that she struggled to offer instead what she saw growing up—a nice and colorful place, a place with families where there was hope (Martinez 2012).

After a pre-credits scene establishes the fraught relationship between Ana (Ferrera) and her mother Carmen (Ontiveros) as the teenager's last day of high school starts, the opening credits are superimposed on the protagonist's journey from her home in Boyle Heights to her school in Beverly Hills. Rhyming with and anticipating her final, much longer trip to New York City, the apparently transitional scene establishes the urban geography of the story and its centrality for an understanding of plot dynamics within an Angeleno context. Boyle Heights and Beverly Hills are offered as Chicano shorthand for the social map that dominates Ana's life and defines her identity. Ana walks to the nearest bus stop, past her

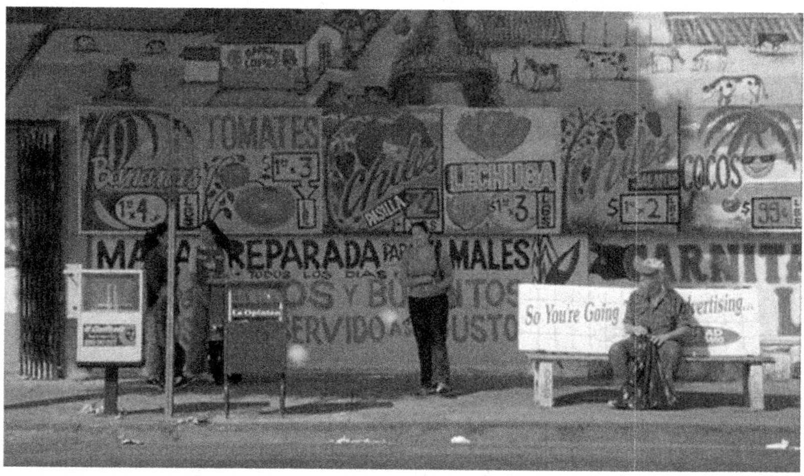

Real Women Have Curves: the colors of the barrio.

neighbors' colorful houses, past street signs that establish the approximate location of the Garcia family's neighborhood (Bailey and Wabash), past some characteristic street murals and bright wall signs written in a mixture of English and Spanish that suggest Cesar Chavez Avenue, and past a group of mariachis and the cupola of the bandstand in the middle of Mariachi Plaza (a location that the film returns to repeatedly). She then crosses 1st Street from the Plaza, framed by the nearby Downtown skyscrapers, and waits for her first bus on the other side, again surrounded by the bright reds, greens, oranges, and blues of the street art, here advertising market products. She later switches buses at Hollywood and Vine (street signs, a poster of *The Lion King*, and the Capitol Records Building for good measure) and turns off Sunset Boulevard at the street where her school is supposed to be (Sunset Plaza Drive). The sequence cannot be more explicit about the textual investment in the urban geography of the story. In more senses than one, the geography is indeed the story.

It is significant that Ana's school is in Beverly Hills, home of the stars and the wealthy, perhaps the most iconic part of the Westside, just as Boyle Heights is seen as the heart of the eastern side of the river, or, to all effects, the wrong side of the tracks. The distance between her point of departure and her point of destination is not just the approximately 11 miles that separate the two locations—we might as well be talking about two different worlds, with various third borders in between, including such iconic dividing lines as the river and La Brea, Robertson, and La

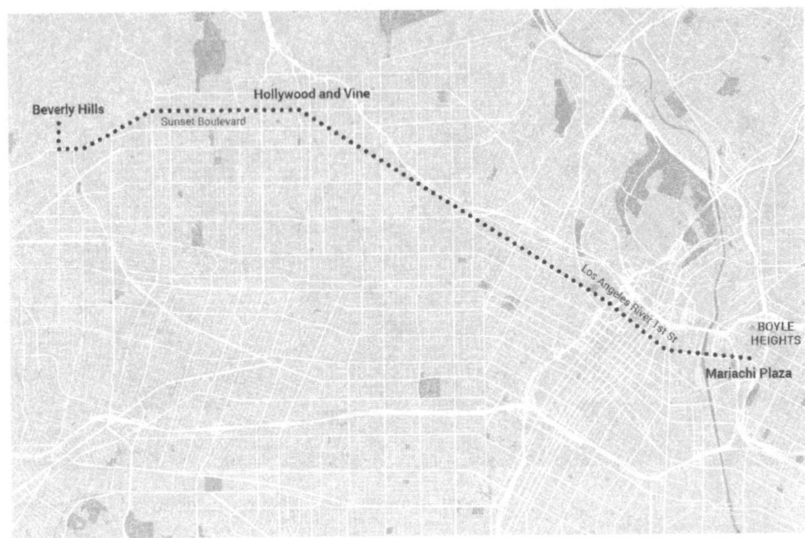

Map 7. Ana's daily bus ride from Boyle Heights to Beverly Hills: across multiple third borders in *Real Women Have Curves*. Map by Francesc Terrades.

Cienega Boulevards, familiar from other movies analyzed here. In going to school every day Ana is not only crossing several urban boundaries but also struggling against various types of resistances, starting with her own mother and finishing with the wealthier kids at school. Her habitual movement along this east-west axis is the decisive component of her sense of self, one that aspires to represent a historically constructed and historically and geographically specific Chicana identity. *Real Women* furthers the notion of East LA as a crucial part of the social identity of many Chicanas and Chicanos (Gámez 2002, 95–96), but it also underlines that the manifold ways in which they move around the cosmopolis and leave their imprint in other areas of the city are just as important.

In *Luminarias* Andrea tries to explain to her son the rage that torments her as a Chicana, one that has to do with her experience as an inhabitant of the borderlands, as being two things and none at the same time, as living with a constant feeling of injustice. Ana's adolescent anxieties, here partly encapsulated in the shape of her body, are comparable. Like Valenzuela, López considers this doubleness, this simultaneous inhabiting of two worlds, and this capacity to integrate herself into a hybrid culture the defining factor of Chicana identity, but she chooses to focus on its more empowering dimensions. She further interprets both worlds as the

Mexican sense of community on the one hand and the Anglo belief in standing up and speaking up for oneself on the other (Urtiaga 2016, 266). Although this articulation of a group identity, like any other, verges dangerously on the kind of stereotype that Chicanos try to resist and fight against, if taken in the most abstract terms possible, it does convey some sense of the particularity of those who are nothing if not two things at the same time. Ana's ability to negotiate the two worlds at both ends of her daily route singles her out as a privileged Chicana and as a role model for young women like her.

This positive articulation of a group identity that achieves social visibility and cultural prestige is reinforced at this early point by casting. Ana's favorite teacher, Mr. Guzman, is played by George Lopez, the popular comedian who was at the time about to become one of the first Latino actors to produce, write, and star in a sitcom, *George Lopez*, which would run for six consecutive seasons on ABC (2002–2007). Since then, Lopez has consolidated himself both as a mainstream comedian, through various television shows, and as an active representative and spokesman of the Chicano community, not unlike Cheech Marin, whose presence in *Luminarias* was used for similar purposes. No explanation is provided for Mr. Guzman's presence as a teacher at the predominantly Anglo school, a lack of explanation that confers a sense of normality to his part. Mr. Guzman, whose journey to the institution must have been more difficult than Ana's, given that he belongs to an older generation, silently and powerfully speaks to the visibility and social mainstreaming that Chicano cinema and, in more general terms, Chicano politics have sought and demanded for decades.

Once the name and location of Ana's school are revealed, *Real Women* loses interest in the Westside and returns to it only a couple more times, notably when Ana decides to lose her virginity with her Anglo classmate Jimmy (Brian Sites), another explicit sign of her restlessness and her refusal to stay on her side of the line. For the rest of the time, the film remains close to Ana's house in Boyle Heights. Visually, Beverly Hills is a lot flatter and unappealing than the barrio. Ana may balk at much of what she sees around her, at home and at her sister's factory, but she is different from Sofia in *Luminarias*, who has to learn to return to the world that she had forsaken for the sake of social and economic success. In purely filmic terms, Ana does not have to abandon her origins because, first, they are more appealing than what she finds on the Westside and, second, her energy and intelligence allow her to make the journey to and fro feasible, if never easy, and so she does not feel the need to give up on either of them. She learns and teaches us that she can inhabit both worlds at the same time and that someone who can be such a proficient citizen of the borderlands is indeed blessed.

In the film's discourse, however, Ana is not just a citizen of the borderlands because of her individual talent at negotiating borders and her general mobility; she is a resident of Boyle Heights. Perhaps evoking the neighborhood's multicultural past, before it became predominantly Latino (Lewthwaite 2010, 41–42; G. Sánchez 2004, 633), *Real Women* posits its real and fictional space as paradigmatic of the city's diversity, if only because of the radical contrast it offers with dominant cinematic representations of LA. This project is subtly but forcefully suggested in the scene that narrates Ana's first date with Jimmy. Most of the scene takes place at one of the few fictional spaces constructed by the film, Café María, where a statue of the Virgin Mary presides over the patio where the couple have a drink. Jimmy has no difficulty understanding that, rather than a symbol of religious faith or even of ethnicity, the statue, along with the lights that decorate the trees, is part of the magic space that Ana offers for their romantic meeting, one designed to pull him out of his Anglo environment and appreciate the values of an alternative world.

In the meantime, the song "Minha Galera" is playing in the background. In the DVD commentary López explains how well the song works as a lullaby, suggesting that the romantic relationship Ana is initiating is a soothing counterpoint to her conflictive relationship with her mother. The song, however, offers further meanings. Manu Chao, the singer of "Minha Galera," is a Spanish-French musician who sings indistinctly in Spanish, French, English, Portuguese, Italian, and other languages, often mixing them in the same song and habitually alternating between them. He often sings about borders and immigrants, in songs such as "Clandestino" (available on the soundtrack) and especially "Bienvenida a Tijuana/Welcome to Tijuana." Although of European origin, Chao has spent long periods in Latin America and has supported various political causes related to the Latino population. "Minha Galera," sung by a cosmopolitan artist in Portuguese to a reggae beat, spells out the meanings that the filmmakers wish to put forward. The term *minha galera*, signifying loosely "my group" or "my friends," can be taken in the context of *Real Women* as signifying Ana's multicultural world.

Because of its strong and detailed sense of place, the movie's celebration of diversity is also the celebration of a city that can encompass this multiplicity, openness, and forward-looking vision, as seen from a Chicano perspective. Yet all is not well in the buoyant paradise of the film. The conflict between Ana and Carmen energizes the narrative, but Ana herself introduces a wider conflict, which remains muffled in the course of the story but keeps returning in various ways: the repressed underside of a feel-good tale always remaining too close to the surface for comfort. Ana spells it out when, reluctant to work in her sister's sewing factory, especially when she learns that she will not be paid straight away, she complains that it is dirty work and shouts, "This is a sweatshop. You are all cheap labor for Bloomingdale's." Estela (Ingrid Oliu) resents and rejects the accusation. In the DVD commentary López insists that Estela's is indeed not a sweatshop, and she praises the realism of Brigitte Broch's production design and its attention to details such as the dirtiness of a workplace. However, the shadow of the maquiladora never quite abandons the story.

Ana's first significant journey, discussed earlier, is soon followed by a second one. The morning after the end of the school year, she goes to work at her sister's factory. Replacing cinematic clichés with the statistic realities of working-class Latinos, the women in the family are seamstresses and the men are gardeners. Ana's father, Raúl (Jorge Cervera Jr.), owns a truck; gardeners' trucks, or *trocas*, are among the most familiar sights on LA's surface roads, particularly around the more affluent areas of the Westside. On his way to work, Raúl gives the three women a ride to the factory. This trip is shorter than Ana's earlier one but is visualized with equally precise detail. To a lively Mexican tune, the truck covers the distance between their house and the Garment District, where Estela's business is located. Although she is initially downcast at the prospect of working with her family, it takes Ana only a few seconds to look out the window and start enjoying the sights. They first drive through Boyle Heights, past the inevitable street murals and shop fronts with Spanish or Spanglish signs, then again along 1st Street to Mariachi Plaza and beyond, crossing the river on the First Street Bridge, and then Little Tokyo, already in the Downtown area, and finally south to the Garment District, the popular *callejones* where many Angeleno Latinos buy their clothes. We assume that the men will drive on west to their daily gardening work. The women get off, and we see the outside and the sign of Estela's little building and then the inside, where much of the film's action takes place.

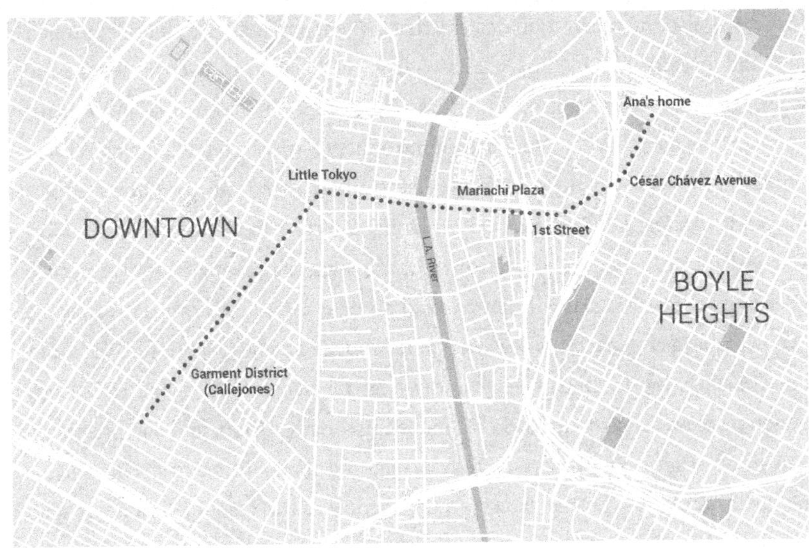

Map 8. A short car ride away: from Ana's family home to the factory in the *callejones* in *Real Women Have Curves*. Map by Francesc Terrades.

The Garment District, situated in the southeastern part of Downtown, is a densely built-up area, often with packed streets, with lines of cut-price garment stores in the front and many abandoned-looking buildings behind. Frequent visitors to the area know that many of those buildings house sweatshops and are part of the informal economy theorized by Saskia Sassen (2006, 161–62) and others. These establishments, catering both to the *callejones* and to the more upmarket stores, have many features in common with the maquiladoras south of the border, the assembly plants massively established in northern Mexico to take advantage of trade agreements and cheap Mexican labor to assemble foreign parts into products that are sold around the world (Kun 2010, 323; R. Sánchez 2001, 526). With the intensification of migration to the north in recent decades, many of the conditions of the maquiladoras are increasingly being reproduced north of the border, particularly in Los Angeles. This area of the city contributes to the social and cultural complexity of Downtown because of its links with the new Financial District, a few streets away, its proximity to Skid Row, and the massive presence in it of Latino and Latina Angelenos. In more general terms, the Bunker Hill–Garment District area exemplifies Sassen's (1998, xxi) view of the workings of advanced capitalism and of global cities as privileged sites of its operations, with corporate actors and disadvantaged workers as equally crucial products of and players in this type of economy. Estela and her employees are part of this cycle, one that, at various points in its trajectory, demands the exploitation of migrant and, particularly in Los Angeles, Latina workers. In the movie this meaning is intensified because of the factory's location in the Garment District.

The women's arrival is visualized through a series of shots that include two recognizable shots of the Garment District, one of Ana looking at the buildings, and one of the truck turning a corner and arriving at its destination. The space portrayed by these last two shots seems different from the previous ones: more open streets and lower buildings. In a section of the interview with Urtiaga that was not published, López explains that the factory scenes were in fact shot in Boyle Heights. In the original play the factory was indeed located in Boyle Heights, but for some unexplained reason the filmmakers decided to relocate it to the Downtown area, a decision from which López seeks to distance herself: "I had never intended it to be in the Garment District; they just put it there. . . . In Downtown, you have mostly big factories; they don't have the little ones I've seen here" (Rosa Urtiaga, interview by Josefina López, 2016; used by permission). The implications of the change are important. López's account of the factory is autobiographical; Estela's is a fictionalization of her own sister's experience, who was, like her mother, also a seamstress and bought and ran a factory in the neighborhood where she treated the workers with respect. By taking the factory out of the barrio and relocating it Downtown, *Real Women* contradicts its own construction of this space, delineating a type of operation and working relationship between employers and employees that may be credible in Boyle Heights but are much less likely to happen in the Garment District. López is aware that this change lends more credibility to Ana's accusation of the place being a sweatshop and that it deconstructs her own much more positive construction of it. Although there may be many similarities between the buildings situated on both sides of the river, the Downtown area gives darker connotations to Estela's factory, evoking if only indirectly the conditions and well-documented experiences of immigrant women in the maquiladoras south of the border, most notoriously in Ciudad Juárez. As she herself admits, worker exploitation is likely in the Garment District; for instance, the employers tend to belong to a different ethnic group than the workers, unlike in the barrio.

Verisimilitude is therefore strained with the move. At the same time, however,

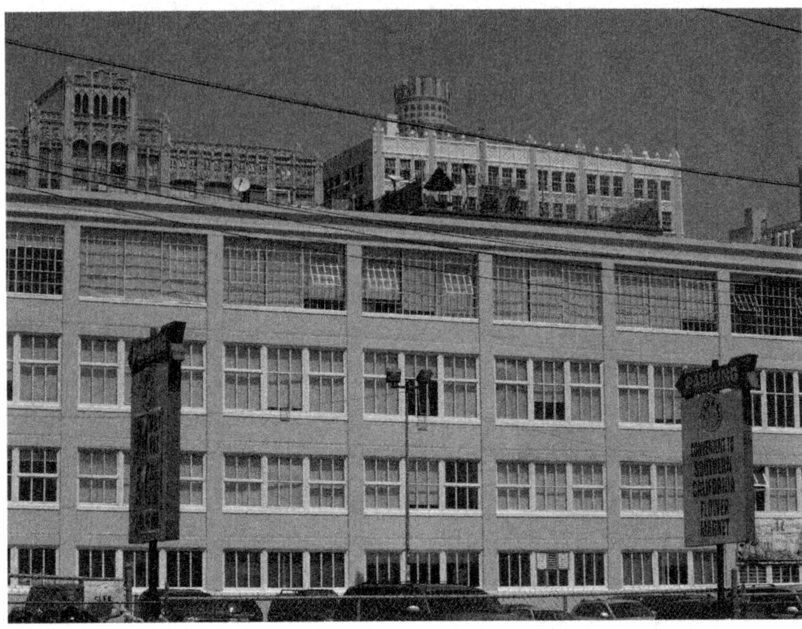

Downtown layers: a building in the Flower District, with the old and the new financial districts in the background.

the film turns the potential contradiction into a mixture of registers that makes both its protagonist and its ideological discourse more complex and, paradoxically, more credible. In the familial atmosphere Ana can lead the celebration of Latina identity in a comic register, especially in the scene in which she persuades the other women to strip down to their underwear. At the same time, she can vent her rage, like Andrea in *Luminarias*, at the long-standing discrimination suffered by Latina women. On the other hand, the movie plants the seed of its own deconstruction: The women in the factory are happy enough with their work, but their complaints, which may seem minor in the context of the story, acquire more pointed social undertones because of their geographic proximity to the exploitation suffered by other Latina workers at the urban sweatshops, themselves mirror images of the infamous maquiladoras. These real women represent the vitality and buoyancy of a group striving to be acknowledged within its most immediate urban context, but their images are haunted by the precariousness and extreme vulnerability of the millions of Latina workers and migrants whom they also stand for.

This ambiguity crystallizes in the final scene. Having made the decision to accept the scholarship offered by Columbia University and having grown as a Latina woman through her experience at the sewing factory, Ana decides to move to New York and start a new life. She tries to get her mother's blessing up until the last minute, but Carmen steadfastly refuses to leave her room and does not say goodbye to her, convinced as she is that her daughter should stay with her family and play the role allotted to traditional Latina women. Recalling the two journeys from the beginning of the film, particularly the second one to the workplace, Ana sits in her father's truck between her father and her grandfather (Felipe de Alba), both supportive of her decision. On the way to the airport, she again looks out the window, this time at the life and childhood she is leaving behind but more specifically at the empty space outside her house where Carmen should have been standing, saying goodbye. Something has broken between them, a rift that goes beyond the mother-daughter relationship and speaks to the doubleness that for López is at the heart of Chicano identity. This sadness contrasts with the final shot, a few seconds later, a long-take tracking shot of Ana coming out of the subway onto Manhattan's Broadway and walking confidently toward the camera and into her future, encompassing the Big Apple with her steady, almost marching gait.

This quick succession of emotions is highlighted during the journey to the airport through the song we hear on the soundtrack, Mexican singer Lila Downs's "La Niña." In purely formal and aesthetic terms this song works well because of the contrast it provides with the soundtrack of the immediately previous scenes. The beginning of "La Niña," performed almost a capella by Downs, brings a transition to the full orchestration and quickening of the pace in the rest of the song. The change of rhythm is made to coincide with the precise moment when the truck starts moving. As Downs's song finds its lively and distinctly Latino pace, it lands on both the protagonist and the spectators that there is no turning back, that Ana's mother and the life she represents are being left behind and the future is rushing to meet her. Thus the song becomes celebratory of the unstoppable power of the young Latina, ready to make an impact in a society for which she still remains largely invisible, the Spanish language and Latin American sound of the track underlining the social over the individual connotations of this climactic narrative moment.

However, the song's lyrics are also significant. They tell of a Latina teenager, one who may well be seen as Ana's shadow, especially in view of Ana's earlier characterization of Estela's business as a sweatshop. Downs's *niña* is a maquiladora worker, and the song evokes her distressing daily routine: She gets up and prays that her day may not be long, then closes her eyes in front of the mirror to avoid seeing how work is destroying her youth, and finally thinks of how all her dreams and hopes, her sweat and strength, have been buried under the oppressive working conditions of the maquiladora. The song, dedicated in the CD's accompanying booklet to all working women, ends with the wish that those days will soon be a bad memory and that she and all the women in her situation will achieve equality. She is a symbol of the oppression and exploitation of women at the border, and the song is a critique of the economic processes that lead to this situation for millions of women around the world. "La Niña" belongs to the album *Border/La Línea*, released in 2001, which includes songs in Spanish, English, and Mayan, several of them dealing with issues of the borderland. Evoking her mixed origin—the Oaxaca-born Downs is the daughter of an indigenous singer and a U.S. film professor—Downs continues here her interest in exploring her country's and her continent's musical traditions and her increasing penchant for fusing traditional and modern forms. This formal hybridity is made to converge with an exploration of the lives of the hybrid people of the border and the various forms of oppression of southern immigrants once they cross the border. In fact, the record is "dedicated to the Mexican migrants, to the spirits of those who have died crossing the line." *Border/La Línea* is the music of the borderland.

"La Niña" captures a particular moment in the economic cycle described by Sassen (1998) in a chapter titled "America's Immigration 'Problem,'" where she explores the economic links between developing and industrialized countries that subsequently produce international migration. Paradoxically, Sassen argues, it is the very conditions that are commonly thought to deter immigration, such as foreign investment and export-oriented growth in developing countries, that cause migratory movements to the industrialized countries. The maquiladoras south of the U.S.-Mexico border are prime examples of the type of industry that first uproots people from their traditional modes of existence and then leaves young workers, typically women, unemployed and unemployable, as export firms hire even younger workers or move production to other countries (Sassen 1998, 34–43). For these women, for whom returning home (to southern Mexico or Central America) is no longer an option, the only alternative is to cross the line and seek work in the great metropolitan cities north of the border. For many of them the nearest of these urban centers is Los Angeles.

The inscription of Downs's bordering music in the text allows *Real Women* to highlight the borderliness of the postmetropolis and to import its social and cultural connotations into is own signifying structure. In superimposing this indictment of global capitalism onto Ana's bildungsroman at this climactic moment, *Real Women* brings the two teenage women together, presenting them as two sides of the same coin, or as two discursive strands of the impact on women of the large migration processes produced by economic globalization. Ana is the bright and lucky young Latina woman who has been given the opportunity to at least aspire to a measure of equality, despite the many problems she may encounter on the way, but in the song another Latina teenager, maybe one working only a few yards away from her sister's factory, has a different story to tell, one of injustice, oppression, and despair. The use of the song at this moment calls our attention to the parallels and continuities between the two, and to their commonalities—to their joint claim of representing the realities of Latina women at the outset of the twenty-first century. The movie's modest success facilitates the access of a larger public, including Anglo and international audiences, to Latino lives in Los Angeles and to their struggle for visibility in light of both continuing injustice and moderate hope for the future.

10

The Border Look and Chicano Los Angeles

In the analysis of *Real Women Have Curves* in Chapter 9, I detected a potential tension between competing voices among the filmmakers. Although this is not unusual in a collective artistic form such as the cinema, the crucial relocation of Estela's factory from Boyle Heights to the Garment District can be conceivably ascribed to the difference in sensibilities between local Chicana Josefina López and the rest of the creative team, especially if we take into consideration that in López's original play the factory was in East LA and that the film was also shot in the heart of the barrio. Inés Valdez, for example, hints at how much is lost in translation from the play to the film in terms of the "subversive potential in the work of Latina/o authors," thus suggesting that because of the nature of the transformations from stage to screen but also because of the ethnic background of the filmmakers, the film may be "less Latino" than the play (2013, 190). From the perspective of Chicano identity, does the fact that the director is Colombian—and even the fact that the other strong creative voice, co-writer and co-producer George LaVoo, is Anglo—disqualify *Real Women* as Chicano cinema in the terms described by Chon Noriega (1992b, xi, xix), or do the transnational cast and crew make it a pan-Latino text, aimed at a more general Latino demographic?

These questions acquire greater momentum in the cases of *Quinceañera* (Richard Glatzer and Wash Westmoreland, 2006) and *A Better Life* (Chris Weitz, 2011). *Quinceañera* was written and directed by Glatzer, a U.S. American, and Westmoreland, a Brit, and was co-produced by maverick independent filmmaker Todd Haynes and others. Following in the steps of *Real Women*, it won the Grand Jury prize and audience award at the Sundance Festival. *A Better Life*, which rose to public attention when actor Demián Bichir was nominated for best actor at the 2012 Academy Awards, was directed by Chris Weitz, co-director with his brother Paul of the teen pic blockbuster *American Pie* (1999) and director of *The Twilight Saga: New Moon* (2009), among other films. Weitz is the grandson of the great Mexican actress Lupita Tovar, who starred in Mexico's first sound film, *Santa* (1932), and many other films. His mother was Hollywood actress Susan Kohner, whose best-known part was that of unfortunate mixed-race Sarah Jane in Douglas Sirk's *Imitation of Life* (1959). Weitz is currently married to Cuban Mexican actress Mercedes Martínez. He is not a Chicano director, yet his Mexican ancestry and links with Mexican, Chicano, and Latino culture bring him closer to the Chicano community, a fact highlighted by the film's marketing campaign. Both *Quinceañera* and *A Better Life* openly attempt to give a cinematic voice to this community, but their own voices are those of outsiders, although they speak from a position of proximity.

The ethnic makeup of the textual or authorial looks at the lives of Chicano and Mexican Angelenos in *Quinceañera* and *A Better Life* may problematize in various ways the authenticity of the stories they narrate, but in a different sense they bring the movies closer to the hybrid experience of the postmetropolis, reinforcing the centrality of the concepts of the border and the borderlands to understand not only the urban dynamics of Los Angeles but, more specifically, the Chicano presence in the city. We might decry the absence of an authentic Chicano look in the two films, but we also might wonder about the extent to which such a look is possible.

Echo Parque

Quinceañera co-directors Glatzer and Westmoreland were living in the very neighborhood they depict when the film was made. Their Waterloo Street home, situated just north of Sunset Boulevard and Echo Park Lake, is at the center of the real location that was used to construct the filmic space. Shortly after the film was completed, their Mexican American neighbors, the Campos family, were, like some of the characters in the film, evicted from their home after many years of living there, victims of gentrification. The directors explain that they arrived in Echo Park and bought their house at a reasonable price when gentrification was just beginning, and they had time to observe the dramatic effects of the process on their Mexican neighbors while they were there. They admit to having said many of the things that the Anglo couple of the film, James (Jason L. Wood) and Gary (David W. Ross), the villains of the story, and their upwardly mobile friends say in the film. When they first arrived, some neighbors asked them to photograph their daughter's *quinceañera*, and several years later the script grew out of that first contact with the tradition (Abcarian 2006, E1; Goldstein 2006, 3; Greenberg

2006, 10). The filmmakers' obvious personal involvement in the story they tell, though remaining outsiders to the community they describe, might explain the ambivalent look of the movie, its combination of an exoticizing look at Mexican customs such as the *quinceañera* parties and its engagement with the plight of the endangered community.

The DVD commentary for *Quinceañera* by its directors and three of its actors ends with the battle cry "Echo Parque," a reminder of the Mexicanness of a neighborhood that was, at the time of the film, becoming rapidly gentrified. Beyond its ambivalent look at the Chicano Angeleno community and its story of a pregnant teenager, *Quinceañera* is an exploration of the impact of gentrification on the working-class areas of the modern city. In the press kit the directors underline the centrality of the Echo Park neighborhood in the film and evoke *Mi Vida Loca* (Allison Anders, 1993), an earlier movie also set in Echo Park. They explain that the neighborhood we see in Anders's film had changed a great deal in the intervening years, with gentrification bringing in gays and artists (Glatzer and Westmoreland 2006, 4).

Mi Vida Loca is concerned with the crippling impact of street gangs on Echo Park. Replicating in many ways the conventions and the visual aesthetic of *Boyz n the Hood*, *Menace II Society*, and other accounts of African American inner-city gang life of its time, Anders's film focuses on female gangbangers in a cinematic space in which everybody appears to be involved with gangs in one way or another. The process of deterioration of local peace seems to run parallel to the intensification of the Mexican presence in the area. One of the female narrators of Anders's movie explains that when she came over from Mexico to Echo Park, all the signs were in English but that now they are in both languages. "You don't need to leave. You can get everything here." The two processes—arrivals from Mexico and gangsterism—are brought together, and one seems the consequence of the other. The outcome is a picture of local life ridden by violence and death, not very different from the South Central of the contemporaneous movies.

Little more than a decade later, gangsterism appears to have receded into the background in *Quinceañera*, even as the Mexicanness of the neighborhood has become compromised by a new social threat: gentrification, presented in the movie as a process of reclamation of the area by the Anglo community from its Chicano inhabitants. During one of the brief montage sequences showing snapshots of the neighborhood, we spot a street sign advertising "Accent elimination. Speak American Standard," a subtle hint at the transformations taking place. In the film's discourse the gradual but unstoppable expansion of this new form of urban upheaval threatens to destroy a way of life that stretches back in history. Yet the gangsterism depicted in Anders's film is not part of this history. Carlos's (Jesse Garcia) petty thefts and his aggressive looks can be seen as a remnant of it, but they are not framed within a local criminal network with any visible impact on the community. The street sign is a visual index of the peaceful invasion of gentrifiers, of which middle-class James and Gary are the ostensible representatives in the plot.

At the beginning of the narrative, the Anglo couple have just purchased a house in the neighborhood and inherited Tío Tomás (Chalo González) as a lodger in an attached cottage. Tío Tomás has lived there for many years and is now sharing the cottage first with younger relative Carlos and then also with the film's co-protagonist, Magdalena (Emily Rios). The two Anglo men embody the exoticizing look of the Mexican community, a look that is openly sexualized as they repeatedly express their sexual preference for young Latino men: "There was this little cute Latin boy at my gym today. Oh my God. Totally little *cholo*," says one of their friends at a dinner party held in their renovated abode. When Gary's "excessive" desire for Carlos threatens the stability of the couple, they summarily and ruthlessly evict Tomás, thus causing, at least indirectly, his death, unable as he is to stand his cruel uprooting from the once gentle community. The film matches scenes of Latino life with the emasculating presence of the new invaders in a melodramatic juxtaposition and does not hide its preferences, even while it sometimes shares the gaze of the invaders.

By the early years of the twenty-first century, Echo Park, situated just north of Downtown, had become an obvious candidate for the expansion of gentrification from the city center. Demographic change in the 2010s indicates a decrease of approximately 10 percent in the Latino population (from 69.8 percent to 58.5 percent) and a simultaneous 10-point growth of "whites" (from 13.2 percent to 23.2 percent), thus reversing the pattern in the city as a whole. In Los Angeles, as in other urban centers, gentrification seems to grow at the same time as multiculturalism, even though both can be seen as opposite processes. Neil Smith (2002) explains how gentrification has been happening on a global level since the 1990s, quickly becoming a crucial urban strategy for city governments in consort with private capital.

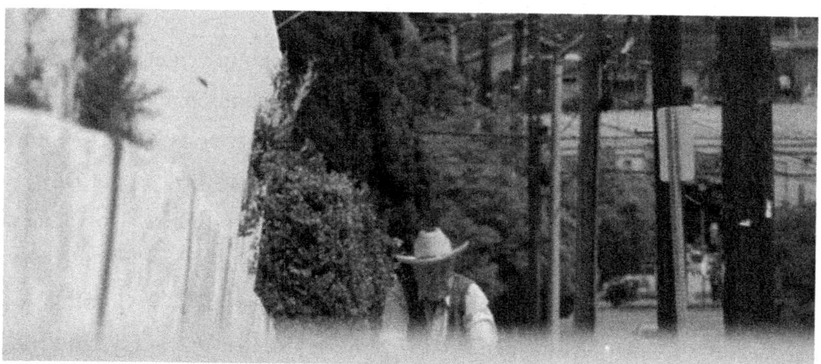

The soul of Echo Park: Tío Tomás in *Quinceañera.*

This latest phase of the process has been characterized, among other things, by an outward diffusion from the urban center in an irregular but inexorable manner whereby, as land and housing prices soar in Downtown areas, districts farther out become caught up in the momentum of gentrification (N. Smith 2002, 440–42).

This does not necessarily rid the cities of their immigrants. In many of the gentrified areas, the previous dwellers often refuse to leave, even though real estate or rented accommodation becomes cost-prohibitive for them, and they find alternative ways of sharing the space with the newcomers. Otherwise, the displaced citizens move farther and farther from the center, to new areas that maybe one day will themselves be gentrified. As Smith and Schaffer explain, visible and invisible borders start to appear in front of those without the economic means, as the metropolitan areas become larger and larger to accommodate its less wealthy citizens in their outer edges (Schaffer and Smith 1986, 347; N. Smith 1982, 139). In *Quinceañera* we overhear a conversation about a character who is moving to Sylmar because she cannot afford to stay in Echo Park anymore. Sylmar is a pleasant neighborhood, situated in the northern tip of the San Fernando Valley, with a majority Latino population, where real estate is still affordable. Depending on the density of the traffic on the crowded freeways, however, it might take up to two hours to drive from Sylmar to the Westside. Gentrification has become a powerful tool of urban development not only in the areas that it affects directly but, more important, in how it redesigns city blueprints, often in unpredictable and uncontrolled ways. Gathering around Tío Tomás and his *champurrado* trolley, which provides an anchor for all the characters, the people of Echo Park ponder the speed at which their neighborhood is changing.

The characters of *Quinceañera* are part of a community caught in the throes of demographic upheaval. Visually, Echo Park is presented through brief montage sequences and even briefer transitional shots between scenes as a quiet, sunny neighborhood with its steep streets that often afford spectacular views of Downtown, its omnipresent lake, and its at times almost rural appearance. Tío Tomás's gait as he leisurely pushes his trolley up- or downhill provides the rhythm of the community. On her dates with boyfriend Herman (or Germán) (J. R. Cruz), Magdalena climbs to their favorite bench on what looks like the edge of Elysian Park, from which they contemplate the city below and discuss plans for the future. The first montage sequence, immediately after the opening *quinceañera*, underlines the Latino quality of the place, with colorful street signs, freshly cut fruit sold on street corners, a mariachi band, and the inevitable picture of the Virgen de Guadalupe, all accompanied in the soundtrack by bolero music. The sequence then segues into Tío Tomás's daily routine: cooking his *champurrado*, tending to his garden, and setting out to walk the streets with his trolley. As he leaves the house, his new landlords are arriving in a red convertible. The speed of the car turning around the corner contrasts with Tomás's slow progress around the neighborhood.

The scene introduces two important and related themes: on the one hand, the threat of gentrification to the lives of the locals, a threat that will, in the case of Tomás, come to fruition at the end of the story; and on the other hand, the narrative importance of the old man's exuberant garden, which he has been lovingly putting together for decades, a veritable sanctuary that can be taken as the spiritual center of the story. This fictional garden is based on and was mostly photographed in another real location: Mexican-born Alberto Hernández's garden in Silver Lake. Ann Herold (2006) describes the real place: "Cascading vines and well-rooted trees draw the earth up to the sky. Sunlight glows through green and gold wine bottles suspended overhead." This is "a place of solace and wonder, a place where saints may walk freely" (F1).

Although this "intoxicatingly Catholic" garden (Herold 2006, F10) can be seen as one of the most explicit instances of the exoticizing gaze of the text, as an expressionistic visual extension of the old man's personality and way of life, it becomes a symptom of the impact of social changes on the community. Not only is the contrast between the garden and the inside of the newcomers' house constantly emphasized, but also, narratively, the garden is the place where Carlos and Magdalena first mourn their great uncle. From what we hear when the Anglo couple discuss it at the end of the film, the garden will soon fall prey to their projected renovations. The garden stands for the old man at first, but it gradually acquires larger connotations: it is the type of urban site that has to be removed as gentrification gathers pace, and therefore it becomes the core of the endangered neighborhood. Herold explains how on Hernández's block there is more than one garden that speaks new money, but it is his garden that fascinates (F10). The same happens in the movie, but the implication is that this fascination will be gone before long, along with the garden itself.

The film mixes two stories: one that relates a generational conflict within a traditional society, which brings it close to *Real Women Have Curves*, and another that explores changes in the contemporary city. The two stories merge and feed off each other, and the fulcrum of this process is again Tío Tomás. It could be argued that this character's death, like Falstaff's in Shakespeare's Plantagenet series, is a sign of social and historical changes beyond his, and indeed any, individual's control. As in Prince Hal's modern Europe, the Anglo middle-class invasion of Echo Park is inevitable and, like Falstaff's medieval worldview, the Mexican community's traditional ways have to eventually give way to progress, however critically that progress is viewed in this film. Despite his age, Tomás does not stand for the type of traditional society that casts out Carlos for his sexual preference and Magdalena for her out-of-wedlock pregnancy. He is in fact the facilitator of a new type of family: He takes the two young people in and with them he forms an alternative family, a "family of exiles" (Rooney 2006, n.p.), that remains a part of the larger familial structure. When Tomás is evicted, Magdalena goes out looking for alternative accommodation for the three of them, and when Herman flees the scene to avoid responsibility for his girlfriend's baby, Carlos offers to act as father to the future baby and help teenage Magdalena get ahead in life. This alternative family is very much in keeping with contemporary discourses on sexuality and sexual identity that find their "natural" ground in independent cinema. Against this paean to tolerance and freedom from tradition, James and Gary's relationship, for all their outward posing and sense of modernity, appears fraught with all the ills of a traditional familial arrangement.

Conversely, whereas Gary and particularly James are given few saving graces in the text, the face of gentrification in the film is not all negative. In her quest to find acceptable new accommodation for Tomás, Carlos, and herself, Magdalena comes across a small house she likes but whose rent is well beyond their means. Using the rhetoric of gentrification, the owner explains that she and her partner put a lot of work and money into it and cannot let it go for less. When Magdalena cannot find anything else, she returns and pleads with the woman, out of quiet desperation. She complains that the neighborhood is changing, that everybody who can afford the prices "is . . . well, white," and offers to do the woman's gardening and house cleaning for free if she can lower the price. When the anonymous Anglo woman hears that Tío Tomás is "that little man that sells *champurrado*," she is moved. Although not Latina, she considers herself a member of the community and likes to think of a sense of continuity with the past. For this reason, she finally agrees to let them have the house. With perfect melodramatic timing—the pathos of the "too late" (Williams 2001, 30–38)—Magdalena runs to break the news to her uncle only to find out that he has just died. It is not clear whether Carlos and Magdalena will still move into the new house—the landlady is present at Magdalena's *quinceañera* in the final scene, taking photos like the filmmakers did at the first *quinceañera*—but in this relatively small detail we find the possibility of a compromise between continuity and change and between the Chicano community and the new members of the neighborhood.

The construction of history is therefore important in *Quinceañera*. Erasing the blight of gangsterism, the film's discourse on Echo Park defends the rights of a community to its place, a particularly patent form of wishful thinking in a city whose history is characterized by ruthless land and real estate speculation, summary destructions of whole neighborhoods, and a volatile sense of spatial belonging. The displacement of Latinos from Echo Park is a milder form of expulsion compared to what happened fifty years earlier in the nearby Chávez Ravine, where three whole working-class neighborhoods of Mexican immigrants, Mexican Americans, and other Latinos were first removed with the promise to rebuild the area with affordable social housing and then saw their houses destroyed to build the new Dodger Stadium, which still occupies the premises (Avila 2006, 146–55; Yosso and García 2007, 146–47). As with the old Chinatown, huge parts of Boyle Heights, and Bunker Hill, real estate interests did not hesitate to shift people out of this area "for the greater good of the city." The article by Yosso and García (2007) is an account of the 2003 Culture Clash play *Chávez Ravine*. Surprisingly, no major film, Chicano or otherwise, has been made yet about this momentous episode in the history of the city. One particularly interesting artistic rendering is Anglo musician Ry Cooder's album *Chávez Ravine* (2006), a musically diverse evocation of the three barrios before the bulldozers arrived, with a perspective not very different from that of *Quinceañera*. Glatzer and Westmoreland's complicity with the Chicano cry "Echo Parque" occupies a similar ideological and cultural space to that of some of Cooder's songs, even as it evokes a more recent and milder form of displacement. They exist in the same historical continuum that features a population at the mercy of capital interests in its diverse forms.

Distributed by Sony Pictures Classics, *Quinceañera* is also a paradigmatic example, industrially, narratively, and discursively, of early-twenty-first-century indie cinema. It invokes and puts into play the conventions of a type of "small" cinema that had become to all effects integrated into the Hollywood industry. This allows the filmmakers to confer a certain degree of cultural legitimacy to their border look at the Latino community of Echo Park. Indirectly inscribing themselves in the narrative through the characters of James and Gary, they ostensibly rest their gaze on the service of the community, borderland dwellers who, in encompassing both closeness to the Other and the exoticizing look, embody the reality as well as the limitations of contemporary Angeleno diversity.

El mero mero sueño Americano

Summit Entertainment, the main production company of *A Better Life* and its distributor in the United States, was an independent company that had recently struck gold with the first two installments of the *Twilight* saga, the first of which had also been directed by Chris Weitz. Commentators noted the pointed contrast between the blockbuster series and the smaller movie (Dargis 2011; Ebert 2011). Although *A Better Life* may be closer to the independent spirit of Indiewood, the *Twilight* movies were also produced independently, that is, outside the major studios. The industrial hybridity of the company at the time and its variety of production and marketing strategies illustrate once again the contradictory nature of much of conglomerate Hollywood. With a different audience in mind from the

Twilight saga, the marketing campaign of *A Better Life*, which included interviews with the director, focused on his Mexican heritage and his family's pedigree in Hollywood and Mexican cinema and emphasized the transnational potential of the industry and its ability to reach out to a variety of audiences, as well as its potentially controversial political content (Brookes 2012; Nicholson 2011). The movie's relatively high profile, especially after Demián Bichir's Oscar nomination, complicates the standing of the film as Chicano cinema. Yet its intense rootedness in Los Angeles speaks to the multiplicity of the city in a direct way. All of this, however, did not prevent *A Better Life* from performing poorly at the box office, with under $2 million in box office receipts in the United States for an estimated budget of $10 million (according to the IMDb). The fact that the melodramatic narrative followed well-trodden conventions, with critics mentioning *Ladri di biciclette* (Vittorio de Sica, 1948) as an overt inspiration, did not prove enough to endear the movie to mainstream audiences. Once again, the invisible barrier was operative.

The melodramatic plot of *A Better Life* starts when gardener Blasco (Joaquín Cosío), who has made enough money in Los Angeles and has decided to return to Mexico, offers to sell his *troca* to his friend and undocumented working hand, Carlos Galindo (Bichir), and pass on to him his list of customers. Although reluctant at the beginning, Carlos decides to accept the offer, but the truck is stolen on his first day as boss. He eventually recovers it with the help of his son, Luis (José Julián), only to find himself stopped by the police, arrested, and summarily deported to Mexico.

When Blasco tries to persuade Carlos to buy the vehicle and take over the business, he paints an optimistic future for his friend, which he summarizes in the phrase, "el mero mero sueño americano" (literally, "the very American dream"). The mention of the phrase *the American dream* in a language other than English points both to its irresistible fascination and the irony of its appropriation by those for whom it was not invented. The term, popularized by James Truslow Adams in a book published in 1931, would become enshrined a few decades later by the mass media as a self-explanatory national motto. Put simply by Adams himself, it is the "dream of a better, richer, and happier life for all our citizens of every rank" (quoted in Cullen 2003, 4). Although the concept has been related to such disparate hopes as religious freedom and ownership of a home but most often to the aspiration of upward mobility, it has been typically understood in terms of economic and/or social progress (Cullen 2003, 1–8). In more general terms, the American dream has been attached to the abstract promise of success, regardless of social, gender, or racial origin (Hochschild 1995, 15–24). Former president Bill Clinton, in a 1993 speech, offered a particularly appealing version of the idea: "The American dream that we were all raised on is a simple but powerful one—if you work hard and play by the rules, you should be given a chance to go as far as your God-given ability will take you" (quoted in Hochschild 1995, 18). An important implication, which goes back to the Declaration of Independence, is that everyone can pursue the dream and that it is the ability and the desire to pursue it that turns people from all over the world into Americans. That is, the American dream is closely tied with national identity and goes a long way toward defining what is special about being a U.S. citizen.

In reality, what decades of recent history and anti-immigrant legislation and cultural texts such as *A Better Life* remind us is that pursuing the American dream is far from enough to become a U.S. citizen and that millions of people who have decided to pursue it are constantly prevented from achieving it. Alongside the admirable democratic ideals established in the Declaration of Independence and the police enforcement of border controls and the clamp-down on immigration, the borderlands, both in the geographic and the legal sense, have become a gray area, inhabited by a special kind of people, not partakers of the American dream but not wholly outside it either. In Los Angeles hundreds of thousands of undocumented workers from Latin America and other parts of the world wait for their increasingly unlikely opportunity to fulfill the American dream, whatever the language of its utterance.

For Carlos, "el mero mero sueño Americano" is embodied in Blasco's truck, yet he hesitates before making the decision. His sense of his real status as an undocumented worker in the country advises him to stay "acá calladito, con la cabeza agachada, tratando de permanecer invisible" ("silent, with my head down, trying to remain invisible"), lying low in the hope that things will change one day, if not for him, then at least for his son, Luis. In the meantime, he remains, to use the words of poet Ricardo Sánchez, "unobtrusive, invisible and acquiescent" (1990, 39–40). *A Better Life* strongly conveys this particular way of inhabiting a space through Carlos's relationship with the real space of LA and carefully maps the city from the perspective and experience of its invisible citizens. In a social and economic sense *A Better Life* delineates the spatial coordinates of the informal economy in Southern California.

As in all the movies mentioned in this final part of this book, most of the faces in *A Better Life* are brown, but there are important differences in the type of society the film depicts. Unlike in *Real Women Have Curves*, *Luminarias*, and *Quinceañera*, the sense of community here is fragile. In *Real Women* we have Ana's family and the sisterhood of workers at Estela's factory. In *Quinceañera* the whole of Echo Park is constructed as a close-knit community that is being threatened by yuppie gentrification. The urgency of this threat is brought most forcefully home through the character of Tío Tomás; he is the living emblem of the barrio, and his death bodes hard times ahead. In *Luminarias* the Mexican restaurant provides the metaphor and the narrative glue for a strong middle-class Mexican American community that aspires to acquire visibility within their own city. These three movies share a strong comic spirit, and in them the conventions of the genre are co-opted to underline the importance of the social group as part of their Chicano agenda. Their common way of explicitly counteracting previous images of the city is by emphasizing not just numbers and statistics but solid alternative urban networks with complex dynamics that are comparable to those of the dominant Anglo community.

By contrast, *A Better Life* features, for the most part, isolated individuals bent exclusively on survival in the hostile city. Such images of the social group are mostly negative, because the only viable group identified here is the street gang, and Luis's proximity to it is seen as something to be avoided at all costs. Intent on making himself invisible, Carlos has relatively slim ties with those around him, even less than loner Nathaniel Ayres in *The Soloist*, for whom, after all, the other homeless in the Nickel are his brothers and sisters. In Weitz's movie sister Anita (Dolores Heredia) provides support both when Carlos needs a loan to buy the truck and when he is deported, by taking care of Luis. Yet she occupies a relatively peripheral position in the narrative, and the strong traditional family that has become such an important feature of the stereotypical depiction of Mexicans in most movies and other cultural texts is considerably blurred here. Once Blasco disappears at the beginning of the story, Carlos has no friends. In fact, given his long working hours and given that he is not even aware of weekends, he has no time for any form of socialization. For the most part, he sees other people from inside his truck. Ana in *Real Women* similarly looks at the world around her from the window of her father's vehicle, but this is a joyous experience that reinforces her sense of belonging. By contrast, Carlos's constant travels to and from work only emphasize his isolation. He is, in the words of Chicana poet Carmen Tafolla, "Alone, like the rest of la raza, / a stranger in my own home" (1985, 184). In historicocultural terms, he embodies the underside of the Chicano and Latino image of a close-knit community.

At the end of the DVD commentary, the director explains how lucky the filmmakers were to be able to shoot the whole film on location in Los Angeles and points out that they used sixty-nine different locations around the city. All these locations play an important role in the narrative and contribute to the articulation of a strong sense of place—LA as seen from the perspective and the living experience of an undocumented worker. Carlos's day starts at the break of dawn in the house he shares with his son on Orme Avenue in Boyle Heights, where he sleeps on the sofa so that Luis can have the only bedroom. It is dark outside both when he leaves and when he returns home, so the spectator is not given the chance to notice exactly where the house is. Yet its location is important, and awareness of it makes the movie's construction of the city richer. Orme Avenue is in the southern end of Boyle Heights, placed underneath a massive freeway exchange where the Pomona, Golden State, and Santa Ana Freeways crisscross. This particular location is an example of the transformations experienced by the neighborhood in the mid-twentieth century when the freeway network was built. As we have seen, to facilitate communication between other neighborhoods, such parts of the city as the surroundings of Orme Street were swallowed up by the roads. As a consequence, the lives of local citizens, at the time and in the future, were significantly affected. Although the freeways are not part of this movie's narrative, this particularly solitary individual lives in their shadow. It can be surmised that Orme Street is both the ideal place for someone to remain invisible and the appropriate spot to convey a sense of a fragmented community and its isolated members. This may not be a visible part of the narrative, yet the link between the film's protagonist and the freeways through the location of his house is consistent with a central part of the city's history, literally the part that became buried under the new transportation system.

When, at the beginning of the movie, we see Carlos travel west, the journey is similar to that of Ana in *Real Women*, except that there are no seamstresses to drop off in the Garment District—the journey continues west, straight to the gardeners' places of work on the Westside. Here we also catch, from his point of view, glimpses of Boyle Heights, although there is no lively Mexican music in the background.

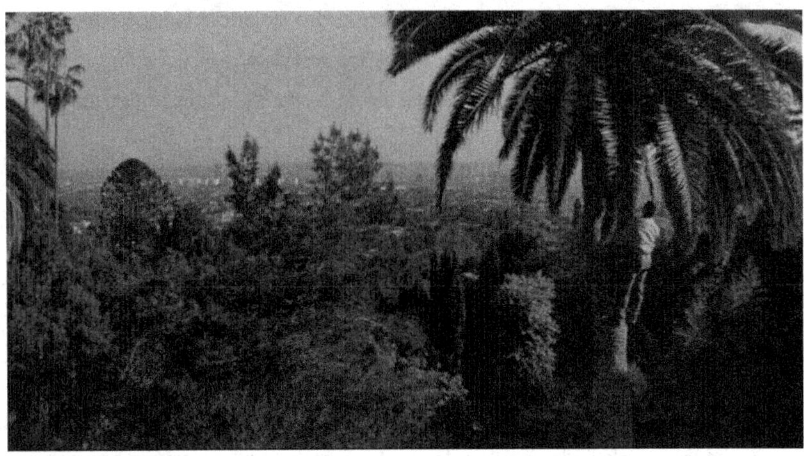

A Better Life: Los Angeles as "el mero mero sueño Americano."

Instead, one of the shots shows Evergreen Cemetery, a central and historically important location of the neighborhood. Next we see the bridge over the river that Carlos and Blasco cross, a lake on the Westside, a private garden probably near Griffith Park, and one more in Malibu, where we see the gardeners fully at work for the first time. These snapshots of the city seem more distant from the subject of the look—Carlos—than in the earlier movie, as though the eye-line matches do not emphasize connection but separation between consecutive shots, as though there is no continuity but constant fragmentation. It is not only that, as in so many other LA movies, the quick montage fails to convey the magnitude of geographic distances in the city, but that no matter how far the protagonist drives his truck, he will always remain distant from the places he looks at.

When Carlos returns home in the evening, we sense the same distance between onlooker and city scenes, except that there are human figures to look at: some surfers returning from the ocean, a young woman jogging with her dog, two young couples meeting outside a Mexican restaurant, a Jewish family leisurely walking in their neighborhood, some people apparently fighting outside a restaurant in Koreatown, a small neighborhood chapel, and a group of young Latino-looking men, maybe gangsters, already east of the river, just before Carlos drives past the sign of his street and arrives home. Maybe the most suggestive of these shots is that of the Mexican restaurant, because the good life apparently enjoyed by the young Anglos in it seems vaguely tied to the protagonist's hardships: Both Mexican culture and

Mexican migrants traveled north as part of the same capitalist rationale, but they remain separate as they facilitate entertainment and cheap labor for other Americans. At one point, perched on the top of a huge palm tree in the Malibu garden, Carlos allows himself a brief moment to admire the city: "Qué bonita es," he says to himself, but during these few seconds, his new partner, Santiago (Carlos Linares), is stealing his hard-earned truck and unleashing the events that will culminate in Carlos's deportation. His sense of the city's beauty is such that he can never take part in it, and even such a moment of humble appreciation of his city is something he cannot afford.

Aware as he is of his lot, Carlos defers his own American dream to his son's future. Yet Luis's experience of the city is markedly different. His girlfriend at school, Ruthie (Chelsea Rendon), happens to be the cousin of one of the leaders of a street gang, Marcelo (Richard Cabral), who is trying to persuade Luis to join them. In one important scene we see Luis at Ruthie's house, surrounded by gang members. This appears to be his natural habitat and where he feels most at home, more so than in his own house. Marcelo hovers near Luis, observing him at close range, waiting for the teenager to give in to peer pressure and join them. Unlike his own family, this one feels real to Luis and one that he might well want to belong to and that would receive him with open arms.

This scene and other gang scenes were shot in Ramona Gardens, at the northern end of Boyle Heights. Like Orme Avenue, Marcelo's neighborhood contributes important connotations to the story. Ramona Gardens has a fraught history. One of the first public housing developments in Los Angeles, it was built in the early 1940s when Boyle Heights was still a relatively ethnically diverse neighborhood. In later decades, already predominantly Mexican, it became notorious for its street violence and racial tension between various gangs, the most notorious of which was Hazard Grande. Alongside this troubled past, the housing project is also renowned for its impressive street art—a series of murals painted on the side of many of its houses, originally created by Chicano artists in the 1970s and kept today in almost mint condition. These murals depict scenes of Chicano life and history and Mexican history and myth, but they also contain memorials to the neighborhood's past. An awe-inspiring fresco shows a Mexican heterosexual couple dressed in zoot suit style, standing proudly against a blue rainbow-like background with the phrase "Hazard Grande" printed above their heads. At the top of the composition, two

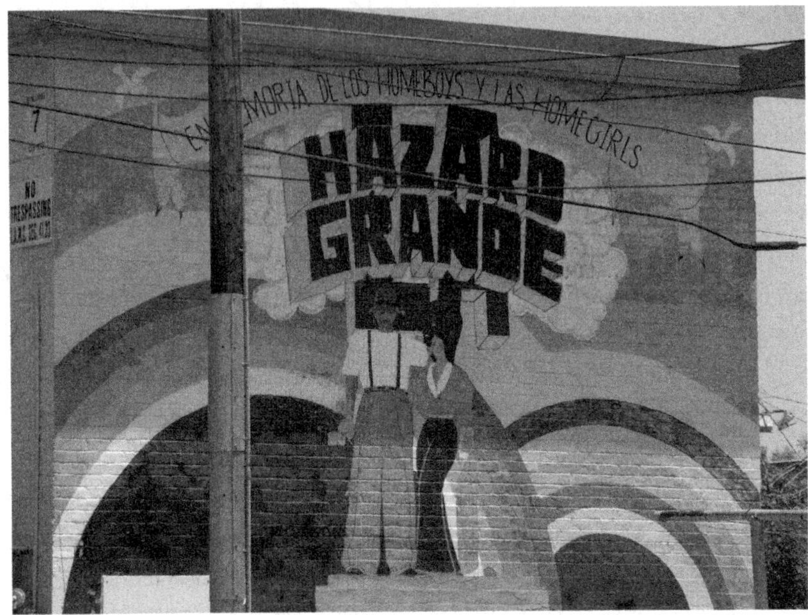

The alternative history of the city in the murals of Ramona Gardens.

white doves hold with their beaks a cloth on which is printed, "En memoria de los homeboys y las homegirls." The mural suggests the complexity of Chicano history in the city, and its specific location provides the ideal background for its ambivalent message: From a Chicano perspective access to the American dream follows a tortuous historical road with stops at the Zoot Suit Riots and gangster culture.

Visiting Ramona Gardens today feels like visiting a street museum, the impressive and impressively kept murals surrounded by everyday scenes of quiet and average family life. It seems hard to believe that this was the location for the type of lives and experiences depicted in movies such as *American Me* and *Blood In Blood Out*. Yet, according to Leandro Sánchez (2000), in his introduction to a photo essay of the neighborhood, the legacy of past life in Ramona Gardens, along with Hazard Grande itself, is still very present, and the young members of the community seem to still be ruled by complex codes of behavior. As Sánchez explains, it is "a surreal place where the past seems to not leave" (2011, n.p.). This location, in which violent past, uncertain present, and hopeful future intermingle in often incomprehensible combinations, goes a long way toward explaining Luis's predicament as the outcome of local geography and history. Although none of this is directly accessible to the spectator of the film, it contributes to the construction of the Chicano teenager's character. It provides depth to his story and, specifically, to the options that are available to him as the son of a Mexican migrant. Luis's walk home from Ramona Gardens encapsulates the enormous distance between the two disparate worlds that he has to juggle daily and the conflictive model of American identity that this experience produces.

In the film's spatial construction, the counterpoint of Ramona Gardens is the *charreada*, the Mexican rodeo that father and son unexpectedly come upon when they are trying to recover the stolen truck. This other slice of Latino life in Los Angeles was shot in Pico Rivera, one of several predominantly Mexican American middle-class neighborhoods in East LA that was featured, less realistically, in *Collateral.* "This is where I'm coming from," says Carlos to his son, whose present life is distant from his father's heritage, a heritage he has trouble understanding. For Luis, as probably for many Angelenos, this show might as well be taking place on the moon. In the film's narrative, however, it is being held next door to the Mexican restaurant and club where father and son finally catch up with the *troca* thief. This is part of the spatial and emotional journey that father and son have undertaken together, a journey that is very much part of their present (without the truck, they have nothing) and their future (*el mero mero sueño Americano*) but also turns out to be a trip to the past, to their Mexican and migrant roots and, more problematically, to those aspects of their common history that separate them.

At the *charreada* Carlos asks Luis to make an effort to understand the Spanish that is being spoken over the loudspeakers. The young man tries, but it is difficult for him, as is his attempt to comprehend why all these poor people have kids, including his own parents. Luis asks his father why he and his mother had him, a question Carlos will not be ready to answer until their final climactic conversation before he is deported. Luis rejects his past, as embodied by his mother, who left them when he was little, and this seems to provide the narrative reason for his distance from his father's culture. In social terms the gap between the two is even wider. When they finally catch up with Santiago, Carlos just wants his truck back but Luis would like to beat the man to death. When, earlier on, he sees undocumented workers waiting for work on a street corner, he despises them. His experience as a young Latino in Los Angeles is fraught with violence and spite, a feeling that is common to other Chicano characters discussed in this book, but, in his case, being at the bottom of the scale, his experience brings him closer to the modes of behavior of street gangs.

Which brings us back to the street corner. Here, near the beginning of the story, before deciding to buy Blasco's truck, Carlos joins other undocumented workers waiting for an employer to come and hire them for the day. This is one of many nondescript corners in the city, where silent people stand or sit patiently and eagerly with their heads down, both afraid of a police raid and aware that the raid is not all that likely to happen because the country's economy needs the cheap labor they offer. When, later on, Luis scorns these workers—"Look at these *pendejos* out here hoin' themselves"—he is not aware that this is exactly what his father has been doing for years. In this Luis is like many real Angelenos, from all walks of life, who choose to ignore this important dimension of their own city. In focusing on this activity and allotting it an important part in its narrative structure, the movie is making a quiet statement and producing urban discourse.

The street corner is where the first contact between Carlos and Santiago takes place. Santiago silently offers Carlos part of his sandwich, and this worker solidarity is what makes Carlos return to the spot when he has work to offer and to choose Santiago to help him with the gardening business—a wrong move, as it turns out. Santiago is Salvadoran and, as father and son follow his tracks to the apartment in South Central where he has been living, we are introduced to the differences between various Latino social groups, not only in the way they speak Spanish but also in terms of the internal social hierarchies that are established among the migrants. As a Central American, or as a *tres veces mojado* (three times a wetback), as Salvadoran migrants are described in a song by Los Tigres del Norte, Santiago is at the bottom of the ladder, and the movie quietly suggests these nuances, which in Los Angeles, as in other parts of the country, operate daily in social relationships. Bichir, Julián, and Linares also incorporate these social differences into their performances, and the film's use of the real LA, as the characters move from Boyle Heights to the Westside and then to South Central, melodramatizes the social hierarchies of the downtrodden.

The street corner is in both dramatic and real terms the location where they all come together. Therefore it stands out as a transfer point in terms of the urban dynamics of the postmetropolis. By using mostly mainstream visual, narrative, and generic protocols, *A Better Life* suggests that Ramona Gardens, Orme Avenue, the *charreada*, and, notably, the street corners where undocumented laborers wait for work are as much part of the city as Hollywood, Venice, or Beverly Hills. Because they are part of the same aesthetic discourse, they also belong to the same urban reality. In a sense, the street corner, where the silent men are "hoin' themselves," is Carlos's true community. This particular community may be difficult to celebrate in terms of Chicano identity, but it is nevertheless an important part of the experiences that recent movies such as those discussed in this chapter and in Chapter 9 portray in their attempt to incorporate Mexican and other Latino identities into cinematic Los Angeles.

Coda
Spanglish

Spanglish (James L. Brooks, 2004) is the title of one of a still few mainstream Hollywood movies dealing with the intricacies of Chicano identity, particularly in its focus on the relationship between narrator Cristina (Shelbie Bruce) and her mother, Flor (Paz Vega), an undocumented migrant who works as a maid for an affluent Anglo family. Beyond the problematic casting of Spanish actress Vega as Mexican Flor, following in a long tradition of "other" casting in Hollywood, I am interested in the title, which encapsulates a central ingredient of Chicano identity. For many Spanish speakers, Spanglish is the term that denotes our tendency to use Spanish pronunciation or intonation patterns and vocabulary and grammatical structures when we speak or write in English, making it incorrect and often difficult to understand. For Mexican Americans and for other Latino groups in the United States, Spanglish has different connotations. For them, it denotes the way they speak or, rather, the various ways in which they speak, and it is one of the most powerful signifiers of their hybrid nature and their bordering status.

In *Borderlands* Gloria Anzaldúa (1999) singles out this particular dimension of her Chicana identity and explains the centrality of what she calls "el lenguaje de la frontera." She lists the many tongues Chicanos speak because they are a complex, heterogeneous people: Standard English, working-class and slang English, Standard Spanish, Standard Mexican Spanish, North Mexican Spanish dialect, Chicano Spanish (with various regional variations), Tex-Mex, and *pachuco* or *caló*. Some of these dialects are spoken more often at home, others in public places; some are more mixed and others are "purer." Spanish words distorted by English influence are frequent, and their standard pronunciation of English bears a strong imprint of Mexican Spanish. Because of the way they use language and the constant code shifting they employ in everyday communication, Chicanos are often derided by both Spanish and English speakers: "*Deslenguadas. Somos los del español deficiente.* We are your linguistic nightmare, your linguistic aberration, your linguistic *mestizaje*, the subject of your *burla*. Because we speak with tongues of fire we are culturally crucified. Racially, culturally and linguistically *somos huérfanos*—we speak an orphan tongue" (Anzaldúa 1999, 80). Yet, for them, their language goes a long way toward explaining who they are: "So, if you want to really hurt me, talk badly about my language. Ethnic identity is twin to linguistic identity. I am my language" (81). Guillermo Gómez-Peña recurrently turns this mixed language into the central feature of his performance art. This is his version of the famous bolero "Bésame mucho": "Kiss me, kiss moi my chola / como si fuera esta noche the last migra raid / kiss me, kiss moi my chola / que tengo miedo perderte somewhere in LA" (Gómez-Peña 1996, 190). Writer and academic Santiago Vaquera-Vásquez introduces himself as a Spanglish speaker. Spanglish is for him, "undomesticated. A tongue-tied language. But if that is my language—after all, I grew up with a wild forked tongue, speaking and mixing Spanish and English constantly—then a malcriado I will be" ("Roundtable Discussion," 2014). As poet Ángela de Hoyos puts it, "I'm Spanglo" (1993, 184).

Films about Mexican Americans, Chicanos, and Latinos in Los Angeles or anywhere else in the country cannot hope to capture and accurately explain the way these people are and relate to one another without reproducing the way they speak. Often driven by commercial considerations, movies have traditionally failed to do this and, for the most part, continue to do so. Charlton Heston's Spanish as Mexican police agent Vargas in *Touch of Evil* (Orson Welles, 1958) is a notorious example. The romantic comedy *From Prada to Nada* (Angel Gracia, 2011), a transposition of Jane Austen's *Sense and Sensibility* to contemporary LA, specifically Beverly Hills and Boyle Heights, is, like the movies discussed in this chapter, an attempt to bring the invisible Chicano community to the fore, this time through a story of class conflict. Although much can be praised in the film in terms of the production of alternative urban discourses that match the realities of the city, it becomes problematic from a Chicano perspective in its casting of Camilla Belle as Nora Domínguez, who is supposed to be fluent in Spanish but is not (she is Brazilian American), and Alexa Pena Vega as her sister Mary, who is meant to have linguistic difficulties when they have to move to Boyle Heights but speaks perfect Spanish. Neither of them speaks like the middle-class Chicanas they are supposed to be.

This linguistic inaccuracy is immediately noticeable to a Spanish speaker, and especially to a Chicano audience, who is particularly sensitive to these matters, and problematizes the credibility of the movie's character construction. Even though it is understandable that filmmakers work with many constraints and that casting decisions must be based on many different considerations, the result in this case is that

From Prada to Nada joins the crammed ranks of movies and other narrative texts that bypass the centrality of Spanglish to understand Chicano society and therefore, for the concerns of this book, Angeleno society.

The movies discussed in the final part of this book, on the other hand, all place Spanglish at the center of their stories and all manage to render accurately the various combinations of English and Spanish that are available to their characters depending on their respective positions in the borderlands. In fact, given the difficulties in defining what Chicano cinema is, we could do a lot worse than place linguistic accuracy at the center of any workable definition of the concept. A good example of this is the dialogues between mother and daughter in *Real Women Have Curves*, the mother speaking mostly Spanish and the daughter mostly English, both with acceptable Chicano or Mexican accents but both interspersing words from the other language in their utterances and both shifting to the other language as the occasion requires. The constant changing and mixing at Estela's factory also rings true. As a general rule, among Chicanos and Mexicans, the older generations, who were often born south of the border, communicate in Spanish, whereas the younger characters speak mostly English but with many inserted Spanish terms in their discourse. They are all capable of switching from one code to another depending on whom they are speaking to.

Carlos's *troca*, a perfectly normal term in Mexican American Spanish but nonexistent outside the United States, is a good example of Chicano Spanish, a linguistic variety characterized by translating literally from English and constantly creating new words and set phrases by mixing both languages. "Ahí te watcho"—a combination of a Mexican turn of phrase, an English verb (not the exact same one that would be used in English), and its Spanish conjugation, meaning approximately "see you later"—which various characters in these films say—also illustrates how language works in the borderlands. Given that they all narrate intergenerational conflicts, the movies analyzed here follow the same pattern in the linguistic profiles of their characters: As in *Real Women*, mother and daughter in *Quinceañera* mix their languages, with Magdalena speaking mostly in English and María (Araceli Guzman-Rico) in Spanish. Tío Tomás, like Ana's grandfather in *Real Women*, speaks almost exclusively Spanish, and when he speaks English, he does it with a Mexican rather than a Chicano accent. In *A Better Life* the undocumented workers who have lived in LA for decades speak Spanish among themselves, but when they speak English, they reflect a middle-of-the-road position, with an English accent that is much less obviously "foreign" than that of the older generation and much closer to that of Chicanos. Mexican Demián Bichir excels at producing this particular register when he speaks English to his son, Luis, neither fully Chicano nor fully Mexican, reflecting where Chicano English comes from. His English, as that of his character, Juárez policeman Marco Ruiz, in the series *The Bridge* (2013–2014), can be taken as an exemplar of the agglomeration of linguistic registers that characterize Chicano identity. In this it contrasts with the carelessness displayed by the more popular and prestigious series *Breaking Bad* (2008–2013), where various supposedly Mexican or Chicano characters speak Spanish with openly foreign accents. Carlos's "bilingualism" in *A Better Life*, natively Mexican when he speaks Spanish, openly Chicanoized when he uses English, embodies the transitional nature of Chicano linguistic identity, moving along a complex axis between English and Spanish, and of the linguistic borderlands. On the opposite end of the spectrum from this cultural tolerance toward language patterns is the street advertisement in *Quinceañera* that publicizes "Accent Elimination. Speak American Standard," quietly suggesting the consequences of the changes taking place in Echo Park (or Echo Parque).

Standard American English symbolizes the other side of the coin of the cultural diversity of the postmetropolis that has become part of the dominant urban discourse of post-1992 Los Angeles. Mind-boggling linguistic diversity is a clear manifestation of the heterogeneity of the city; between eighty-six and ninety-two languages are spoken at Angeleno schools, depending on the year of publication of the sources of the figures (Gottlieb 2007, 7; Hayden 1995, 83; Jencks 1996, 48). Contradicting the spurious linguistic purity constructed by most Hollywood movies about LA and promoted by various legislative initiatives in the recent past, these films attempt to capture the linguistic reality of one part of this urban heterogeneity. The varieties of Spanglish spoken in these movies may not add up to the eight different languages hyperbolically listed by Anzaldúa (1999), but they do suggest that those eighty-six or ninety-two different languages illustrate a much greater variety, one that becomes even greater when we factor in, for example, the influence of African American slang on Chicano teenagers: In *A Better Life* Chicano school kids use expressions such as "Who he down with?" or "Yo, my man." Both assimilation into a problematic American Standard English and mongrelization of linguistic practices are important discourses in cultural representations of the city and, as such, constitute one more area of discursive struggle. When comedian George Lopez, in one of his most famous stand-up performances, his HBO solo debut in Phoenix, asserts that English as the official language will never work because Chicanos will always speak Spanglish, he is not so much describing reality as making discourse and openly counterattacking English-only policies (G. Lopez 2007). In a less overt way, through their explicit vocation as realistic accounts of urban life, the movies analyzed here perform the same operation.

The proliferation of linguistic varieties found in these movies evokes the sounds one can hear at Norm's, the traditional Angeleno diner featured at the beginning of my Introduction. The underlying assumption in this book has been that Norm's is closer to the reality of the city than, say, the Downtown depicted in *(500) Days of Summer*. In fact, the cinematic landscape of the last two decades may well be better represented by *(500) Days* than by *Real Women Have Curves*, yet a close look at the ways in which contemporary movies have engaged with the real LA reveals multiple nuances and the irresistible push of the diversity discourse. From the discussions of individual movies offered here, we can conclude that the city always finds ways to reveal itself in its complexities, contradictions, and anxieties, whether in direct or indirect ways, often as much through what is hidden or repressed as through what is shown and celebrated. Contemporary cinematic Los Angeles is both indebted to its own past and necessarily open to its current cultural context. The invisible presence of Ramona Gardens on the narrative surface of *A Better Life* may be an apt closing illustration of the ways in which the city that never ceases to fascinate makes its way into filmic representations, iceberg-like, and once and again asserts its power to produce meaning in a technologically globalized world in which borders, whether geographic, political, or, indeed, textual, will inexorably be crossed. In the last reading, contemporary Los Angeles movies are fictional and cultural transpositions of the ever-growing borderlands.

Works Cited

Abbas, Ackbar. 2003. "Cinema, the City, and the Cinematic." In Linda Krause and Patrice Petro, eds., *Global Cities: Cinema, Architecture, and Urbanism in a Digital Age*, 142–56. New Brunswick, NJ: Rutgers University Press.

Abcarian, Robin. 2006. "Coming of Age During an Era of Great Change." *Los Angeles Times* (January 21): E1, E24.

Abelmann, N., and Lie, J. 1995. *Blue Dreams: Korean Americans and the Los Angeles Riots*. Cambridge, MA: Harvard University Press.

Abramowitz, Rachel. 2004. "Staring into Darkness." *Los Angeles Times* (June 13): E1, E4.

Acuña, Rodolfo E. 1996. *Anything but Mexican: Chicanos in Contemporary Los Angeles*. London: Verso.

Ailworth, Erin. 2004. "It's Time to Hit the Town." *Los Angeles Times* (August 5): E12.

Ames, Christopher. 1997. *Movies About Movies: Hollywood Reflected*. Lexington: University Press of Kentucky.

Anderson, Susan. 1996. "A City Called Heaven: Black Enchantment and Despair in Los Angeles." In Allen J. Scott and Edward W. Soja, eds., *The City: Los Angeles and Urban Theory at the End of the Twentieth Century*, 336–64. Berkeley: University of California Press.

Andrew, Geoff. 1993. "Sitting on D-Fens." *Time Out* (June 2–9): 1–2.

Andrews, David. 2004. "An Oneiric Fugue: The Various Logics of *Mulholland Drive*." *Journal of Film and Video* 56.1: 25–40.

Anzaldúa, Gloria. 1999 [1987]. *Borderlands/La Frontera: The New Mestiza*. San Francisco: Aunt Lute Books.

Aoun, Steven. 2003. "Film of the Quarter: *Mulholland Drive*." *Metro Magazine: Media and Education Magazine* 136: 204.

Atkinson, Michael. 2004. "Mann on Fire." *Village Voice* (August 4): 72.

Augé, Marc. 1995. *Non-Places: Introduction to an Anthropology of Supermodernity*. London: Verso.

Avila, Eric. 1998. "The Folklore of the Freeway: Space, Culture, and Identity in Postwar Los Angeles." *Aztlán* 23.1: 14–31.

———. 2006. *Popular Culture in the Age of White Flight: Fear and Fantasy in Suburban Los Angeles*. Berkeley: University of California Press.

———. 2010. "Social Flashpoints." In William Deverell and Greg Hise, eds., *A Companion to Los Angeles*, 95–109. Malden, MA: Wiley Blackwell.

Works Cited

Azcona, María del Mar. 2010. *The Multi-Protagonist Film*. Malden, MA: Wiley Blackwell.

———. 2015. "'We Are All Uxbal': Narrative Complexity in the Borderlands in *Biutiful*." *Journal of Film and Video* 67.1: 3–13.

Baca, Judith F. 2002. "Public Participation in Conservation I: *The Great Wall of Los Angeles*." In Hafthor Yngvason, ed., *Conservation and Maintenance of Contemporary Public Art: A Conference Hosted by the Cambridge Arts Council*, 21–29. Cambridge, MA: Archetype.

Badillo, Juan Manuel. 2013. "Quebró la productora Cha Cha Cha de los 'Tres Amigos' del cine mexicano." *Corre Cámara*. www.correcamara.com.mx/inicio/int.php?mod=noticias_detalle&id_noticia=4310 (accessed October 22, 2014).

Baker, Bob. 1993. "The Urban Reality: Why Love L.A.?" *Los Angeles Times* (March 15): F1, F6.

Barragan, Bianca. 2015. "An Introduction to Googie, SoCal's Signature Architectural Style." *Curbed Los Angeles* (January 16). la.curbed.com/archives/2015/01/an_introduction_to_googie_socals_signature_architectural_style.php (accessed April 22, 2015).

Bates, David. 2011. "*The Big Sleep*." In Gabriel Solomons, ed., *World Film Locations: Los Angeles*, 18–19. Bristol: Intellect Books.

Baudrillard, Jean. 1989. *America*, trans. Chris Turner. London: Verso.

Bell, James. 2014. "Computer Love." *Sight & Sound* 24.1: 20–25.

Benito, Jesús, and Manzanas, Ana María. 2011. *Cities, Borders, and Spaces in Intercultural American Literature and Film*. New York: Routledge.

Berrettini, Mark L. 1999. "Private Knowledge, Public Space: Investigation and Navigation in *Devil in a Blue Dress*." *Cinema Journal* 39.1: 74–89.

Bhabha, Homi. 1994. *The Location of Culture*. London: Routledge.

Blackwelder, R. 2004. "*Collateral*." *Video Librarian* (November–December): 20.

Bordwell, David. 1988 [1985]. *Narration in the Fiction Film*. London: Routledge.

———. 2006. *The Way Hollywood Tells It: Story and Style in Modern Movies*. Berkeley: University of California Press.

Branigan, Edward. 1992. *Narrative Comprehension and Film*. London: Routledge.

Braudy, Leo. 2010. "Cultures and Communities." In William Deverell and Greg Hise, eds., *A Companion to Los Angeles*, 269–88. Malden, MA: Wiley Blackwell.

———. 2011. *The Hollywood Sign*. New Haven, CT: Yale University Press.

Brookes, Julian. 2012. "Oscars: How A Better Life's Chris Weitz and Demian Bichir Got Political." *Rolling Stone* (February 24). www.rollingstone.com/politics/news/oscars-how-a-better-lifes-chris-weitz-and-demian-bichir-got-political-20120224 (accessed September 7, 2015).

Bruns, John. 2008. "The Polyphonic Film." *New Review of Film and Television Studies* 6.2: 189–212.

Carson, Tom. 1992. "Mannish Boys." *L.A. Weekly* (April 3): 33.

Cooper, Anthony, and Rumford, Chris. 2011. "Cosmopolitan Borders: Bordering as Connectivity." In Maria Rovisco and Magdalena Nowicka, eds., *The Ashgate Research Companion to Cosmopolitanism*, 261–76. London: Ashgate.

Cullen, Jim. 2003. *The American Dream: A Short History of an Idea That Shaped a Nation*. Oxford, UK: Oxford University Press.

Culver, Lawrence. 2010. "America's Playground: Recreation and Race." In William Deverell and Greg Hise, eds., *A Companion to Los Angeles*, 421–37. Malden, MA: Wiley Blackwell.

Dargis, Manohla. 1996. "*Devil in a Blue Dress*." *Sight and Sound* 6.1: 38.

———. 2001. "Truly Sad, Truly Monstrous: David Lynch's *Mulholland Drive*." *L.A. Weekly* (October 17). www.laweekly.com/2001-10-25/news/truly-sad-truly-monstrous/ (accessed September 17, 2014).

———. 2011. "Drifting Apart, Struggling Together." *New York Times* (June 23). www.nytimes.com/2011/06/24/movies/a-better-life-directed-by-chris-weitz-review.html?_r=0 (accessed September 7, 2015).

Davies, Jude. 1995. "Gender, Ethnicity, and Cultural Crisis in *Falling Down* and *Groundhog Day*." *Screen* 36.3: 214–32.

Davis, Mike. 1996. "How Eden Lost Its Garden: A Political History of the Los Angeles Landscape." In Allen J. Scott and Edward W. Soja, eds., *The City: Los Angeles and Urban Theory at the End of the Twentieth Century*, 160–85. Berkeley: University of California Press.

———. 1998. *Ecology of Fear: Los Angeles and the Imagination of Disaster*. London: Picador.

———. 2000. *Magical Urbanism: Latinos Reinvent the U.S. City*. London: Verso.

———. 2001. "Bunker Hill: Hollywood's Dark Shadow." In Mark Shiel and Tony Fitzmaurice, eds., *Cinema and the City: Film and Urban Societies in a Global Context*, 33–45. Oxford, UK: Blackwell.

———. 2006 [1990]. *City of Quartz: Excavating the Future of Los Angeles*. London: Verso.

Dawes, Amy. 2005. "*Collateral*." *Variety* (January 4): xi.

Dear, Michael. 1996. "In the City, Time Becomes Visible: Intentionality and Urbanism in Los Angeles, 1781–1991." In Allen J. Scott and Edward W. Soja, eds., *The City: Los Angeles and Urban Theory at the End of the Twentieth Century*, 76–105. Berkeley: University of California Press.

de Certeau, Michel. 1984. *The Practice of Everyday Life*, trans. Steven Randall. Berkeley: University of California Press.

de Hoyos, Angela. 1993. "La Gran Ciudad (for Mireya Robles)." In Tey Diana Rebolledo and Eliana S. Rivero, eds., *Infinite Divisions: An Anthology of Chicana Literature*, 184. Phoenix: University of Arizona Press.

de la Campa, Román. 2001. "Latinos and the Crossover Aesthetic." Foreword to Mike Davis, *Magical Urbanism: Latinos Reinvent the U.S. City*, i–xviii. London: Verso.

Deleyto, Celestino. 2009. *The Secret Space of Romantic Comedy*. Manchester, UK: Manchester University Press.

Denby, David. 1999. "San Fernando Aria." *The New Yorker* (December 20): 102–3.

Diawara, Manthia. 1993. "Black American Cinema: The New Realism." In Manthia Diawara, ed., *Black American Cinema*, 3–25. London: Routledge.

Dickey, J. D. 2008. *The Rough Guide to Los Angeles and Southern California*. New York: Rough Guides.

Dillman, Joanne Clarke. 2010. "Twelve Characters in Search of a Televisual Text: *Magnolia* Masquerading as Soap Opera." *Journal of Popular Film and Television* 33.3: 142–50.

DiMassa, Cara Mia. 2006. "Differing Views of Race in L.A. Collide in 'Crash.'" *Los Angeles Times* (March 2): A1, A23.

Dimendberg, Edward. 1995. "The Will to Motorization: Cinema, Highways, and Modernity. *October* 73: 91–137.

———. 2010. "Cinema and the Making of a Modern City." In William Deverell and Greg Hise, eds., *A Companion to Los Angeles*, 346–64. Malden, MA: Wiley Blackwell.

Douglas, Kirk. 1993. "My Son Is the Villain, Not the Hero, of Urban Drama." *Los Angeles Times* (March 22): F3.

Drake, Philip. 2008. "Distribution and Marketing in Contemporary Hollywood." In Paul McDonald and Janet Wasko, eds., *The Contemporary Hollywood Industry*, 63–82. Malden, MA: Blackwell.

Du Bois, W. E. B. 1994. *The Souls of Black Folk*. New York: Gramercy Books.

Dyer, Richard. 1997. *White*. London: Routledge.

———. 1998. "Introduction to Film Studies." In John Hill and Pamela Church Gibson, eds., *The Oxford Guide to Film Studies*, 3–10. Oxford, UK: Oxford University Press.

Ebert, Roger. 2011. "*A Better Life*." RogerEbert.com (July 6). www.rogerebert.com/reviews/a-better-life-2011 (accessed September 7, 2015).

Erie, Steven P., and MacKenzie, Scott. 2010. "Crown Jewels: Infrastructure and Growth." In William Deverell and Greg Hise, eds., *A Companion to Los Angeles*, 216–32. Malden, MA: Wiley Blackwell.

Estrada, William David. 2008. *The Los Angeles Plaza: Sacred and Contested Space*. Austin: University of Texas Press.

Ethington, Philip J. 2010. "Ab Urbis Condita: Regional Regimes Since 13,000 Before

Present." In William Deverell and Greg Hise, eds., *A Companion to Los Angeles*, 177–215. Malden, MA: Wiley Blackwell.

Everett, Wendy. 2005. "Fractal Films and the Architecture of Complexity." *Studies in European Cinema* 2.3: 159–71.

Faludi, Susan. 2000 [1999]. *Stiffed: The Betrayal of Modern Man*. London: Vintage.

Farber, Stephen. 2000. "Their Reputation Precedes Them, Alas." *Los Angeles Times* (January 30): 4, 28, 30–32.

Fojas, Camilla. 2006. "Border Cinema and the Global City (of Angels)." *Aztlán: A Journal of Chicano Studies* 31.1: 7–31.

French, Philip. 2002. "Lynch's Law and Disorder." *The Guardian* (January 6). www.theguardian.com/film/2002/jan/06/davidlynch.philipfrench (accessed September 15, 2014).

Fuller, Graham. 2001. "Babes in Babylon." *Sight and Sound* 11.12: 14–17.

Gabriel, John. 1996. "What Do You Do When Minority Means You? *Falling Down* and the Construction of 'Whiteness.'" *Screen* 37.2: 129–51.

Galbraith, Jane. 1992. "Selling Sweat." *Los Angeles Times*, Calendar section (April 19): 27–28.

Gámez, José Luis. 2002. "Representing the City: The Imagination and Critical Practice in East Los Angeles." *Aztlan* 27.1: 95–120.

García Canclini, Néstor. 2001 [1990]. *Culturas Híbridas: Estrategias para entrar y salir de la modernidad*. Buenos Aires: Paidós.

Ginsberg, Merle, and Baum, Gary. 2013. "Budget Cuts." *Hollywood Reporter* (August 22). www.hollywoodreporter.com/news/las-famous-500-days-summer-611391 (accessed May 13, 2015).

Glatzer, Richard, and Westmoreland, Wash. 2006. Press kit for *Quinceañera*. Sony Pictures Classics.

Gledhill, Christine. 1980. "*Klute* 1: A Contemporary Film Noir and Feminist Criticism." In E. Ann Kaplan, ed., *Women in Film Noir*, 6–21. London: British Film Institute.

Glixman, Elizabeth P. 2007. "An Interview with Karen Tei Yamashita." *Eclectica Magazine* 11.4 (October–November). www.eclectica.org/v11n4/glixman_yamashita.html (accessed March 5, 2014).

Goldman, Michael. 2004. "Building *Collateral*." *Millimeter* 32.8 (August): 49–54.

Goldstein, Gregg. 2006. "SPC Wins Rights to *Quinceañera*." *Hollywood Reporter* (March 13): 3, 30.

Gómez-Peña, Guillermo. 1988. "Documented/Undocumented." In Rick Simonson and Scott Walker, eds., *The Graywolf Annual Five: Multi-Cultural Literacy, Opening the American Mind*, 130–31. Saint Paul, MN: Graywolf Press, 1988.

———. 1996. *The New World Border: Prophecies, Poems, and Loqueras for the End of the Century*. San Francisco: City Lights.

Goodridge, Mike. 2002. "Crowd-Pleaser Confirms HBO's Indie Influence." *Screen International* (January 25): 19.

Gottlieb, Robert. 2007. *Reinventing Los Angeles: Nature and Community in the Global City*. Cambridge, MA: MIT Press.

Greenberg, James. 2006. "*Quinceañera*." *Hollywood Reporter* (January 30): 10, 20.

Greimas, A. J. 1986 [1966]. *Sémantique structurale*. Paris: Presses universitaires de France.

Guerrero, Ed. 1996. "*Devil in a Blue Dress*." *Cineaste* 22.1: 38, 40–41.

Harmon, Amy. 1993. "Fed Up with 'Down.'" *Los Angeles Times* (March 1): D1–D2.

Harris, Dana. 2002. "HBO 'Curves' into Distribution." *Variety* (July 31): 1, 17.

Hartig, Anthea. 2010. "'A Most Advantageous Spot on the Map': Promotion and Popular Culture." In William Deverell and Greg Hise, eds., *A Companion to Los Angeles*, 289–312. Malden, MA: Wiley Blackwell.

Hawthorne, Christopher. 2006. "Typecast in an Urban Drama." *Los Angeles Times* (March 5). articles.latimes.com/2006/mar/05/entertainment/ca-hawthorne5 (accessed July 6, 2016).

———. 2009. "L.A. as Filtered by Love in *(500) Days of Summer*." *Los Angeles Times* (July 31). www.latimes.com/entertainment/arts/la-et-500days-2009jul31-story.html#page=1 (accessed May 7, 2015).

———. 2010. "Contemporary Voice: Thickets of Diversity, Swaths of Emptiness." In William Deverell and Greg Hise, eds., *A Companion to Los Angeles*, 479–93. Malden, MA: Wiley Blackwell.

Hayden, Dolores. 1995. *The Power of Place: Urban Landscapes as Public History*. Cambridge, MA: MIT Press.

Heath, Stephen. 1981. *Questions of Cinema*. Bloomington: Indiana University Press, 1981.

Herold, Ann. 2006. "Grace in Leaf and Stone." *Los Angeles Times* (September 14): F1, F10.

Hise, Greg. 2010. "Situating Stories: What Has Been Said About Landscape and the Built Environment." In William Deverell and Greg Hise, eds., *A Companion to Los Angeles*, 393–420. Malden, MA: Wiley Blackwell.

Hoberman, J. 2001. "Point of No Return." *Village Voice* (October 2). www.villagevoice.com/2001-10-02/film/points-of-no-return/2/ (accessed September 11, 2014).

Hochschild, Jennifer L. 1995. *Facing Up to the American Dream: Race, Class, and the Soul of the Nation*. Princeton, NJ: Princeton University Press.

Hoffmann, Jessica. 2007. "LAPD Gentrifies Skid Row." *Color Lines: News for Action* (October 3). colorlines.com/archives/2007/10/lapd_gentrifies_skid_row.html (accessed March 4, 2014).

Hogen-Esch, Tom. 2010. "Consolidation, Fragmentation, and New Fiscal Federalism." In William Deverell and Greg Hise, eds., *A Companion to Los Angeles*, 233–49. Malden, MA: Wiley Blackwell.

Hohenadel, Kristin. 2001. "Real L.A., the One That's Lived In." *New York Times* (October 7). www.nytimes.com/2001/10/07/movies/real-la-the-one-that-s-lived-in.html (accessed September 11, 2014).

Honeycutt, Kirk. 1993. "Getting Down on 'Falling Down.'" *Hollywood Reporter* (March 2): 3, 81.

———. 2000. "*Luminarias*." *Hollywood Reporter* (May 3): 11–12.

Hsu, Hsuan. 2006. "Racial Privacy, the L.A. Ensemble Film, and Paul Haggis's *Crash*." *Film Criticism* 31.1–2: 132–56.

Hudson, Jennifer A. 2004. "'*No Hay Banda*, and Yet We Hear a Band': David Lynch's Reversal of Coherence in *Mulholland Drive*." *Journal of Film and Video* 56.1: 17–24.

Hunter, James. 2000. "It's a Mann's Mann's Mann's World." *Village Voice* (February 15): 109, 115.

James, Caryn. 1992. "What Gives 'White Men' Its Spring." *New York Times* (April 26). www.nytimes.com/1992/04/26/movies/film-view-what-gives-white-men-its-spring.html (accessed July 6, 2016).

James, David E. 2005. *The Most Typical Avant-Garde: History and Geography of Minor Cinemas in Los Angeles*. Berkeley: University of California Press.

Jameson, Fredric. 1984. "Postmodernism, or, the Cultural Logic of Late Capitalism." *New Left Review* 146: 53–92.

Jeffers McDonald, Tamar. 2007. *Romantic Comedy: Boy Meets Girls Meets Genre*. London: Wallflower.

Jencks, Charles. 1996. "Hetero-Architecture and the L.A. School." In Allen J. Scott and Edward W. Soja, eds., *The City: Los Angeles and Urban Theory at the End of the Twentieth Century*, 47–75. Berkeley: University of California Press.

Jew, Victor. 2010. "The Anti-Chinese Massacre of 1871 and Its Strange Career." In William Deverell and Greg Hise, eds., *A Companion to Los Angeles*, 110–28. Malden, MA: Wiley Blackwell.

Karlamanga, Soumya, and Reyes, Emily Alpert. 2015. "Norm's Restaurant Moves Closer to Designation as L.A. Historic Monument." *Los Angeles Times* (March 19). www.latimes.com/local/lanow/la-me-ln-norms-restaurant-historic-monument-20150319-story.html (accessed April 22, 2015).

Kaufman, Anthony. 2002. "Thinking Inside the Box." *Village Voice* (March): 124.

King, Geoff, Molloy, Claire, and Tzioumakis, Yannis, eds. 2012. *American Independent Cinema: Indie, Indiewood, and Beyond*. London: Routledge.

King, Loren. 2002. "America the Beautiful." *Boston Globe* (November 10): N11, N13.

King, Peter H. 1993. "A Walk Across the City." *Los Angeles Times* (March 7). articles.

latimes.com/1993-03-07/news/mn-8334_1_los-angeles (accessed July 6, 2016).
Kotler, Steven 2004. "*Collateral*." *Variety* (December 16). variety.com/2004/film/awards/michael-mann-1117915104/ (accessed July 6, 2016).
Kun, Josh. 2010. "Tijuana and the Borders of Race." In William Deverell and Greg Hise, eds., *A Companion to Los Angeles*, 313–26. Malden, MA: Wiley Blackwell.
Kurashige, Scott. 2010. "Between 'White Spot' and 'World City': Racial Integration and the Roots of Multiculturalism." In William Deverell and Greg Hise, eds., *A Companion to Los Angeles*, 56–71. Malden, MA: Wiley Blackwell.
Lack, Roland-François. 2016. "The Map and the Territory." *Sight and Sound* 26.3: 60.
Laine, Tarja. 2009. "Affective Telepathy, or the Intuition of the Heart: *Persona* with *Mulholland Drive*." *New Review of Film and Television Studies* 7.3: 325–38.
Lane, Christina. 2011. *Magnolia*. Malden, MA: Wiley-Blackwell.
LeElef, Ner, comp. 2001. "World Jewish Population." www.simpletoremember.com/vitals/world-jewish-population.htm (accessed October 1, 2014).
Lefebvre, Henri. 1991 [1974]. *The Production of Space*, trans. Donald Nicholson-Smith. Oxford, UK: Blackwell.
Levine, Stuart. 2004. "The Contenders." *Variety* (November 9): 18–19.
Levy, Emmanuel. 2006. "*Mulholland Drive*." *Cinema 24/7* (March 28). emanuellevy.com/review/mulholland-drive-3/ (accessed September 11, 2014).
Lewthwaite, Stephanie. 2010. "Race, Place, and Ethnicity in the Progressive Era." In William Deverell and Greg Hise, eds., *A Companion to Los Angeles*, 40–44. Malden, MA: Wiley Blackwell.
Limón, José E. 1992. "Stereotyping and Chicano Resistance: An Historical Dimension." In Chon Noriega, ed., *Chicanos and Film: Representation and Resistance*, 3–17. Minneapolis: University of Minnesota Press.
Lobato, Ramon. 2008. "Crimes Against Urbanity: The Concrete Soul of Michael Mann." *Continuum: Journal of Media and Cultural Studies* 22.3: 341–52.
Lopate, Philip. 2001. "Welcome to L.A.: Hollywood Outsider David Lynch Plunges into Tinseltown's Dark Psyche." *Film Comment* 37.5: 44–50.
Lopez, George. 2007. "George Lopez: America's Mexican." HBO. www.youtube.com/watch?v=n8x_Z0kG8q4 (accessed May 29, 2014).
Lopez, Steve. 2005. "Down in This 'Crash.'" *Los Angeles Times* (May 13): B1, B10.
———. 2006a. "Getting a 'Crash' Course on Race." *Los Angeles Times* (March 12): B1, B7.
———. 2006b. "Misses the Big Picture." *Los Angeles Times* (March 8): B1, B11.
———. 2008. *The Soloist: A Lost Dream, an Unlikely Friendship, and the Redemptive Power of Music*. London: Penguin.
López Calvo, Ignacio. 2011. *Latino Los Angeles in Film and Fiction: The Cultural Production of Social Anxiety*. Tucson: University of Arizona Press.

Los Angeles 2020 Commission. 2013. "A Time for Truth" (December). www.la2020reports.org/reports/A-Time-For-Truth.pdf (accessed July 7, 2016).

Martinez, Kevin. 2012. "Boyle Heights Beat: East L.A. Residents Claim Hollywood Depicts Latinos Solely in Stereotypes." *Latinovoices* (April 11). www.huffingtonpost.com/2012/04/11/hollywood-stereotypes-depictions-of-latinos-east-los-angeles_n_1415238.html (accessed August 31, 2015).

Maslin, Janet. 1999. "*Magnolia.*" *New York Times* (December 17): E15.

Massey, Doreen. 2005. *For Space*. Los Angeles: Sage.

McArthur, Colin. 1997. "Chinese Boxes and Russian Dolls: Tracking the Elusive Cinematic City." In David B. Clarke, ed., *The Cinematic City*, 19–45. London: Routledge.

McBride, Dave. 2010. "Counterculture." In William Deverell and Greg Hise, eds., *A Companion to Los Angeles*, 327–45. Malden, MA: Wiley Blackwell.

McCarthy, Todd. 2001. "Mysterious Curves Drive Lynch Thriller 'Mulholland.'" *Variety* (May 21–27): 15, 24.

———. 2004. "*Collateral.*" *Variety* (August 2–8): 27–28.

———. 2009. "*The Soloist.*" *Variety* (April 16). variety.com/2009/film/reviews/the-soloist-1200474532/ (accessed May 25, 2015).

McDonald, Paul, and Wasko, Janet. 2008. "Introduction: The New Contours of the Hollywood Film Industry." In Paul McDonald and Janet Wasko, eds., *The Contemporary Hollywood Industry*, 1–9. Malden, MA: Blackwell.

McFly, Marty. 2013. "Filming Locations: *Magnolia* (1999)." *San Fernando Valley Blog*. sanfernandovalleyblog.blogspot.com.es/2013/12/filming-locations-magnolia-1999.html (accessed June 26, 2014).

McGowan, Todd. 2004. "Lost on Mulholland Drive: Navigating David Lynch's Panegyric to Hollywood." *Cinema Journal* 43.2: 67–89.

McLean, Adrienne L. 2004. *Being Rita Hayworth: Labor, Identity, and Hollywood Stardom*. New Brunswick, NJ: Rutgers University Press.

McWilliams, Carey. 2010 [1946]. *Southern California: An Island on the Land*. Salt Lake City: Peregrine Smith.

Mennel, Barbara. 2008. *Cities and Cinema*. London: Routledge.

Metz, Walter. 2006. "Woody's Melindas and Todd's Stories: Complex Film Narratives in the Light of Literary Modernism." *Film Criticism* 31.1–2: 107–31.

Meyer, Carla. 2002. "Mom, Teen Square Off in 'Real Women': Funny, Engaging Drama About Latino Family in L.A." *San Francisco Chronicle* (October 25). www.sfgate.com/movies/article/Mom-teen-square-off-in-Real-Women-Funny-2759799.php (accessed April 8, 2014).

Moore, Solomon. 2007. "Some Respite, if Little Cheer, for Skid Row Homeless." *New York Times* (October 31). www.nytimes.com/2007/10/31/us/31skidrow.html

(accessed March 4, 2014).

Mosley, Walter. 2010 [1990]. *Devil in a Blue Dress*. London: Serpent's Tail.

Muñoz, Lorenza. 2000. "Latinas' Love Story Is Just the Tip of *Luminarias* Message." *Los Angeles Times* (May 3): F2, F6.

Naremore, James. 1998. *More than Noir: Film Noir and Its Contexts*. Berkeley: University of California Press.

Neustadter, Scott. 2009. "*(500) Days of Summer*: Revenge Is Writing a Film About a Girl Who Dumped You." *Daily Mail* (28 August). www.dailymail.co.uk/tvshowbiz/article-1209556/500-Days-Summer-Revenge-writing-film-girl-dumped-you.html (accessed May 7, 2015).

Newman, David. 2007. "The Lines That Continue to Separate Us: Borders in Our 'Borderless World.'" In Johan Schimanski and Stephen Wolfe, eds., *Border Poetics De-Limited*, 27–57. Hannover, Germany: Wehrhahn.

Newman, Kathleen. 1992. "Latino Sacrifice in the Discourse of Citizenship: Acting Against the 'Mainstream,' 1985–1988." In Chon Noriega, ed., *Chicanos and Film: Representation and Resistance*, 59–72. Minneapolis: University of Minnesota Press.

Newman, Kim. 2002. "*Mulholland Dr.*" *Sight & Sound* 12.1: 50–51.

———. 2014. "Street Legal." *Sight & Sound* 24.2: 34–37.

Nichols, Chris. 2015. "Norm's Restaurant Chain Has Sold." *Los Angeles Magazine* (January 9). www.lamag.com/askchris/norms-restaurant-chain-sold/ (accessed April 22, 2015).

Nicholson, Amy. 2011. "Interview: 'A Better Life' Director Chris Weitz on Gangs, Oscars, and His Gardener's Revenge" (June 21). pro.boxoffice.com/articles/2011-06-chris-weitz-on (accessed September 7, 2015).

Nieland, Justus J. 1999. "Race-ing *Noir* and Re-placing History: The Mulatta and Memory in *One False Move* and *Devil in a Blue Dress*." *Velvet Light Trap* 43 (spring): 63–77.

Nochimson, Martha P. 2002. "*Mulholland Drive*." *Film Quarterly* 56.1: 37–45.

Noriega, Chon. 1992a. "Between a Weapon and a Formula: Chicano Cinema and Its Contexts." In Chon Noriega, ed., *Chicanos and Film: Representation and Resistance*, 141–67. Minneapolis: University of Minnesota Press.

———, ed. 1992b. *Chicanos and Film: Representation and Resistance*. Minneapolis: University of Minnesota Press.

Nowell-Smith, Geoffrey. 2001. "Cities: Real and Imagined." In Mark Shiel and Tony Fitzmaurice, eds., *Cinema and the City: Film and Urban Societies in a Global Context*, 99–108. Oxford, UK: Blackwell.

Olalquiaga, Celeste. 1992. *Megalopolis: Contemporary Cultural Sensibilities*. Minneapolis: University of Minnesota Press.

Olsen, Mark. 2000. "Singing in the Rain." *Sight and Sound* 10.3: 26–28.

Ong, Paul, and Blumenberg, Evelyn. 1996. "Income and Racial Inequality in Los Angeles." In Allen J. Scott and Edward W. Soja, eds., *The City: Los Angeles and Urban Theory at the End of the Twentieth Century*, 311–35. Berkeley: University of California Press.

Painter Young, Jamie. 2002. "America Ferrera and Lupe Ontiveros Redefine the Leading Lady." *Backstage West* (October 17): 1, 6.

Palaversich, Diana. 2003. "La vuelta a Tijuana en seis escritores." *Aztlán* 28.1: 97–125.

Park, Jeana H. 1993. "Portrayal of a Store Owner Seen as Volatile Stereotype." *Los Angeles Times* (March 22): F3.

Parson, Don. 1993. "'This Modern Marvel': Bunker Hill, Chavez Ravine, and the Politics of Modernism in Los Angeles." *Southern California Quarterly* 75.3–4: 333–50.

Pastor, Manuel. 2010. "Contemporary Voice: Contradictions, Coalitions, and Common Ground." In William Deverell and Greg Hise, eds., *A Companion to Los Angeles*, 250–65. Malden, MA: Wiley Blackwell.

Peña Ovalle, Priscilla. 2011. *Dance and the Hollywood Latina: Race, Sex, and Stardom*. New Brunswick, NJ: Rutgers University Press.

Posner, Ellen. 1997. "Introduction." In Robert Geddes, ed., *Cities in Our Future*, 1–11. Washington, DC: Island Press.

Pratt, Mary Louise. 1991. "Arts of the Contact Zone." *Profession* 91: 33–40.

Puig, Claudia. 2002. "'Real Women' Reflects the Real World." *USA Today* (October 24). usatoday30.usatoday.com/life/movies/reviews/2002-10-24-real-women_x.htm (accessed March 8, 2014).

Pye, Douglas, and Walker, Michael. 2010. "Editorial." *Movie: A Journal of Film Criticism* 1 (August). www2.warwick.ac.uk/fac/arts/film/movie/contents/editorial.pdf (accessed April 20, 2015).

Quart, Alyssa. 2005. "Networked: Don Roos and *Happy Endings*." *Film Comment* 41.4: 48–51

Rafferty, Terrence. 1992. "The Current Cinema." *New Yorker* (April 6): 80–82.

Ramírez Berg, Charles. 2002. *Latino Images in Film: Stereotypes, Subversion, Resistance*. Austin: University of Texas Press.

———. 2006. "A Taxonomy of Alternative Plots in Recent Films: Classifying the 'Tarantino Effect.'" *Film Criticism* 31.1–2: 5–61.

Reinhold, Robert. 1993. "Horror for Hollywood: Film Hits a Nerve with Its Grim View of Hometown." *New York Times* (March 29): A11.

Relph, Edward. 2008 [1976]. *Place and Placelessness*. London: Pion.

Renninger, Bryce J. 2013. "Spike Jonze, Why Are There No Brown People in Your Future Los Angeles?" *IndieWire* (June 10). www.indiewire.com/article/spike-jonze-why-are-there-no-brown-people-in-your-future-los-angeles (accessed June 10, 2014).

Rhodes, John David, and Gorfinkel, Elena. 2011. "Introduction: The Matter of Places." In John David Rhodes and Elena Gorfinkel, eds., *Taking Place: Location and the Moving Image*, vii–xxix. Minneapolis: University of Minnesota Press.

Rich, B. Ruby. 1995. "Dumb Lugs and Femmes Fatales." *Sight and Sound* 5.11: 6–10.

Riley, Jenelle. 2002. "The Women Behind *Real Women*." *Back Stage Week Drama-Logue* (October 17). www.backstage.com/news/the-women-behind-real-women_2/ (accessed July 14, 2016).

Rooney, David. 1999. "*Luminarias*." *Variety* (October 11–17). variety.com/1999/film/reviews/luminarias-1200459573/ (accessed July 6, 2016).

———. 2006. "*Quinceañera*." *Variety* (January 23). variety.com/2006/film/markets-festivals/quinceanera-1200519110/ (accessed July 6, 2016).

"A Roundtable Discussion with Daniel Alarcón, Eduardo Halfon, and Santiago Vaquera-Vásquez." 2014. *Believer* 107 (May). www.believermag.com/issues/201002/?read=roundtable#.U4TF2l65KRw (accessed May 27, 2014).

Rumford, Chris. 2008. "Bordering and Connectivity: Cosmopolitan Opportunities." In Gerard Delanty, ed., *Routledge Handbook of Cosmopolitan Studies*, 245–53. London: Routledge.

Saldívar, José David. 1997. *Border Matters: Remapping American Cultural Studies*. Berkeley: University of California Press.

Sánchez, George J. 2004. "'What's Good for Boyle Heights Is Good for the Jews': Creating Multiculturalism on the East Side During the 1950s." *American Quarterly* 56.3: 633–61.

———. 2010. "Disposable People, Expendable Neighborhoods." In William Deverell and Greg Hise, eds., *A Companion to Los Angeles*, 129–46. Malden, MA: Wiley Blackwell.

Sánchez, Leandro. 2011. "Ramona Gardens." www.behance.net/gallery/RAMONA-GARDENS-by-Leandro-Sanchez/1485117 (accessed May 22, 2014).

Sánchez, Ricardo. 1990. *Eagle-Visioned/Feathered Adobes*. El Paso, TX: Cinco Puntos Press.

Sánchez, Rosaura. 2001. "Mapping the Spanish Language Along the Multiethnic and Multilingual Border." In Chon A. Noriega, Eric R. Avila, Karen Mary Davalos, Chela Sandoval, and Rafael Pérez-Torres, eds., *The Chicano Studies Reader: An Anthology of Aztlán*, 515–55. Los Angeles: UCLA Chicano Studies Research Center.

Sassen, Saskia. 1998. *Globalization and Its Discontents: Essays on the New Mobility of People and Money*. New York: New Press.

———. 2006 [1991]. *Cities in a World Economy*. Thousand Oaks, CA: Pine Forge Press.

Saul, Scott. 2010. "Gridlock of Rage: The Watts and Rodney King Riots." In William

Deverell and Greg Hise, eds., *A Companion to Los Angeles*, 147–67. Malden, MA: Wiley Blackwell.

Schaffer, R., and Smith, Neil. 1986. "The Gentrification of Harlem?" *Annals of the Association of American Geographers* 76.3: 347–65.

Schatz, Tom. 2008. "The Studio System and Conglomerate Hollywood." In Paul McDonald and Janet Wasko, eds., *The Contemporary Hollywood Industry*, 13–42. Malden: Blackwell.

Schimanski, Johan, and Wolfe, Stephen, eds. 2007a. *Border Poetics De-Limited*. Hannover, Germany: Wehrhahn.

———. 2007b. "Entry Points: An Introduction." In Johan Schimanski and Stephen Wolfe, eds., *Border Poetics De-Limited*, 9–26. Hannover, Germany: Wehrhahn.

Sconce, Jeffrey. 2002. "Irony, Nihilism, and the New American 'Smart' Film." *Screen* 43.4: 349–63.

Scott, Allen J. 1996. "High-Technology Industrial Development in the San Fernando Valley and Ventura County: Observations on Economic Growth and the Evolution of Urban Form." In Allen J. Scott and Edward W. Soja, eds., *The City: Los Angeles and Urban Theory at the End of the Twentieth Century*, 276–310. Berkeley: University of California Press.

Seabrook, J. 2008. *Ciutats*. Barcelona: Edicions Intermón Oxfam.

Sennett, Richard D. 2002. "Cosmopolitanism and the Social Experience of Cities." In Steven Vertovec and Robin Cohen, eds., *Conceiving Cosmopolitanism: Theory, Context, and Practice*, 42–47. Oxford, UK: Oxford University Press.

Shaw, Deborah. 2013. *The Three Amigos: The Transnational Filmmaking of Guillermo del Toro, Alejandro González Iñárritu, and Alfonso Cuarón*. Manchester, UK: Manchester University Press.

Shefrin, Elana. 2005. "*Le Noir et le Blanc*: Hybrid Myths in *Devil in a Blue Dress* and *L.A. Confidential*." *Literature/Film Quarterly* 33.3: 172–81.

Shiel, Mark. 2001. "Cinema and the City in History and Theory." In Mark Shiel and Tony Fitzmaurice, eds., *Cinema and the City: Film and Urban Societies in a Global Context*, 1–18. Oxford, UK: Blackwell.

———. 2012. *Hollywood Cinema and the Real Los Angeles*. London: Reaktion Books.

Shipman, David. 1989. *The Great Movie Stars: The Golden Years*, 2nd rev. ed. London: Macdonald.

Silver, Alan, and Ursini, James. 2005. *L.A. Noir: The City as Character*. Los Angeles: Santa Monica Press.

Smith, Gavin. 2004. "Join Tom Cruise for a Nocturnal White-Knuckle Thriller Ride." *Film Comment* 40.4: 14.

Smith, Neil. 1982. "Gentrification and Uneven Development." *Economic Geography* 58.2: 139–55.

———. 2002. "New Globalism, New Urbanism: Gentrification as Global Strategy." *Antipode* 34.3: 427–50.

Soja, Edward W. 1996. "Los Angeles, 1965–1992: From Crisis-Generated Restructuring to Restructuring-Generated Crisis." In Allen J. Scott and Edward W. Soja, eds., *The City: Los Angeles and Urban Theory at the End of the Twentieth Century*, 426–62. Berkeley: University of California Press.

———. 2000. *Postmetropolis: Critical Studies of Cities and Regions*. Malden, MA: Blackwell.

Soja, Edward W., and Scott, Allen J. 1996. "Introduction to Los Angeles: City and Region." In Allen J. Scott and Edward W. Soja, eds., *The City: Los Angeles and Urban Theory at the End of the Twentieth Century*, 1–21. Berkeley: University of California Press.

SPARC (Social and Public Art Resource Center). 2014. "The Great Wall: History and Description." sparcinla.org/the-great-wall-part-2/ (accessed March 25, 2014).

Tafolla, Carmen. 1985. "At the Very Last Battle." In Santiago Daydí-Tolson, ed., *Five Poets of Aztlan*, 184. Tempe, AZ: Bilingual Review Press.

Taylor, Ella. 2004. "Night Cruise: Michael Mann's Nerve-Rattling *Collateral*." *L.A. Weekly* (August 6): 40.

Thomas, Deborah. 2001. *Reading Hollywood: Spaces and Meanings in American Film*. London: Wallflower.

Thomas, Kevin. 2000. "*Luminarias*, a Sharp Fresh Look at the Latino Experience." *Los Angeles Times* (May 5).

Thompson, Anne. 2008. "Wright's 'Soloist' Won't Play Holiday." *Variety* (October 19). variety.com/2008/film/awards/wright-s-soloist-won-t-play-holiday-1117994310/ (accessed May 25, 2015).

Thompson, Luke Y. 1999. "The Not-So-Magnificent Anderson." *New Times Los Angeles* (December 16–22): 40, 42.

Thomson, David. 2001. "The Ultimate Road Movie About LA's Ultimate Road." *The Independent* (November 4). www.independent.co.uk/arts-entertainment/films/features/the-ultimate-road-movie-about-las-ultimate-road-9268876.html (accessed July 6, 2016).

Tröhler, Margrit. 2007. *Offene Welten ohne Helden: Plurale Figuren-Konstellationen im Film*. Marburg, Germany: Schüren Presseverlag.

Tuan, Yi-Fu. 1977. *Space and Place: The Perspective of Experience*. Minneapolis: University of Minnesota Press.

Tzioumakis, Yannis. 2006. *American Independent Cinema: An Introduction*. New Brunswick, NJ: Rutgers University Press.

Urtiaga, Rosa. 2016. "Border Women: An Interview with Josefina López." *Latino Studies* 14.2: 265–71.

Valdez, Inés. 2013. "Reel Latinas? Race, Gender, and Asymmetric Recognition in Contemporary Film." *Politics, Groups, and Identities* 1.2: 181–98.

Vass, Michael. 2005. "Cinematic Meaning in the Work of David Lynch: Revisiting *Twin Peaks: Fire Walk with Me*, *Lost Highway*, and *Mulholland Drive*." *Cineaction* 67: 12–23.

Voss, Karen. 1998. "Replacing L.A.: *Mi Familia*, *Devil in a Blue Dress*, and Screening the Other Los Angeles." *Wide Angle* 20.3: 157–81.

Wachs, Martin. 1996. "The Evolution of Transportation Policy in Los Angeles: Images of Past Policies and Future Prospects." In Allen J. Scott and Edward W. Soja, eds., *The City: Los Angeles and Urban Theory at the End of the Twentieth Century*, 106–59. Berkeley: University of California Press.

Weaver, John D. 1980. *Los Angeles: The Enormous Village, 1781–1981*. Santa Barbara, CA: Capra Press.

Weinstein, Richard. 1997. "Los Angeles: The First American City." In Robert Geddes, ed., *Cities in Our Future*, 69–98. Washington, DC: Island Press.

Westwater, Brady. 2006. "Handing Skid Row to the Drug Dealers." *Los Angeles Times* (September 20). articles.latimes.com/2006/sep/20/opinion/oe-westwater20 (accessed March 4, 2014).

Williams, Linda. 2001. *Playing the Race Card: Melodramas of Black and White from Uncle Tom to O. J. Simpson*. Princeton, NJ: Princeton University Press.

Wolch, Jennifer. 1996. "From Global to Local: The Rise of Homelessness in Los Angeles During the 1980s." In Allen J. Scott and Edward W. Soja, eds., *The City: Los Angeles and Urban Theory at the End of the Twentieth Century*, 390–425. Berkeley: University of California Press.

Yamashita, Karen Tei. 1997. *Tropic of Orange*. Minneapolis: Coffee House Press.

Yosso, Tara J., and García, David G. 2007. "'This Is No Slum!' A Critical Race Theory Analysis of Community Cultural Wealth and Culture Clash's *Chávez Ravine*." *Aztlán* 32.1: 145–79.

Zilberg, Elana. 1998. "*Falling Down* in *El Norte*: A Cultural Politics and Spatial Poetics in the ReLatinization of Los Angeles." *Wide Angle* 20.3: 183–209.

Index

Page numbers in *italics* refer to images.

CPSIA information can be obtained
at www.ICGtesting.com
Printed in the USA
FSOW04n0430270217
31195FS

9 780814 339855